Dokebi Bride

Vol. 6

MARLEY

NETCOMICS

Dokebi Bride Vol. 6

Story and Art by Marley

English translation rights in USA,
Canada, UK, NZ, Australia arranged by
Ecomix Media Company
395-21 Seogyo-dong, Mapo-gu, Seoul, Korea 121-840
info@ecomixmedia.com

- Produced by **Ecomix Media Company**
- Translator Soyoung Jung
- Editor Jim Scaife
- Managing Editor Soyoung Jung
- Cover Designer purj
- Graphic Designers Hyelim Oh, Hyekyoung Choi
- President & Publisher Heewoon Chung

P.O. Box 3036, Jersey City, NJ 07303-3036
info@netcomics.com
www.NETCOMICS.com

ISBN: 978-1-60009-080-6

First printing: August 2007
10 9 8 7 6 5 4 3 2 1
Printed in Korea

CONTENTS

From the Author

When I wrote the preface for volume 5 wishing you good fortune in the new year, it would seem I promised a near future next-meeting. But here I am saying hello in the middle of the summer, far past a year from then, feeling small.

During the long hiatus, watching "Dokebi Bride" appear less frequently in the search engines, many questions popped out of my mind. It was also a year in which I turned these questions about my own identity into a flower arrangement

While working on Dokebi Bride, "Korean" and "Korean shamanism" were terms that seemed most like shackles to me. Even when I whipped my hand around to find out what they were, no solid chunks could be caught. Yet these terms had something strong about them, and every time I brought the story to mind they would drag me down like a hook around my legs. It made me think that they were shackles I put around myself while brandishing a smile, perhaps because most of the encouragements I had received alluded to those subjects.

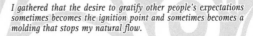

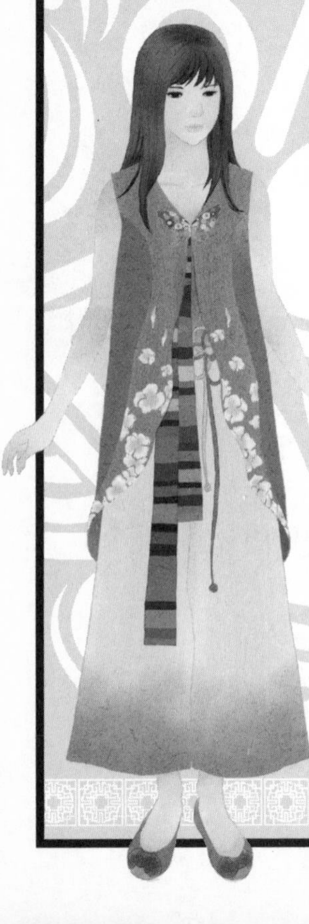

I gathered that the desire to gratify other people's expectations sometimes becomes the ignition point and sometimes becomes a molding that stops my natural flow.

There was a time when I reflected carefully about what it means to say something is "Korean." I thought it probably isn't when we deal with specific traditional subjects, but rather when we come into contact with our "true-form," which we've obtained knowingly and unknowingly. (And one's growth is attained not only by understanding and accepting the true form that one belongs to, but also by a vivacious counter-point of bold shattering, as with a hammer, and reconstructing, I thought.)

The answer I gave myself is that perhaps we can find ourselves in "the moving, breathing, changing and pulsating present"—a large circle that unites diverse and heterogeneous things and where we absorb nourishment as a baby suckles at its mother's breasts—not in the taxidermic homogeneity found in the diagrams or stereotypes from any one life, race, job, or religion.

And our life's journeys may be all sorts of multifarious things... but what about our grand spiritual journeys?

I threw my hands up in the direction of this question when I began working on "Dokebi Bride," and planted its question mark once again last year at this time. As such, I surrender to the heavens my petitions that my journey be one where I arrive at the final destination naturally, without difficulties.

The days are becoming sweltering.
This summer, I hope you won't be infected by the prevalent anxiety and edginess, but instead will soak up the jaunty sound of the waves wherever you are..

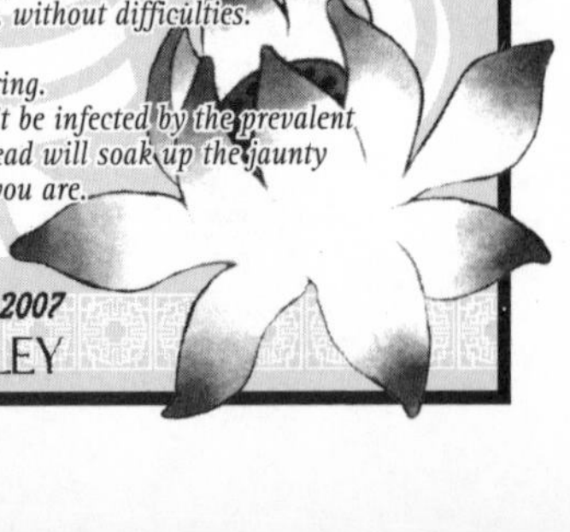

August 2007
MARLEY

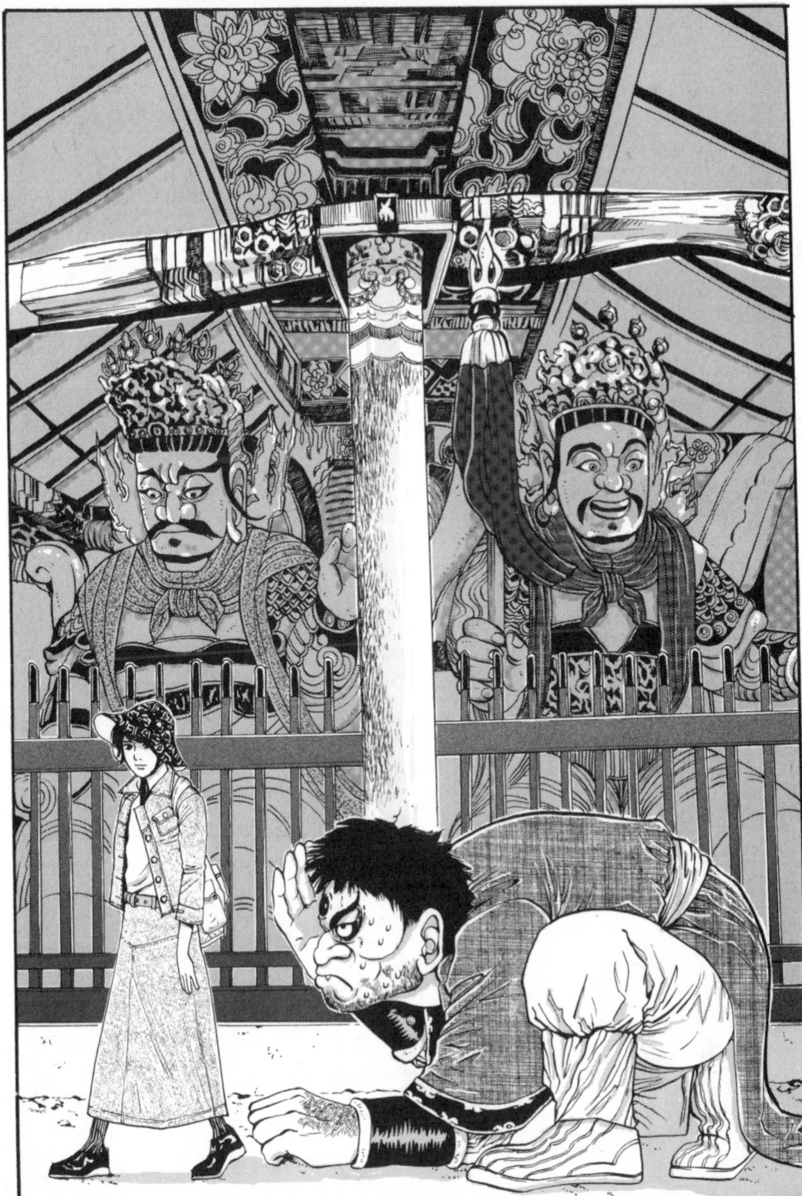

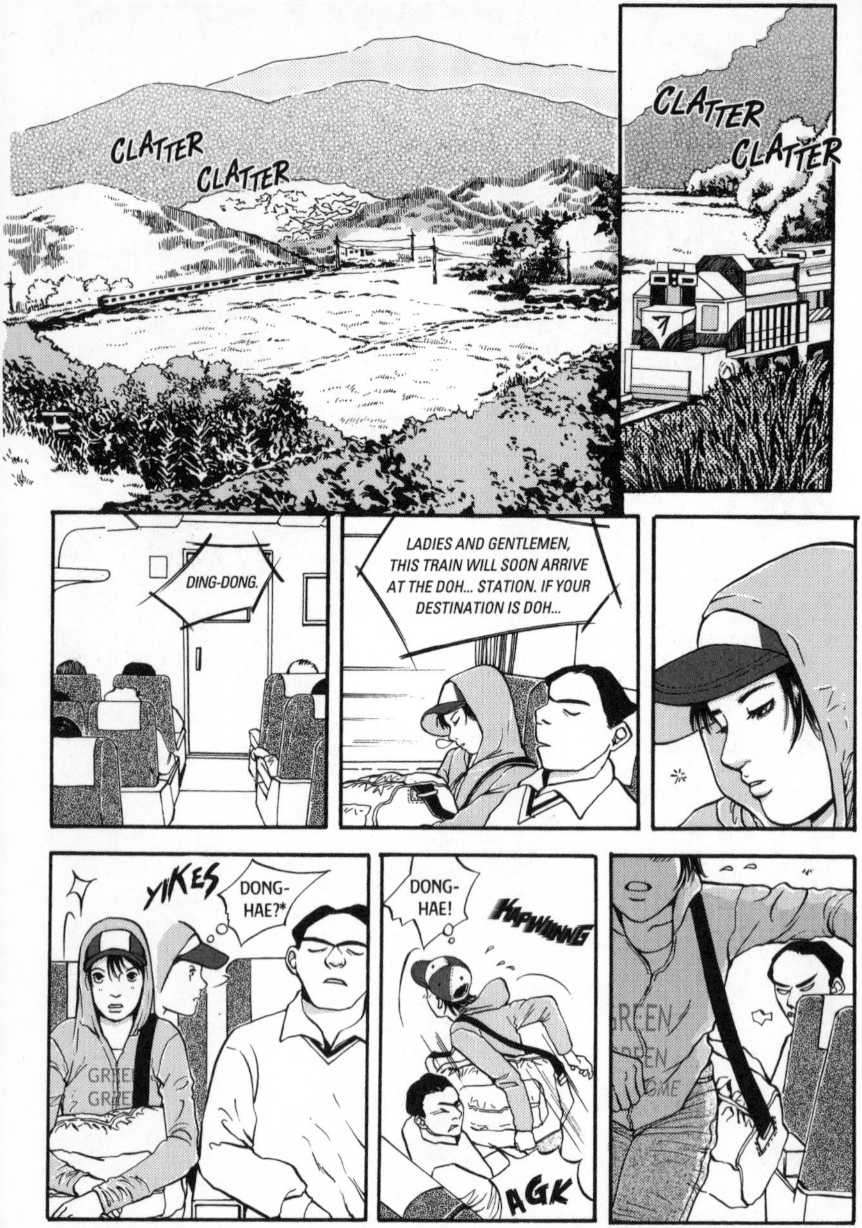
CLATTER
CLATTER
CLATTER
CLATTER
DING-DONG.
LADIES AND GENTLEMEN, THIS TRAIN WILL SOON ARRIVE AT THE DOH... STATION. IF YOUR DESTINATION IS DOH...
YIKES
DONG-HAE?*
DONG-HAE!
KAPWUNNG
AGK

* "EASTERN SEA"

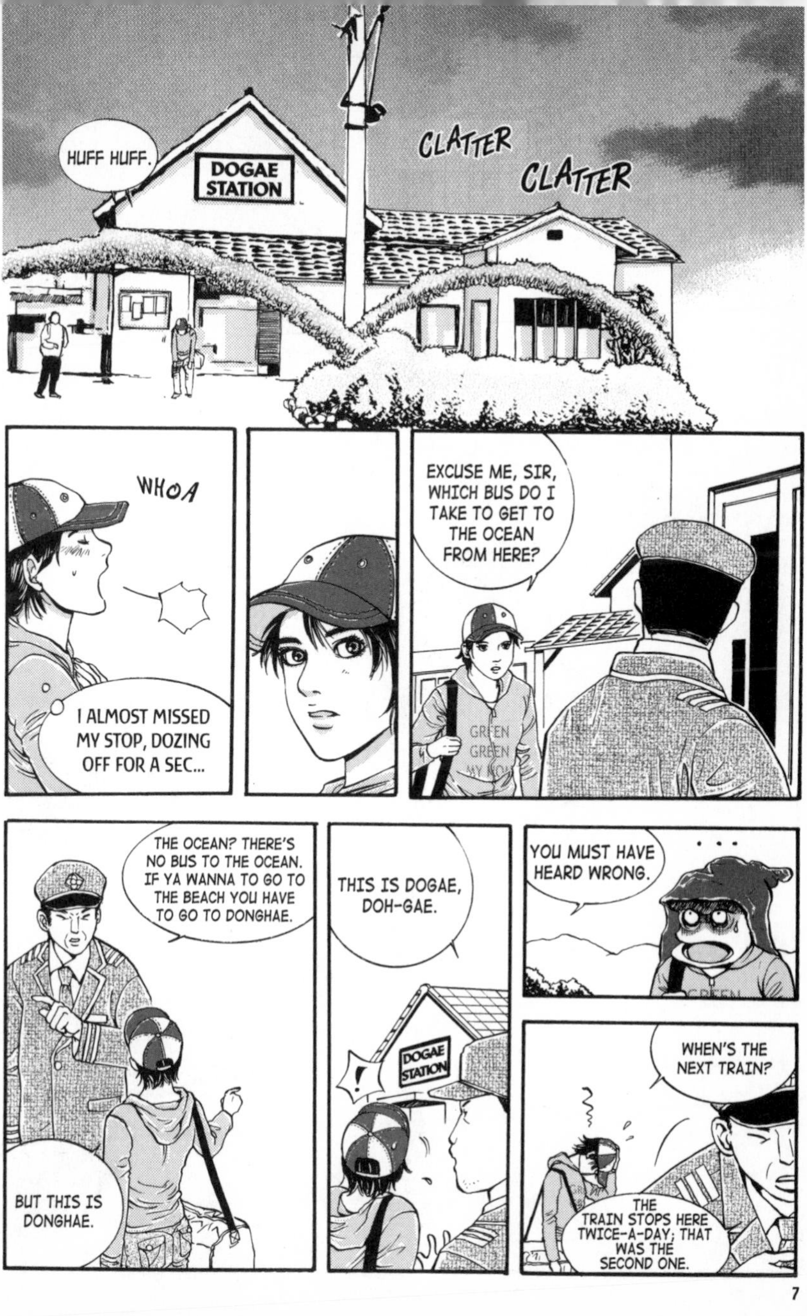
HUFF HUFF.
DOGAE STATION
CLATTER
CLATTER
WHOA
I ALMOST MISSED MY STOP, DOZING OFF FOR A SEC...
EXCUSE ME, SIR, WHICH BUS DO I TAKE TO GET TO THE OCEAN FROM HERE?
GREEN GREEN
THE OCEAN? THERE'S NO BUS TO THE OCEAN. IF YA WANNA TO GO TO THE BEACH YOU HAVE TO GO TO DONGHAE.
BUT THIS IS DONGHAE.
THIS IS DOGAE, DOH-GAE.
DOGAE STATION
!
YOU MUST HAVE HEARD WRONG.
...
WHEN'S THE NEXT TRAIN?
THE TRAIN STOPS HERE TWICE-A-DAY; THAT WAS THE SECOND ONE.

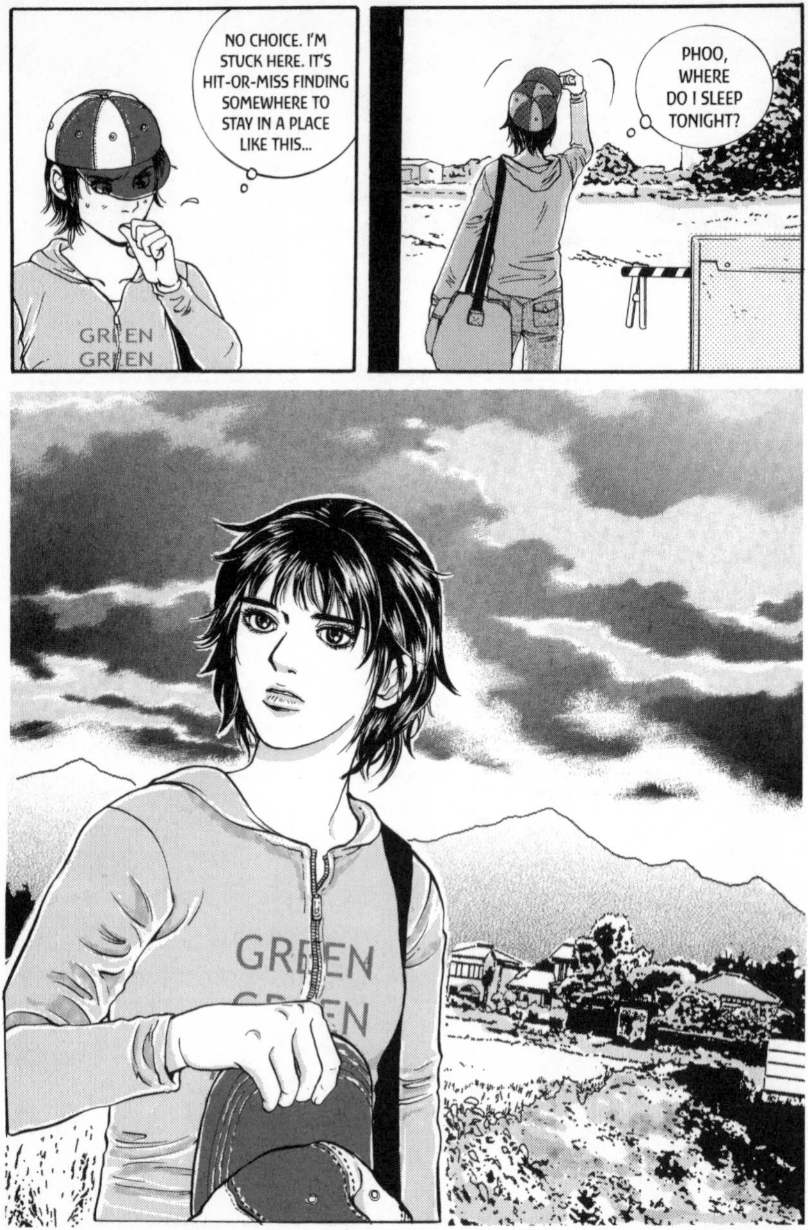
NO CHOICE. I'M STUCK HERE. IT'S HIT-OR-MISS FINDING SOMEWHERE TO STAY IN A PLACE LIKE THIS...
GREEN GREEN
PHOO, WHERE DO I SLEEP TONIGHT?
GREEN GREEN

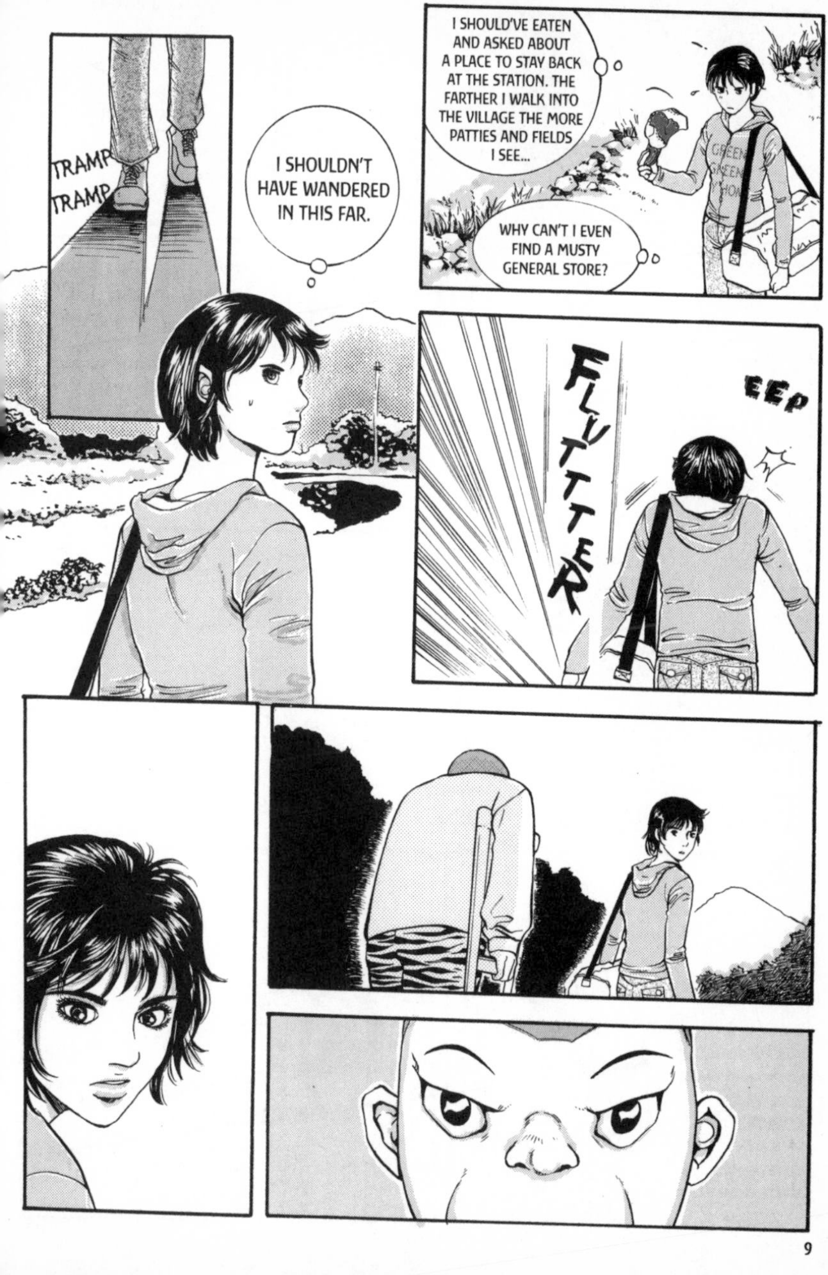
TRAMP
TRAMP
I SHOULDN'T HAVE WANDERED IN THIS FAR.
I SHOULD'VE EATEN AND ASKED ABOUT A PLACE TO STAY BACK AT THE STATION. THE FARTHER I WALK INTO THE VILLAGE THE MORE PATTIES AND FIELDS I SEE...
WHY CAN'T I EVEN FIND A MUSTY GENERAL STORE?
FLUTTTER
EEP

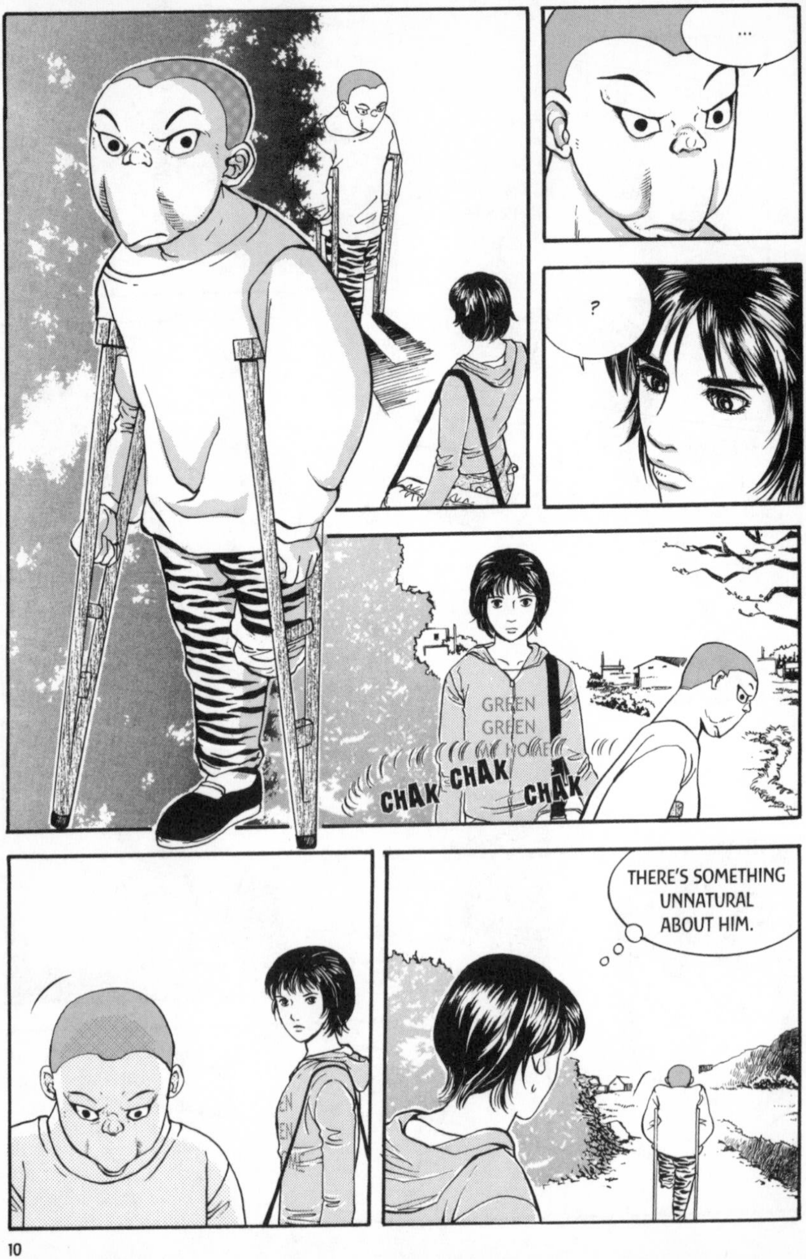
...
?
GREEN
GREEN
CHAK
CHAK
CHAK
THERE'S SOMETHING UNNATURAL ABOUT HIM.

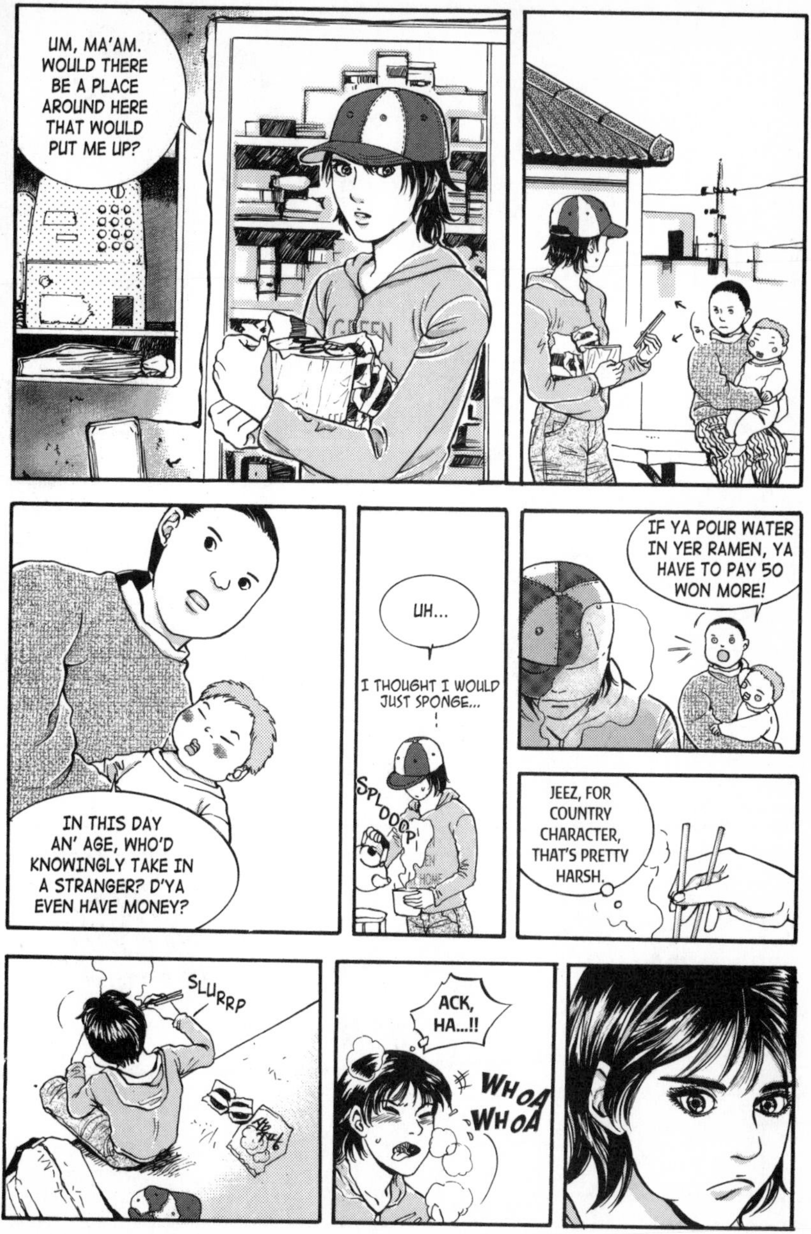
UM, MA'AM. WOULD THERE BE A PLACE AROUND HERE THAT WOULD PUT ME UP?
IN THIS DAY AN' AGE, WHO'D KNOWINGLY TAKE IN A STRANGER? D'YA EVEN HAVE MONEY?
UH...
I THOUGHT I WOULD JUST SPONGE...
SPLOOOP
IF YA POUR WATER IN YER RAMEN, YA HAVE TO PAY 50 WON MORE!
JEEZ, FOR COUNTRY CHARACTER, THAT'S PRETTY HARSH.
SLURRP
ACK, HA...!!
WHOA WHOA

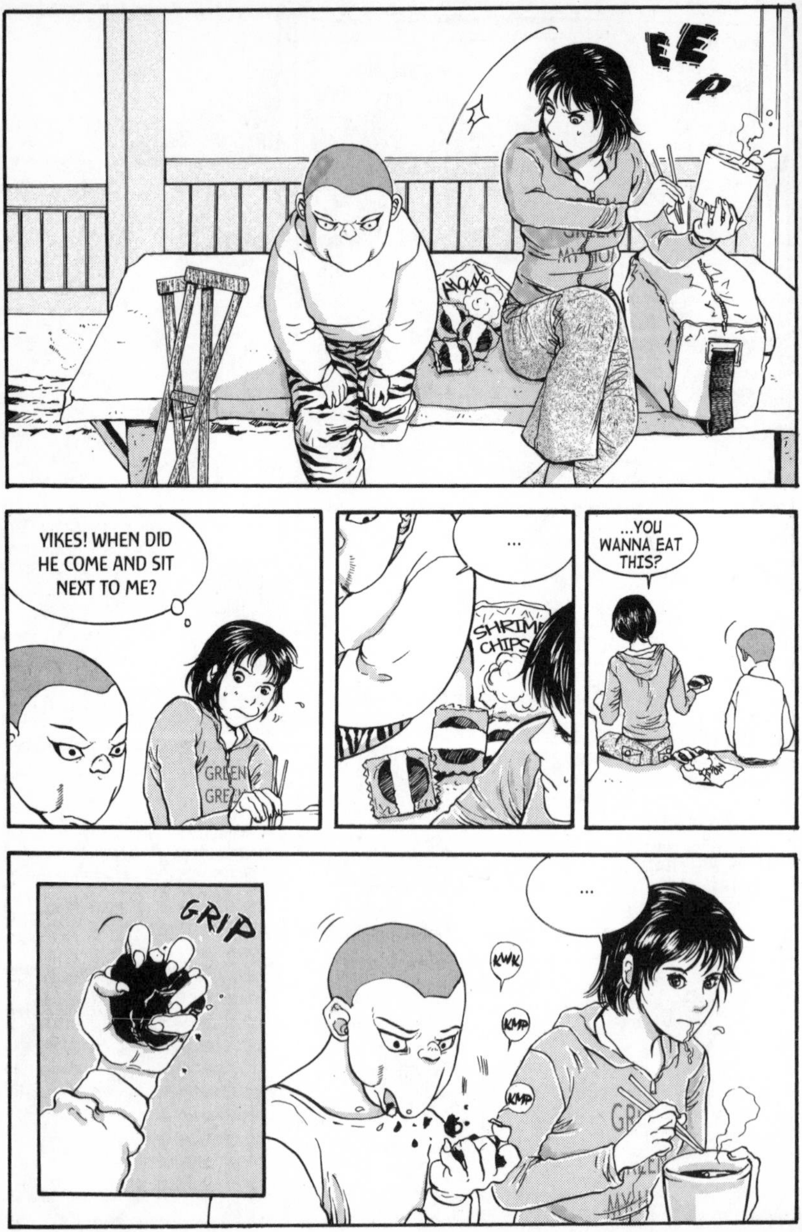
EEP
YIKES! WHEN DID HE COME AND SIT NEXT TO ME?
...
...YOU WANNA EAT THIS?
GRIP
...
KWK
KMP
KMP

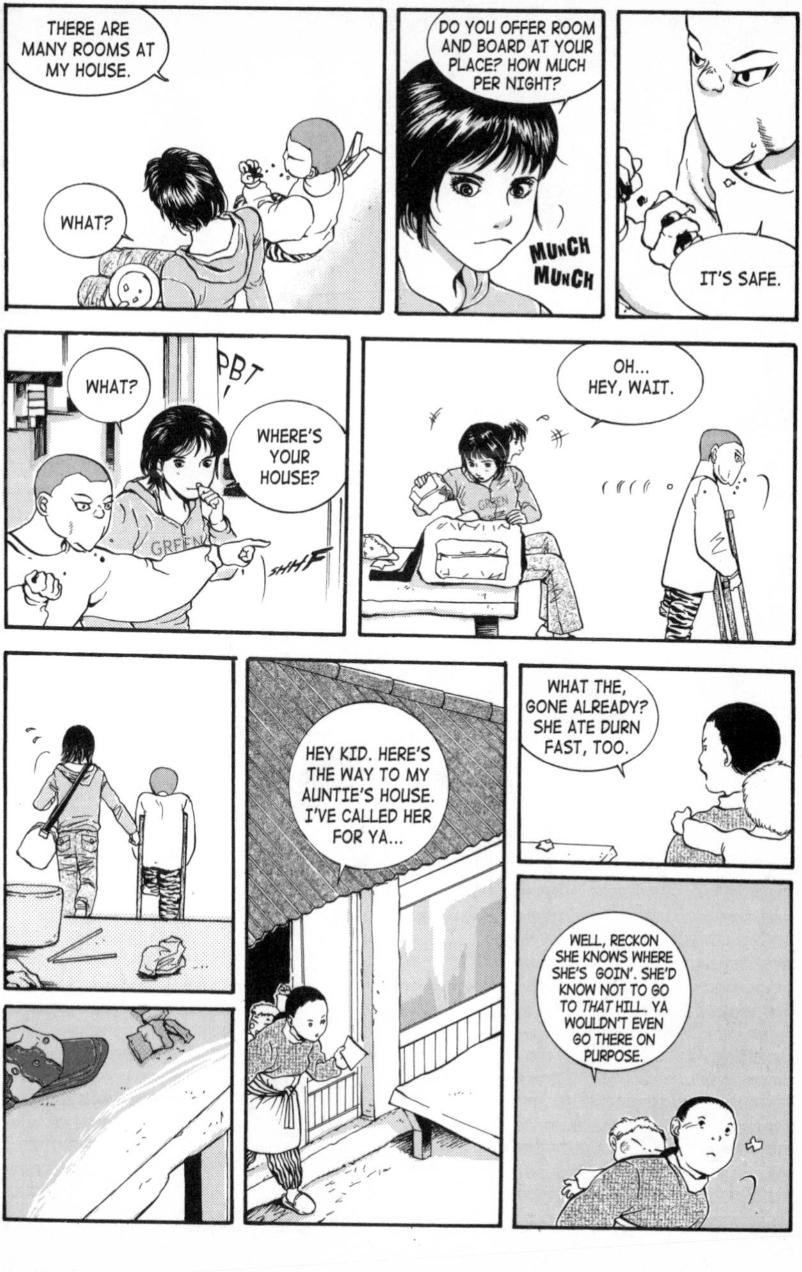
THERE ARE MANY ROOMS AT MY HOUSE.
WHAT?
DO YOU OFFER ROOM AND BOARD AT YOUR PLACE? HOW MUCH PER NIGHT?
MUNCH MUNCH
IT'S SAFE.
WHAT?
PBT
WHERE'S YOUR HOUSE?
SHHF
OH... HEY, WAIT.
HEY KID. HERE'S THE WAY TO MY AUNTIE'S HOUSE. I'VE CALLED HER FOR YA...
WHAT THE, GONE ALREADY? SHE ATE DURN FAST, TOO.
WELL, RECKON SHE KNOWS WHERE SHE'S GOIN'. SHE'D KNOW NOT TO GO TO *THAT* HILL. YA WOULDN'T EVEN GO THERE ON PURPOSE.

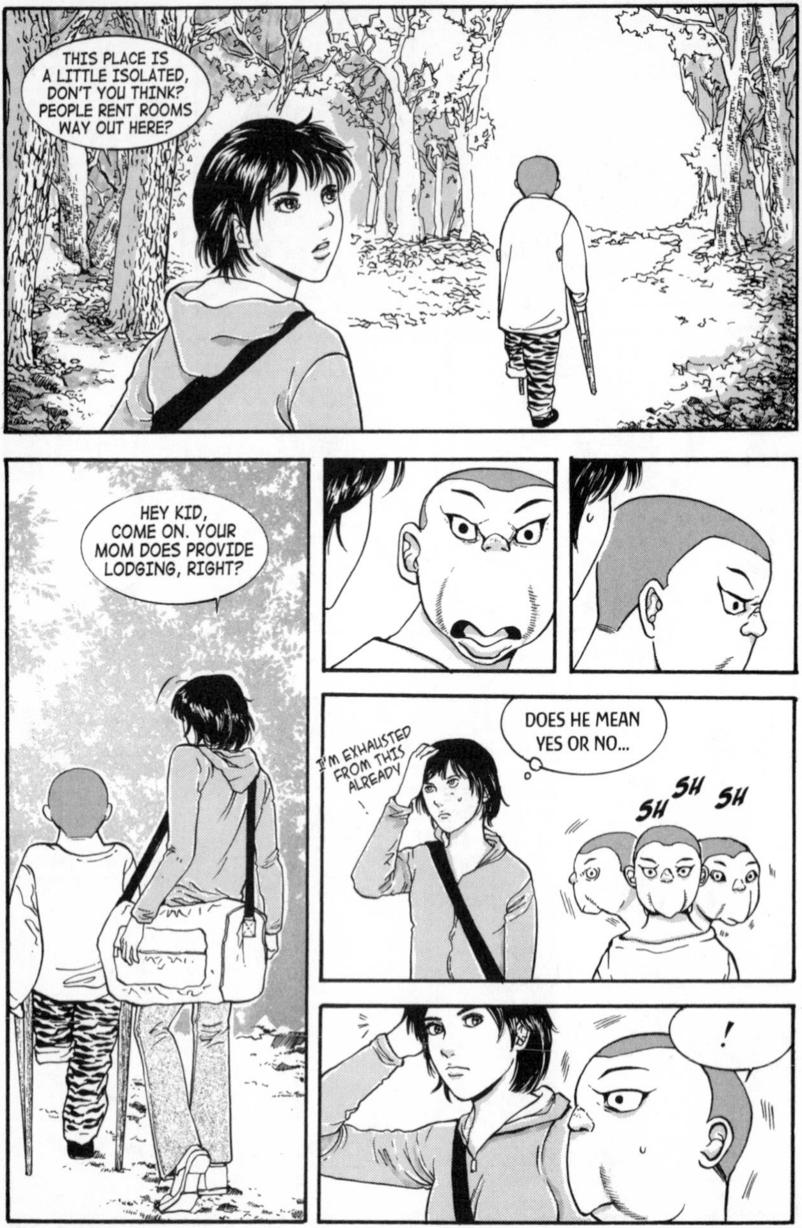
THIS PLACE IS A LITTLE ISOLATED, DON'T YOU THINK? PEOPLE RENT ROOMS WAY OUT HERE?
HEY KID, COME ON. YOUR MOM DOES PROVIDE LODGING, RIGHT?
I'M EXHAUSTED FROM THIS ALREADY
DOES HE MEAN YES OR NO...
SH SH SH
!

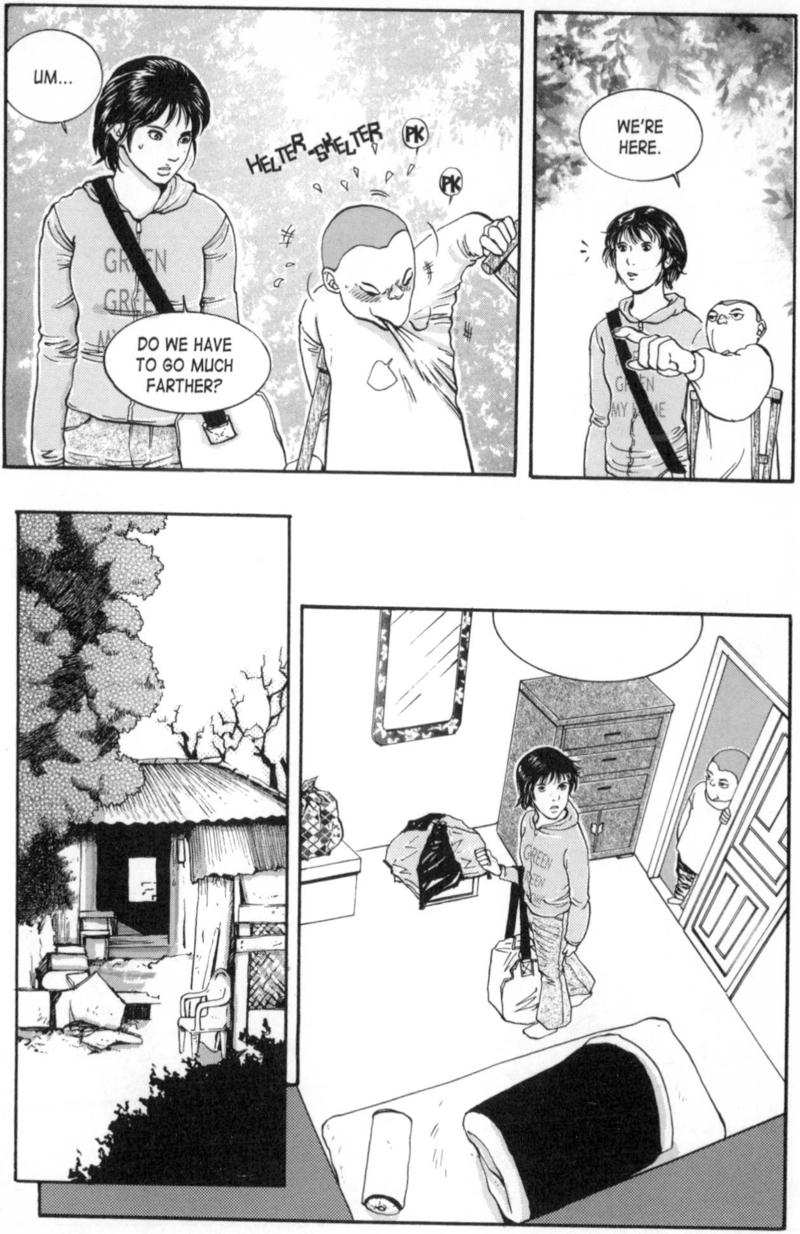
UM...
HELTER-SKELTER
PK
PK
DO WE HAVE TO GO MUCH FARTHER?
WE'RE HERE.

YOUR PARENTS AREN'T HOME? I'M NOT SURE I CAN JUST WALTZ IN LIKE THIS AND STAY.

WHAT'S THAT? IS THAT FOOD? YOU'RE A REAL HOME-MAKER, HUH?

I ATE RAMEN, THOUGH.

NOD

THANKS, I'LL ENJOY IT.

SHHF

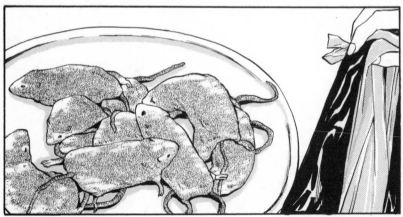

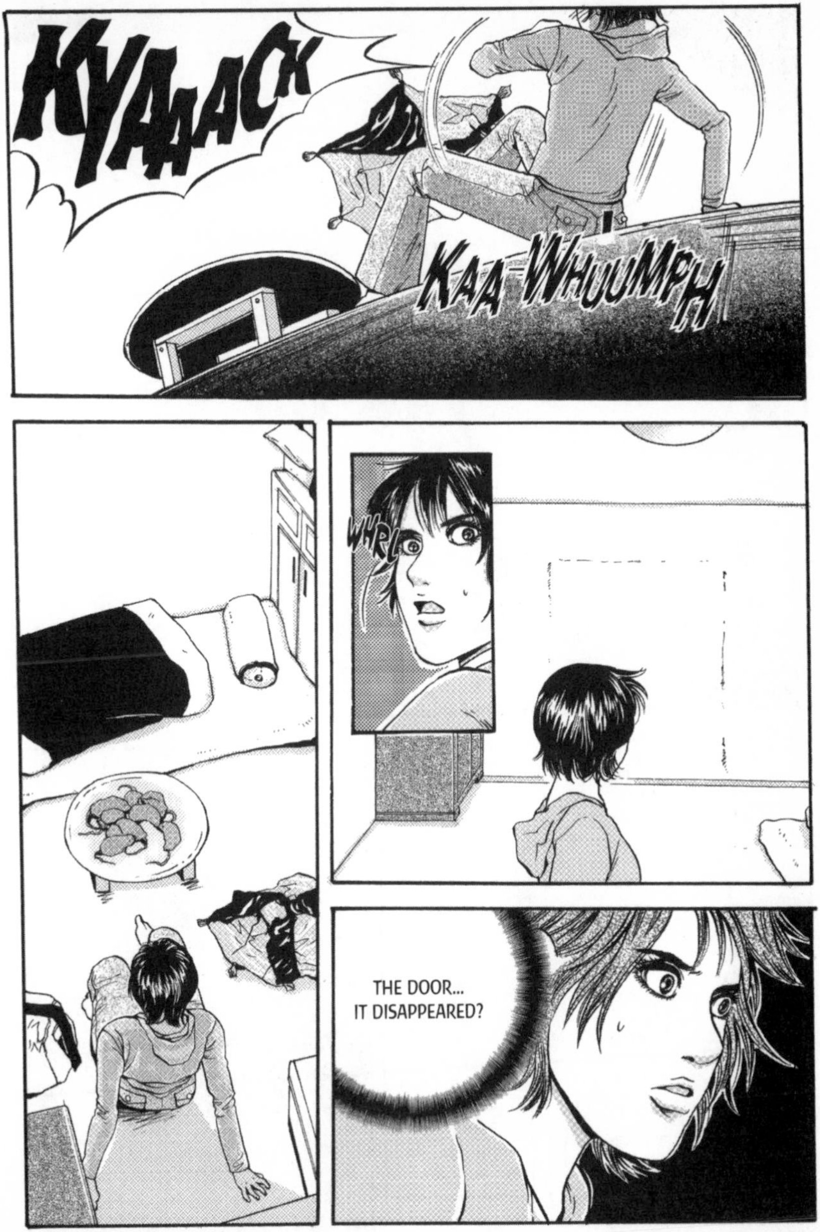
KYAAACK
KAA WHUUMPH
WHRL
THE DOOR...
IT DISAPPEARED?

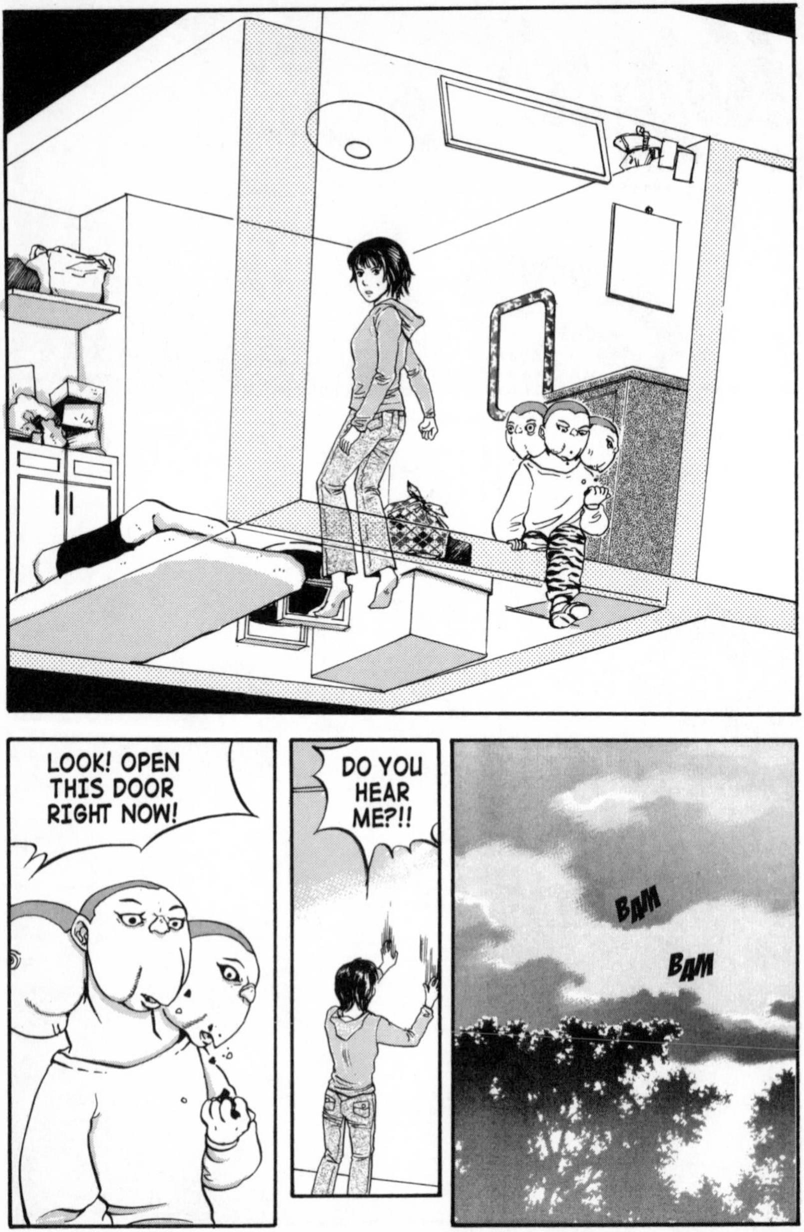

LOOK! OPEN THIS DOOR RIGHT NOW!
DO YOU HEAR ME?!!
BAM
BAM

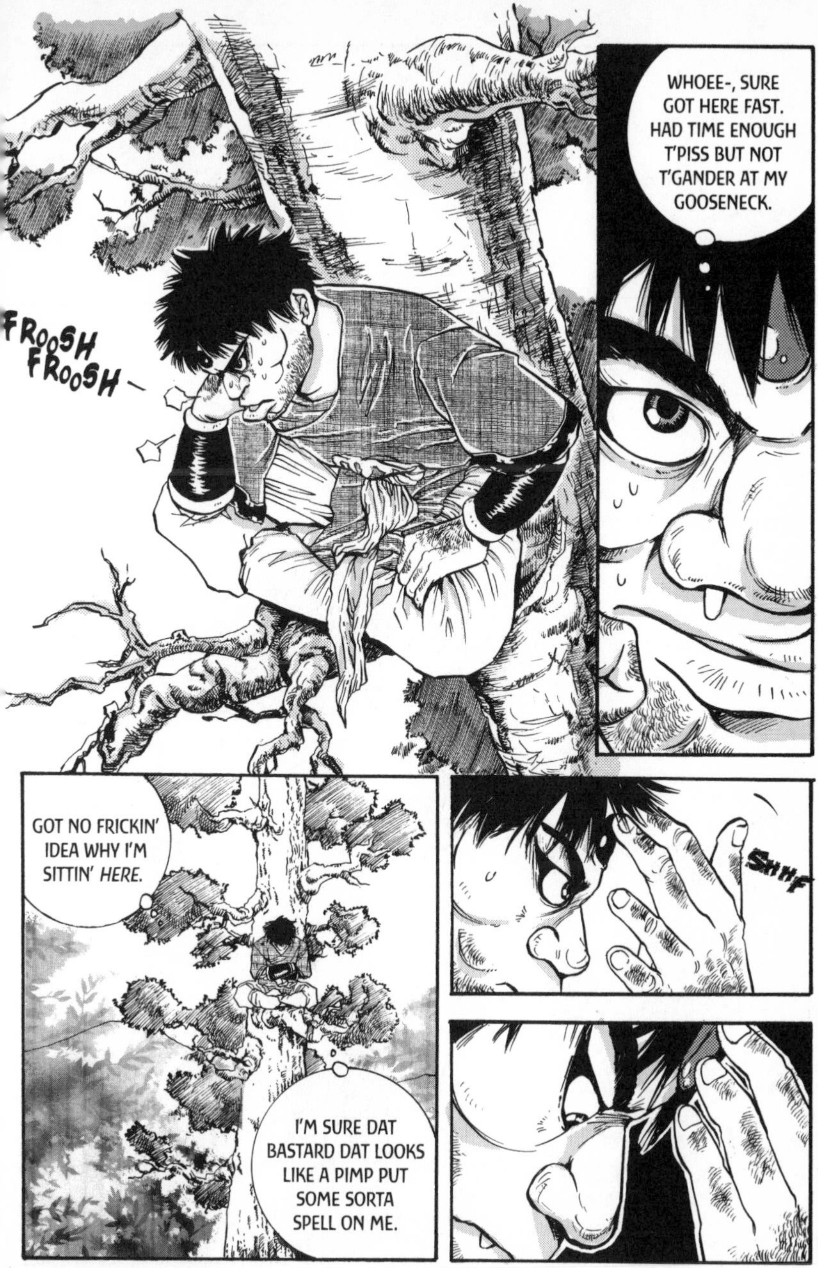
WHOEE-, SURE GOT HERE FAST. HAD TIME ENOUGH T'PISS BUT NOT T'GANDER AT MY GOOSENECK.
FROOSH FROOSH
GOT NO FRICKIN' IDEA WHY I'M SITTIN' *HERE*.
I'M SURE DAT BASTARD DAT LOOKS LIKE A PIMP PUT SOME SORTA SPELL ON ME.
SHHF

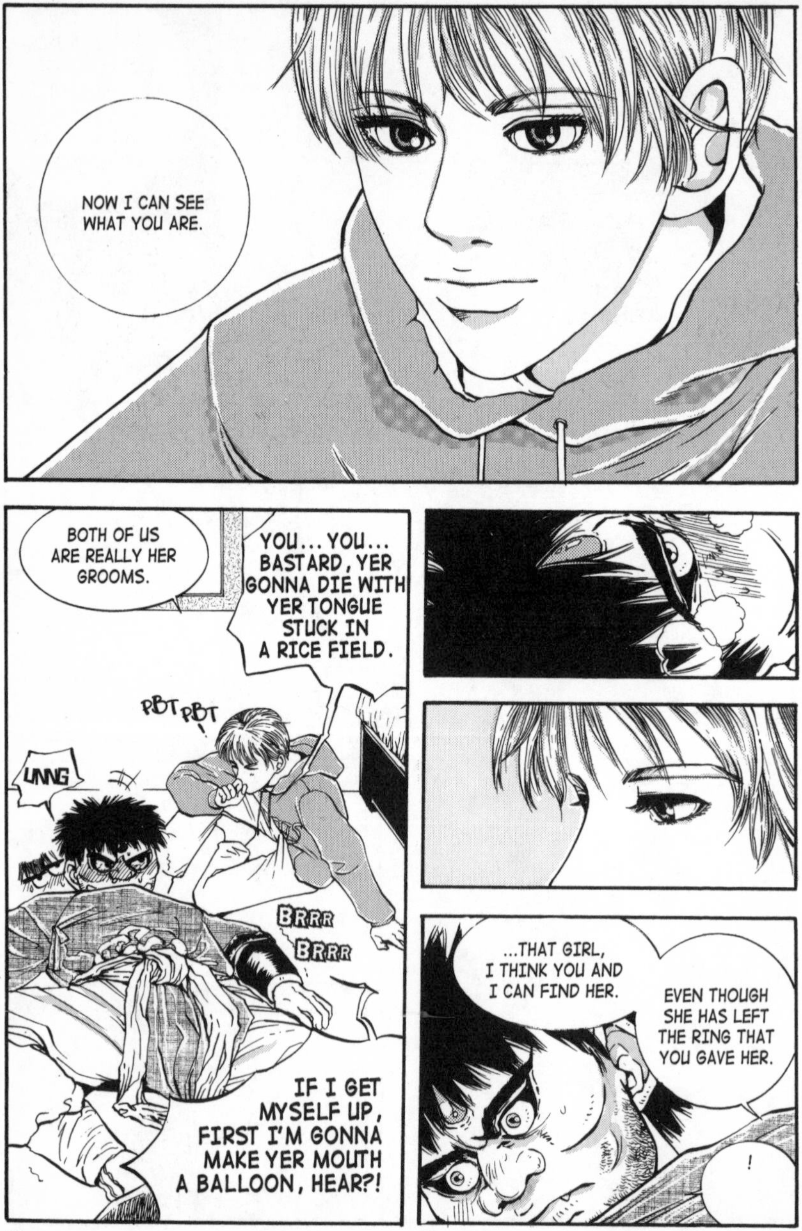
NOW I CAN SEE WHAT YOU ARE.
BOTH OF US ARE REALLY HER GROOMS.
YOU... YOU... BASTARD, YER GONNA DIE WITH YER TONGUE STUCK IN A RICE FIELD.
PBT PBT
UNNG
BRRR
BRRR
IF I GET MYSELF UP, FIRST I'M GONNA MAKE YER MOUTH A BALLOON, HEAR?!
...THAT GIRL, I THINK YOU AND I CAN FIND HER.
EVEN THOUGH SHE HAS LEFT THE RING THAT YOU GAVE HER.
!

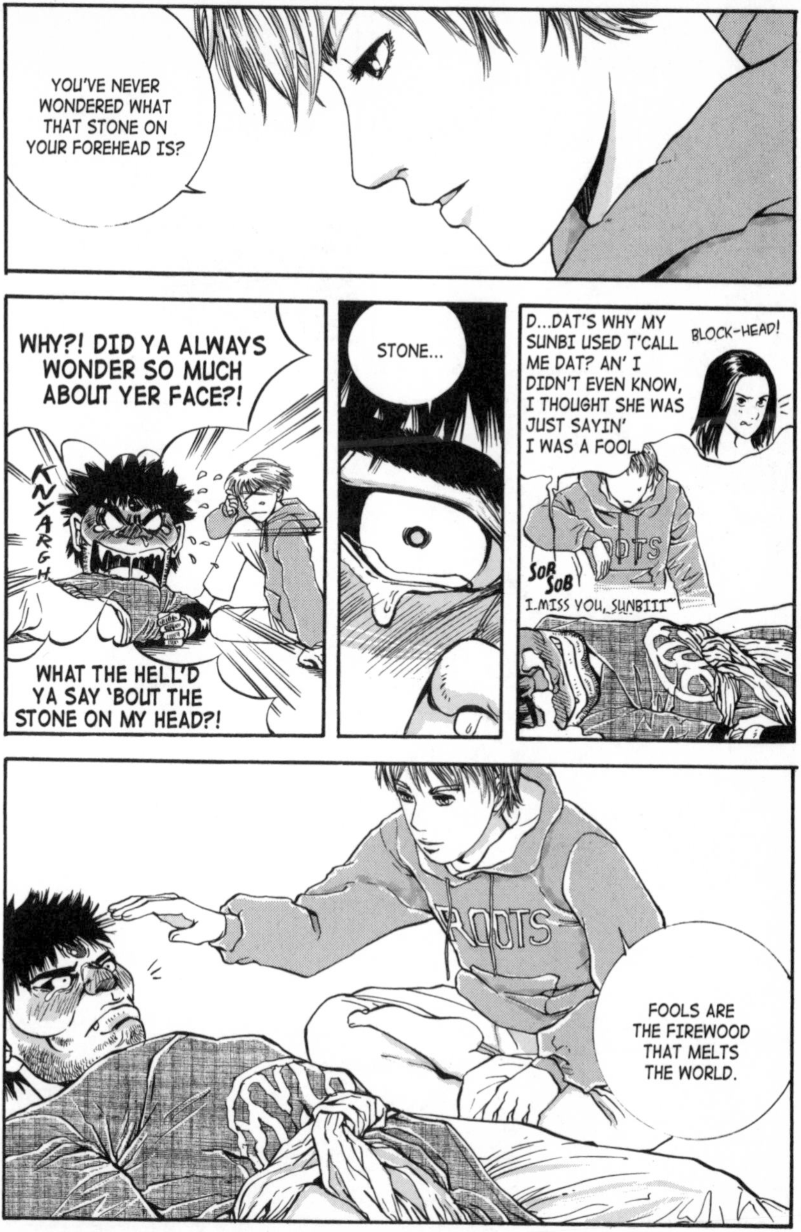
YOU'VE NEVER WONDERED WHAT THAT STONE ON YOUR FOREHEAD IS?
WHY?! DID YA ALWAYS WONDER SO MUCH ABOUT YER FACE?!
KNYARGH
WHAT THE HELL'D YA SAY 'BOUT THE STONE ON MY HEAD?!
STONE...
D...DAT'S WHY MY SUNBI USED T'CALL ME DAT? AN' I DIDN'T EVEN KNOW, I THOUGHT SHE WAS JUST SAYIN' I WAS A FOOL.
BLOCK-HEAD!
SOB SOB
I MISS YOU, SUNBIII~
FOOLS ARE THE FIREWOOD THAT MELTS THE WORLD.

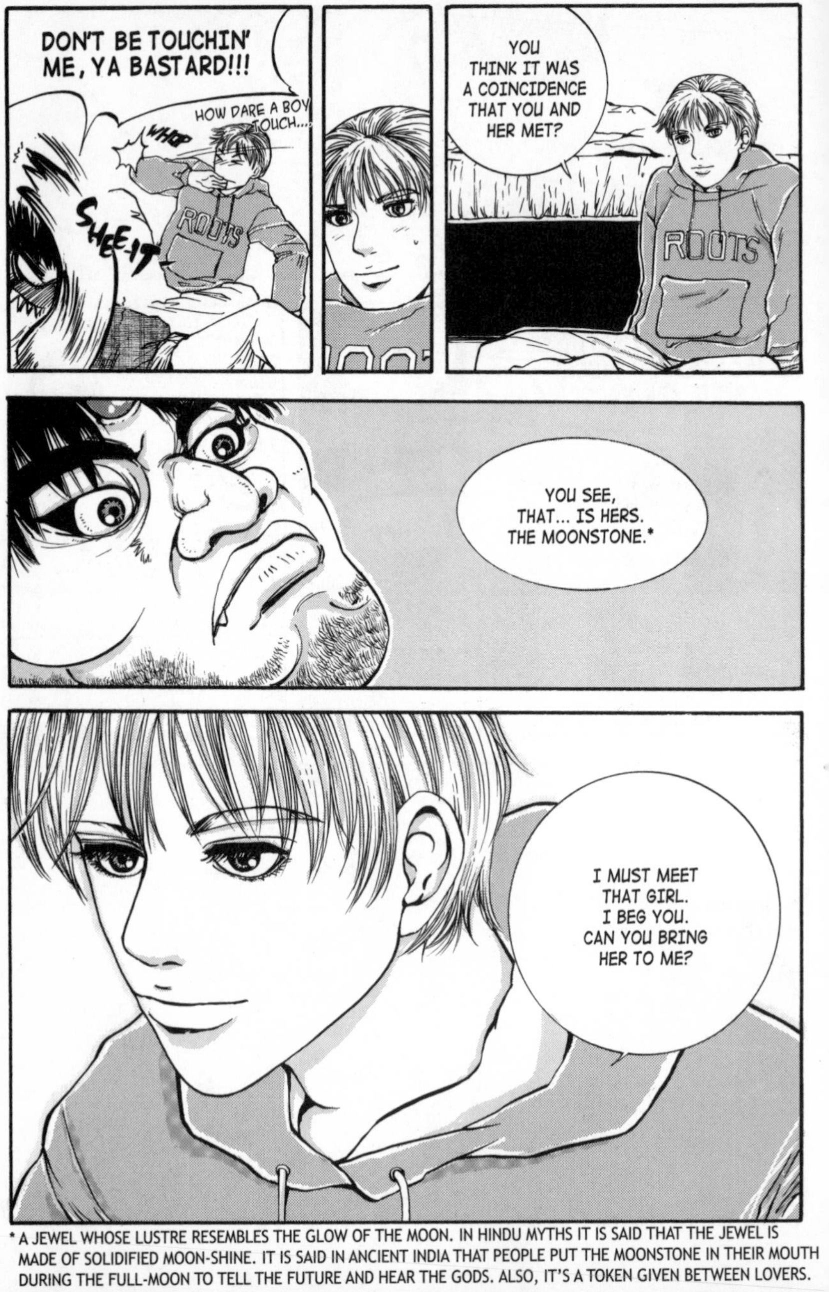
DON'T BE TOUCHIN' ME, YA BASTARD!!!
HOW DARE A BOY TOUCH...
WHIP
SHEE-IT
YOU THINK IT WAS A COINCIDENCE THAT YOU AND HER MET?
YOU SEE, THAT... IS HERS. THE MOONSTONE.*
I MUST MEET THAT GIRL. I BEG YOU. CAN YOU BRING HER TO ME?

* A JEWEL WHOSE LUSTRE RESEMBLES THE GLOW OF THE MOON. IN HINDU MYTHS IT IS SAID THAT THE JEWEL IS MADE OF SOLIDIFIED MOON-SHINE. IT IS SAID IN ANCIENT INDIA THAT PEOPLE PUT THE MOONSTONE IN THEIR MOUTH DURING THE FULL-MOON TO TELL THE FUTURE AND HEAR THE GODS. ALSO, IT'S A TOKEN GIVEN BETWEEN LOVERS.

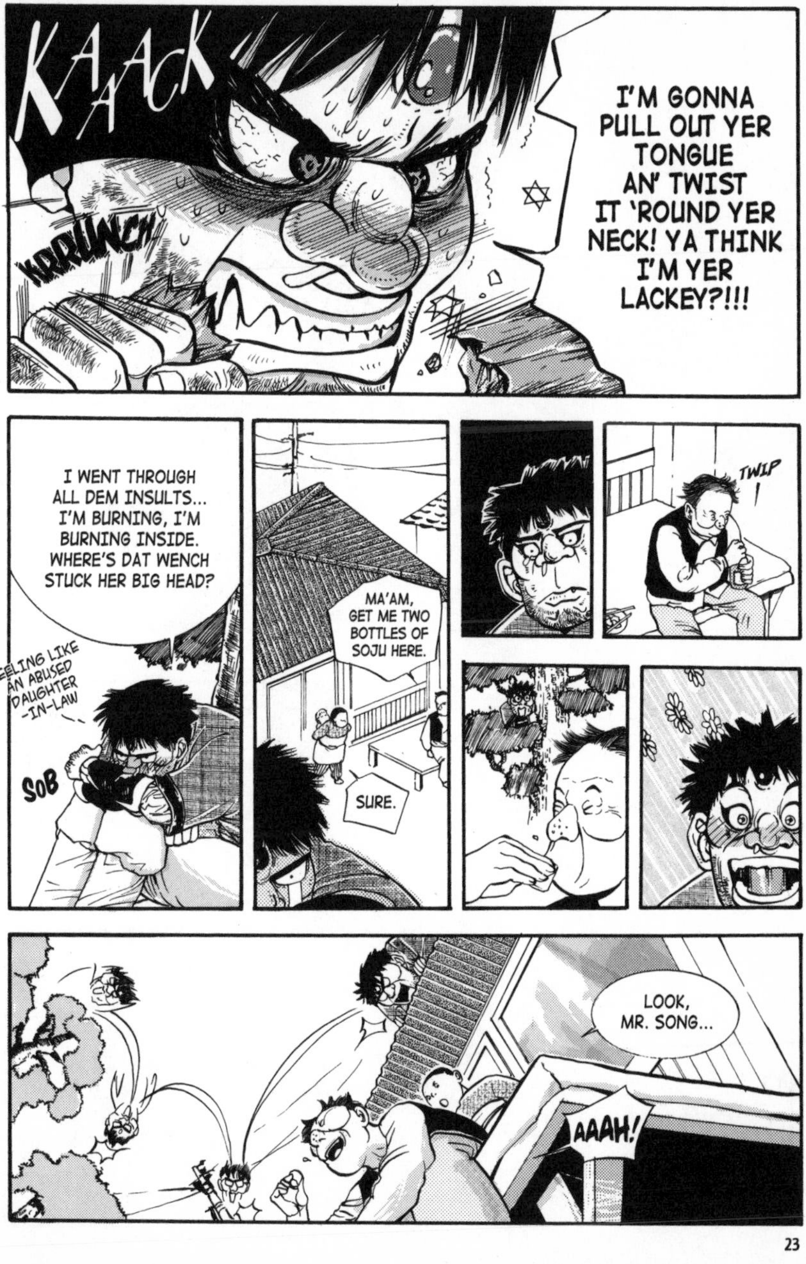
KAAACK
KRRUNCH
I'M GONNA PULL OUT YER TONGUE AN' TWIST IT 'ROUND YER NECK! YA THINK I'M YER LACKEY?!!!
I WENT THROUGH ALL DEM INSULTS... I'M BURNING, I'M BURNING INSIDE. WHERE'S DAT WENCH STUCK HER BIG HEAD?
FEELING LIKE AN ABUSED DAUGHTER -IN-LAW
SOB
MA'AM, GET ME TWO BOTTLES OF SOJU HERE.
SURE.
TWIP
LOOK, MR. SONG...
AAAH!

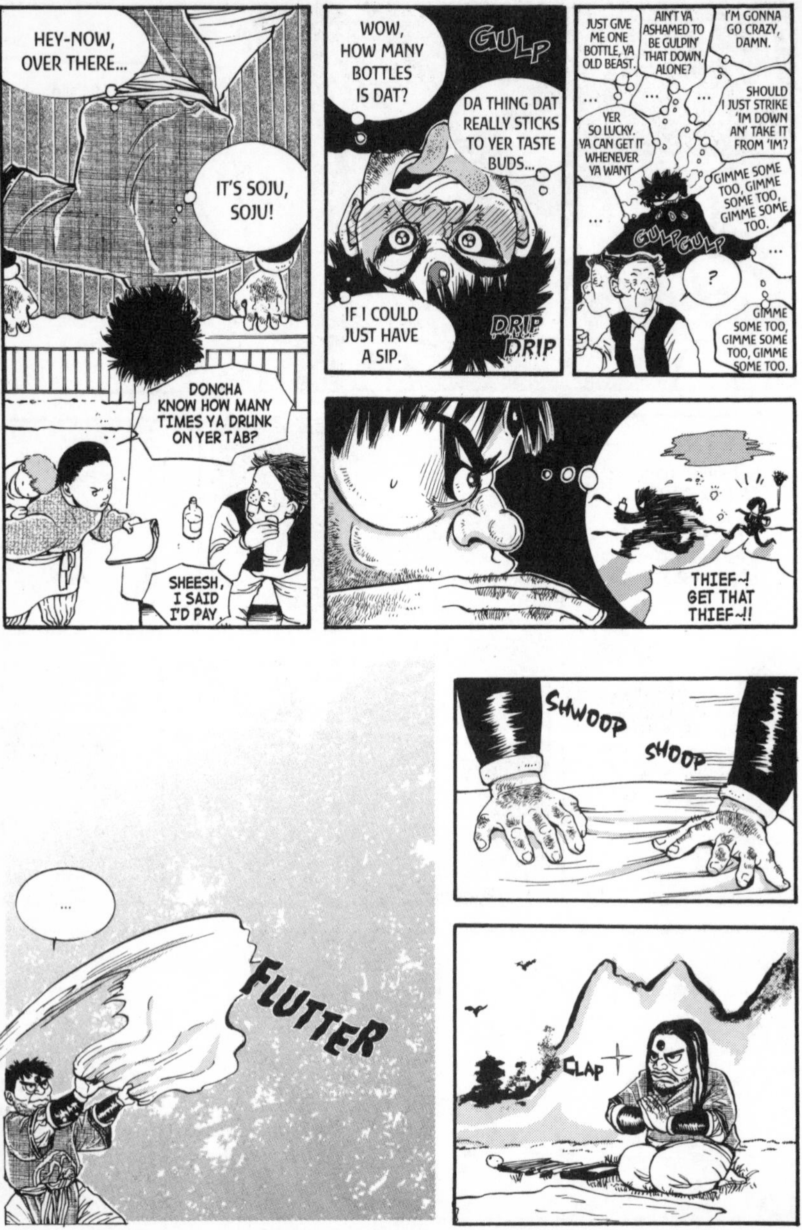
HEY-NOW, OVER THERE...
IT'S SOJU, SOJU!
DONCHA KNOW HOW MANY TIMES YA DRUNK ON YER TAB?
SHEESH, I SAID I'D PAY.
WOW, HOW MANY BOTTLES IS DAT?
GULP
DA THING DAT REALLY STICKS TO YER TASTE BUDS...
IF I COULD JUST HAVE A SIP.
DRIP DRIP
JUST GIVE ME ONE BOTTLE, YA OLD BEAST.
AIN'T YA ASHAMED TO BE GULPIN' THAT DOWN, ALONE?
I'M GONNA GO CRAZY, DAMN.
...
...
...
SHOULD I JUST STRIKE 'IM DOWN AN' TAKE IT FROM 'IM?
YER SO LUCKY. YA CAN GET IT WHENEVER YA WANT
GIMME SOME TOO, GIMME SOME TOO, GIMME SOME TOO.
...
GULP GULP
...
?
GIMME SOME TOO, GIMME SOME TOO, GIMME SOME TOO.
THIEF~! GET THAT THIEF~!!
SHWOOP
SHOOP
...
FLUTTER
CLAP

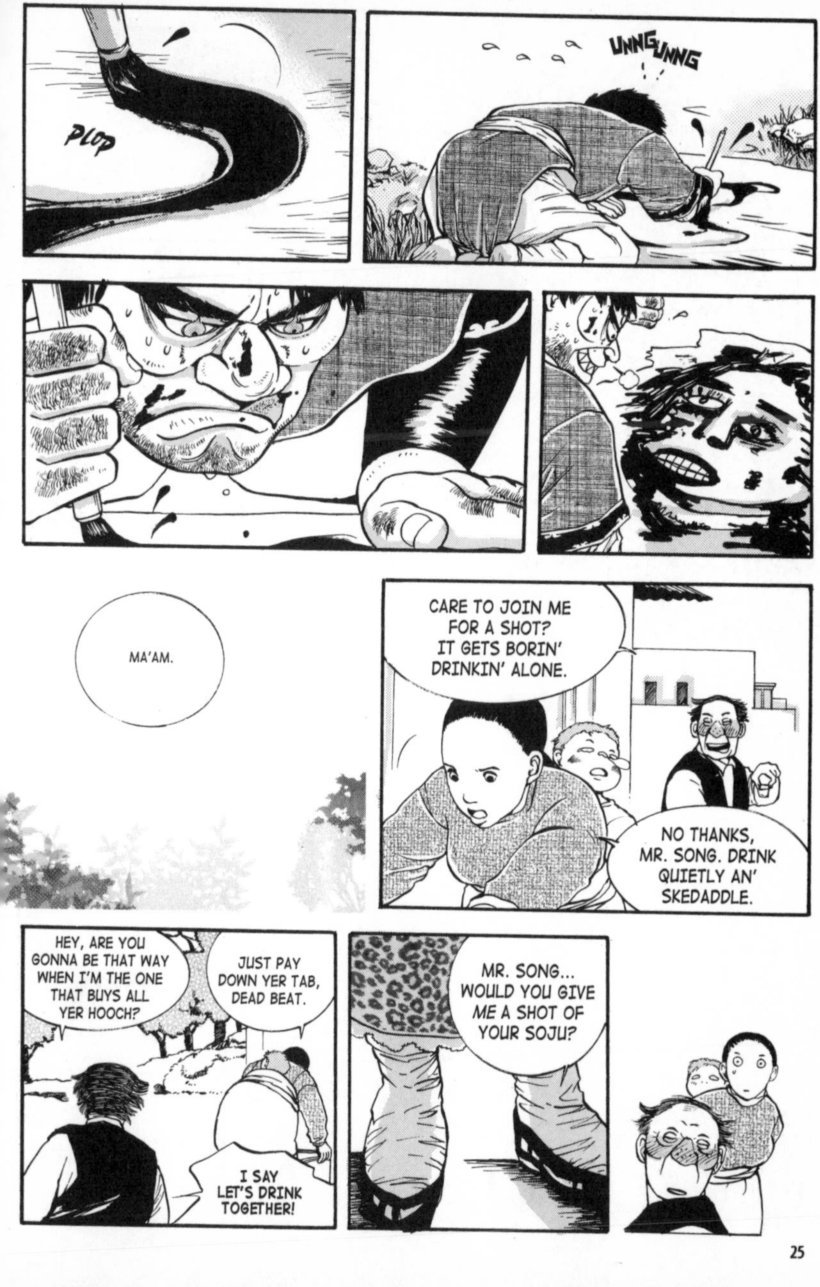
PLOP
UNNG UNNG
MA'AM.
CARE TO JOIN ME FOR A SHOT? IT GETS BORIN' DRINKIN' ALONE.
NO THANKS, MR. SONG. DRINK QUIETLY AN' SKEDADDLE.
HEY, ARE YOU GONNA BE THAT WAY WHEN I'M THE ONE THAT BUYS ALL YER HOOCH?
JUST PAY DOWN YER TAB, DEAD BEAT.
I SAY LET'S DRINK TOGETHER!
MR. SONG... WOULD YOU GIVE *ME* A SHOT OF YOUR SOJU?

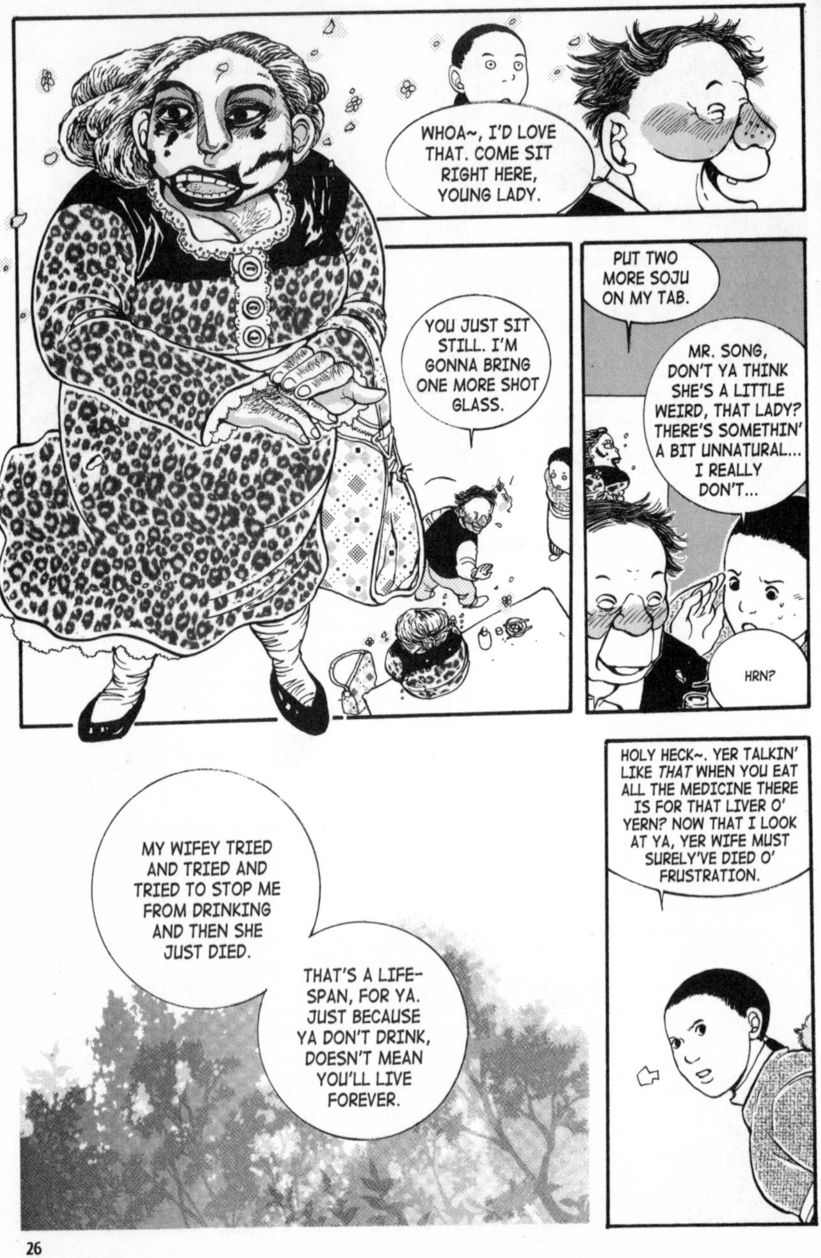
WHOA~, I'D LOVE THAT. COME SIT RIGHT HERE, YOUNG LADY.
YOU JUST SIT STILL. I'M GONNA BRING ONE MORE SHOT GLASS.
PUT TWO MORE SOJU ON MY TAB.
MR. SONG, DON'T YA THINK SHE'S A LITTLE WEIRD, THAT LADY? THERE'S SOMETHIN' A BIT UNNATURAL... I REALLY DON'T...
HRN?
HOLY HECK~. YER TALKIN' LIKE *THAT* WHEN YOU EAT ALL THE MEDICINE THERE IS FOR THAT LIVER O' YERN? NOW THAT I LOOK AT YA, YER WIFE MUST SURELY'VE DIED O' FRUSTRATION.
MY WIFEY TRIED AND TRIED AND TRIED TO STOP ME FROM DRINKING AND THEN SHE JUST DIED.
THAT'S A LIFE-SPAN, FOR YA. JUST BECAUSE YA DON'T DRINK, DOESN'T MEAN YOU'LL LIVE FOREVER.

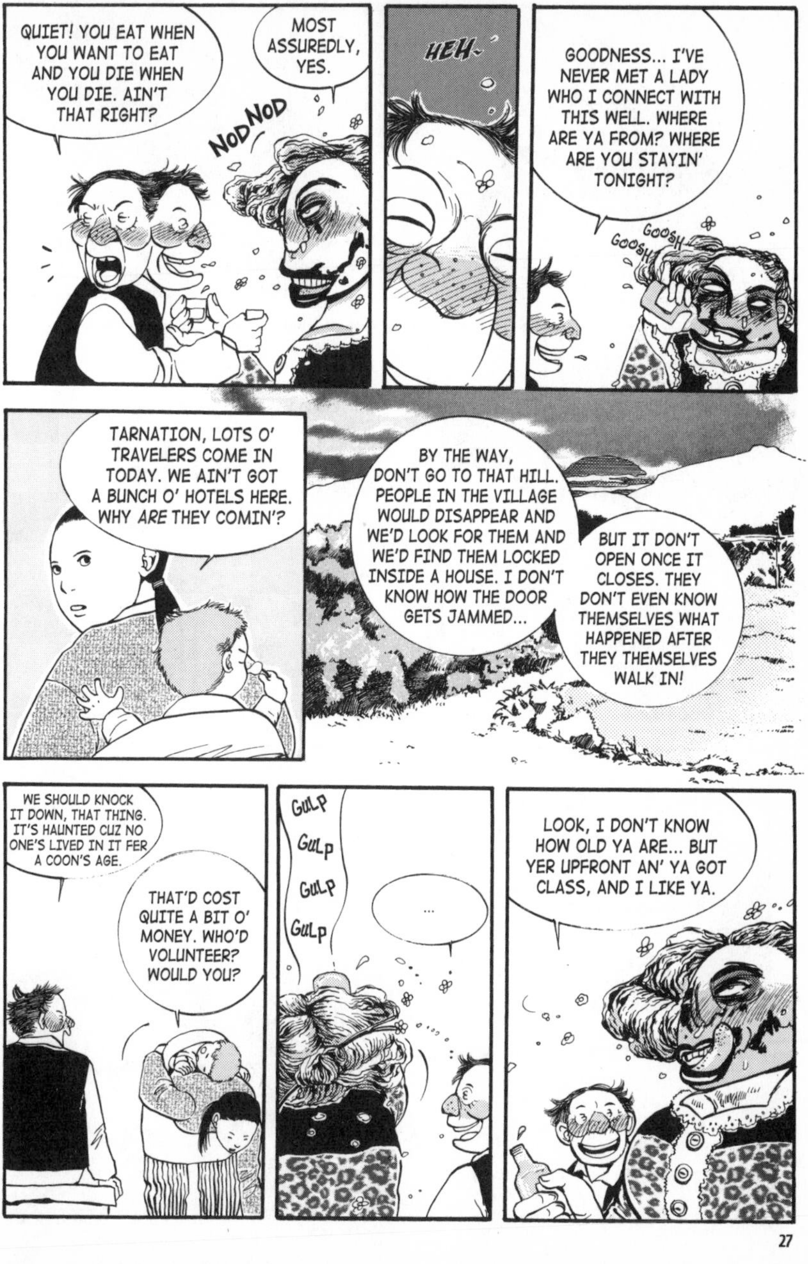
QUIET! YOU EAT WHEN YOU WANT TO EAT AND YOU DIE WHEN YOU DIE. AIN'T THAT RIGHT?
MOST ASSUREDLY, YES.
NOD NOD
HEH~
GOODNESS... I'VE NEVER MET A LADY WHO I CONNECT WITH THIS WELL. WHERE ARE YA FROM? WHERE ARE YOU STAYIN' TONIGHT?
GOOSH GOOSH
TARNATION, LOTS O' TRAVELERS COME IN TODAY. WE AIN'T GOT A BUNCH O' HOTELS HERE. WHY *ARE* THEY COMIN'?
BY THE WAY, DON'T GO TO THAT HILL. PEOPLE IN THE VILLAGE WOULD DISAPPEAR AND WE'D LOOK FOR THEM AND WE'D FIND THEM LOCKED INSIDE A HOUSE. I DON'T KNOW HOW THE DOOR GETS JAMMED...
BUT IT DON'T OPEN ONCE IT CLOSES. THEY DON'T EVEN KNOW THEMSELVES WHAT HAPPENED AFTER THEY THEMSELVES WALK IN!
WE SHOULD KNOCK IT DOWN, THAT THING. IT'S HAUNTED CUZ NO ONE'S LIVED IN IT FER A COON'S AGE.
THAT'D COST QUITE A BIT O' MONEY. WHO'D VOLUNTEER? WOULD YOU?
GULP
GULP
GULP
GULP
...
LOOK, I DON'T KNOW HOW OLD YA ARE... BUT YER UPFRONT AN' YA GOT CLASS, AND I LIKE YA.

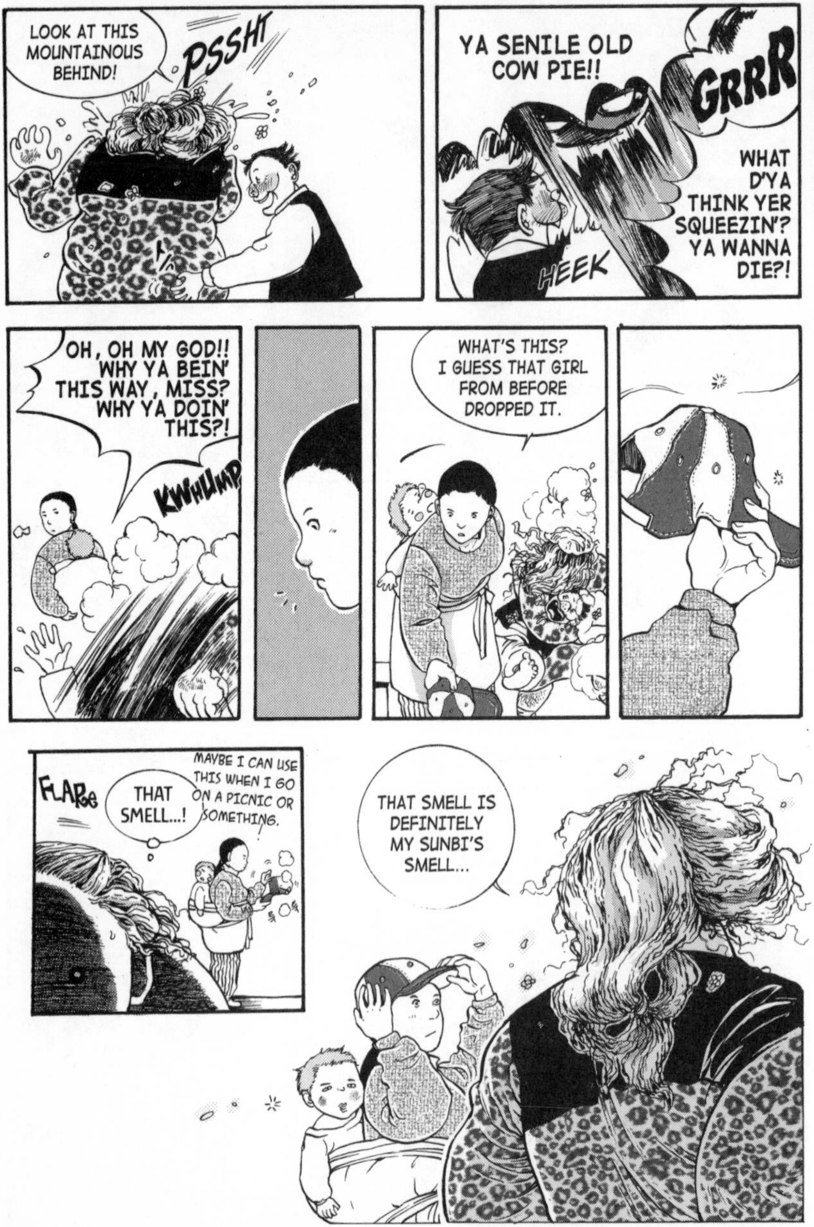
LOOK AT THIS MOUNTAINOUS BEHIND!
PSSHT
YA SENILE OLD COW PIE!!
GRRR
WHAT D'YA THINK YER SQUEEZIN'? YA WANNA DIE?!
HEEK
OH, OH MY GOD!! WHY YA BEIN' THIS WAY, MISS? WHY YA DOIN' THIS?!
KWHUMP
WHAT'S THIS? I GUESS THAT GIRL FROM BEFORE DROPPED IT.
FLAP
THAT SMELL...!
MAYBE I CAN USE THIS WHEN I GO ON A PICNIC OR SOMETHING.
THAT SMELL IS DEFINITELY MY SUNBI'S SMELL...

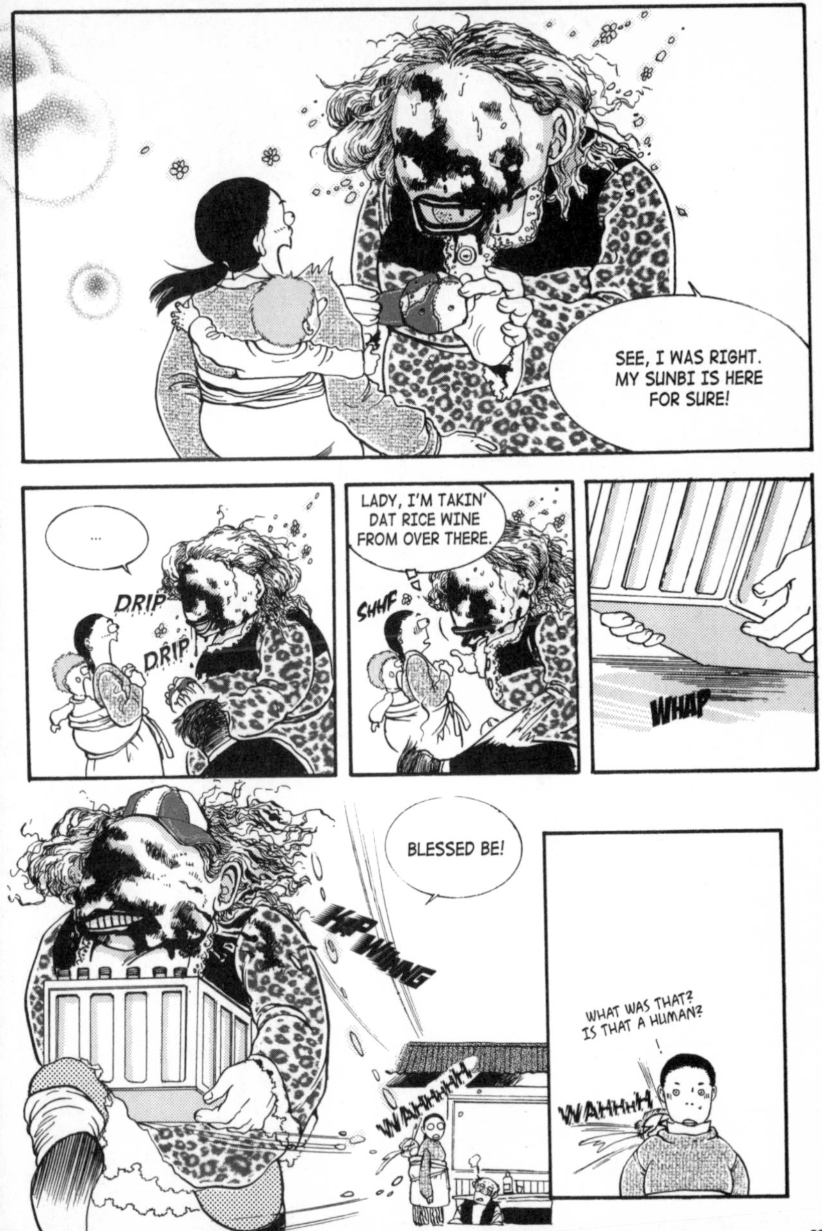
SEE, I WAS RIGHT. MY SUNBI IS HERE FOR SURE!
...
DRIP
DRIP
LADY, I'M TAKIN' DAT RICE WINE FROM OVER THERE.
SHUF
WHAP
BLESSED BE!
FWOOSH
WAHHHH
WHAT WAS THAT? IS THAT A HUMAN?
!
WAHHHH

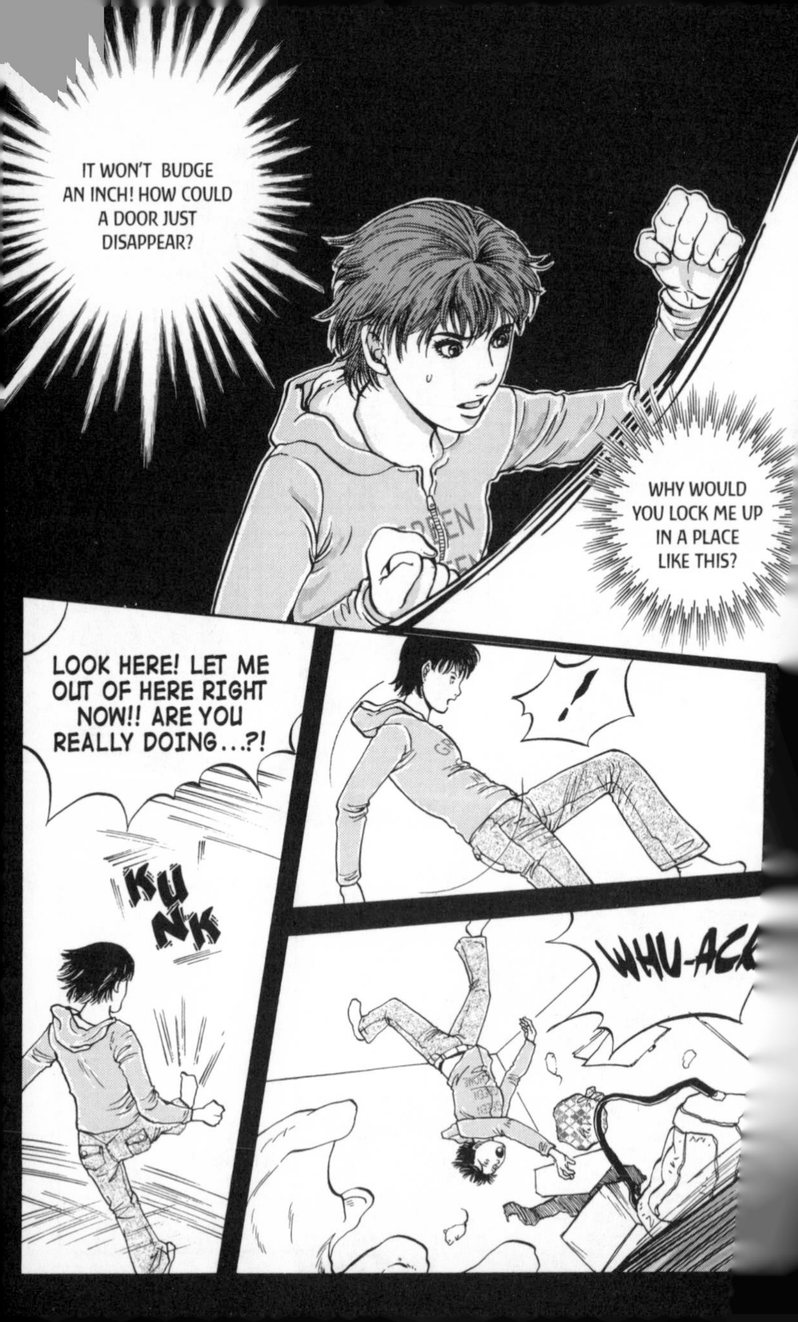
IT WON'T BUDGE AN INCH! HOW COULD A DOOR JUST DISAPPEAR?
WHY WOULD YOU LOCK ME UP IN A PLACE LIKE THIS?
LOOK HERE! LET ME OUT OF HERE RIGHT NOW!! ARE YOU REALLY DOING...?!
!
KUNK
WHU-ACK

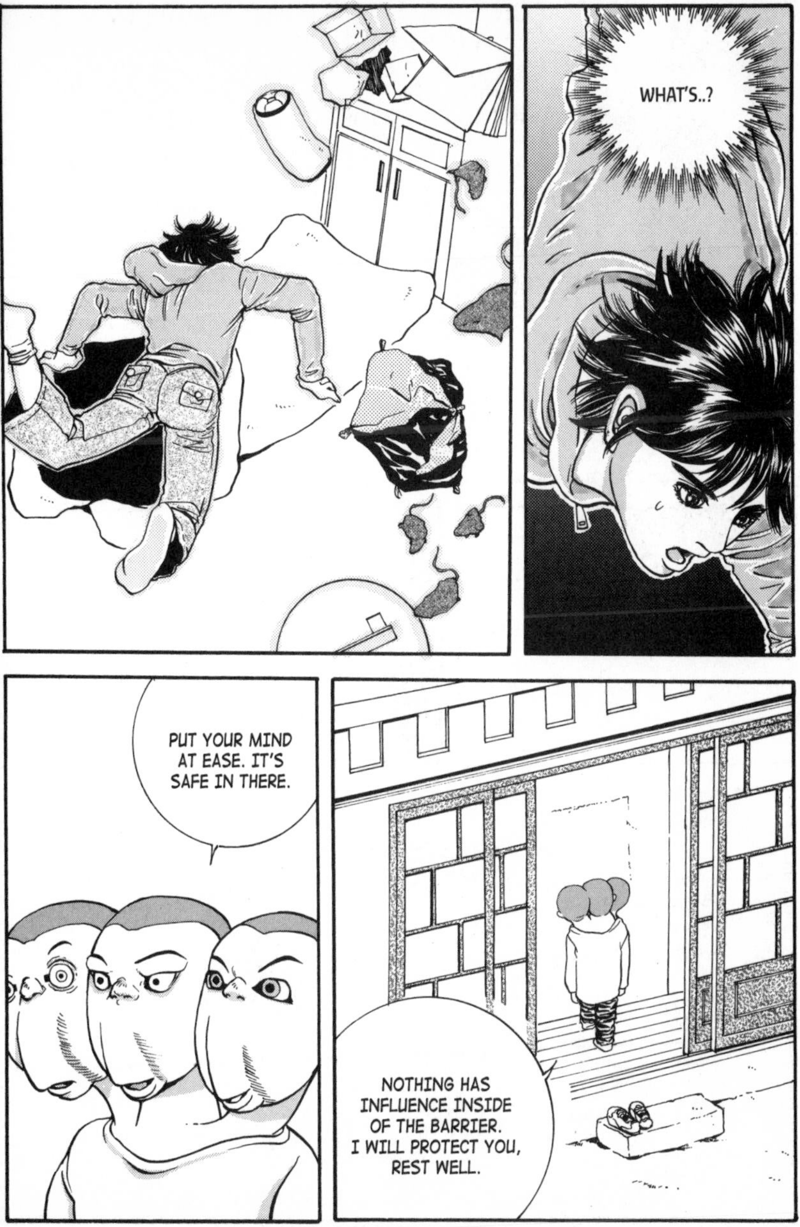
WHAT'S..?
PUT YOUR MIND AT EASE. IT'S SAFE IN THERE.
NOTHING HAS INFLUENCE INSIDE OF THE BARRIER. I WILL PROTECT YOU, REST WELL.

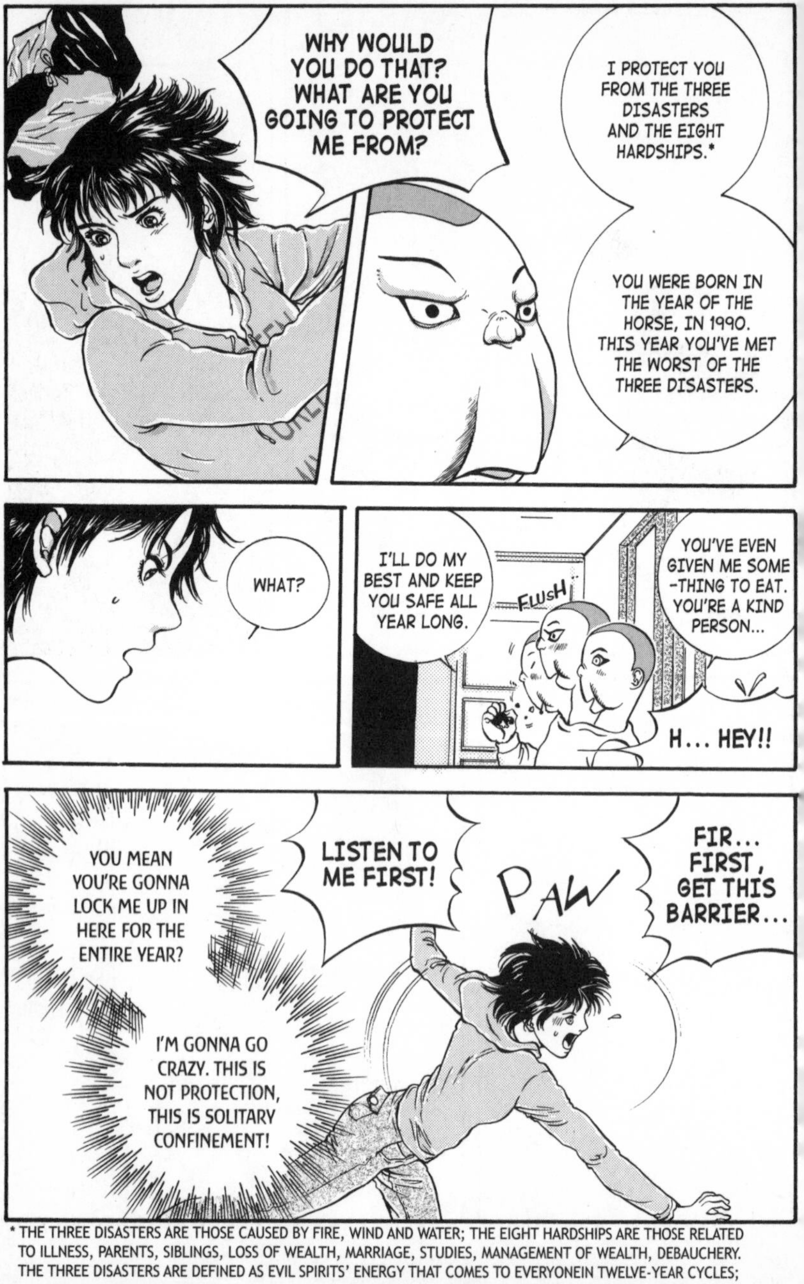
WHY WOULD YOU DO THAT? WHAT ARE YOU GOING TO PROTECT ME FROM?
I PROTECT YOU FROM THE THREE DISASTERS AND THE EIGHT HARDSHIPS.*
YOU WERE BORN IN THE YEAR OF THE HORSE, IN 1990. THIS YEAR YOU'VE MET THE WORST OF THE THREE DISASTERS.
WHAT?
I'LL DO MY BEST AND KEEP YOU SAFE ALL YEAR LONG.
FLUSH
YOU'VE EVEN GIVEN ME SOME-THING TO EAT. YOU'RE A KIND PERSON...
H... HEY!!
YOU MEAN YOU'RE GONNA LOCK ME UP IN HERE FOR THE ENTIRE YEAR?
I'M GONNA GO CRAZY. THIS IS NOT PROTECTION, THIS IS SOLITARY CONFINEMENT!
LISTEN TO ME FIRST!
PAW
FIR... FIRST, GET THIS BARRIER...

* THE THREE DISASTERS ARE THOSE CAUSED BY FIRE, WIND AND WATER; THE EIGHT HARDSHIPS ARE THOSE RELATED TO ILLNESS, PARENTS, SIBLINGS, LOSS OF WEALTH, MARRIAGE, STUDIES, MANAGEMENT OF WEALTH, DEBAUCHERY. THE THREE DISASTERS ARE DEFINED AS EVIL SPIRITS' ENERGY THAT COMES TO EVERYONEIN TWELVE-YEAR CYCLES;

KYACK

WARL

SO, NOTHING CAN INFLUENCE THIS AREA?

I'M GONNA FREAK OUT. NO GRAVITY? THAT MAKES NO SENSE.

!

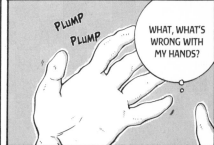

PLUMP PLUMP

WHAT, WHAT'S WRONG WITH MY HANDS?

EACK

WHILE IT STAYS WITH YOU FOR THREE YEARS. THE FIRST YEAR IS CALLED "ENTERING THE THREE DISASTERS", THE SECOND YEAR IS CALLED "IN THE THREE DISASTERS" AND THE THIRD YEAR IS CALLED "LEAVING THE THREE DISASTERS." THE EXPERTS WARN AGAINST ACCEPTING THIS TIME AS A DIFFICULT PERIOD; THEY RECOMMEND ACCEPTING IT AS A PREPARATION PERIOD FOR THE FUTURE.

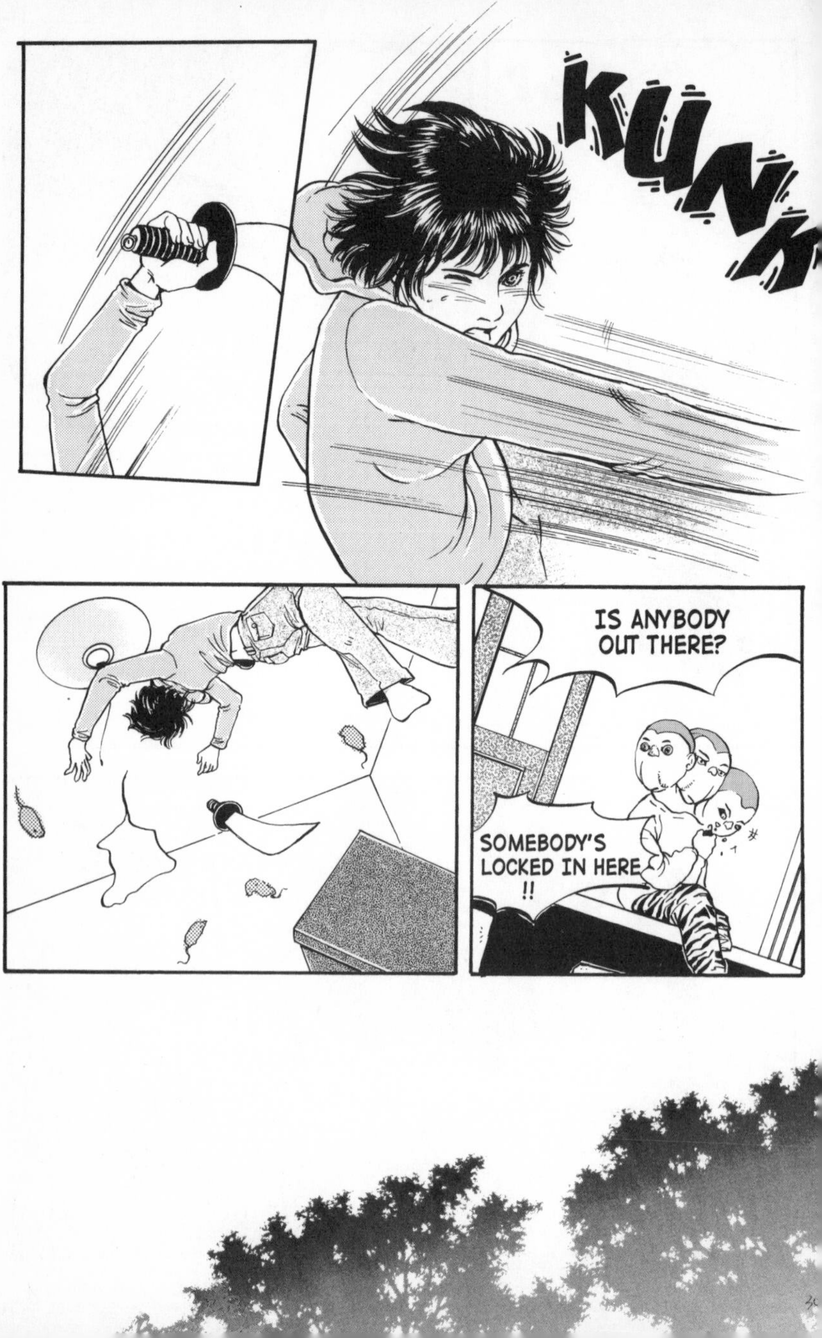
KUNK
IS ANYBODY OUT THERE?
SOMEBODY'S LOCKED IN HERE!!

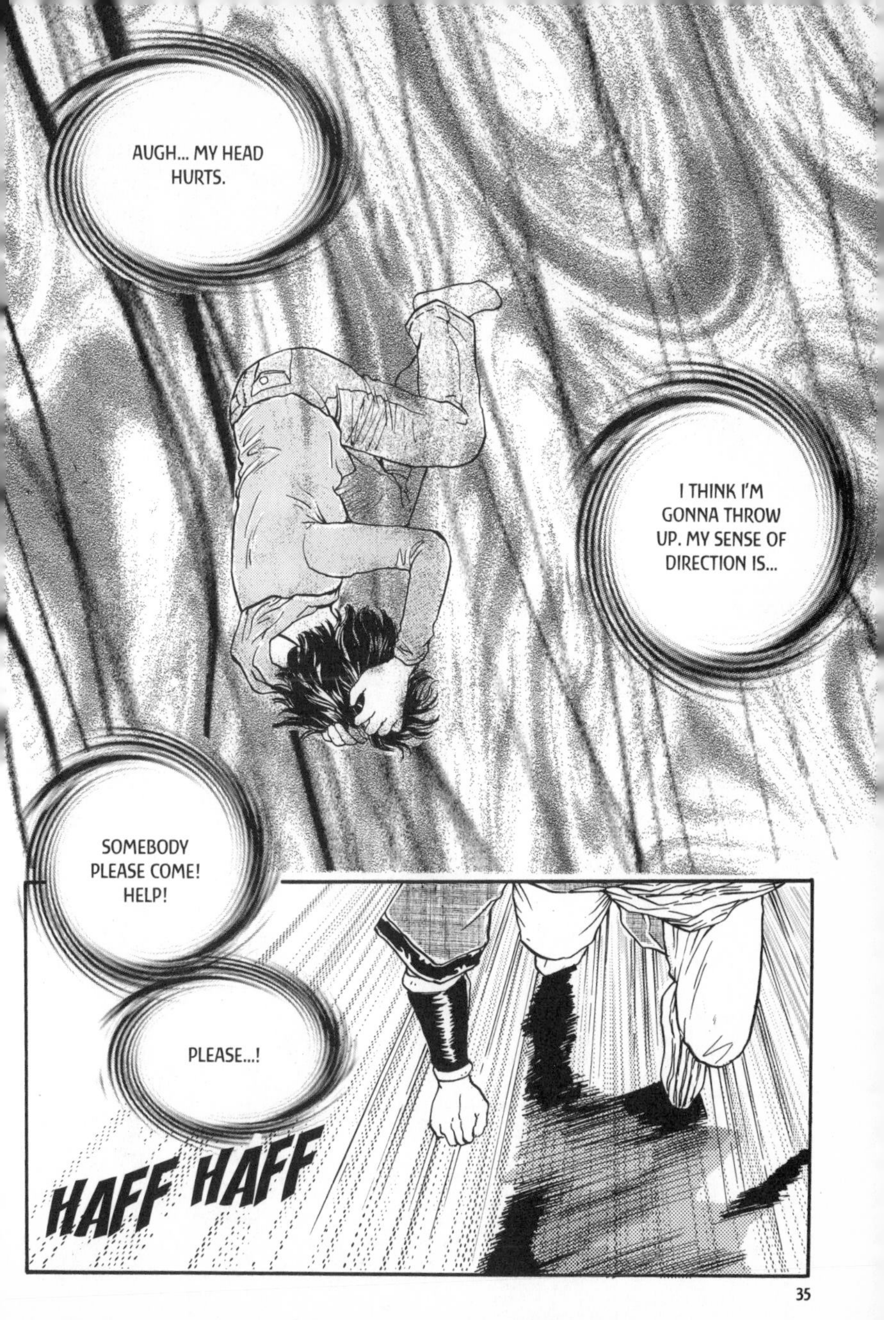
AUGH... MY HEAD HURTS.
I THINK I'M GONNA THROW UP. MY SENSE OF DIRECTION IS...
SOMEBODY PLEASE COME! HELP!
PLEASE...!
HAFF HAFF

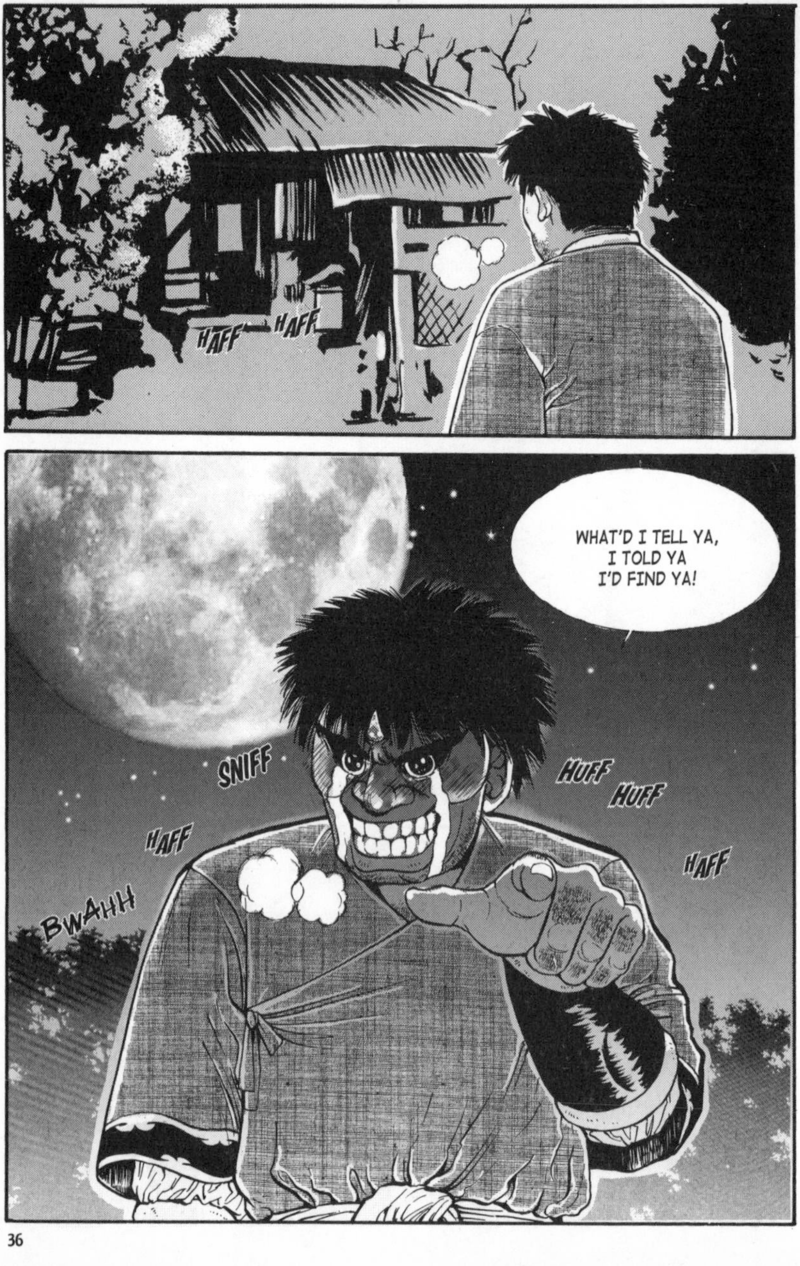
HAFF HAFF
WHAT'D I TELL YA, I TOLD YA I'D FIND YA!
SNIFF
HUFF HUFF
HAFF
HAFF
BWAHH

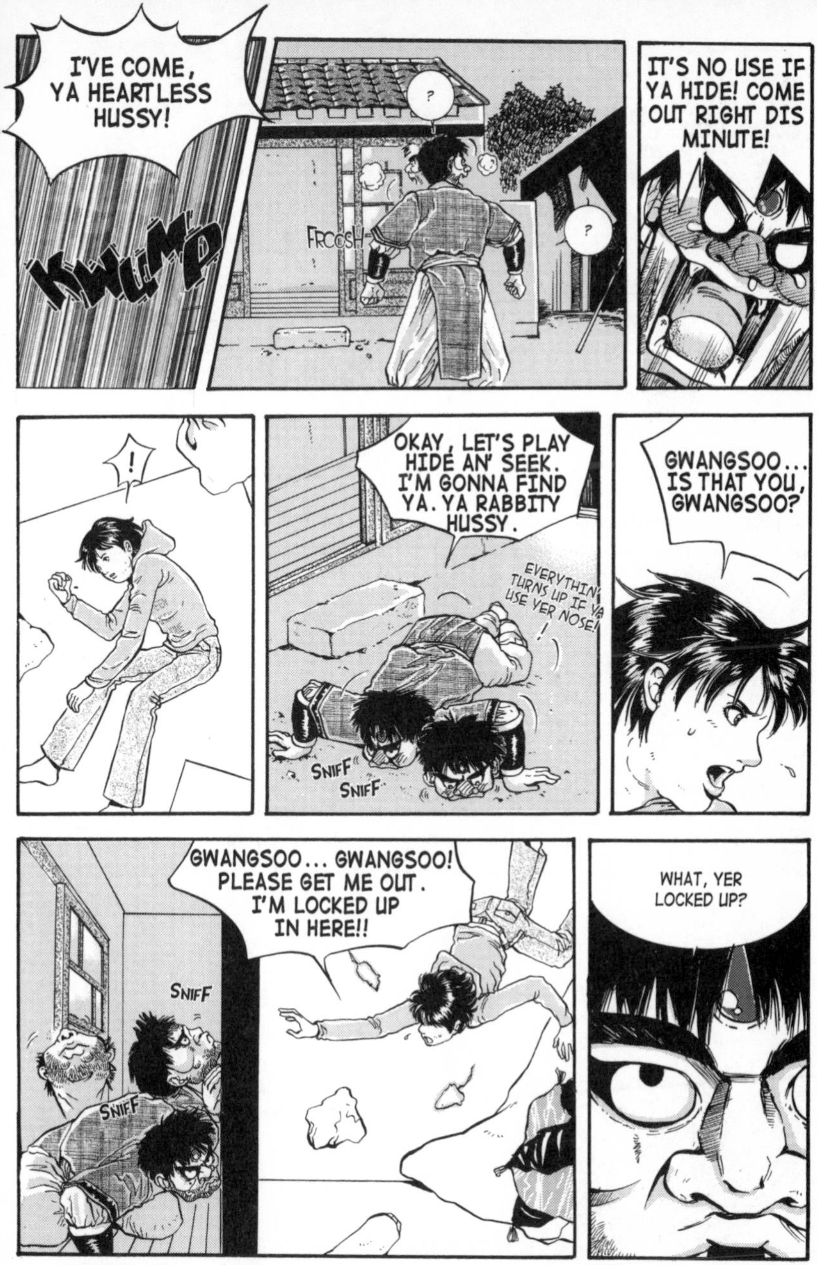
I'VE COME, YA HEARTLESS HUSSY!
KWUMP
?
FRCOSH
?
IT'S NO USE IF YA HIDE! COME OUT RIGHT DIS MINUTE!
!
OKAY, LET'S PLAY HIDE AN' SEEK. I'M GONNA FIND YA. YA RABBITY HUSSY.
EVERYTHIN' TURNS UP IF YA USE YER NOSE!
SNIFF SNIFF
GWANGSOO... IS THAT YOU, GWANGSOO?
GWANGSOO... GWANGSOO! PLEASE GET ME OUT. I'M LOCKED UP IN HERE!!
SNIFF
SNIFF
WHAT, YER LOCKED UP?

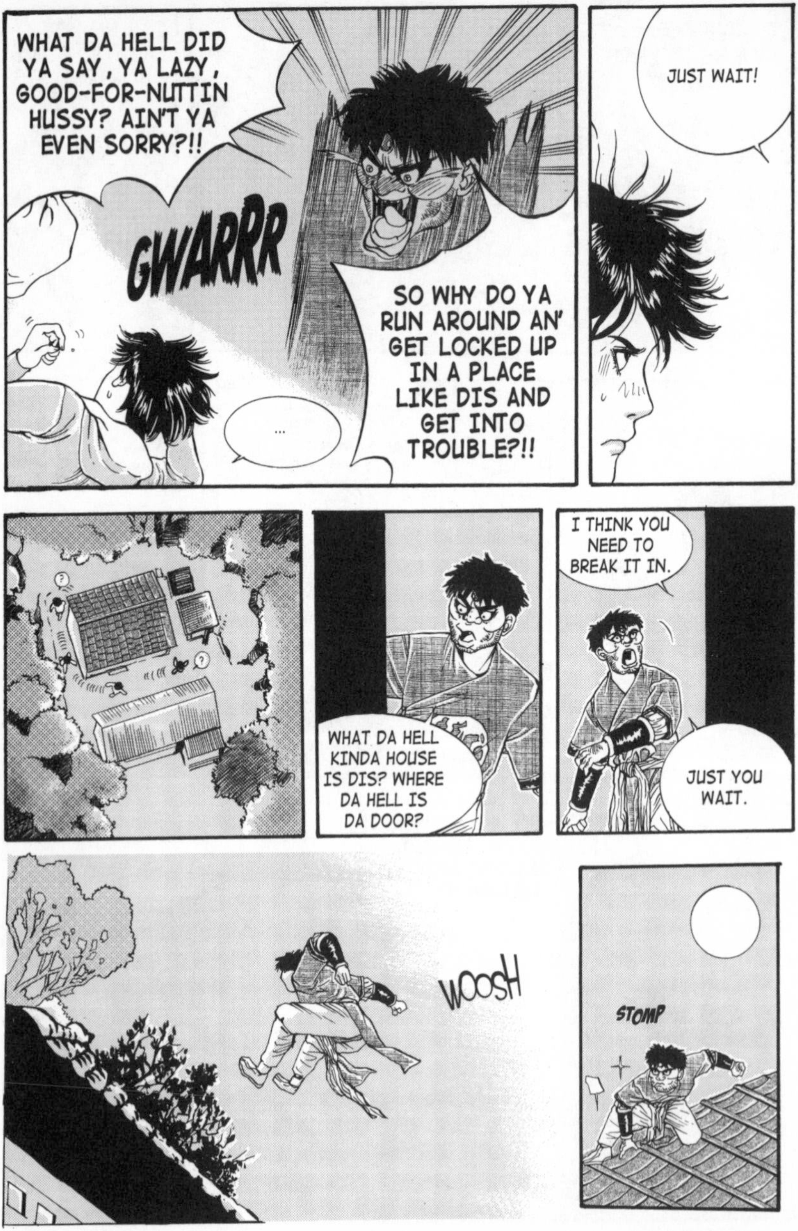
WHAT DA HELL DID YA SAY, YA LAZY, GOOD-FOR-NUTTIN HUSSY? AIN'T YA EVEN SORRY?!!
GWARRR
...
SO WHY DO YA RUN AROUND AN' GET LOCKED UP IN A PLACE LIKE DIS AND GET INTO TROUBLE?!!
JUST WAIT!
WHAT DA HELL KINDA HOUSE IS DIS? WHERE DA HELL IS DA DOOR?
I THINK YOU NEED TO BREAK IT IN.
JUST YOU WAIT.
WOOSH
STOMP

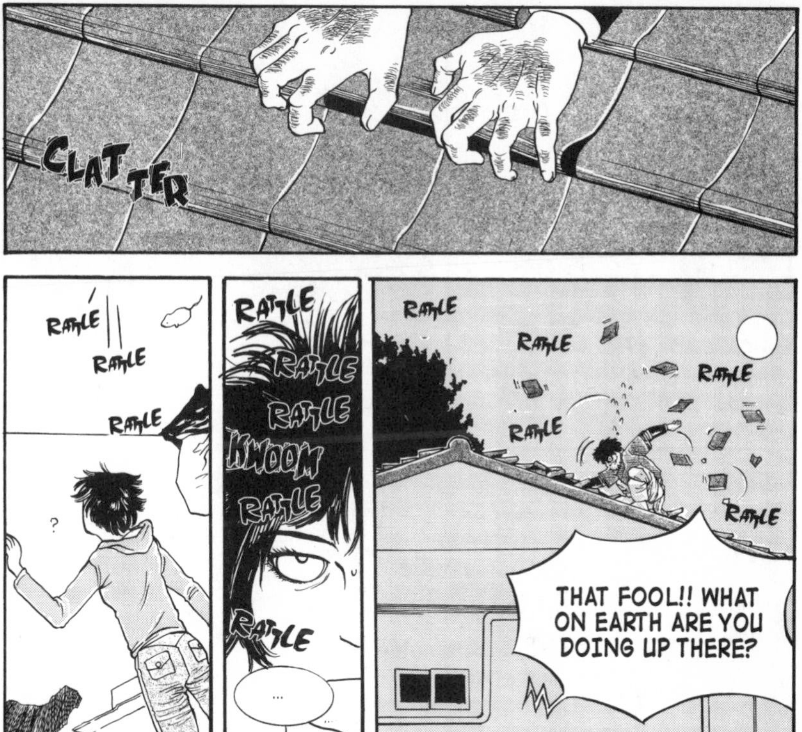
CLATTER
RATTLE
RATTLE
RATTLE
?
RATTLE
RATTLE
RATTLE
KWOOM
RATTLE
RATTLE
...
RATTLE
RATTLE
RATTLE
RATTLE
RATTLE
THAT FOOL!! WHAT ON EARTH ARE YOU DOING UP THERE?

"LIKE A DOKEBI TEARING UP THE ROOFTILES" IS A KOREAN EXPRESSION USED WHEN ONE IS DOING BUSY-WORK, OR WHEN ONE FINDS HIMSELF RUMMAGING WITHOUT KNOWING WHY.

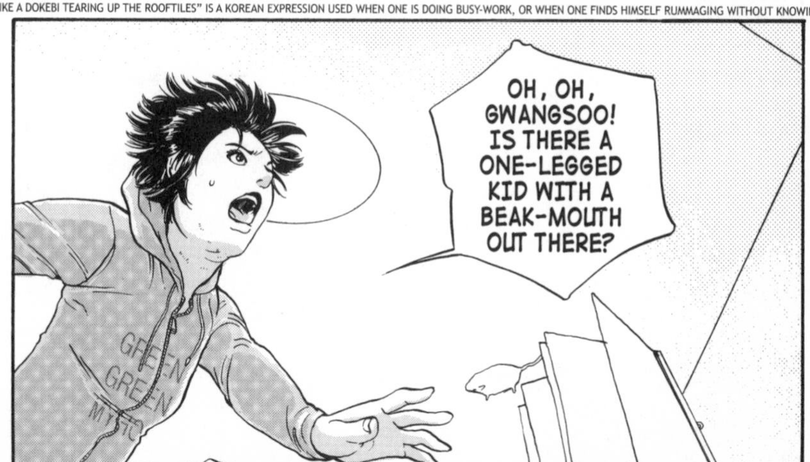
OH, OH, GWANGSOO! IS THERE A ONE-LEGGED KID WITH A BEAK-MOUTH OUT THERE?

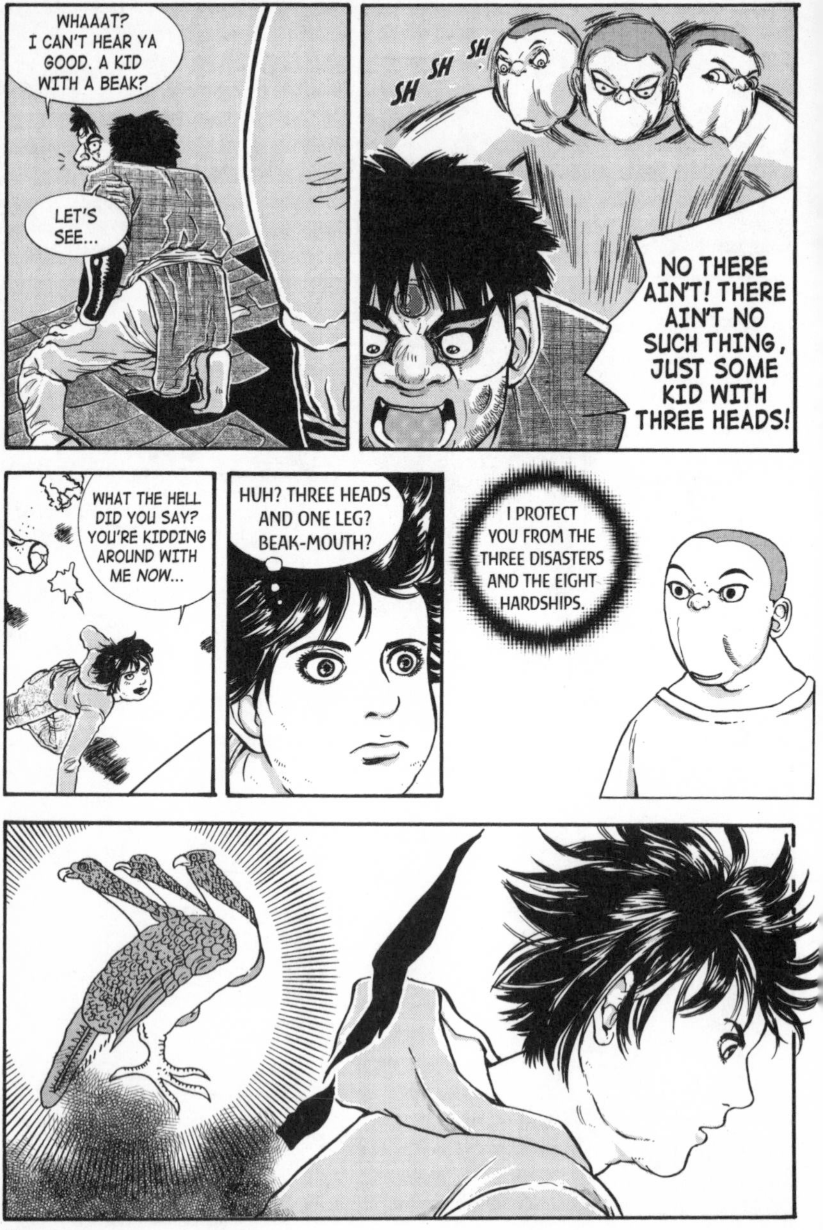
WHAAAT? I CAN'T HEAR YA GOOD. A KID WITH A BEAK?
LET'S SEE...
SH SH SH
NO THERE AIN'T! THERE AIN'T NO SUCH THING, JUST SOME KID WITH THREE HEADS!
WHAT THE HELL DID YOU SAY? YOU'RE KIDDING AROUND WITH ME *NOW*...
HUH? THREE HEADS AND ONE LEG? BEAK-MOUTH?
I PROTECT YOU FROM THE THREE DISASTERS AND THE EIGHT HARDSHIPS.

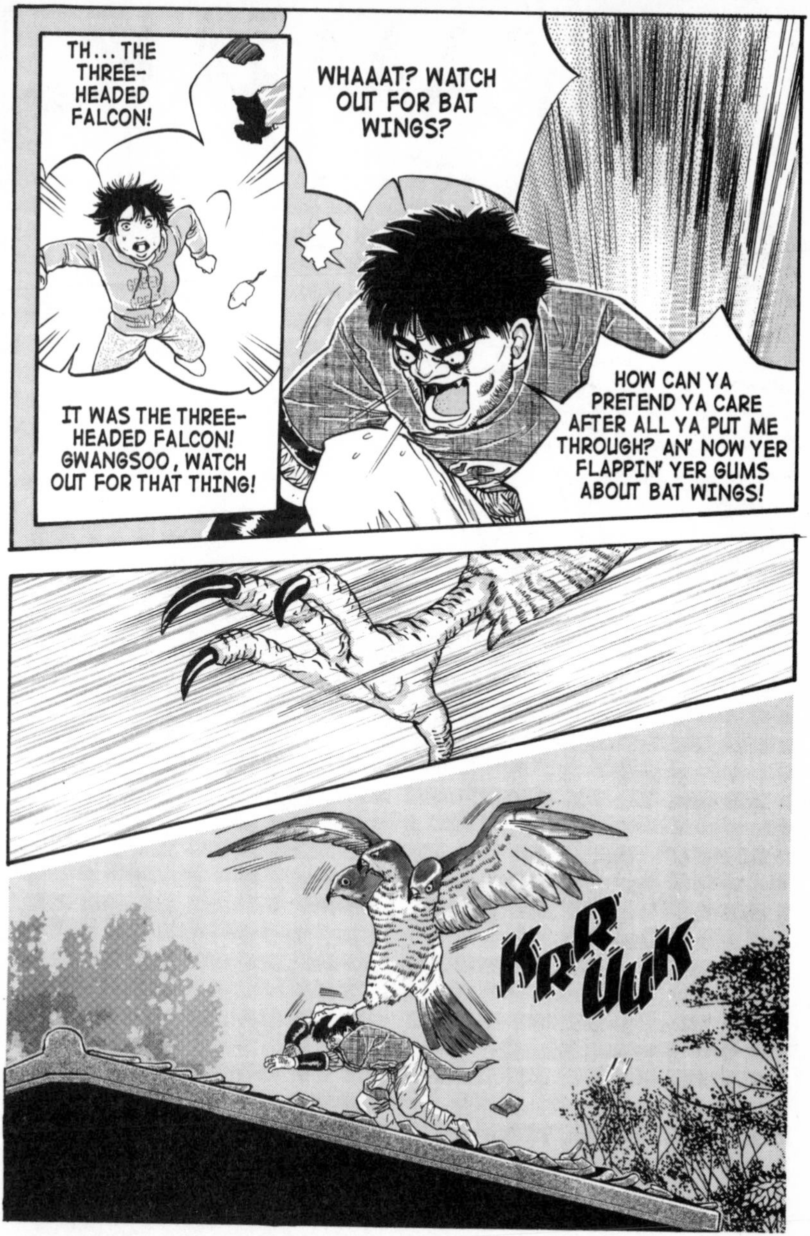

TH... THE THREE-HEADED FALCON!
IT WAS THE THREE-HEADED FALCON! GWANGSOO, WATCH OUT FOR THAT THING!
WHAAAT? WATCH OUT FOR BAT WINGS?
HOW CAN YA PRETEND YA CARE AFTER ALL YA PUT ME THROUGH? AN' NOW YER FLAPPIN' YER GUMS ABOUT BAT WINGS!
KRRUUK

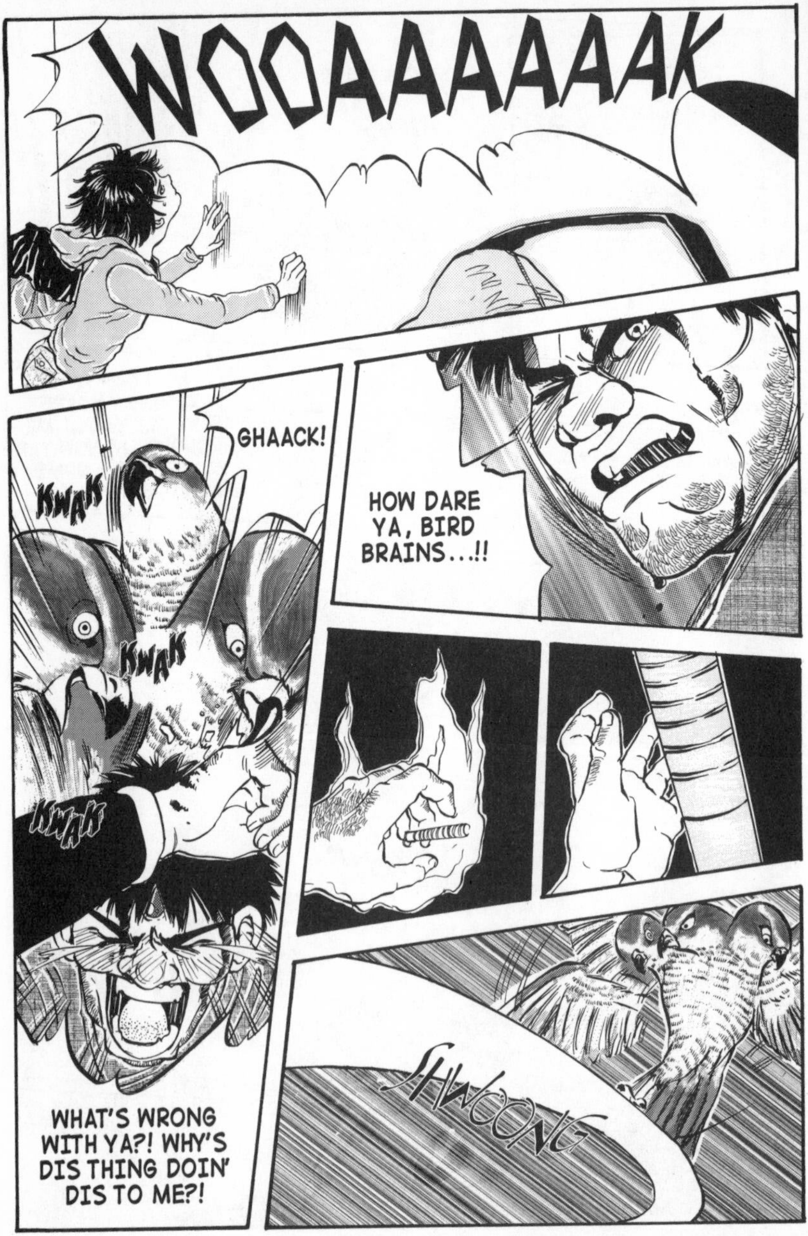
WOOAAAAAAK
HOW DARE YA, BIRD BRAINS...!!
GHAACK!
KWAK
KWAK
KWAK
WHAT'S WRONG WITH YA?! WHY'S DIS THING DOIN' DIS TO ME?!
SHWOONG

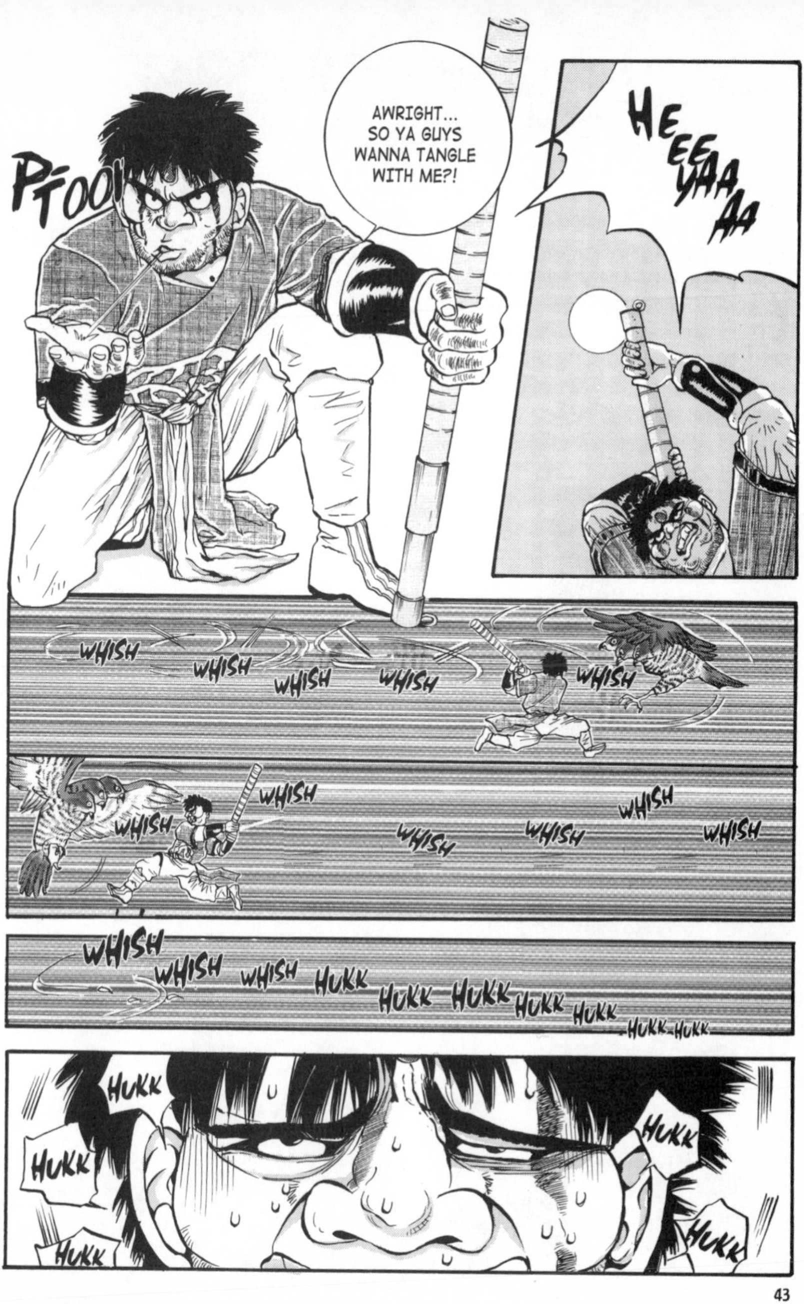
PTOOI
AWRIGHT... SO YA GUYS WANNA TANGLE WITH ME?!
HEEEYAAAAA
WHISH
WHISH
WHISH
WHISH
WHISH
WHISH
WHISH
WHISH
WHISH
WHISH
WHISH
WHISH
WHISH
WHISH
HUKK
HUKK
HUKK
HUKK
HUKK
HUKK-HUKK
HUKK
HUKK
HUKK
HUKK
HUKK

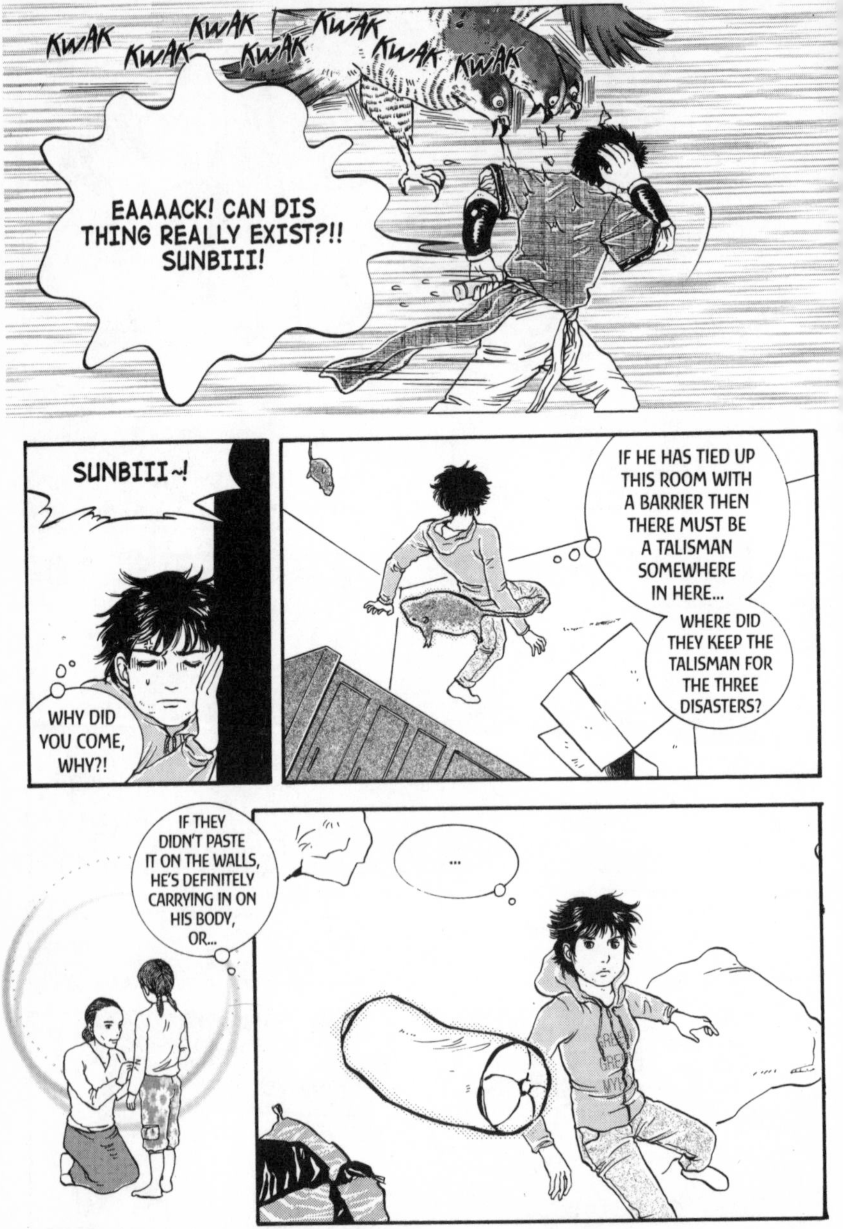
KWAK KWAK KWAK KWAK KWAK KWAK KWAK
EAAAACK! CAN DIS THING REALLY EXIST?!! SUNBIII!
SUNBIII~!
WHY DID YOU COME, WHY?!
IF HE HAS TIED UP THIS ROOM WITH A BARRIER THEN THERE MUST BE A TALISMAN SOMEWHERE IN HERE...
WHERE DID THEY KEEP THE TALISMAN FOR THE THREE DISASTERS?
IF THEY DIDN'T PASTE IT ON THE WALLS, HE'S DEFINITELY CARRYING IN ON HIS BODY, OR...
...

FWOOM

FSHOO

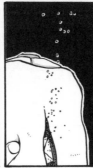

FOUND IT!!

WHAP

KIIEE KP

?

KIIEEK

CRRME

45

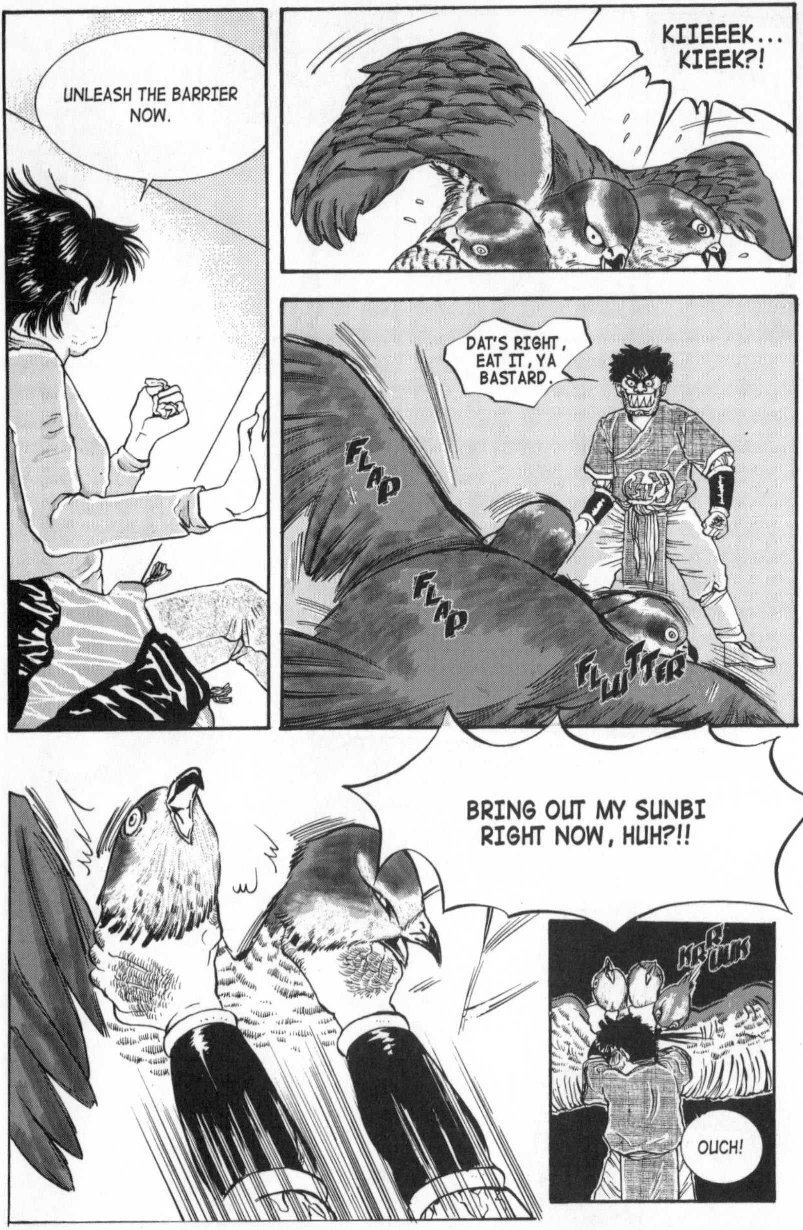
UNLEASH THE BARRIER NOW.
KIIEEEK... KIEEK?!
DAT'S RIGHT, EAT IT, YA BASTARD.
FLAP
FLAP
FLUTTER
BRING OUT MY SUNBI RIGHT NOW, HUH?!!
OUCH!

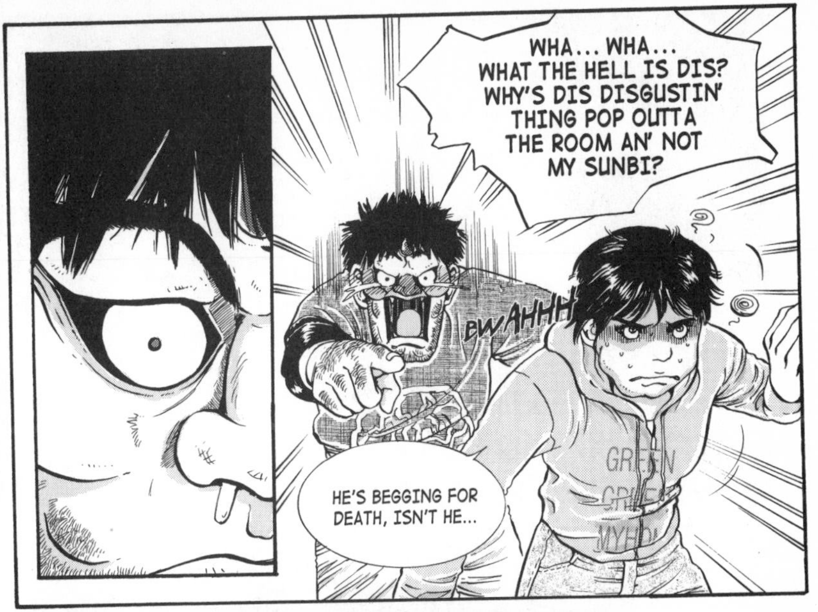
WHA... WHA...
WHAT THE HELL IS DIS? WHY'S DIS DISGUSTIN' THING POP OUTTA THE ROOM AN' NOT MY SUNBI?
BWAHHH
HE'S BEGGING FOR DEATH, ISN'T HE...

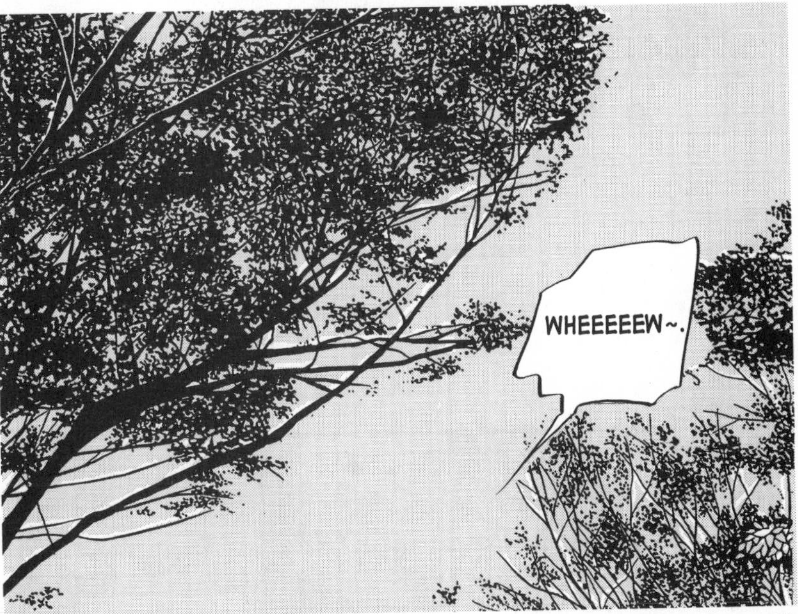
WHEEEEEW~.

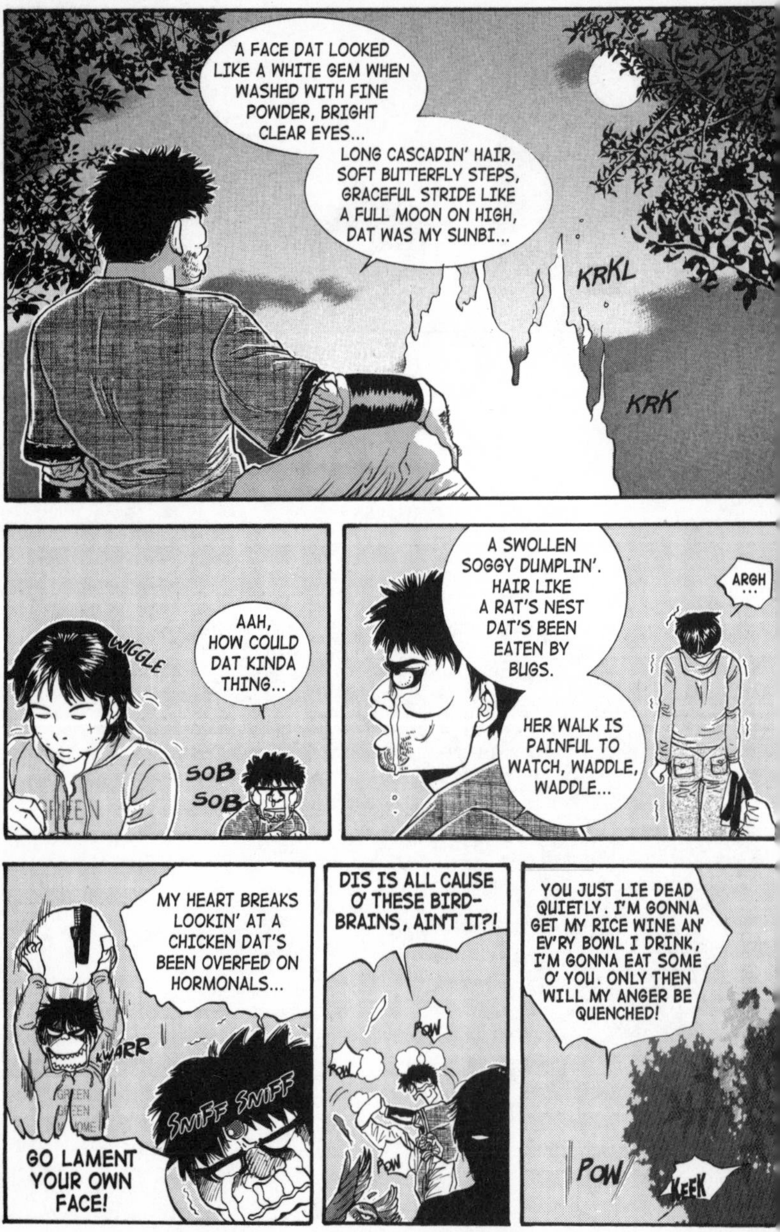
A FACE DAT LOOKED LIKE A WHITE GEM WHEN WASHED WITH FINE POWDER, BRIGHT CLEAR EYES...
LONG CASCADIN' HAIR, SOFT BUTTERFLY STEPS, GRACEFUL STRIDE LIKE A FULL MOON ON HIGH, DAT WAS MY SUNBI...
KRKL
KRK
WIGGLE
AAH, HOW COULD DAT KINDA THING...
SOB SOB
A SWOLLEN SOGGY DUMPLIN'. HAIR LIKE A RAT'S NEST DAT'S BEEN EATEN BY BUGS.
HER WALK IS PAINFUL TO WATCH, WADDLE, WADDLE...
ARGH ...
MY HEART BREAKS LOOKIN' AT A CHICKEN DAT'S BEEN OVERFED ON HORMONALS...
KWARR
SNIFF SNIFF
GO LAMENT YOUR OWN FACE!
DIS IS ALL CAUSE O' THESE BIRD-BRAINS, AIN'T IT?!
POW
POW
POW
YOU JUST LIE DEAD QUIETLY. I'M GONNA GET MY RICE WINE AN' EV'RY BOWL I DRINK, I'M GONNA EAT SOME O' YOU. ONLY THEN WILL MY ANGER BE QUENCHED!
POW
KEEK

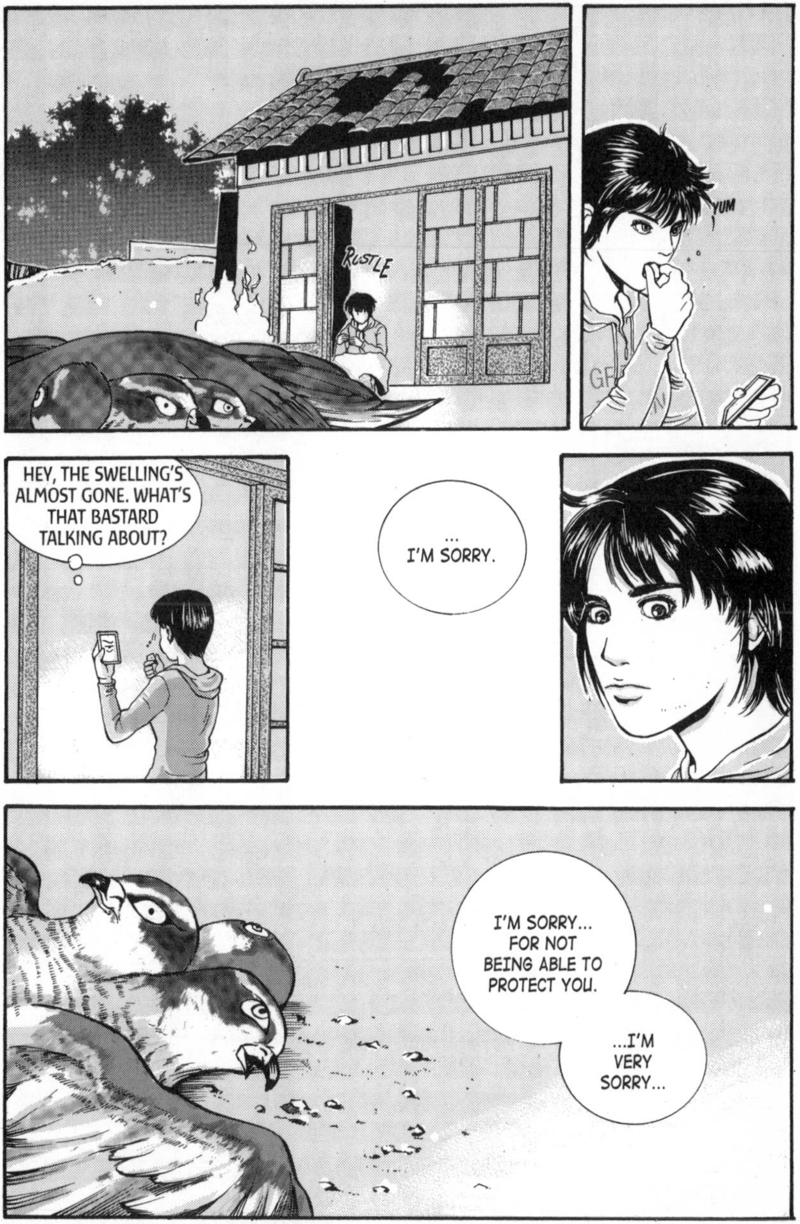
RUSTLE
YUM
HEY, THE SWELLING'S ALMOST GONE. WHAT'S THAT BASTARD TALKING ABOUT?
... I'M SORRY.
I'M SORRY... FOR NOT BEING ABLE TO PROTECT YOU.
...I'M VERY SORRY...

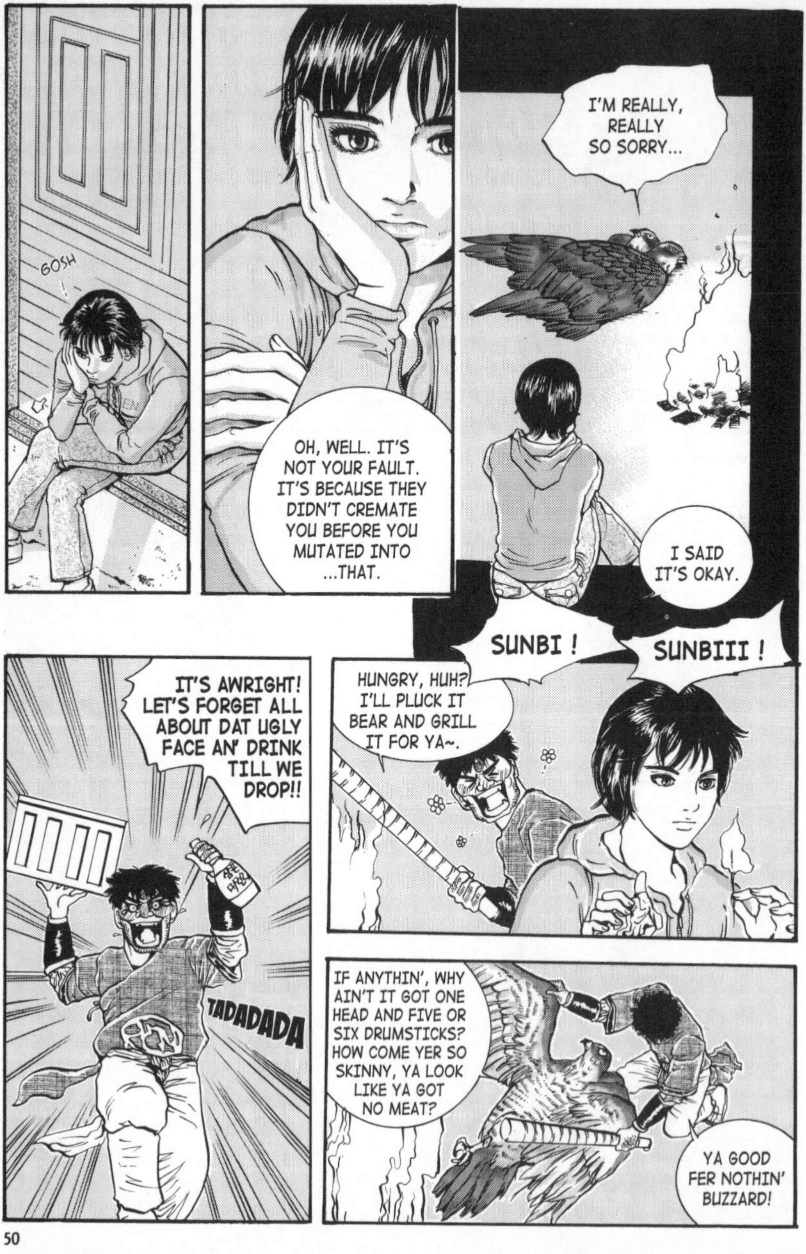
GOSH
OH, WELL. IT'S NOT YOUR FAULT. IT'S BECAUSE THEY DIDN'T CREMATE YOU BEFORE YOU MUTATED INTO ...THAT.
I'M REALLY, REALLY SO SORRY...
I SAID IT'S OKAY.
SUNBI !
SUNBIII !
HUNGRY, HUH? I'LL PLUCK IT BEAR AND GRILL IT FOR YA~.
IT'S AWRIGHT! LET'S FORGET ALL ABOUT DAT UGLY FACE AN' DRINK TILL WE DROP!!
TADADADA
IF ANYTHIN', WHY AIN'T IT GOT ONE HEAD AND FIVE OR SIX DRUMSTICKS? HOW COME YER SO SKINNY, YA LOOK LIKE YA GOT NO MEAT?
YA GOOD FER NOTHIN' BUZZARD!

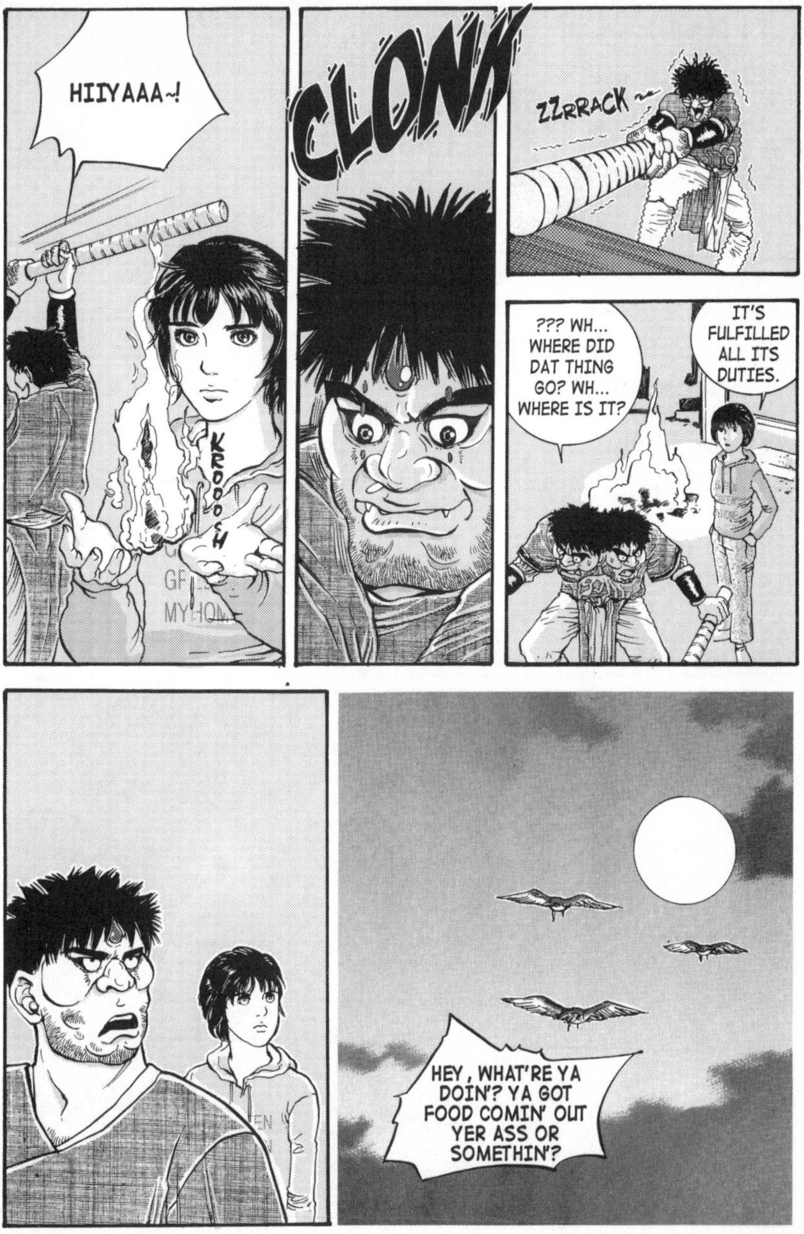
HIIYAAA~!
CLONK
ZZRRACK ~
KROOOOSH
GF
MYHOM
??? WH... WHERE DID DAT THING GO? WH... WHERE IS IT?
IT'S FULFILLED ALL ITS DUTIES.
HEY, WHAT'RE YA DOIN'? YA GOT FOOD COMIN' OUT YER ASS OR SOMETHIN'?

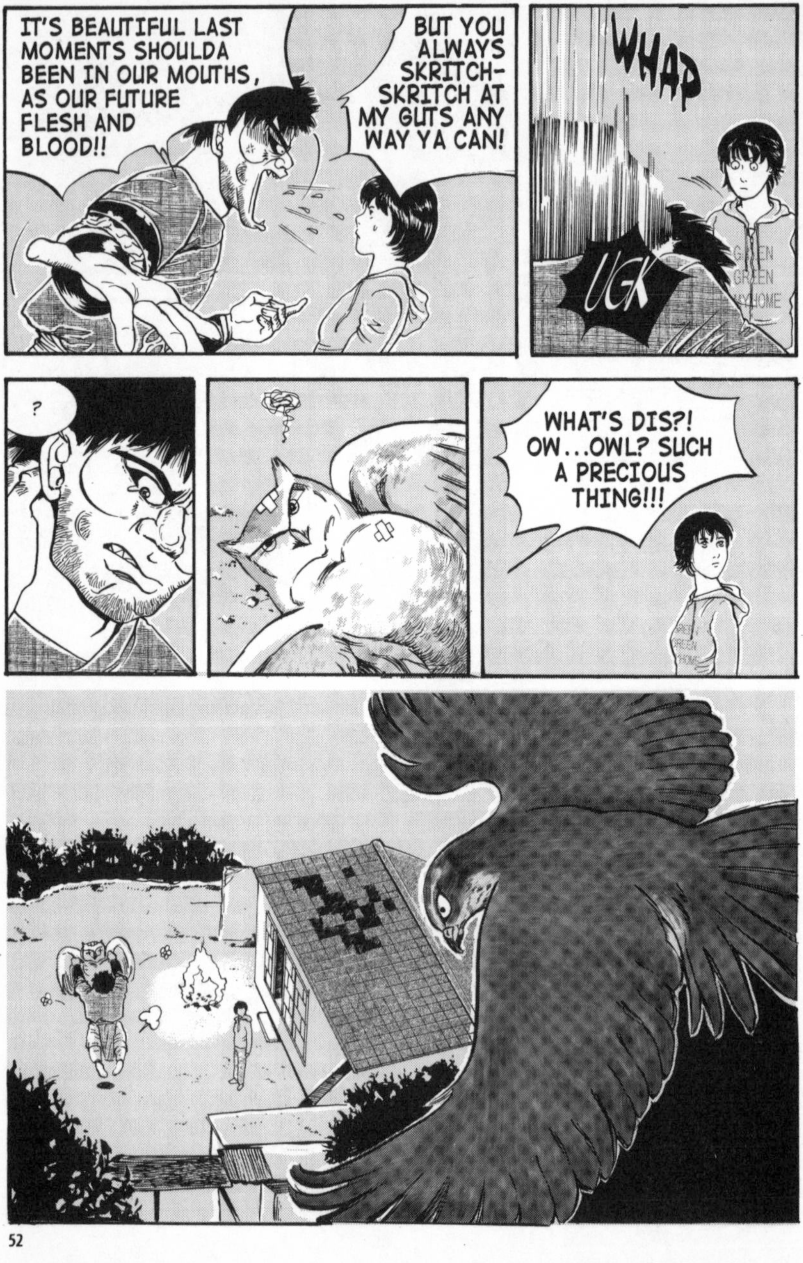
IT'S BEAUTIFUL LAST MOMENTS SHOULDA BEEN IN OUR MOUTHS, AS OUR FUTURE FLESH AND BLOOD!!
BUT YOU ALWAYS SKRITCH-SKRITCH AT MY GUTS ANY WAY YA CAN!
WHAP
UGK
GREEN GREEN MY HOME
?
WHAT'S DIS?! OW...OWL? SUCH A PRECIOUS THING!!!

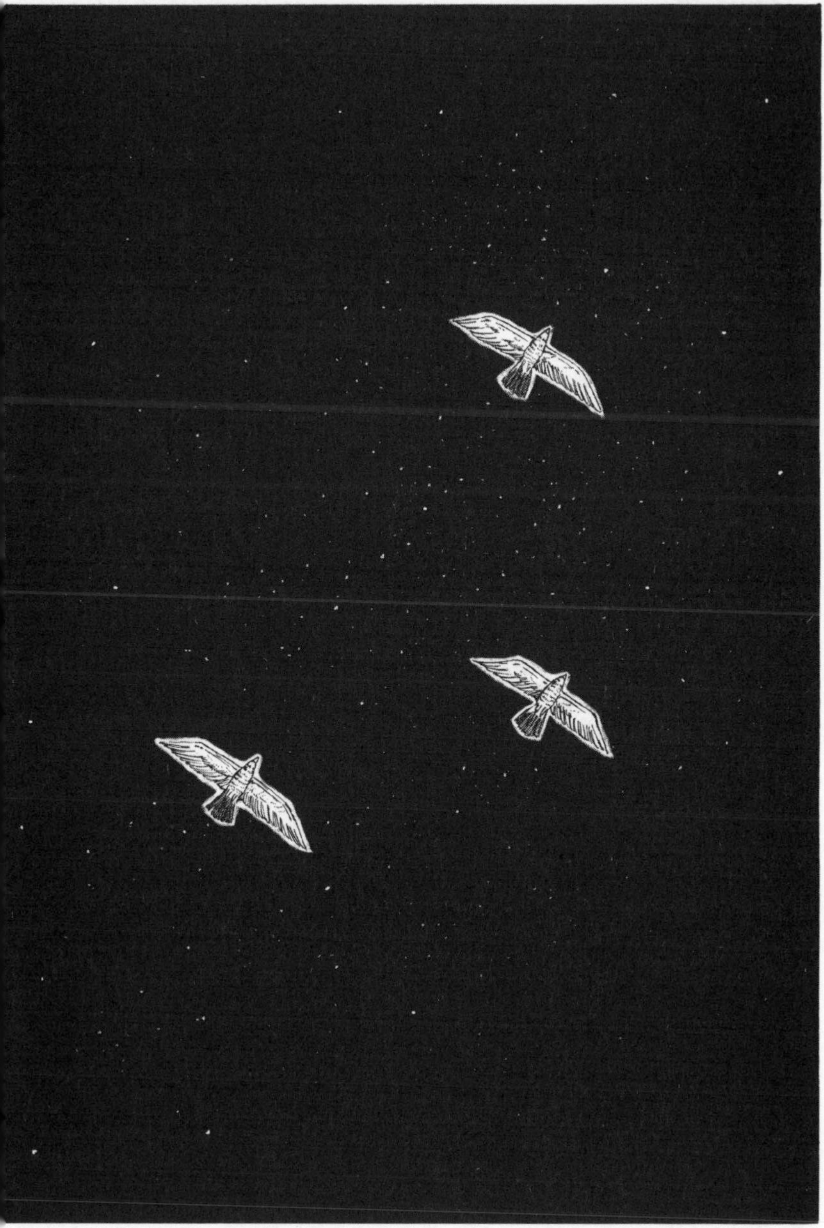

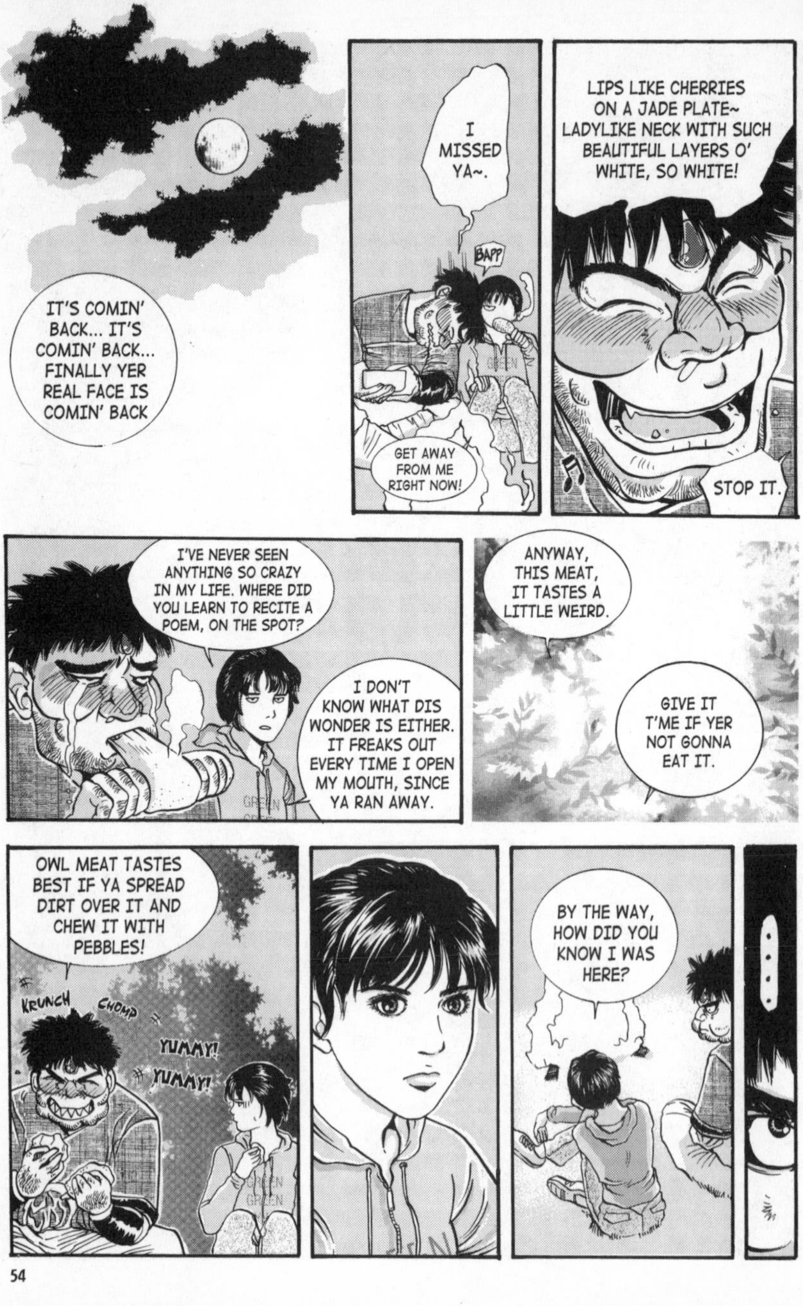
IT'S COMIN' BACK... IT'S COMIN' BACK... FINALLY YER REAL FACE IS COMIN' BACK
I MISSED YA~.
BAPP
GET AWAY FROM ME RIGHT NOW!
LIPS LIKE CHERRIES ON A JADE PLATE~ LADYLIKE NECK WITH SUCH BEAUTIFUL LAYERS O' WHITE, SO WHITE!
STOP IT.
I'VE NEVER SEEN ANYTHING SO CRAZY IN MY LIFE. WHERE DID YOU LEARN TO RECITE A POEM, ON THE SPOT?
I DON'T KNOW WHAT DIS WONDER IS EITHER. IT FREAKS OUT EVERY TIME I OPEN MY MOUTH, SINCE YA RAN AWAY.
ANYWAY, THIS MEAT, IT TASTES A LITTLE WEIRD.
GIVE IT T'ME IF YER NOT GONNA EAT IT.
OWL MEAT TASTES BEST IF YA SPREAD DIRT OVER IT AND CHEW IT WITH PEBBLES!
KRUNCH
CHOMP
YUMMY!
YUMMY!
BY THE WAY, HOW DID YOU KNOW I WAS HERE?
....

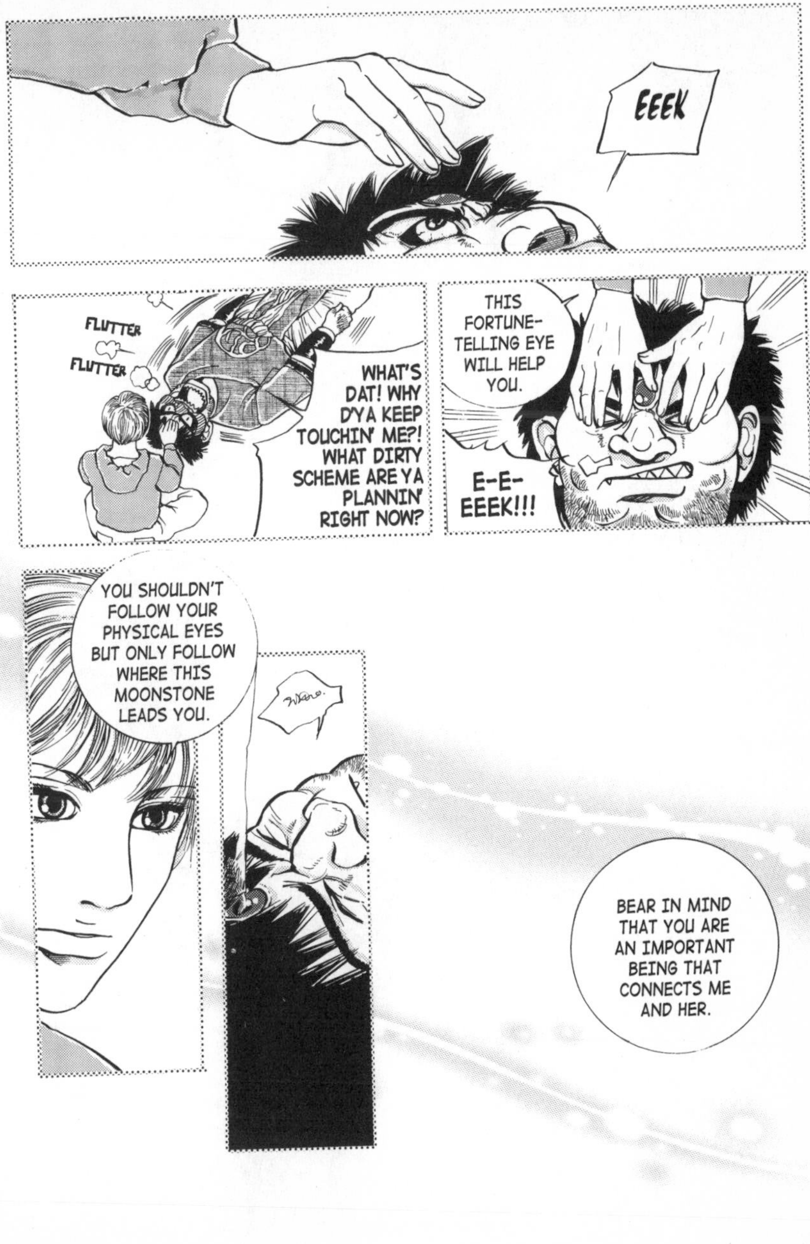
EEEK
FLUTTER
FLUTTER
WHAT'S DAT! WHY D'YA KEEP TOUCHIN' ME?! WHAT DIRTY SCHEME ARE YA PLANNIN' RIGHT NOW?
THIS FORTUNE-TELLING EYE WILL HELP YOU.
E-E-EEEK!!!
YOU SHOULDN'T FOLLOW YOUR PHYSICAL EYES BUT ONLY FOLLOW WHERE THIS MOONSTONE LEADS YOU.
BEAR IN MIND THAT YOU ARE AN IMPORTANT BEING THAT CONNECTS ME AND HER.

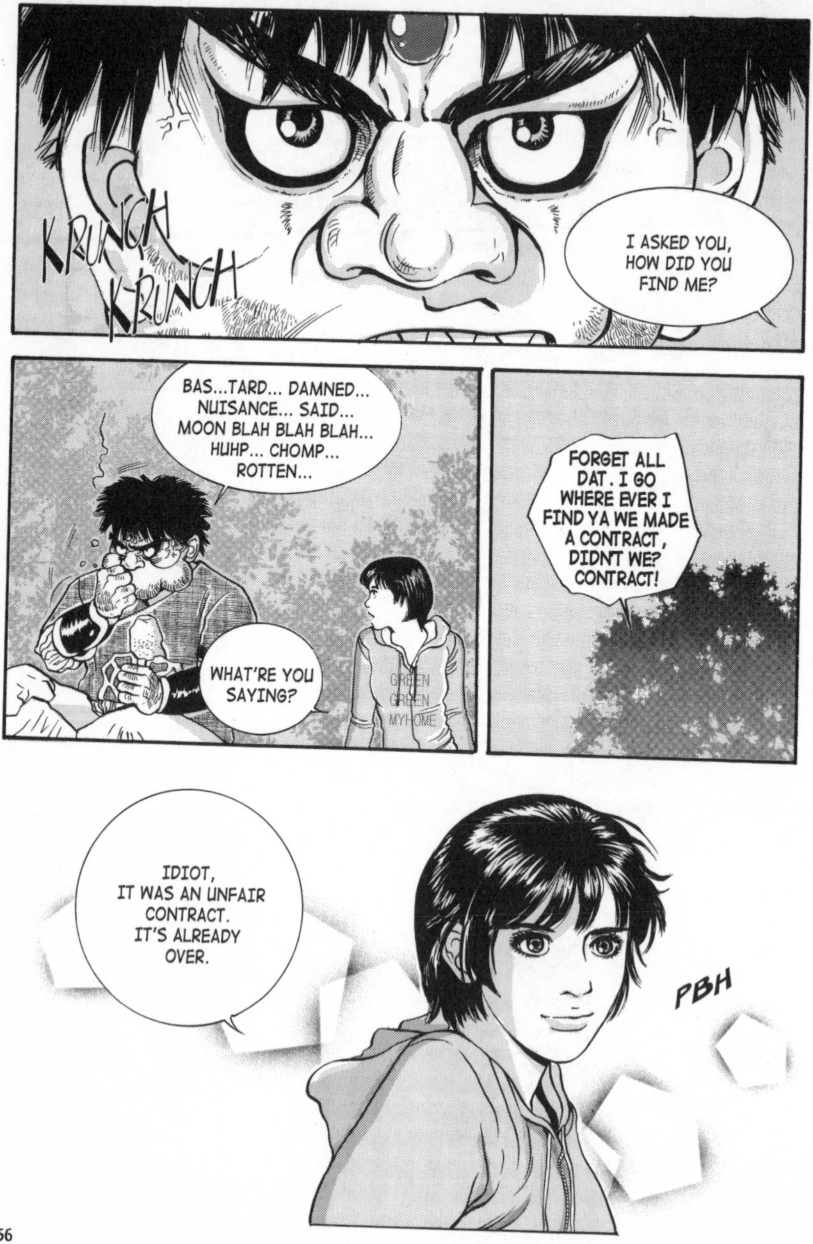
KRUNCH KRUNCH
I ASKED YOU, HOW DID YOU FIND ME?
BAS...TARD... DAMNED... NUISANCE... SAID... MOON BLAH BLAH BLAH... HUHP... CHOMP... ROTTEN...
WHAT'RE YOU SAYING?
GREEN GREEN MYHOME
FORGET ALL DAT. I GO WHERE EVER I FIND YA WE MADE A CONTRACT, DIDN'T WE? CONTRACT!
IDIOT, IT WAS AN UNFAIR CONTRACT. IT'S ALREADY OVER.
PBH

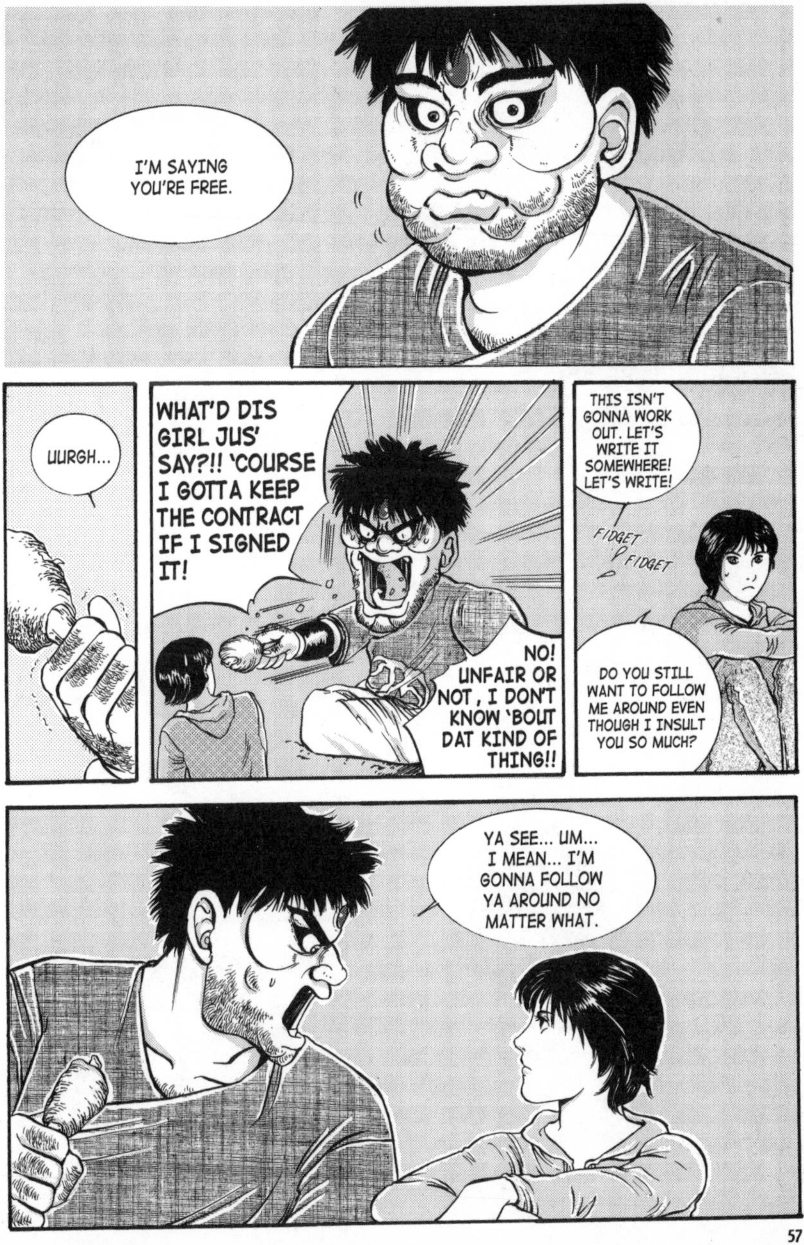

I'M SAYING YOU'RE FREE.
UURGH...
WHAT'D DIS GIRL JUS' SAY?!! 'COURSE I GOTTA KEEP THE CONTRACT IF I SIGNED IT!
NO! UNFAIR OR NOT, I DON'T KNOW 'BOUT DAT KIND OF THING!!
THIS ISN'T GONNA WORK OUT. LET'S WRITE IT SOMEWHERE! LET'S WRITE!
FIDGET FIDGET
DO YOU STILL WANT TO FOLLOW ME AROUND EVEN THOUGH I INSULT YOU SO MUCH?
YA SEE... UM... I MEAN... I'M GONNA FOLLOW YA AROUND NO MATTER WHAT.

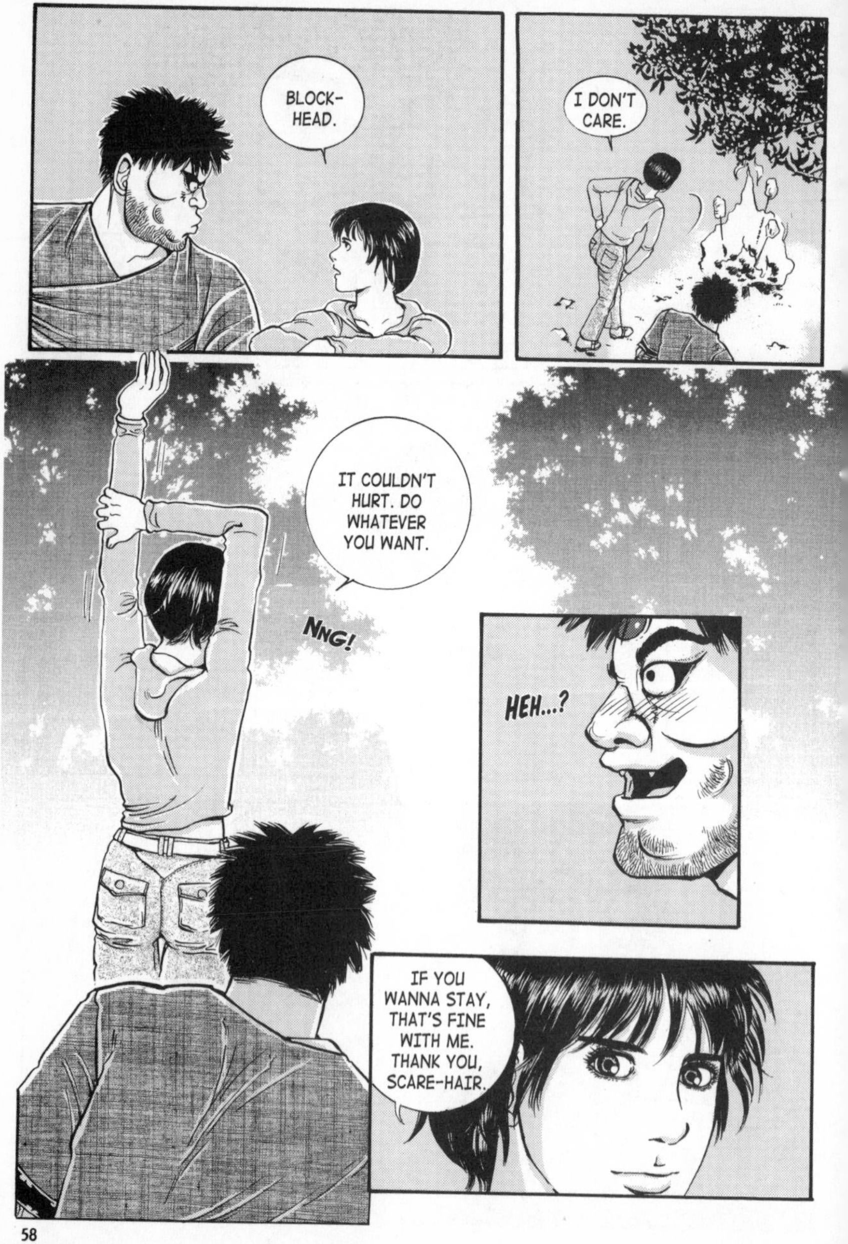
BLOCK-HEAD.
I DON'T CARE.
IT COULDN'T HURT. DO WHATEVER YOU WANT.
NNG!
HEH...?
IF YOU WANNA STAY, THAT'S FINE WITH ME. THANK YOU, SCARE-HAIR.

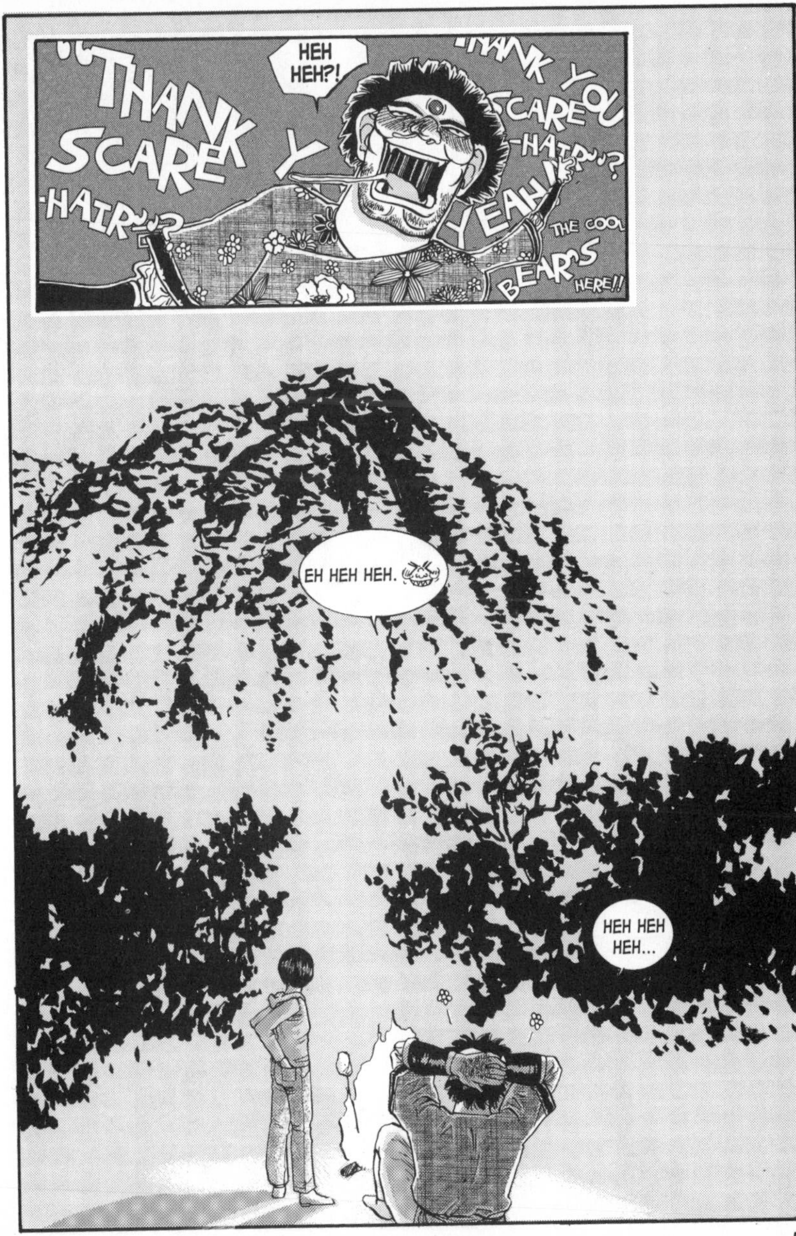
"THANK SCARE Y -HAIR-..?
HEH HEH?!
THANK YOU SCARE-HAIR..?
YEAH! THE COOL BEAR'S HERE!!
EH HEH HEH.
HEH HEH HEH...

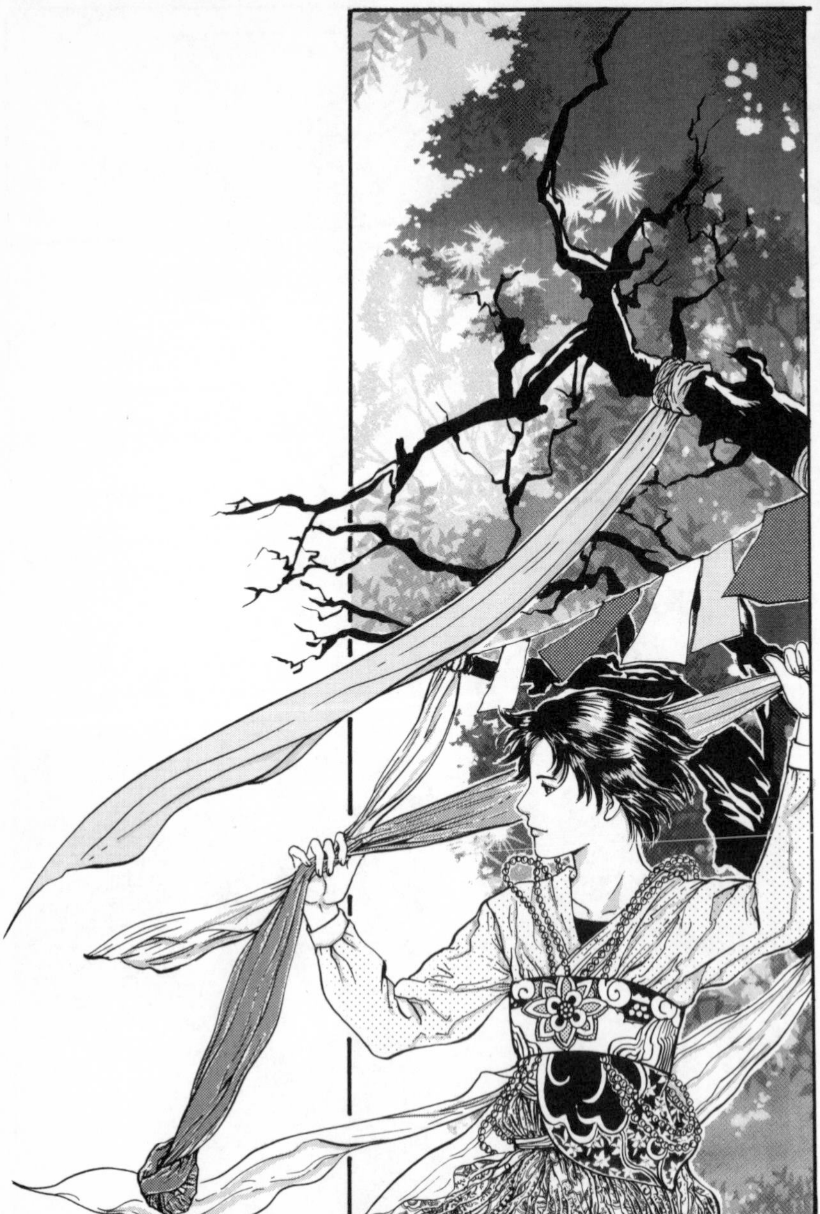

MY MUTE HUNCHBACK MOTHER

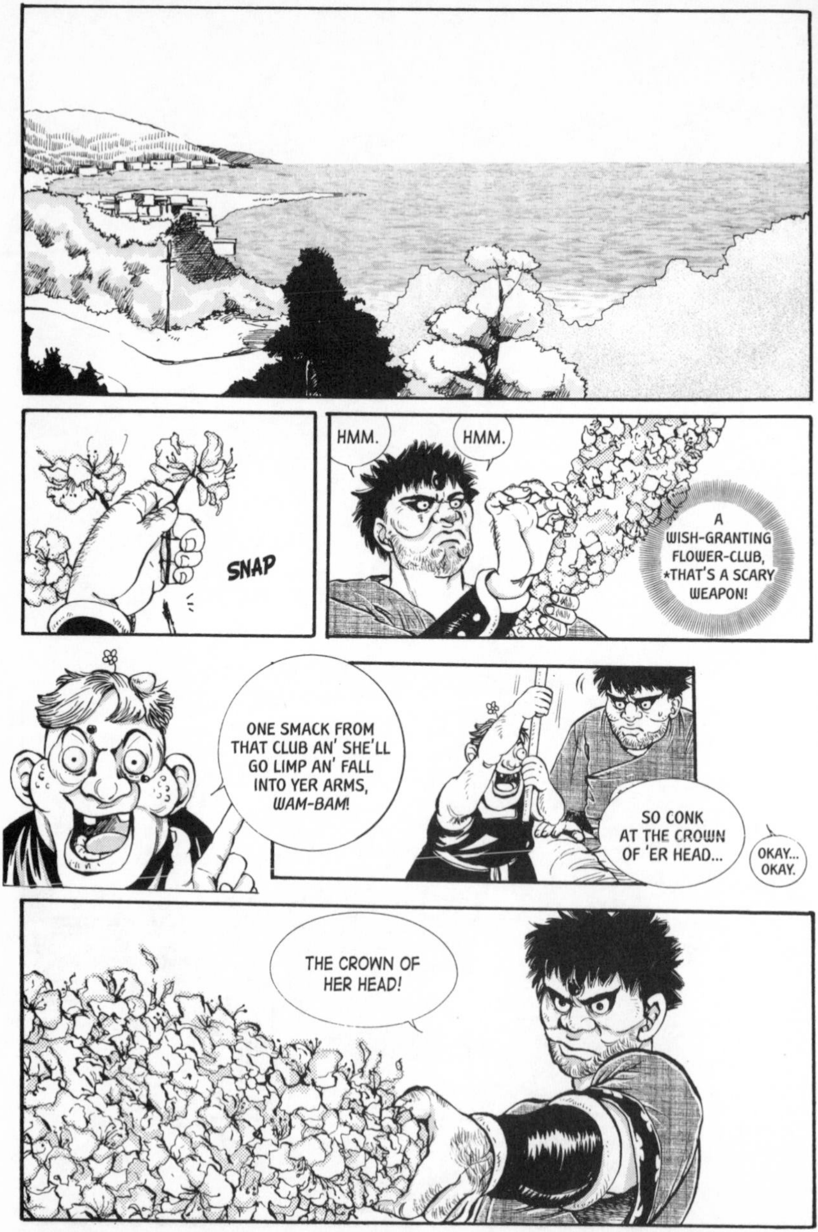
SNAP
HMM.
HMM.
A WISH-GRANTING FLOWER-CLUB, *THAT'S A SCARY WEAPON!
ONE SMACK FROM THAT CLUB AN' SHE'LL GO LIMP AN' FALL INTO YER ARMS, *WAM-BAM*!
SO CONK AT THE CROWN OF 'ER HEAD...
OKAY... OKAY.
THE CROWN OF HER HEAD!

* IT IS SAID THAT IF ONE MAKES A FLOWER CLUB OUT OF BEAUTIFUL AZALEAS AND HITS A WOMAN ON THE BACK OR TOP OF HER HEAD THEN SHE WILL FALL IN LOVE WITH HIM/HER.

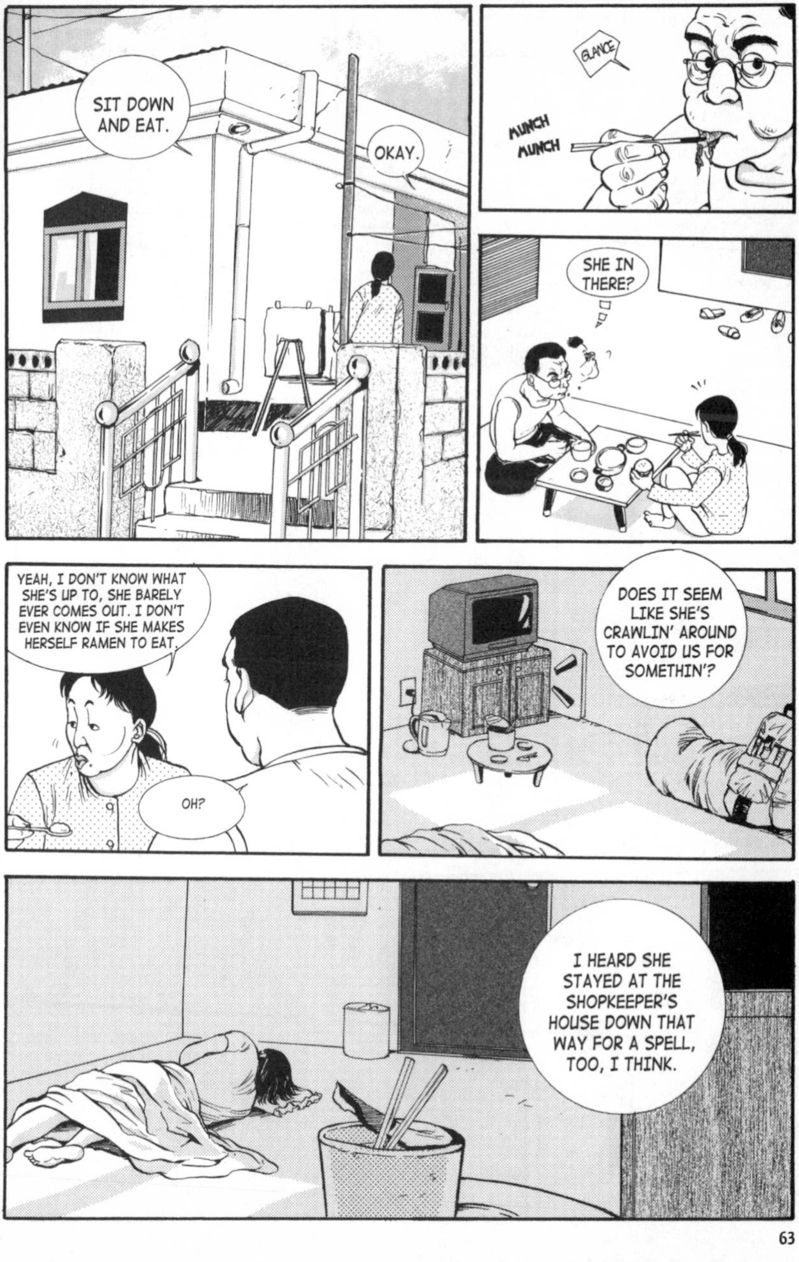
SIT DOWN AND EAT.
OKAY.
GLANCE
MUNCH MUNCH
SHE IN THERE?
YEAH, I DON'T KNOW WHAT SHE'S UP TO, SHE BARELY EVER COMES OUT. I DON'T EVEN KNOW IF SHE MAKES HERSELF RAMEN TO EAT.
OH?
DOES IT SEEM LIKE SHE'S CRAWLIN' AROUND TO AVOID US FOR SOMETHIN'?
I HEARD SHE STAYED AT THE SHOPKEEPER'S HOUSE DOWN THAT WAY FOR A SPELL, TOO, I THINK.

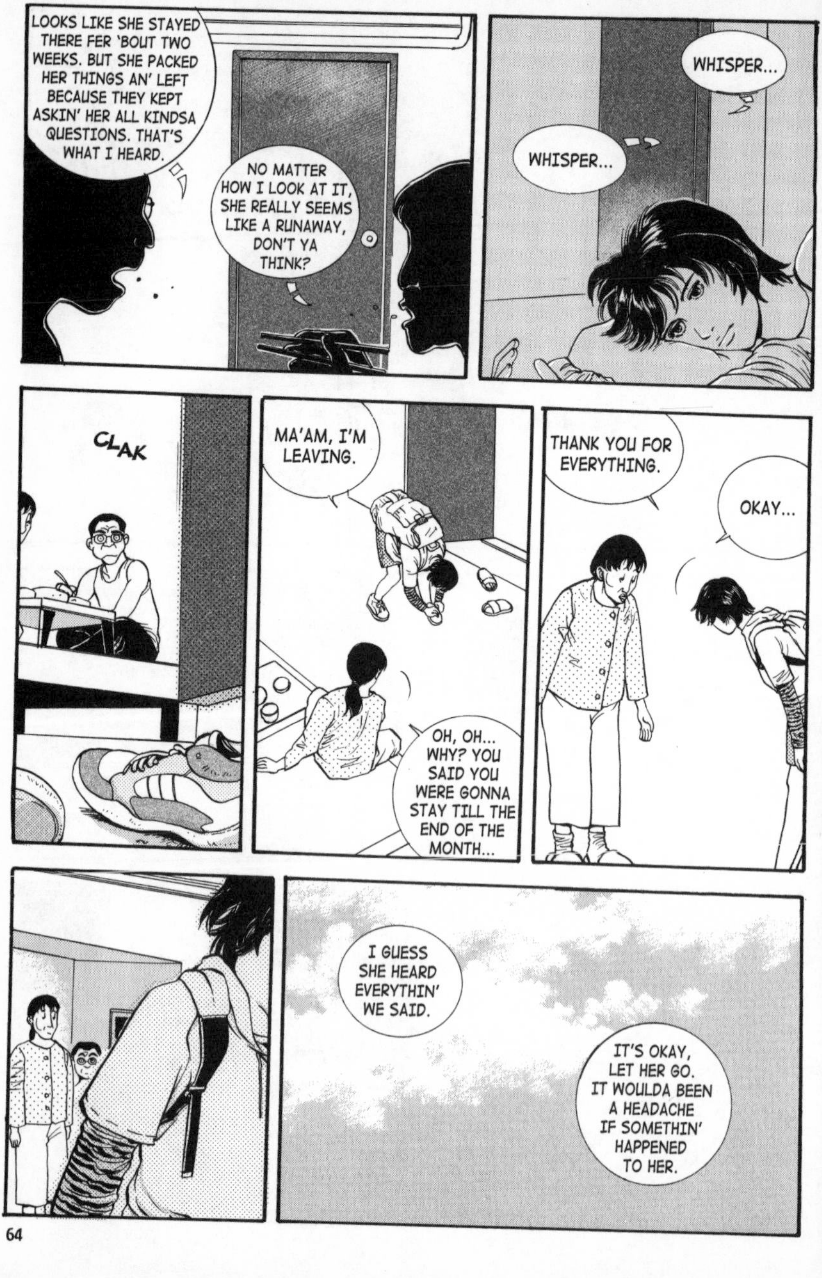

LOOKS LIKE SHE STAYED THERE FER 'BOUT TWO WEEKS. BUT SHE PACKED HER THINGS AN' LEFT BECAUSE THEY KEPT ASKIN' HER ALL KINDSA QUESTIONS. THAT'S WHAT I HEARD.
NO MATTER HOW I LOOK AT IT, SHE REALLY SEEMS LIKE A RUNAWAY, DON'T YA THINK?
WHISPER...
WHISPER...
CLAK
MA'AM, I'M LEAVING.
OH, OH... WHY? YOU SAID YOU WERE GONNA STAY TILL THE END OF THE MONTH...
THANK YOU FOR EVERYTHING.
OKAY...
I GUESS SHE HEARD EVERYTHIN' WE SAID.
IT'S OKAY, LET HER GO. IT WOULDA BEEN A HEADACHE IF SOMETHIN' HAPPENED TO HER.

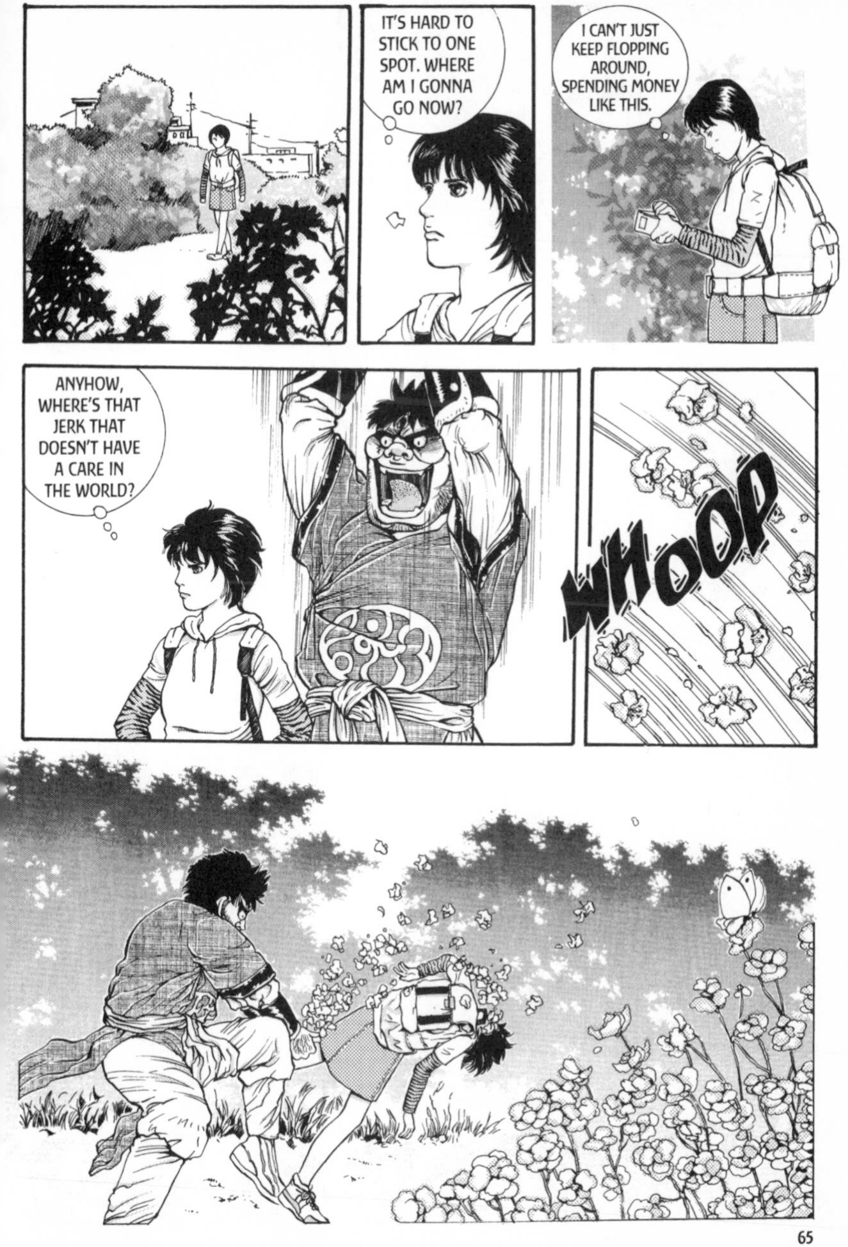

IT'S HARD TO STICK TO ONE SPOT. WHERE AM I GONNA GO NOW?
I CAN'T JUST KEEP FLOPPING AROUND, SPENDING MONEY LIKE THIS.
ANYHOW, WHERE'S THAT JERK THAT DOESN'T HAVE A CARE IN THE WORLD?
WHOOP

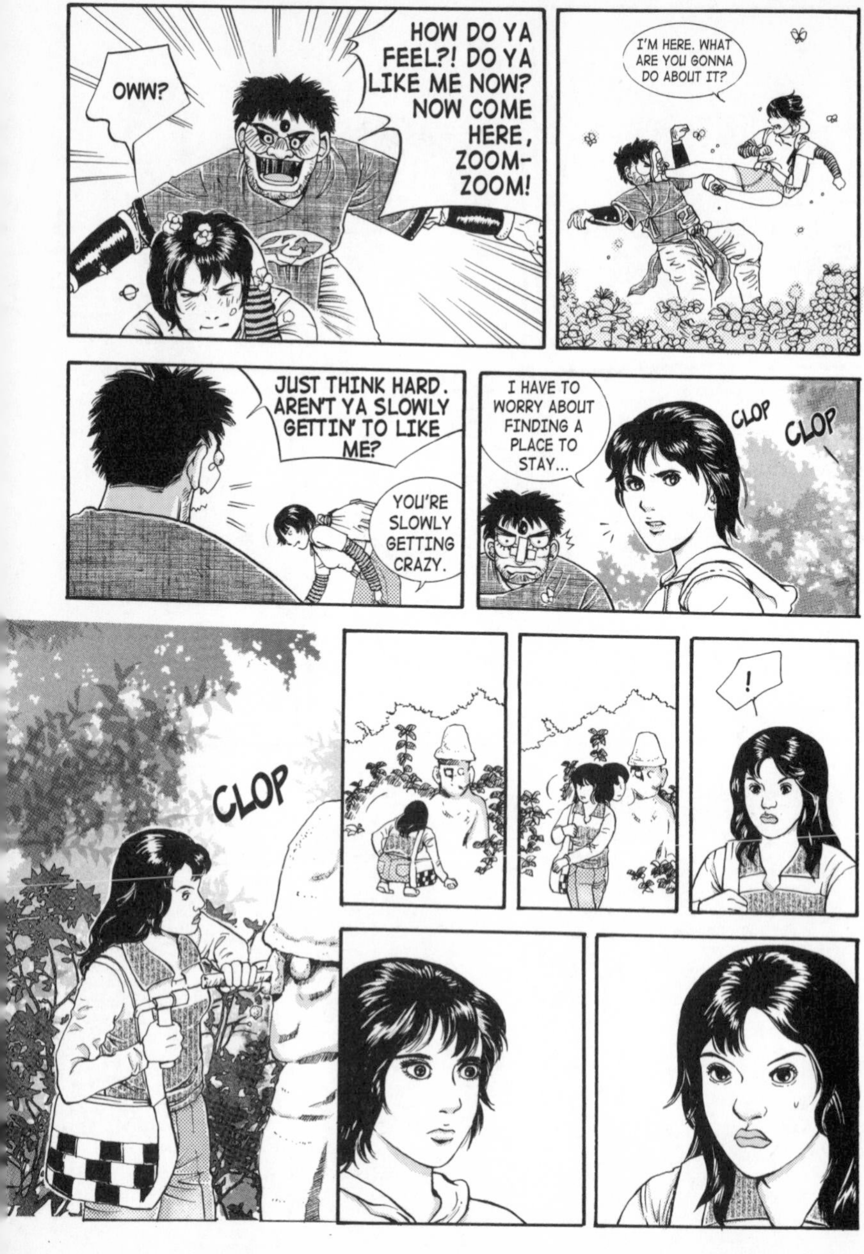
HOW DO YA FEEL?! DO YA LIKE ME NOW? NOW COME HERE, ZOOM-ZOOM!
OWW?
I'M HERE. WHAT ARE YOU GONNA DO ABOUT IT?
JUST THINK HARD. AREN'T YA SLOWLY GETTIN' TO LIKE ME?
YOU'RE SLOWLY GETTING CRAZY.
I HAVE TO WORRY ABOUT FINDING A PLACE TO STAY...
CLOP
CLOP
CLOP
!

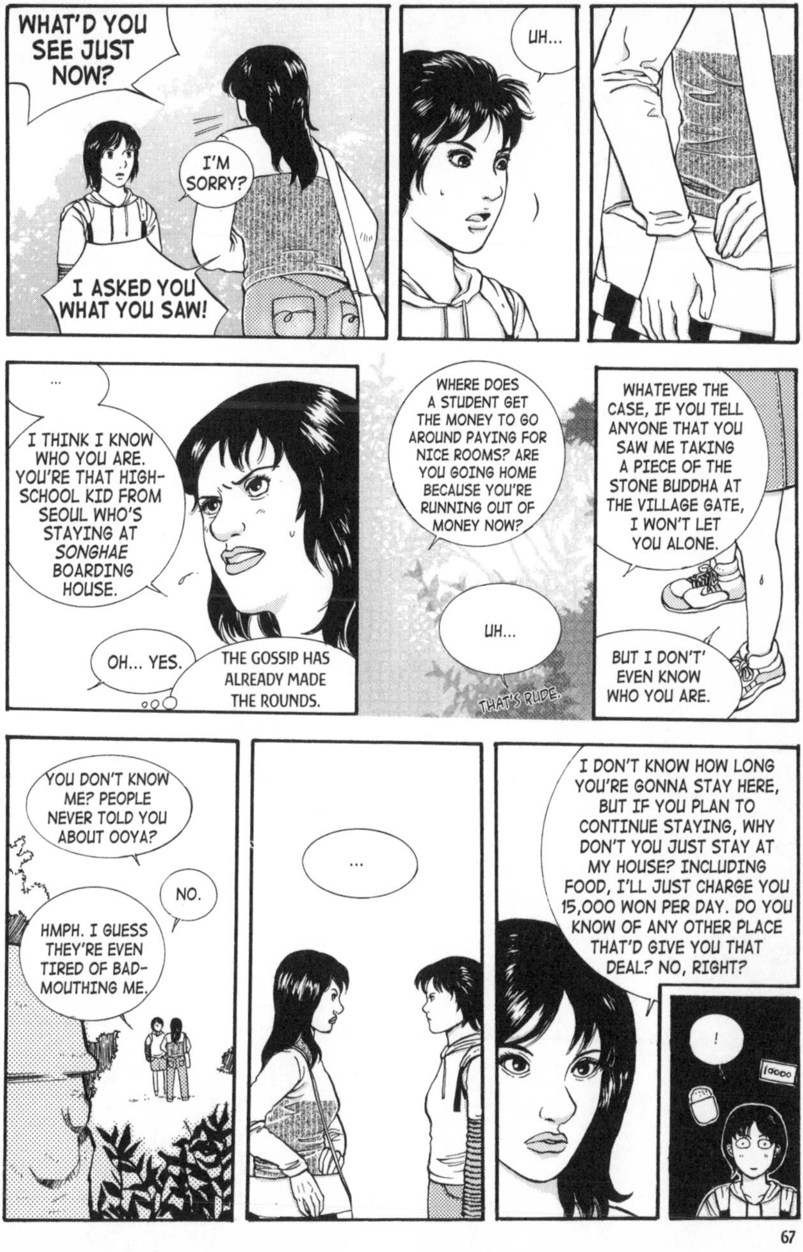
WHAT'D YOU SEE JUST NOW?
I'M SORRY?
I ASKED YOU WHAT YOU SAW!
UH...
...
I THINK I KNOW WHO YOU ARE. YOU'RE THAT HIGH-SCHOOL KID FROM SEOUL WHO'S STAYING AT *SONGHAE* BOARDING HOUSE.
OH... YES.
THE GOSSIP HAS ALREADY MADE THE ROUNDS.
WHERE DOES A STUDENT GET THE MONEY TO GO AROUND PAYING FOR NICE ROOMS? ARE YOU GOING HOME BECAUSE YOU'RE RUNNING OUT OF MONEY NOW?
UH...
THAT'S RUDE.
WHATEVER THE CASE, IF YOU TELL ANYONE THAT YOU SAW ME TAKING A PIECE OF THE STONE BUDDHA AT THE VILLAGE GATE, I WON'T LET YOU ALONE.
BUT I DON'T' EVEN KNOW WHO YOU ARE.
YOU DON'T KNOW ME? PEOPLE NEVER TOLD YOU ABOUT OOYA?
NO.
HMPH. I GUESS THEY'RE EVEN TIRED OF BAD-MOUTHING ME.
...
I DON'T KNOW HOW LONG YOU'RE GONNA STAY HERE, BUT IF YOU PLAN TO CONTINUE STAYING, WHY DON'T YOU JUST STAY AT MY HOUSE? INCLUDING FOOD, I'LL JUST CHARGE YOU 15,000 WON PER DAY. DO YOU KNOW OF ANY OTHER PLACE THAT'D GIVE YOU THAT DEAL? NO, RIGHT?
!
10000

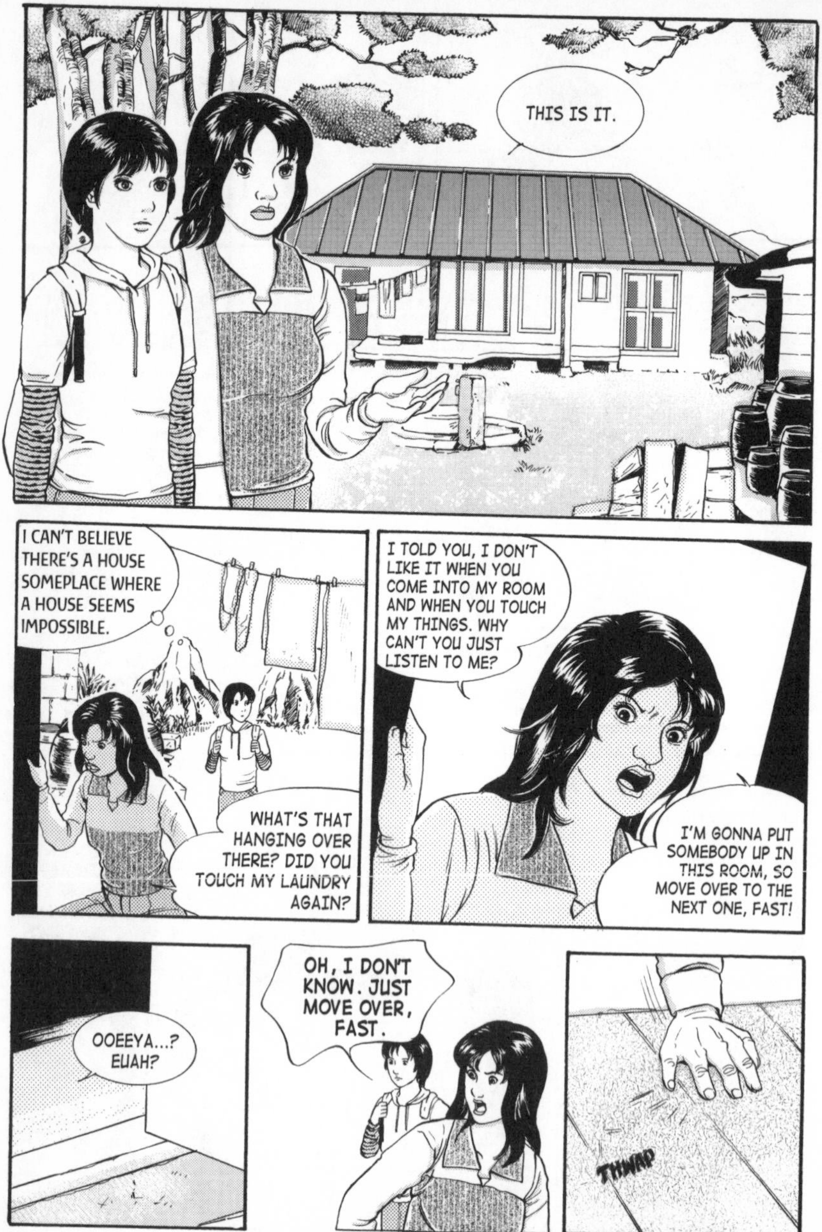

THIS IS IT.
I CAN'T BELIEVE THERE'S A HOUSE SOMEPLACE WHERE A HOUSE SEEMS IMPOSSIBLE.
WHAT'S THAT HANGING OVER THERE? DID YOU TOUCH MY LAUNDRY AGAIN?
I TOLD YOU, I DON'T LIKE IT WHEN YOU COME INTO MY ROOM AND WHEN YOU TOUCH MY THINGS. WHY CAN'T YOU JUST LISTEN TO ME?
I'M GONNA PUT SOMEBODY UP IN THIS ROOM, SO MOVE OVER TO THE NEXT ONE, FAST!
OOEEYA...? EUAH?
OH, I DON'T KNOW. JUST MOVE OVER, FAST.
THWAP

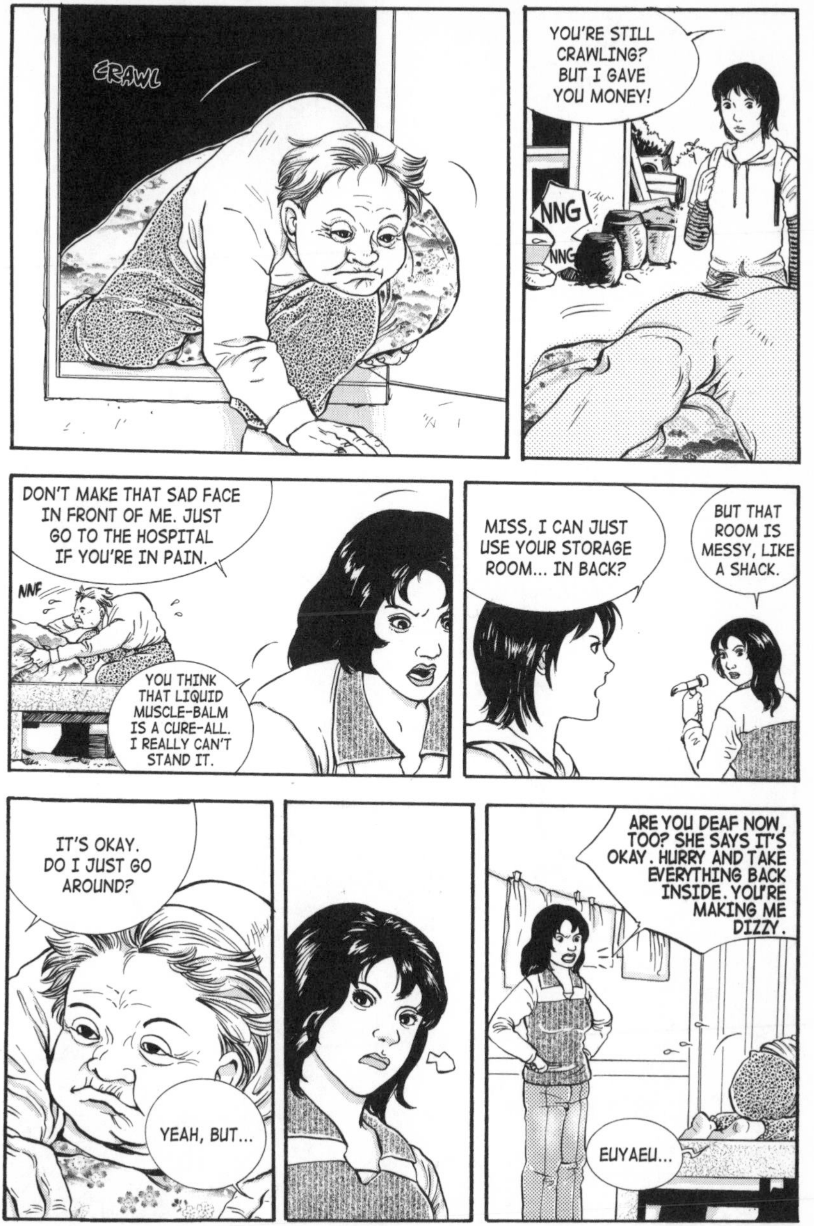
CRAWL
YOU'RE STILL CRAWLING? BUT I GAVE YOU MONEY!
NNG
NNG
DON'T MAKE THAT SAD FACE IN FRONT OF ME. JUST GO TO THE HOSPITAL IF YOU'RE IN PAIN.
NNF
YOU THINK THAT LIQUID MUSCLE-BALM IS A CURE-ALL. I REALLY CAN'T STAND IT.
MISS, I CAN JUST USE YOUR STORAGE ROOM... IN BACK?
BUT THAT ROOM IS MESSY, LIKE A SHACK.
IT'S OKAY. DO I JUST GO AROUND?
YEAH, BUT...
ARE YOU DEAF NOW, TOO? SHE SAYS IT'S OKAY. HURRY AND TAKE EVERYTHING BACK INSIDE. YOU'RE MAKING ME DIZZY.
EUYAEU...

CLOP CLOP KOOM

CLOP

CLOP

CLOP

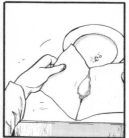

...

KOFF UGH

DAMN STUFF. OF COURSE, CRUSHED STONE WON'T GO EASILY DOWN MY THROAT.

FINE, I TELL YOU. JUST GIVE ME A SON, I DON'T CARE IF MY THROAT GETS ALL SCRATCHED UP.

ULP

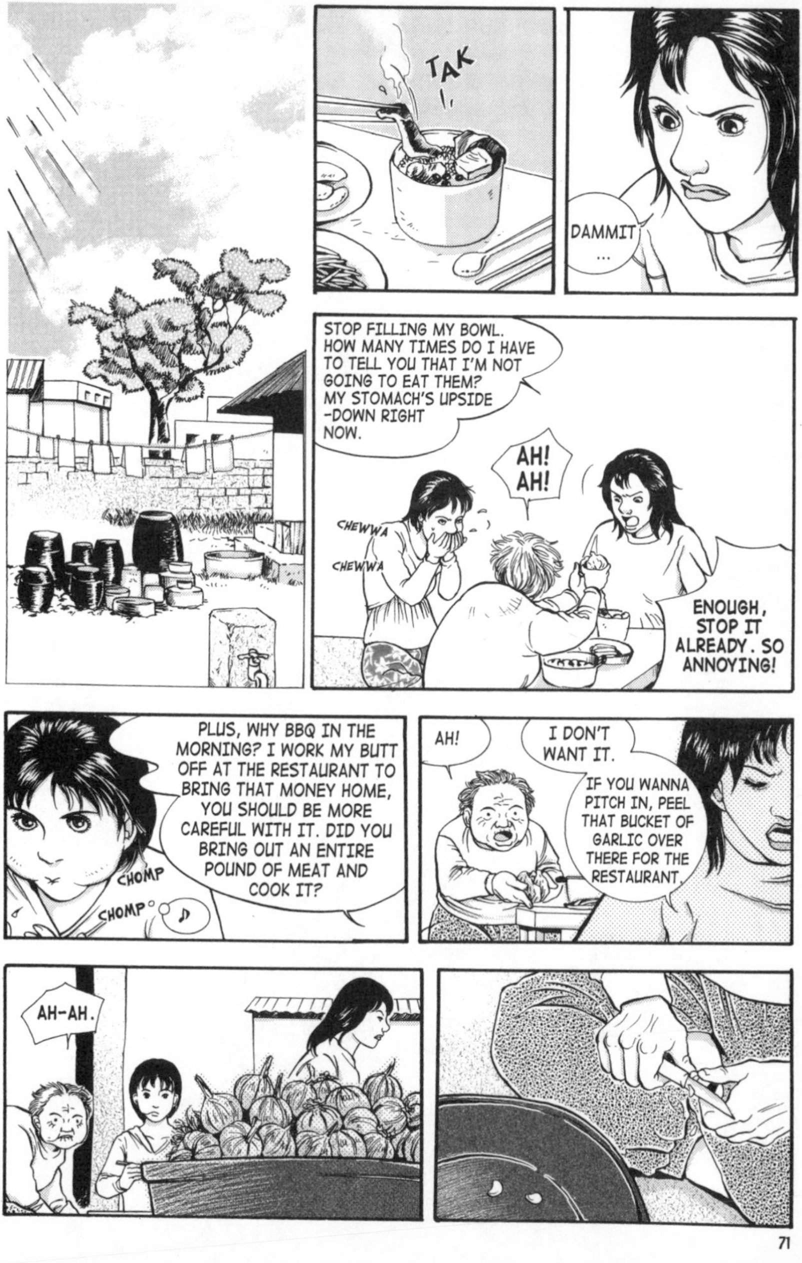
TAK
DAMMIT ...
STOP FILLING MY BOWL. HOW MANY TIMES DO I HAVE TO TELL YOU THAT I'M NOT GOING TO EAT THEM? MY STOMACH'S UPSIDE -DOWN RIGHT NOW.
AH! AH!
CHEWWA
CHEWWA
ENOUGH, STOP IT ALREADY. SO ANNOYING!
PLUS, WHY BBQ IN THE MORNING? I WORK MY BUTT OFF AT THE RESTAURANT TO BRING THAT MONEY HOME, YOU SHOULD BE MORE CAREFUL WITH IT. DID YOU BRING OUT AN ENTIRE POUND OF MEAT AND COOK IT?
CHOMP
CHOMP
♪
AH!
I DON'T WANT IT.
IF YOU WANNA PITCH IN, PEEL THAT BUCKET OF GARLIC OVER THERE FOR THE RESTAURANT.
AH-AH.

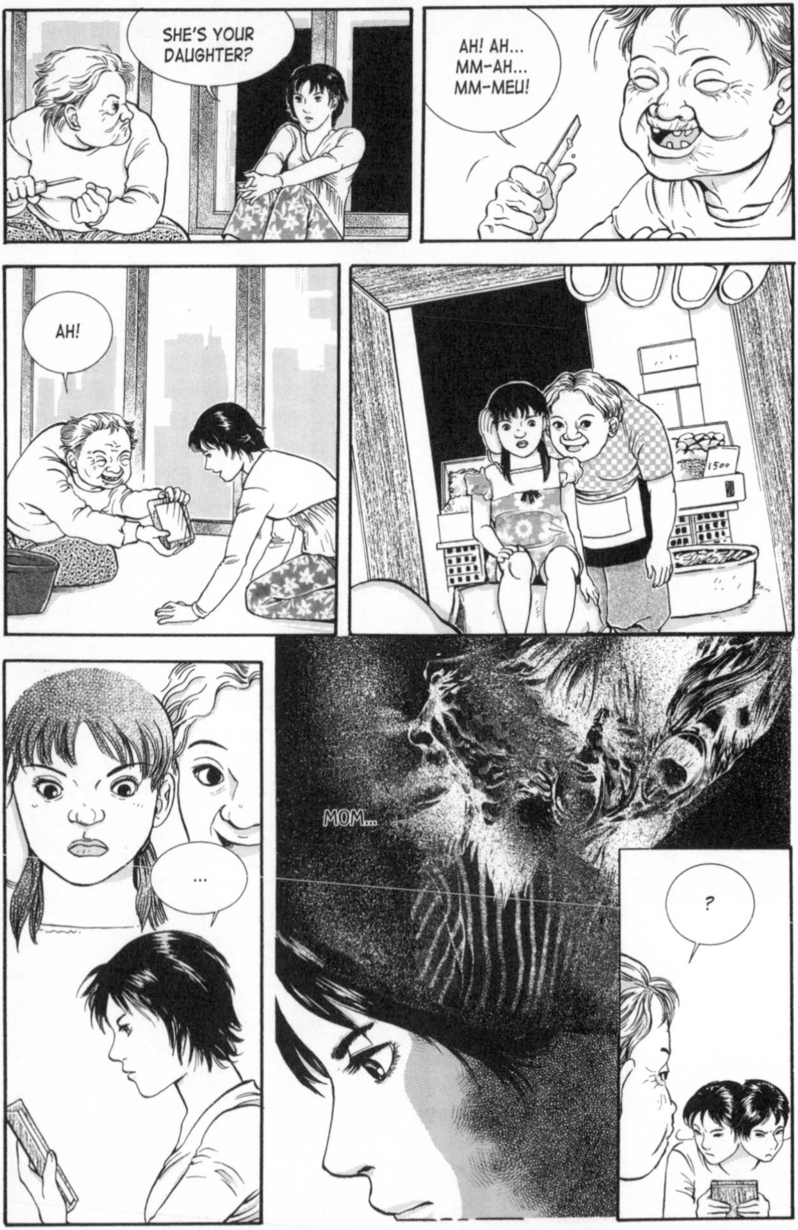
SHE'S YOUR DAUGHTER?
AH! AH... MM-AH... MM-MEU!
AH!
1500
MOM...
...
?

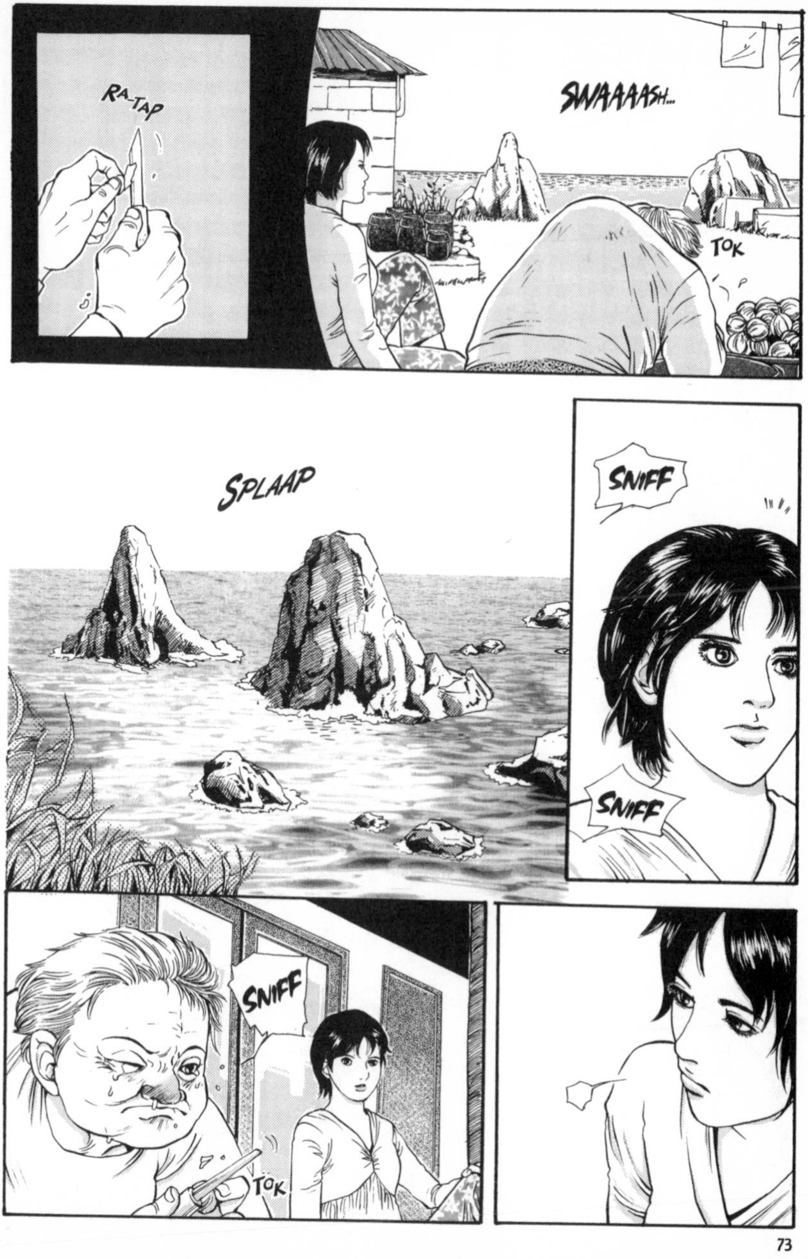
RA-TAP
SWAAAASH...
TOK
SPLAAP
SNIFF
SNIFF
SNIFF
TOK

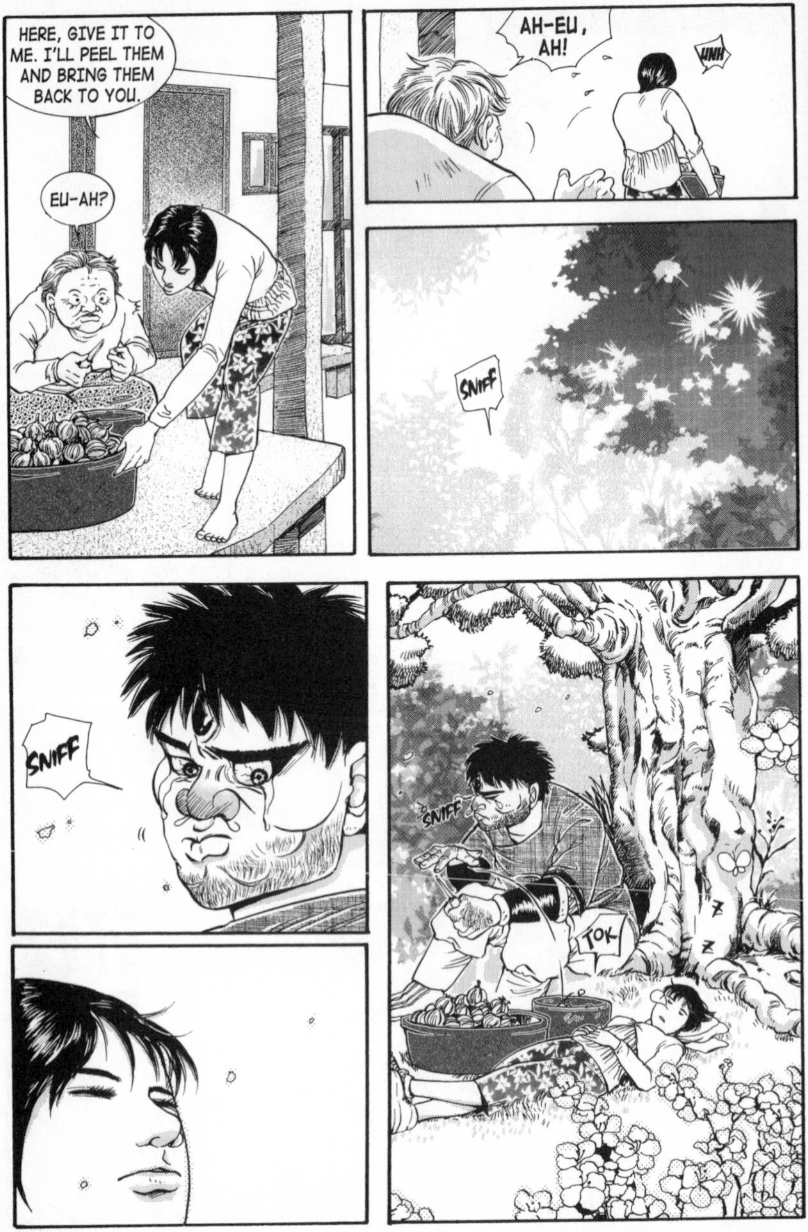
HERE, GIVE IT TO ME. I'LL PEEL THEM AND BRING THEM BACK TO YOU.
EU-AH?
AH-EU, AH!
UNH
SNIFF
SNIFF
SNIFF
TOK
Z
Z

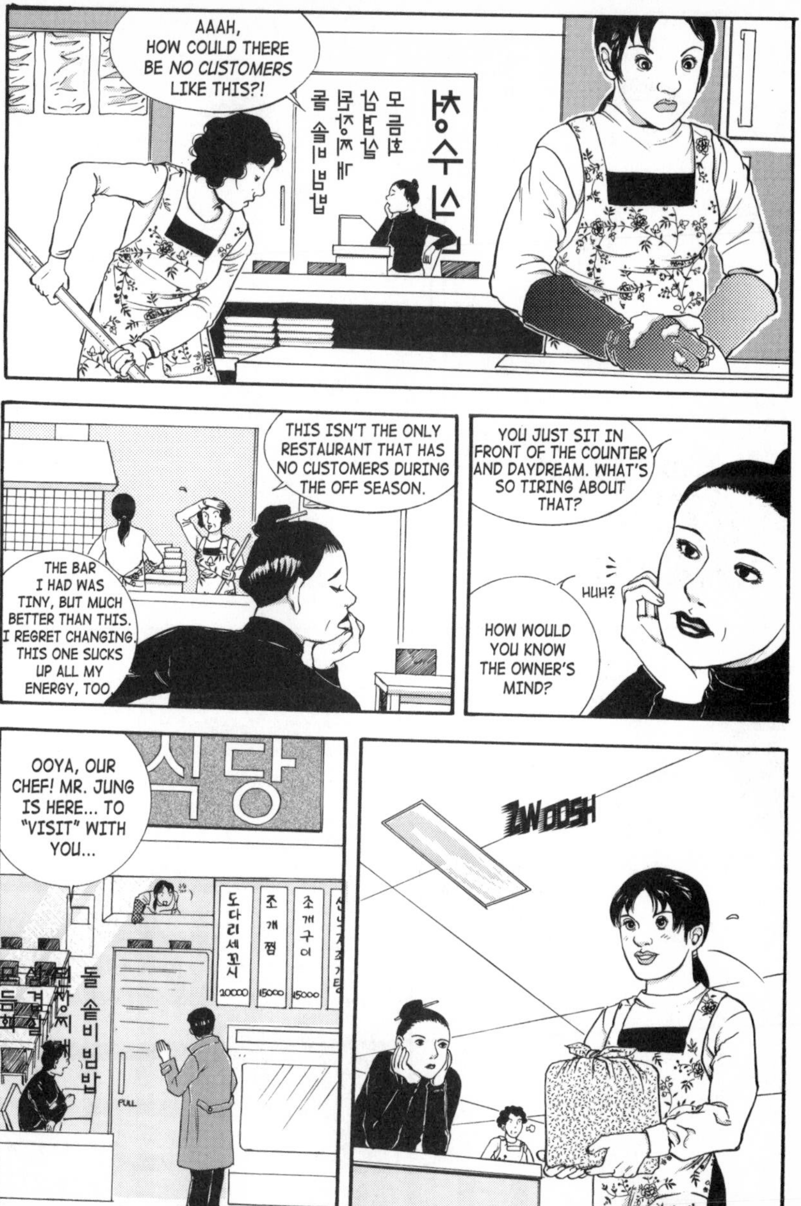
AAAH, HOW COULD THERE BE *NO CUSTOMERS* LIKE THIS?!
THIS ISN'T THE ONLY RESTAURANT THAT HAS NO CUSTOMERS DURING THE OFF SEASON.
THE BAR I HAD WAS TINY, BUT MUCH BETTER THAN THIS. I REGRET CHANGING. THIS ONE SUCKS UP ALL MY ENERGY, TOO.
YOU JUST SIT IN FRONT OF THE COUNTER AND DAYDREAM. WHAT'S SO TIRING ABOUT THAT?
HUH?
HOW WOULD YOU KNOW THE OWNER'S MIND?
식당
OOYA, OUR CHEF! MR. JUNG IS HERE... TO "VISIT" WITH YOU...
도다리세꼬시
10000
조개찜
15000
조개구이
15000
ZWOOSH

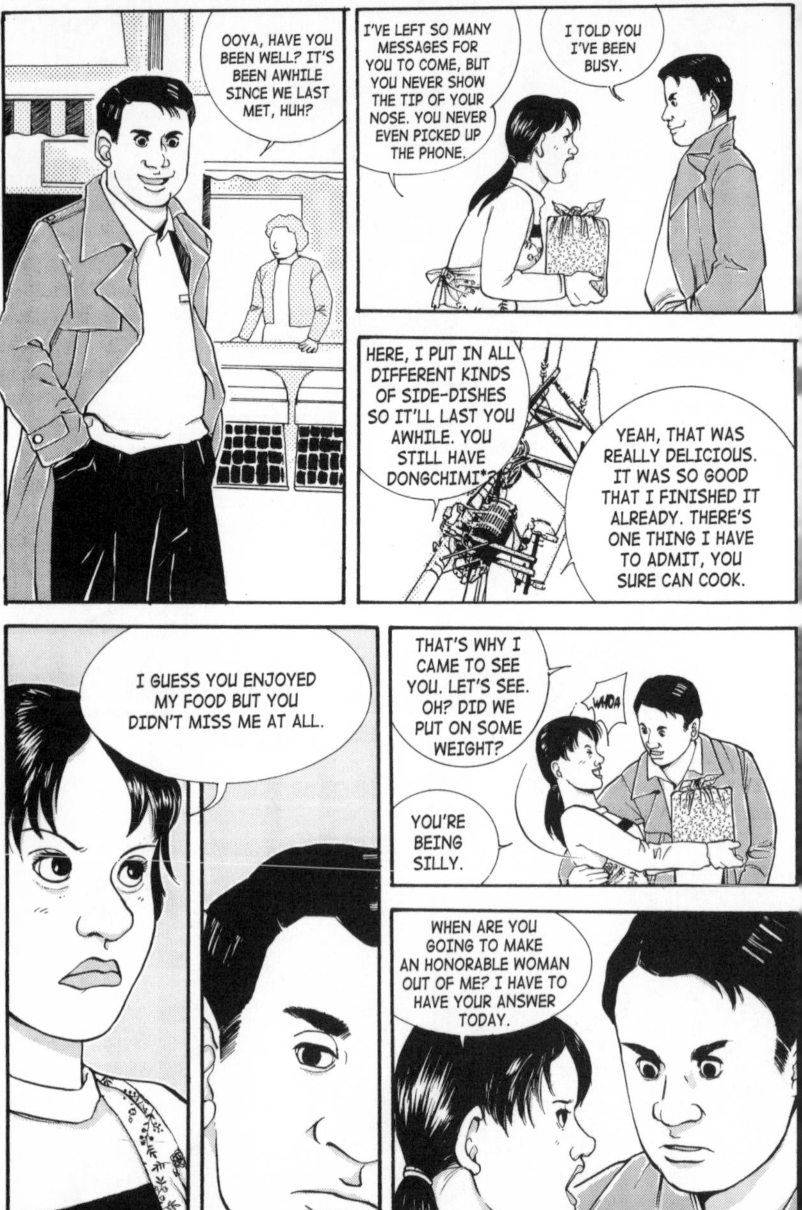
OOYA, HAVE YOU BEEN WELL? IT'S BEEN AWHILE SINCE WE LAST MET, HUH?
I'VE LEFT SO MANY MESSAGES FOR YOU TO COME, BUT YOU NEVER SHOW THE TIP OF YOUR NOSE. YOU NEVER EVEN PICKED UP THE PHONE.
I TOLD YOU I'VE BEEN BUSY.
HERE, I PUT IN ALL DIFFERENT KINDS OF SIDE-DISHES SO IT'LL LAST YOU AWHILE. YOU STILL HAVE DONGCHIMI*?
YEAH, THAT WAS REALLY DELICIOUS. IT WAS SO GOOD THAT I FINISHED IT ALREADY. THERE'S ONE THING I HAVE TO ADMIT, YOU SURE CAN COOK.
I GUESS YOU ENJOYED MY FOOD BUT YOU DIDN'T MISS ME AT ALL.
THAT'S WHY I CAME TO SEE YOU. LET'S SEE. OH? DID WE PUT ON SOME WEIGHT?
WHOA
YOU'RE BEING SILLY.
WHEN ARE YOU GOING TO MAKE AN HONORABLE WOMAN OUT OF ME? I HAVE TO HAVE YOUR ANSWER TODAY.

* GIMCHI MADE WITH CHOPPED RADISHES PICKLED IN SALT WATER

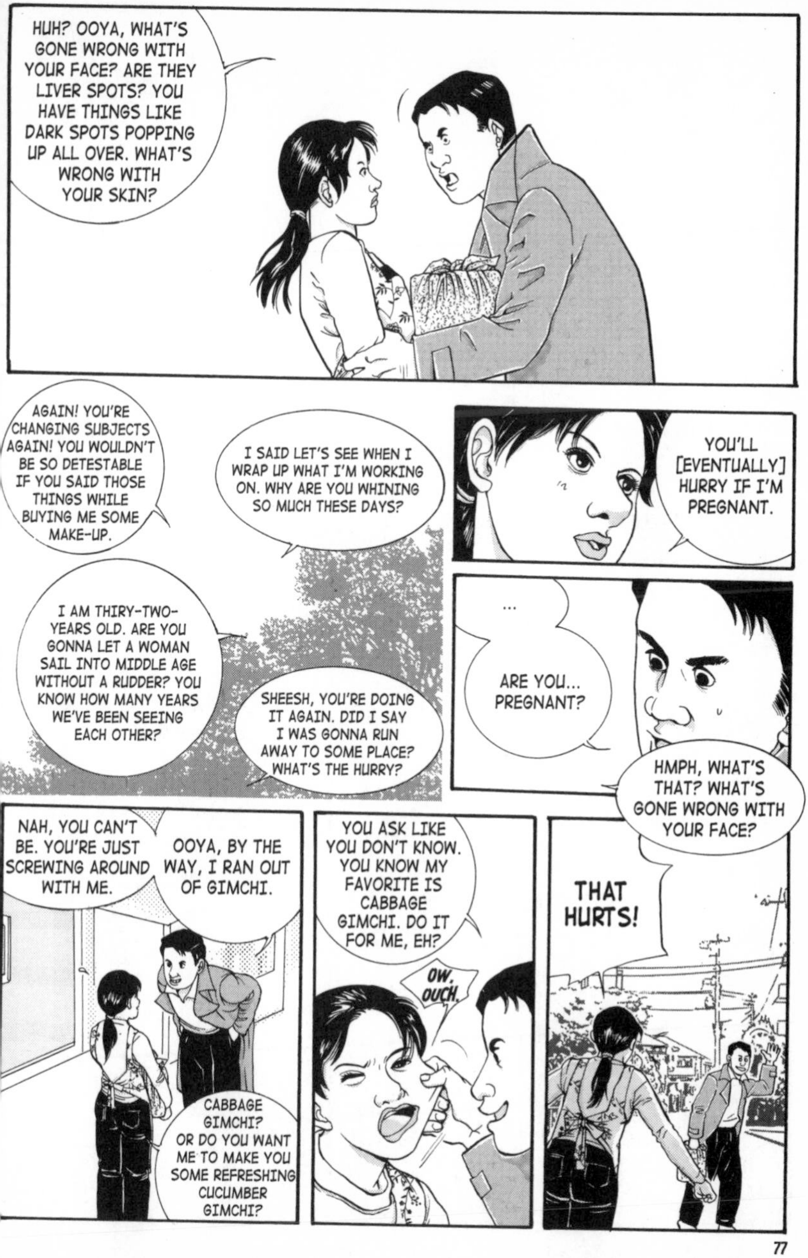
HUH? OOYA, WHAT'S GONE WRONG WITH YOUR FACE? ARE THEY LIVER SPOTS? YOU HAVE THINGS LIKE DARK SPOTS POPPING UP ALL OVER. WHAT'S WRONG WITH YOUR SKIN?
AGAIN! YOU'RE CHANGING SUBJECTS AGAIN! YOU WOULDN'T BE SO DETESTABLE IF YOU SAID THOSE THINGS WHILE BUYING ME SOME MAKE-UP.
I SAID LET'S SEE WHEN I WRAP UP WHAT I'M WORKING ON. WHY ARE YOU WHINING SO MUCH THESE DAYS?
I AM THIRY-TWO-YEARS OLD. ARE YOU GONNA LET A WOMAN SAIL INTO MIDDLE AGE WITHOUT A RUDDER? YOU KNOW HOW MANY YEARS WE'VE BEEN SEEING EACH OTHER?
SHEESH, YOU'RE DOING IT AGAIN. DID I SAY I WAS GONNA RUN AWAY TO SOME PLACE? WHAT'S THE HURRY?
YOU'LL [EVENTUALLY] HURRY IF I'M PREGNANT.
...
ARE YOU... PREGNANT?
HMPH, WHAT'S THAT? WHAT'S GONE WRONG WITH YOUR FACE?
NAH, YOU CAN'T BE. YOU'RE JUST SCREWING AROUND WITH ME.
OOYA, BY THE WAY, I RAN OUT OF GIMCHI.
CABBAGE GIMCHI? OR DO YOU WANT ME TO MAKE YOU SOME REFRESHING CUCUMBER GIMCHI?
YOU ASK LIKE YOU DON'T KNOW. YOU KNOW MY FAVORITE IS CABBAGE GIMCHI. DO IT FOR ME, EH?
OW, OUCH.
THAT HURTS!

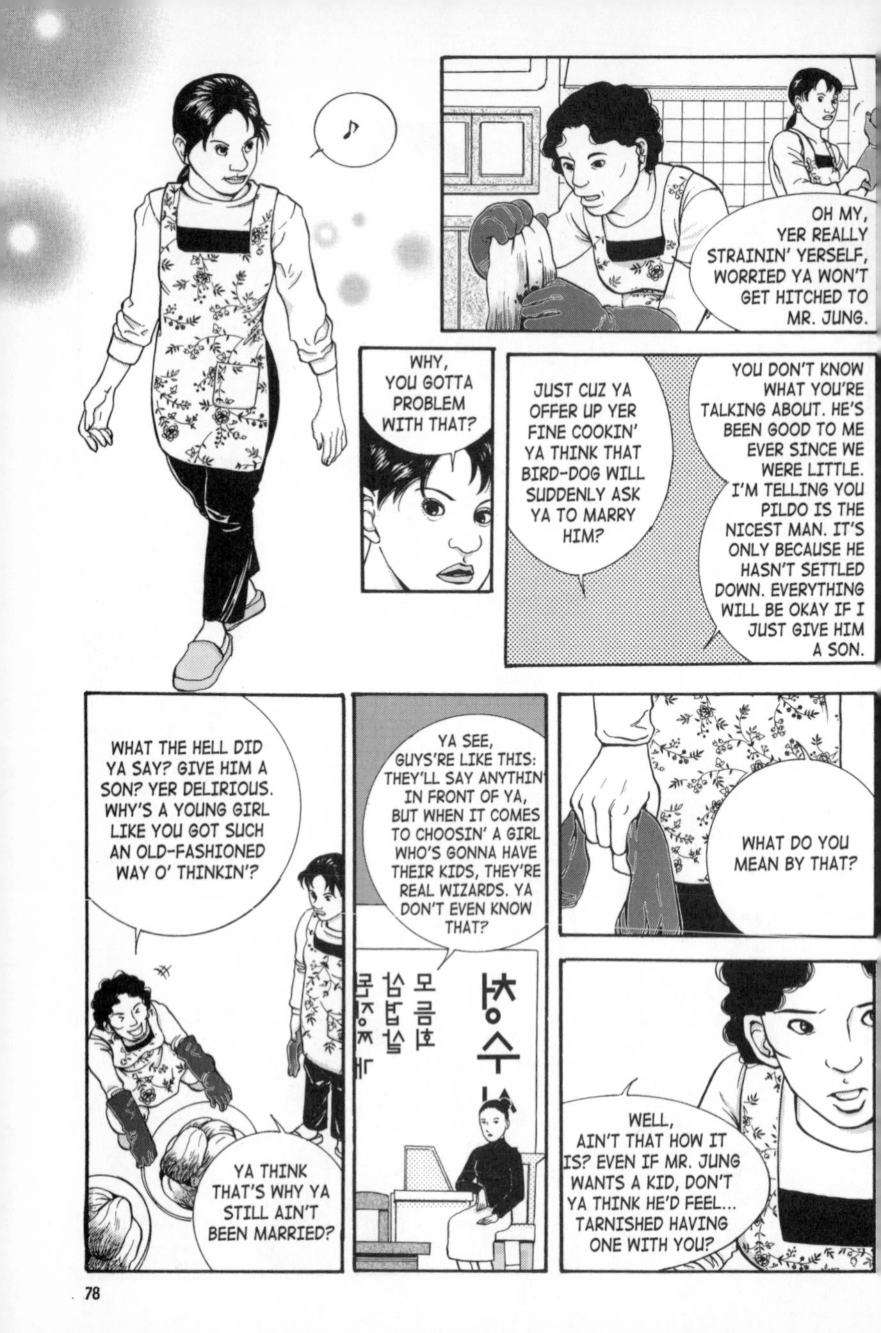
OH MY, YER REALLY STRAININ' YERSELF, WORRIED YA WON'T GET HITCHED TO MR. JUNG.
WHY, YOU GOTTA PROBLEM WITH THAT?
JUST CUZ YA OFFER UP YER FINE COOKIN' YA THINK THAT BIRD-DOG WILL SUDDENLY ASK YA TO MARRY HIM?
YOU DON'T KNOW WHAT YOU'RE TALKING ABOUT. HE'S BEEN GOOD TO ME EVER SINCE WE WERE LITTLE. I'M TELLING YOU PILDO IS THE NICEST MAN. IT'S ONLY BECAUSE HE HASN'T SETTLED DOWN. EVERYTHING WILL BE OKAY IF I JUST GIVE HIM A SON.
WHAT THE HELL DID YA SAY? GIVE HIM A SON? YER DELIRIOUS. WHY'S A YOUNG GIRL LIKE YOU GOT SUCH AN OLD-FASHIONED WAY O' THINKIN'?
YA THINK THAT'S WHY YA STILL AIN'T BEEN MARRIED?
YA SEE, GUYS'RE LIKE THIS: THEY'LL SAY ANYTHIN' IN FRONT OF YA, BUT WHEN IT COMES TO CHOOSIN' A GIRL WHO'S GONNA HAVE THEIR KIDS, THEY'RE REAL WIZARDS. YA DON'T EVEN KNOW THAT?
WHAT DO YOU MEAN BY THAT?
WELL, AIN'T THAT HOW IT IS? EVEN IF MR. JUNG WANTS A KID, DON'T YA THINK HE'D FEEL... TARNISHED HAVING ONE WITH YOU?

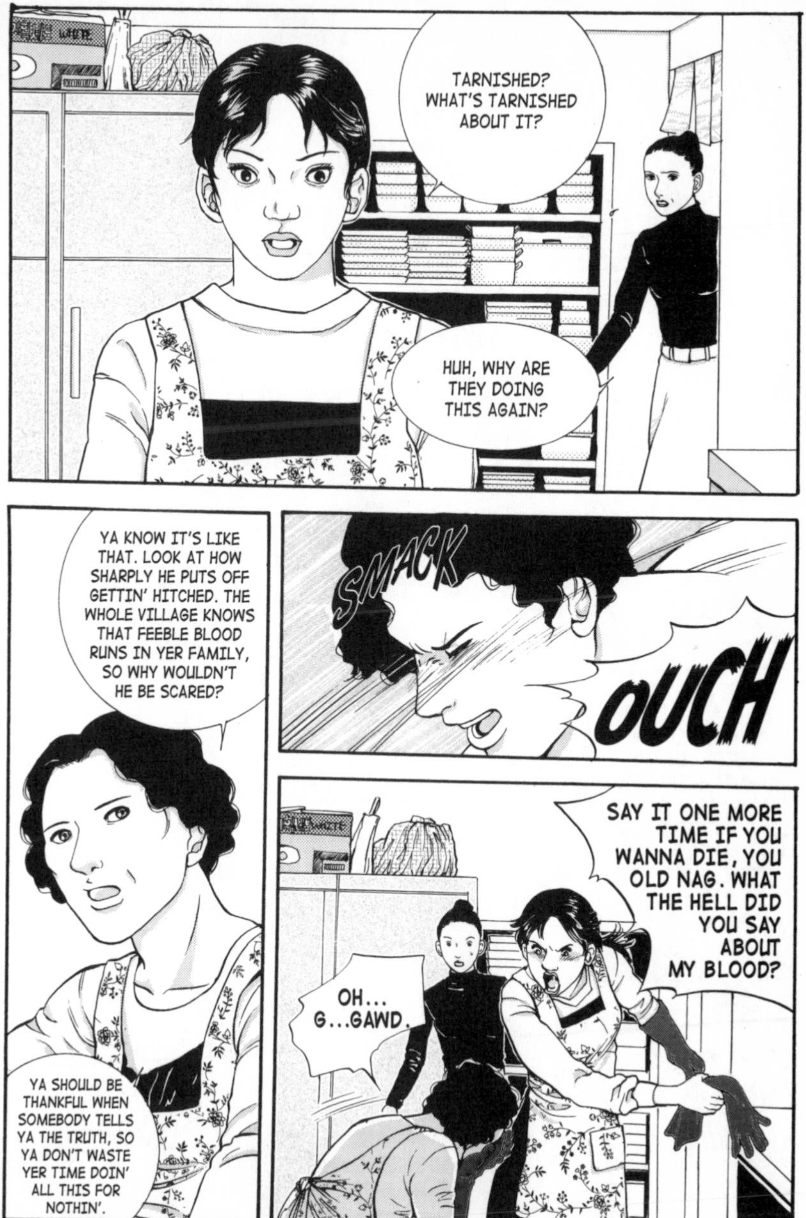
TARNISHED? WHAT'S TARNISHED ABOUT IT?
HUH, WHY ARE THEY DOING THIS AGAIN?
YA KNOW IT'S LIKE THAT. LOOK AT HOW SHARPLY HE PUTS OFF GETTIN' HITCHED. THE WHOLE VILLAGE KNOWS THAT FEEBLE BLOOD RUNS IN YER FAMILY, SO WHY WOULDN'T HE BE SCARED?
YA SHOULD BE THANKFUL WHEN SOMEBODY TELLS YA THE TRUTH, SO YA DON'T WASTE YER TIME DOIN' ALL THIS FOR NOTHIN'.
SMACK
OUCH
SAY IT ONE MORE TIME IF YOU WANNA DIE, YOU OLD NAG. WHAT THE HELL DID YOU SAY ABOUT MY BLOOD?
OH... G...GAWD.

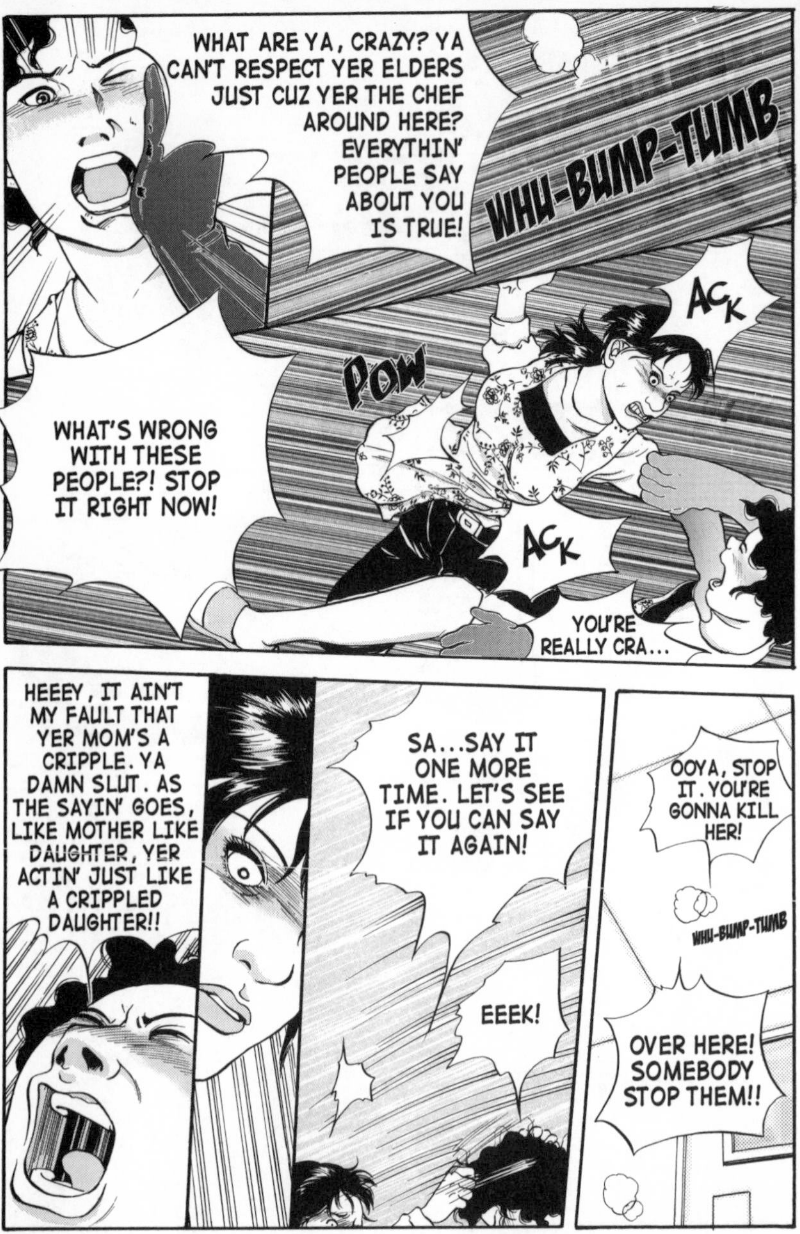
WHAT ARE YA, CRAZY? YA CAN'T RESPECT YER ELDERS JUST CUZ YER THE CHEF AROUND HERE? EVERYTHIN' PEOPLE SAY ABOUT YOU IS TRUE!
WHU-BUMP-TUMB
ACK
POW
WHAT'S WRONG WITH THESE PEOPLE?! STOP IT RIGHT NOW!
ACK
YOU'RE REALLY CRA...
OOYA, STOP IT. YOU'RE GONNA KILL HER!
WHU-BUMP-TUMB
OVER HERE! SOMEBODY STOP THEM!!
SA...SAY IT ONE MORE TIME. LET'S SEE IF YOU CAN SAY IT AGAIN!
EEEK!
HEEEY, IT AIN'T MY FAULT THAT YER MOM'S A CRIPPLE. YA DAMN SLUT. AS THE SAYIN' GOES, LIKE MOTHER LIKE DAUGHTER, YER ACTIN' JUST LIKE A CRIPPLED DAUGHTER!!

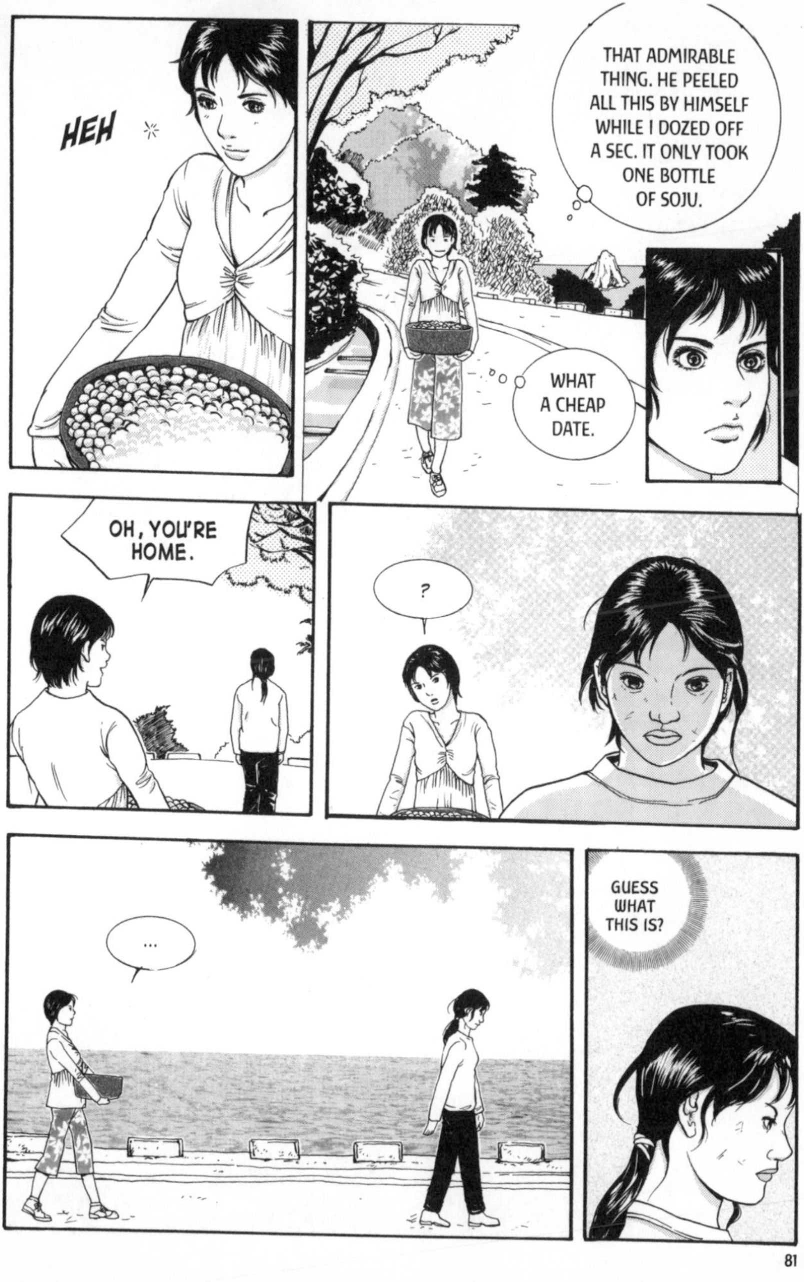
HEH
THAT ADMIRABLE THING. HE PEELED ALL THIS BY HIMSELF WHILE I DOZED OFF A SEC. IT ONLY TOOK ONE BOTTLE OF SOJU.
WHAT A CHEAP DATE.
OH, YOU'RE HOME.
?
...
GUESS WHAT THIS IS?

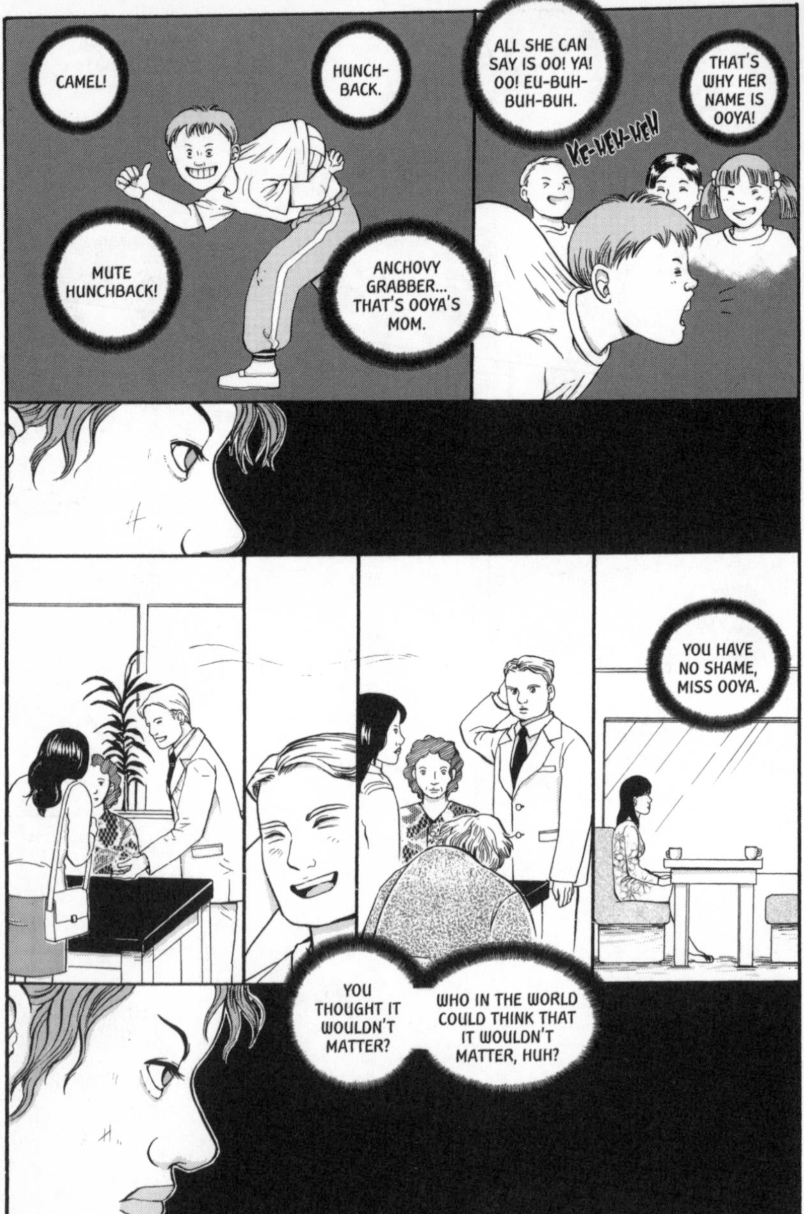
CAMEL!
HUNCH-BACK.
MUTE HUNCHBACK!
ANCHOVY GRABBER... THAT'S OOYA'S MOM.
ALL SHE CAN SAY IS OO! YA! OO! EU-BUH-BUH-BUH.
THAT'S WHY HER NAME IS OOYA!
KE-HEH-HEH
YOU HAVE NO SHAME, MISS OOYA.
YOU THOUGHT IT WOULDN'T MATTER?
WHO IN THE WORLD COULD THINK THAT IT WOULDN'T MATTER, HUH?

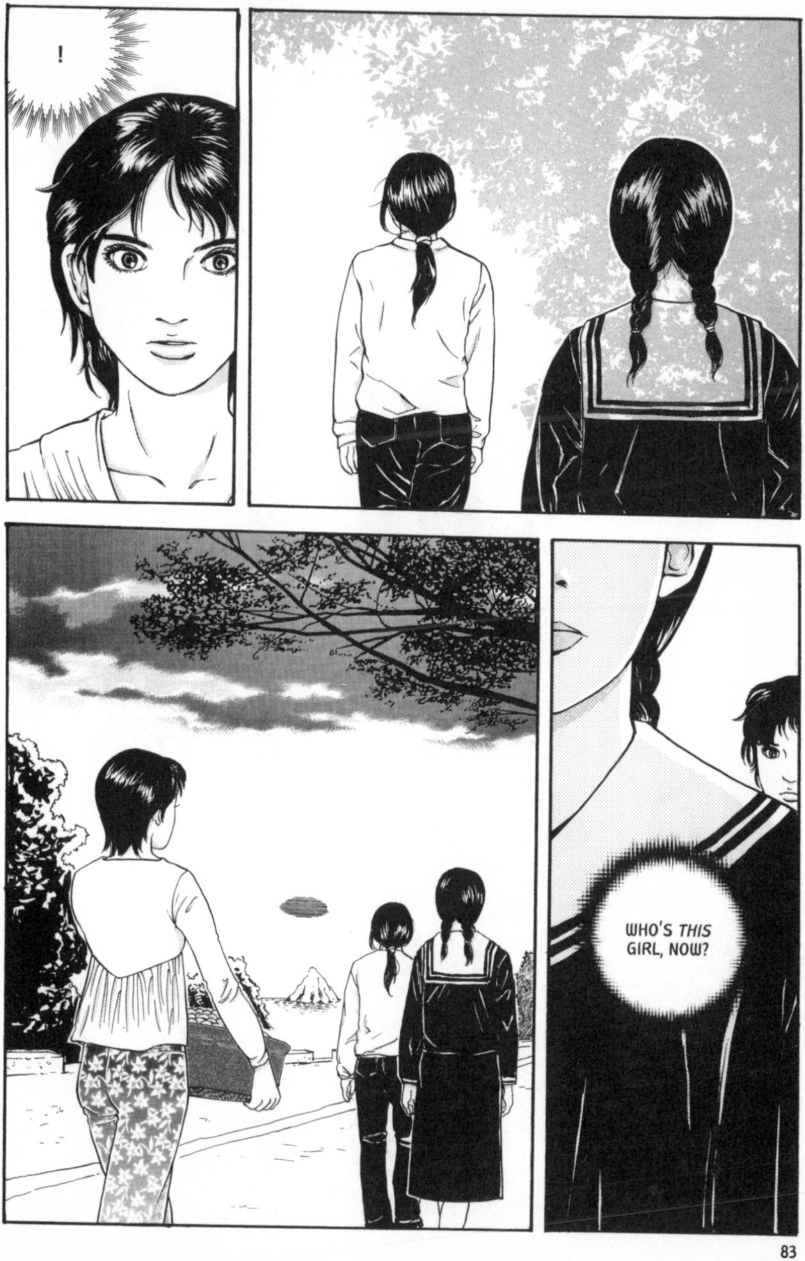
!
WHO'S *THIS* GIRL, NOW?

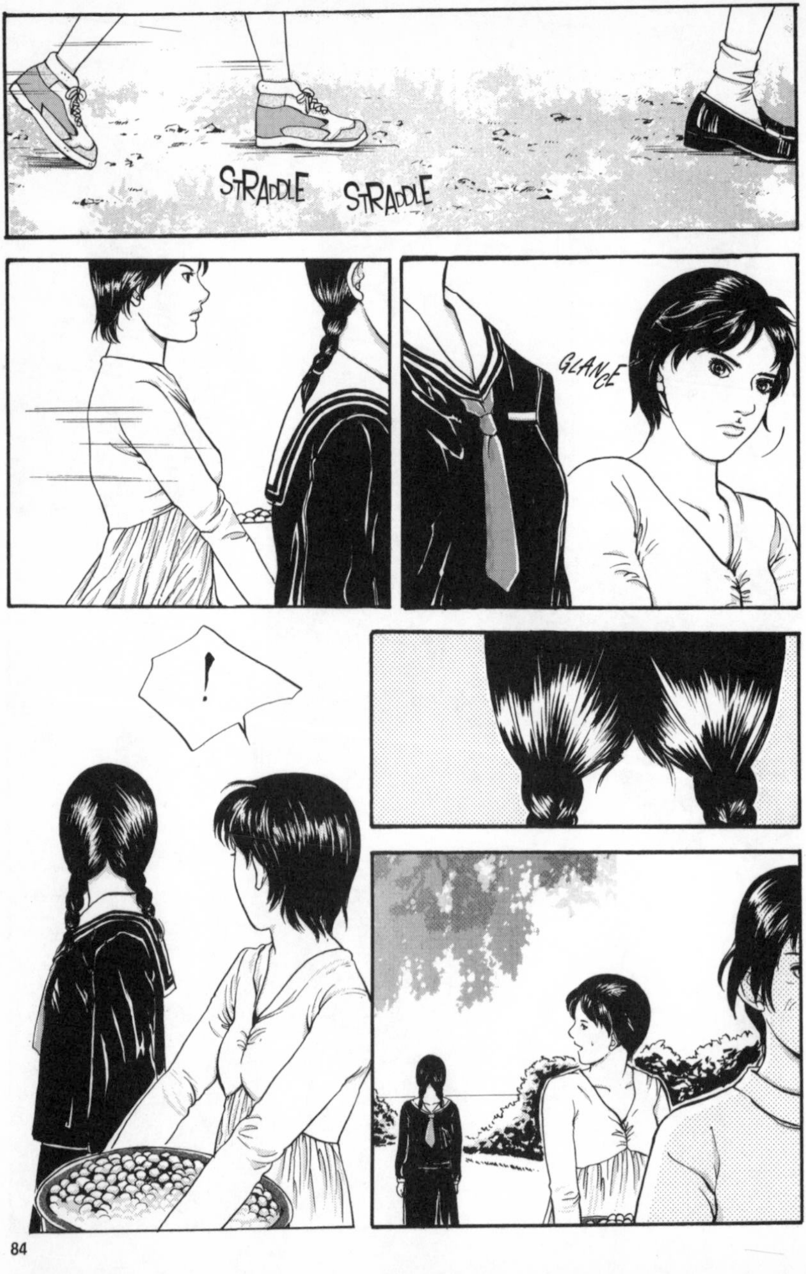
STRADDLE STRADDLE
GLANCE
!

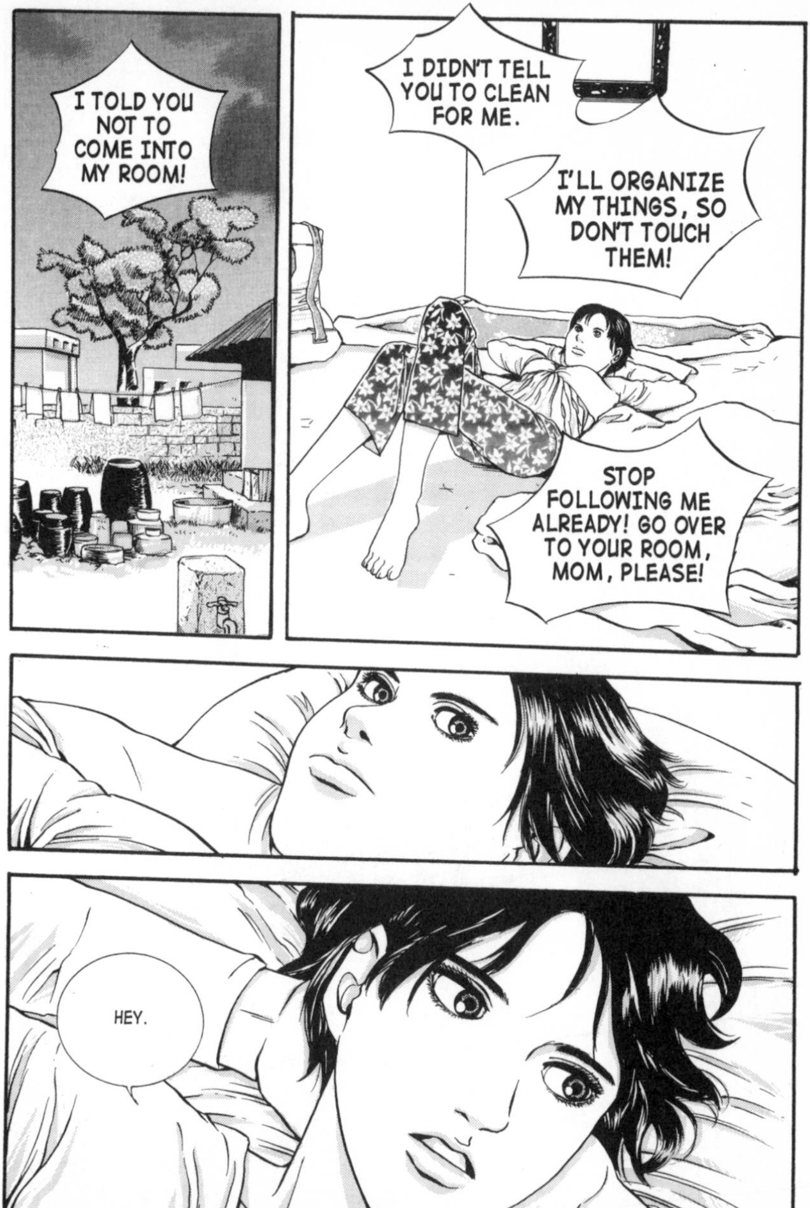
I TOLD YOU NOT TO COME INTO MY ROOM!
I DIDN'T TELL YOU TO CLEAN FOR ME.
I'LL ORGANIZE MY THINGS, SO DON'T TOUCH THEM!
STOP FOLLOWING ME ALREADY! GO OVER TO YOUR ROOM, MOM, PLEASE!
HEY.

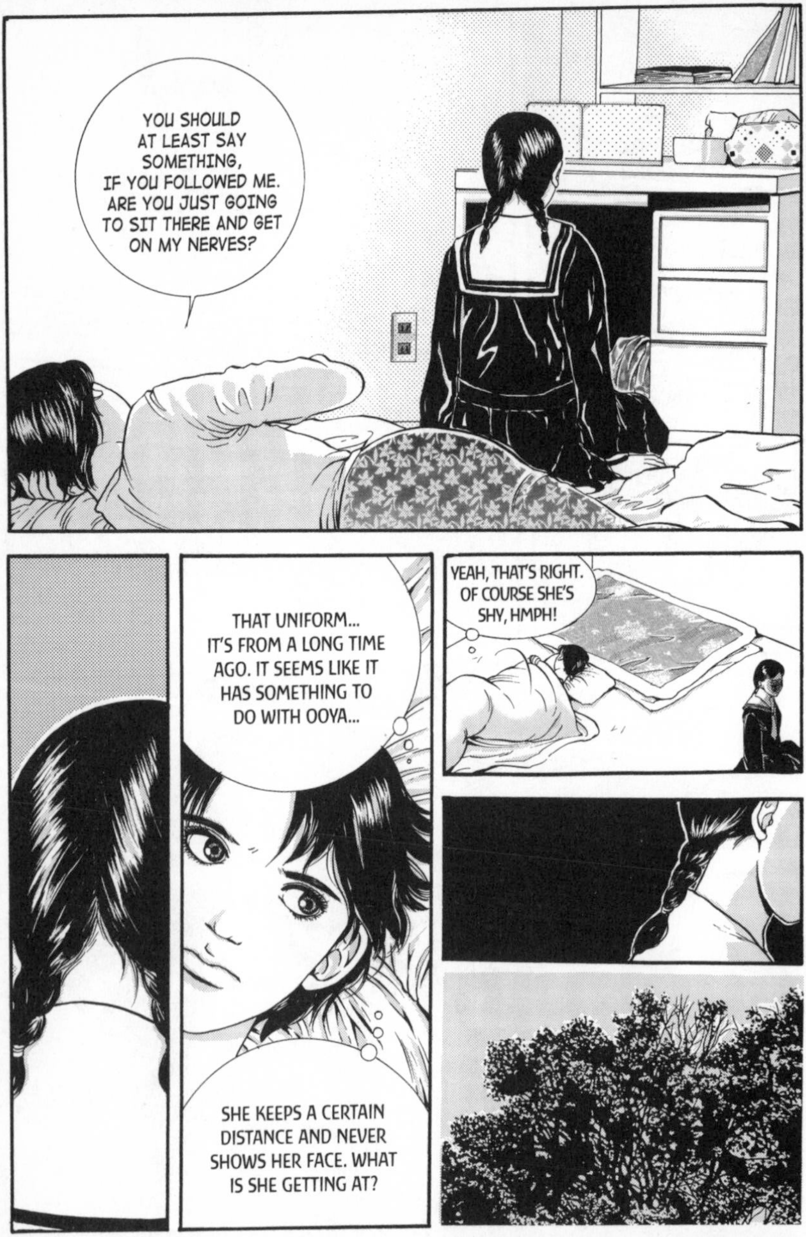
YOU SHOULD AT LEAST SAY SOMETHING, IF YOU FOLLOWED ME. ARE YOU JUST GOING TO SIT THERE AND GET ON MY NERVES?
THAT UNIFORM... IT'S FROM A LONG TIME AGO. IT SEEMS LIKE IT HAS SOMETHING TO DO WITH OOYA...
SHE KEEPS A CERTAIN DISTANCE AND NEVER SHOWS HER FACE. WHAT IS SHE GETTING AT?
YEAH, THAT'S RIGHT. OF COURSE SHE'S SHY, HMPH!

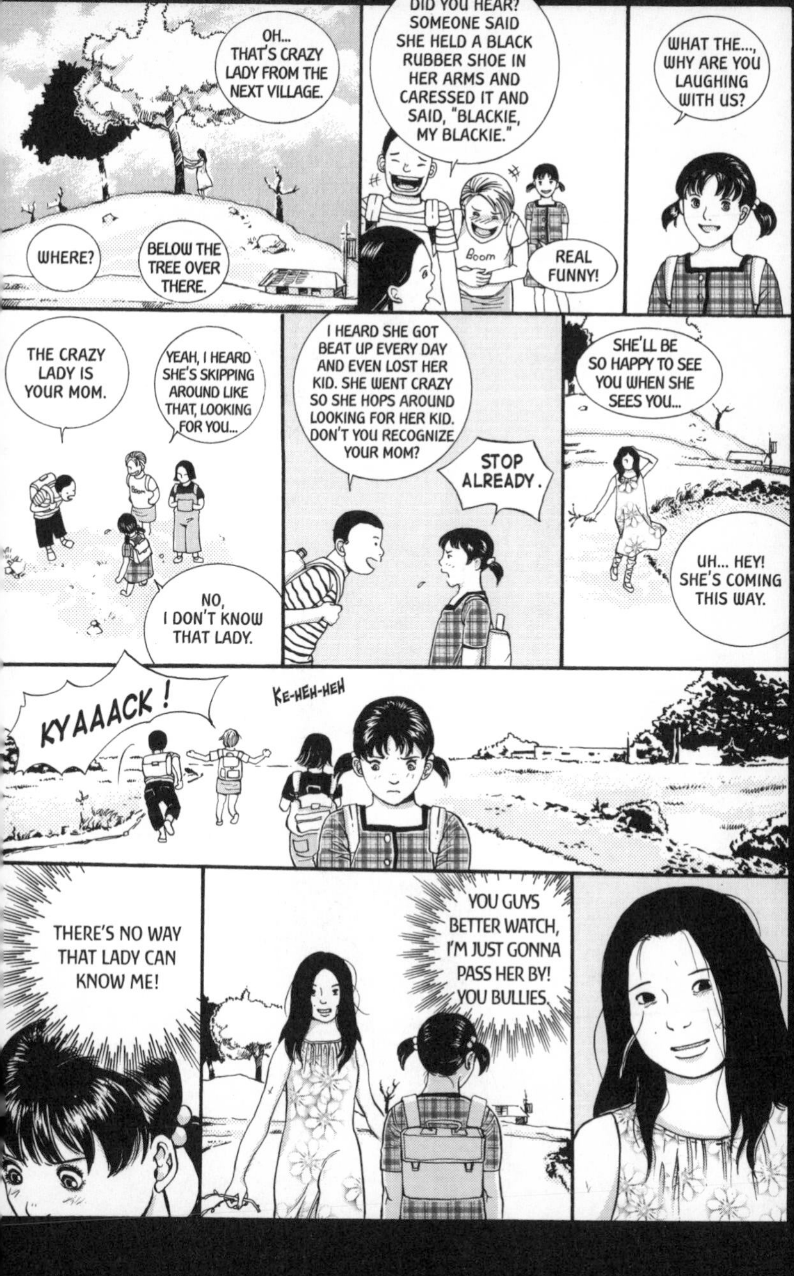
OH... THAT'S CRAZY LADY FROM THE NEXT VILLAGE.
WHERE?
BELOW THE TREE OVER THERE.
DID YOU HEAR? SOMEONE SAID SHE HELD A BLACK RUBBER SHOE IN HER ARMS AND CARESSED IT AND SAID, "BLACKIE, MY BLACKIE."
Boom
REAL FUNNY!
WHAT THE..., WHY ARE YOU LAUGHING WITH US?
THE CRAZY LADY IS YOUR MOM.
YEAH, I HEARD SHE'S SKIPPING AROUND LIKE THAT, LOOKING FOR YOU...
NO, I DON'T KNOW THAT LADY.
I HEARD SHE GOT BEAT UP EVERY DAY AND EVEN LOST HER KID. SHE WENT CRAZY SO SHE HOPS AROUND LOOKING FOR HER KID. DON'T YOU RECOGNIZE YOUR MOM?
STOP ALREADY.
SHE'LL BE SO HAPPY TO SEE YOU WHEN SHE SEES YOU...
UH... HEY! SHE'S COMING THIS WAY.
KYAAACK!
KE-HEH-HEH
THERE'S NO WAY THAT LADY CAN KNOW ME!
YOU GUYS BETTER WATCH, I'M JUST GONNA PASS HER BY! YOU BULLIES.

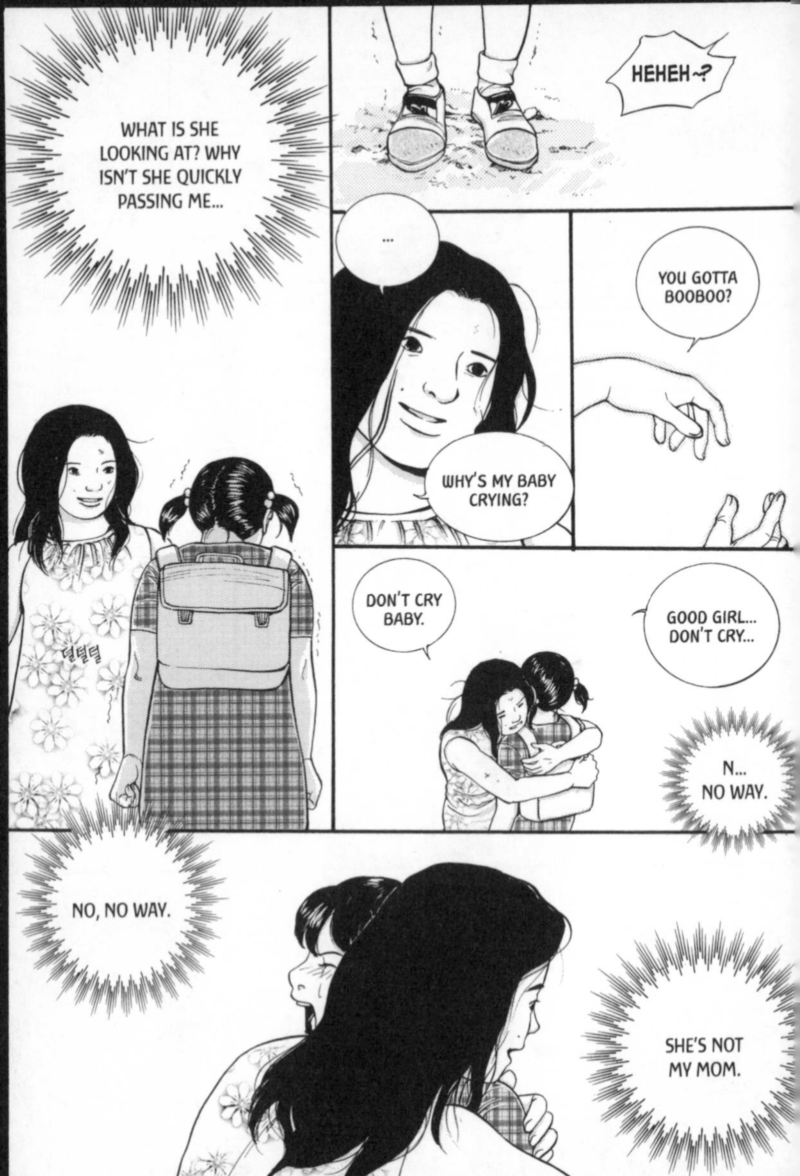
WHAT IS SHE LOOKING AT? WHY ISN'T SHE QUICKLY PASSING ME...
덜덜덜
HEHEH~?
...
WHY'S MY BABY CRYING?
YOU GOTTA BOOBOO?
DON'T CRY BABY.
GOOD GIRL... DON'T CRY...
N... NO WAY.
NO, NO WAY.
SHE'S NOT MY MOM.

EEP, WHAT TIME IS IT?

IT'S DAMP. IT MUST BE RAINING. NO WONDER I FELT RESTLESS.

WHY DO THE MEMORIES FROM MY CHILDHOOD KEEP RESURFACING THESE PAST FEW DAYS?

NOW THAT I LOOK, SHE DISAPPEARED WITHOUT A SOUND. I GUESS I'VE BECOME PRETTY INSENSITIVE, FALLING ASLEEP WITHOUT A CARE.

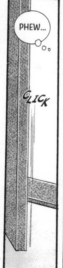

PHEW...

CLICK

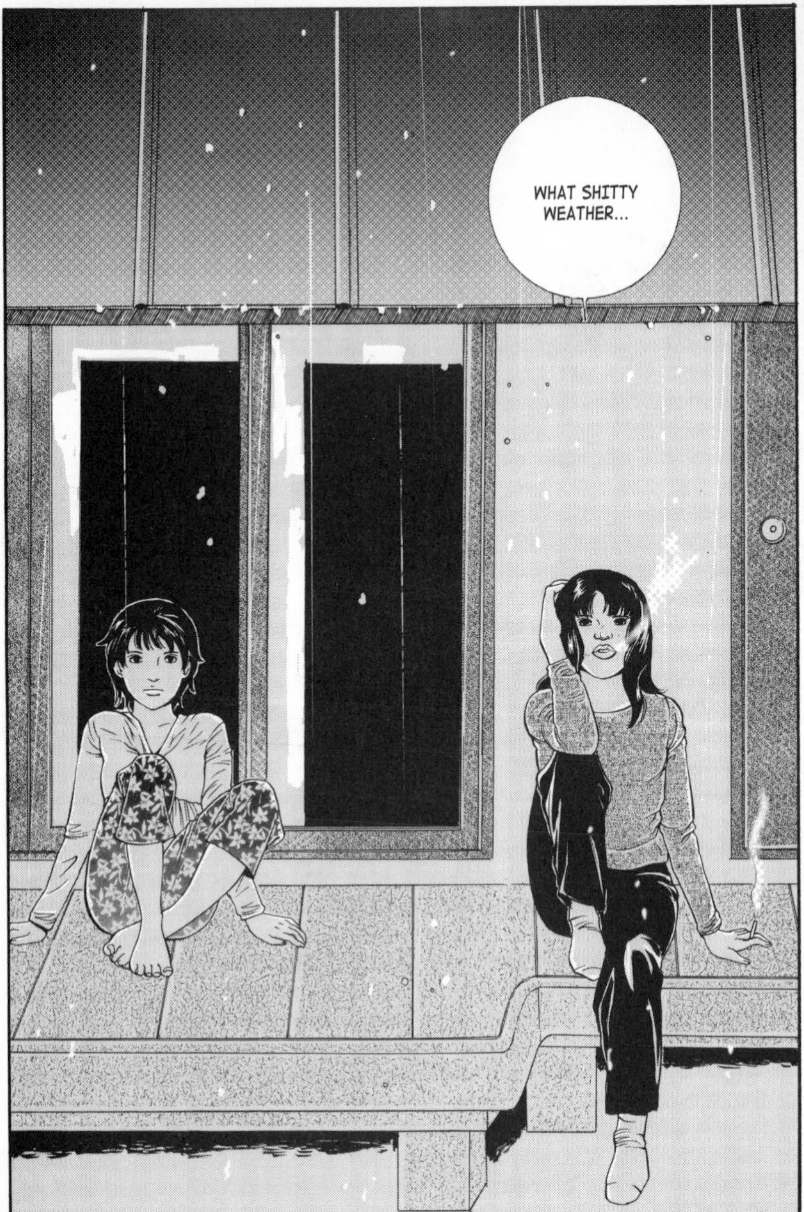
WHAT SHITTY WEATHER...

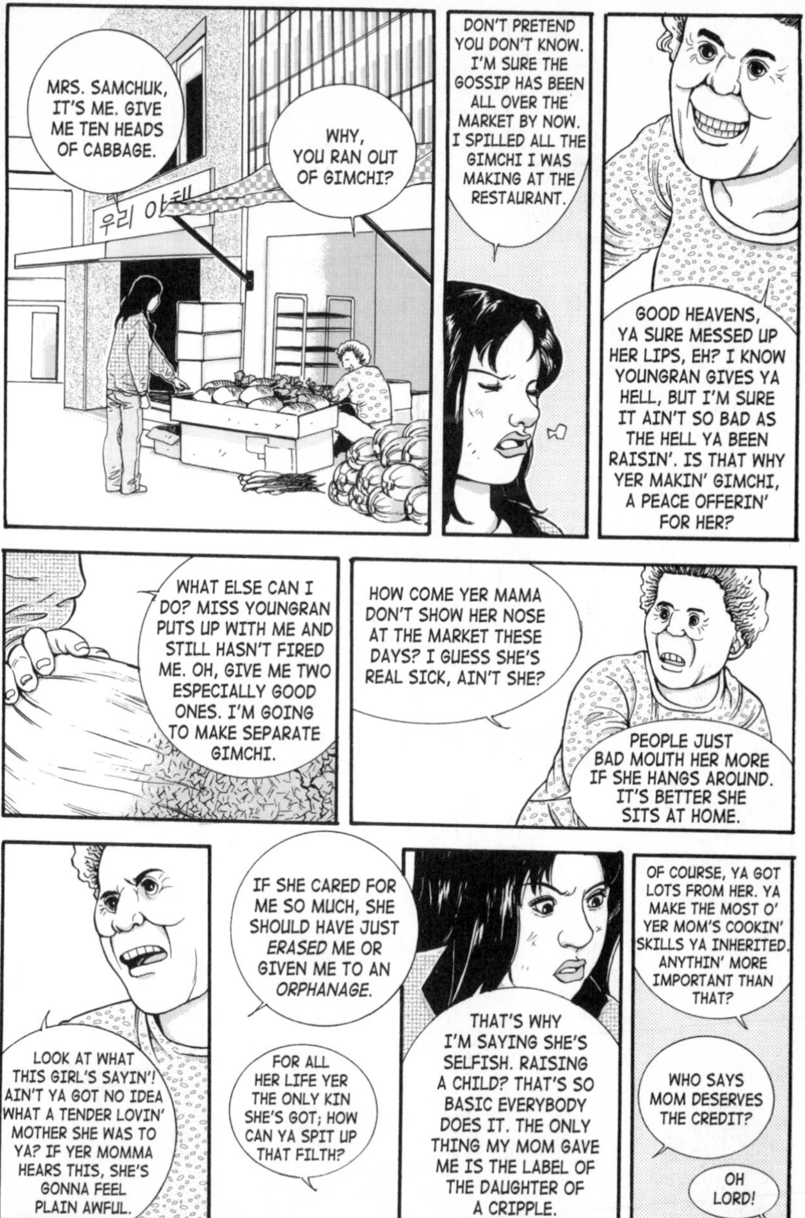

MRS. SAMCHUK, IT'S ME. GIVE ME TEN HEADS OF CABBAGE.
우리 야채
WHY, YOU RAN OUT OF GIMCHI?
DON'T PRETEND YOU DON'T KNOW. I'M SURE THE GOSSIP HAS BEEN ALL OVER THE MARKET BY NOW. I SPILLED ALL THE GIMCHI I WAS MAKING AT THE RESTAURANT.
GOOD HEAVENS, YA SURE MESSED UP HER LIPS, EH? I KNOW YOUNGRAN GIVES YA HELL, BUT I'M SURE IT AIN'T SO BAD AS THE HELL YA BEEN RAISIN'. IS THAT WHY YER MAKIN' GIMCHI, A PEACE OFFERIN' FOR HER?
WHAT ELSE CAN I DO? MISS YOUNGRAN PUTS UP WITH ME AND STILL HASN'T FIRED ME. OH, GIVE ME TWO ESPECIALLY GOOD ONES. I'M GOING TO MAKE SEPARATE GIMCHI.
HOW COME YER MAMA DON'T SHOW HER NOSE AT THE MARKET THESE DAYS? I GUESS SHE'S REAL SICK, AIN'T SHE?
PEOPLE JUST BAD MOUTH HER MORE IF SHE HANGS AROUND. IT'S BETTER SHE SITS AT HOME.
IF SHE CARED FOR ME SO MUCH, SHE SHOULD HAVE JUST *ERASED* ME OR GIVEN ME TO AN *ORPHANAGE*.
LOOK AT WHAT THIS GIRL'S SAYIN'! AIN'T YA GOT NO IDEA WHAT A TENDER LOVIN' MOTHER SHE WAS TO YA? IF YER MOMMA HEARS THIS, SHE'S GONNA FEEL PLAIN AWFUL.
FOR ALL HER LIFE YER THE ONLY KIN SHE'S GOT; HOW CAN YA SPIT UP THAT FILTH?
THAT'S WHY I'M SAYING SHE'S SELFISH. RAISING A CHILD? THAT'S SO BASIC EVERYBODY DOES IT. THE ONLY THING MY MOM GAVE ME IS THE LABEL OF THE DAUGHTER OF A CRIPPLE.
OF COURSE, YA GOT LOTS FROM HER. YA MAKE THE MOST O' YER MOM'S COOKIN' SKILLS YA INHERITED. ANYTHIN' MORE IMPORTANT THAN THAT?
WHO SAYS MOM DESERVES THE CREDIT?
OH LORD!

* THE SIGN READS "OUR VEGETABLES"

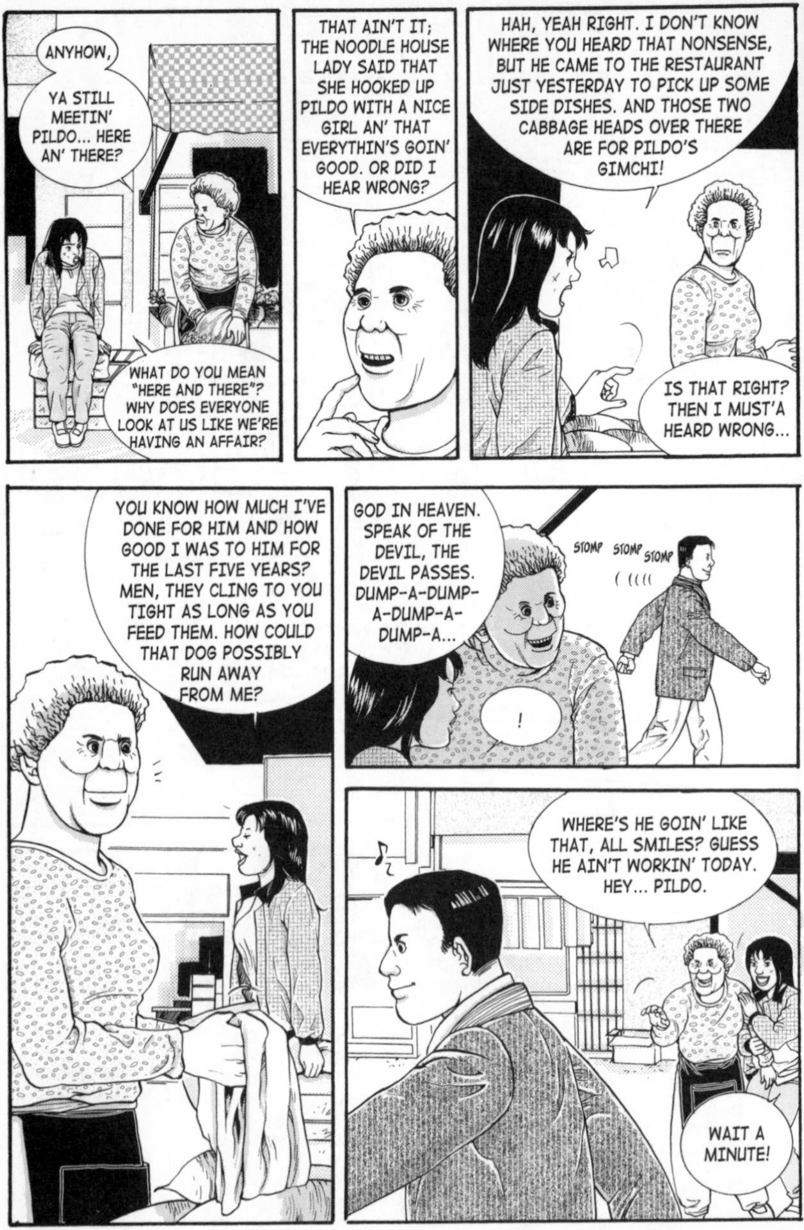

ANYHOW,
YA STILL MEETIN' PILDO... HERE AN' THERE?
WHAT DO YOU MEAN "HERE AND THERE"? WHY DOES EVERYONE LOOK AT US LIKE WE'RE HAVING AN AFFAIR?
THAT AIN'T IT; THE NOODLE HOUSE LADY SAID THAT SHE HOOKED UP PILDO WITH A NICE GIRL AN' THAT EVERYTHIN'S GOIN' GOOD. OR DID I HEAR WRONG?
HAH, YEAH RIGHT. I DON'T KNOW WHERE YOU HEARD THAT NONSENSE, BUT HE CAME TO THE RESTAURANT JUST YESTERDAY TO PICK UP SOME SIDE DISHES. AND THOSE TWO CABBAGE HEADS OVER THERE ARE FOR PILDO'S GIMCHI!
IS THAT RIGHT? THEN I MUST'A HEARD WRONG...
YOU KNOW HOW MUCH I'VE DONE FOR HIM AND HOW GOOD I WAS TO HIM FOR THE LAST FIVE YEARS? MEN, THEY CLING TO YOU TIGHT AS LONG AS YOU FEED THEM. HOW COULD THAT DOG POSSIBLY RUN AWAY FROM ME?
GOD IN HEAVEN. SPEAK OF THE DEVIL, THE DEVIL PASSES. DUMP-A-DUMP-A-DUMP-A-DUMP-A...
STOMP STOMP STOMP
!
WHERE'S HE GOIN' LIKE THAT, ALL SMILES? GUESS HE AIN'T WORKIN' TODAY. HEY... PILDO.
WAIT A MINUTE!

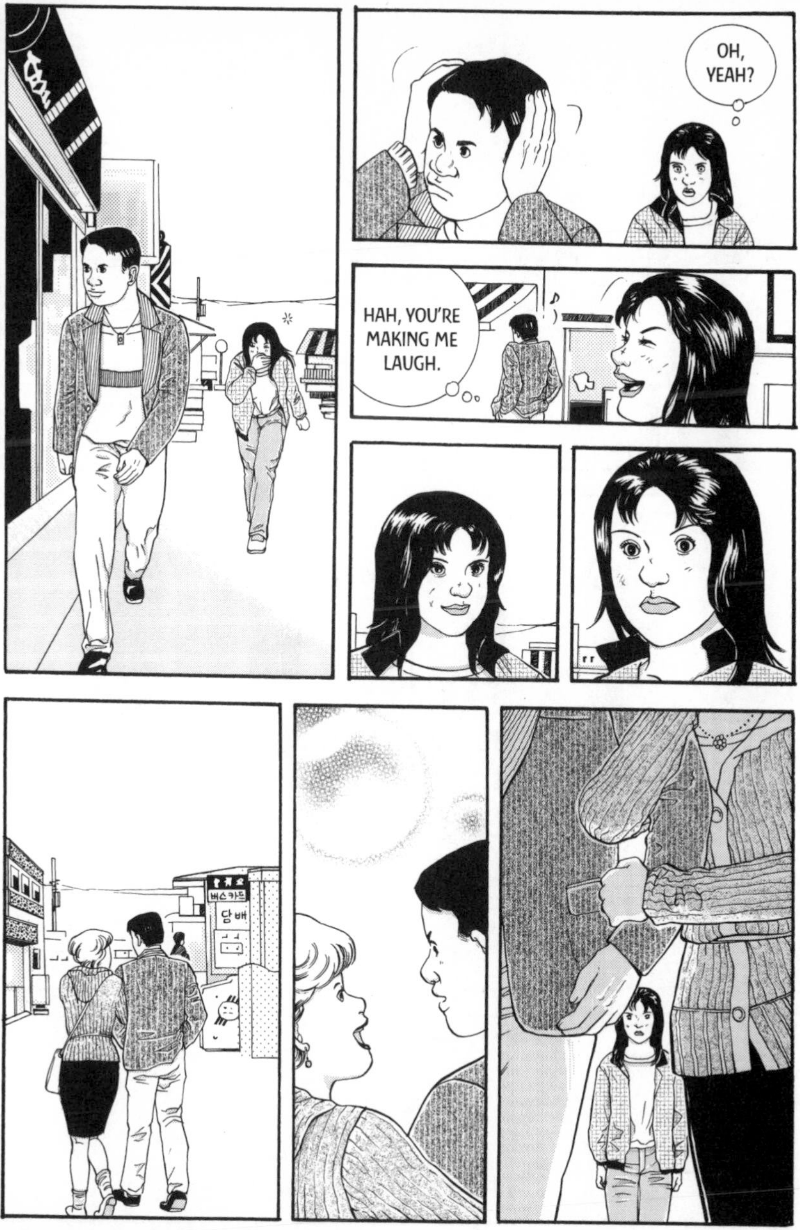
OH, YEAH?
HAH, YOU'RE MAKING ME LAUGH.
버스카드
담배

* THE SIGNS READ "BUS PASS" AND "CIGARETTES"

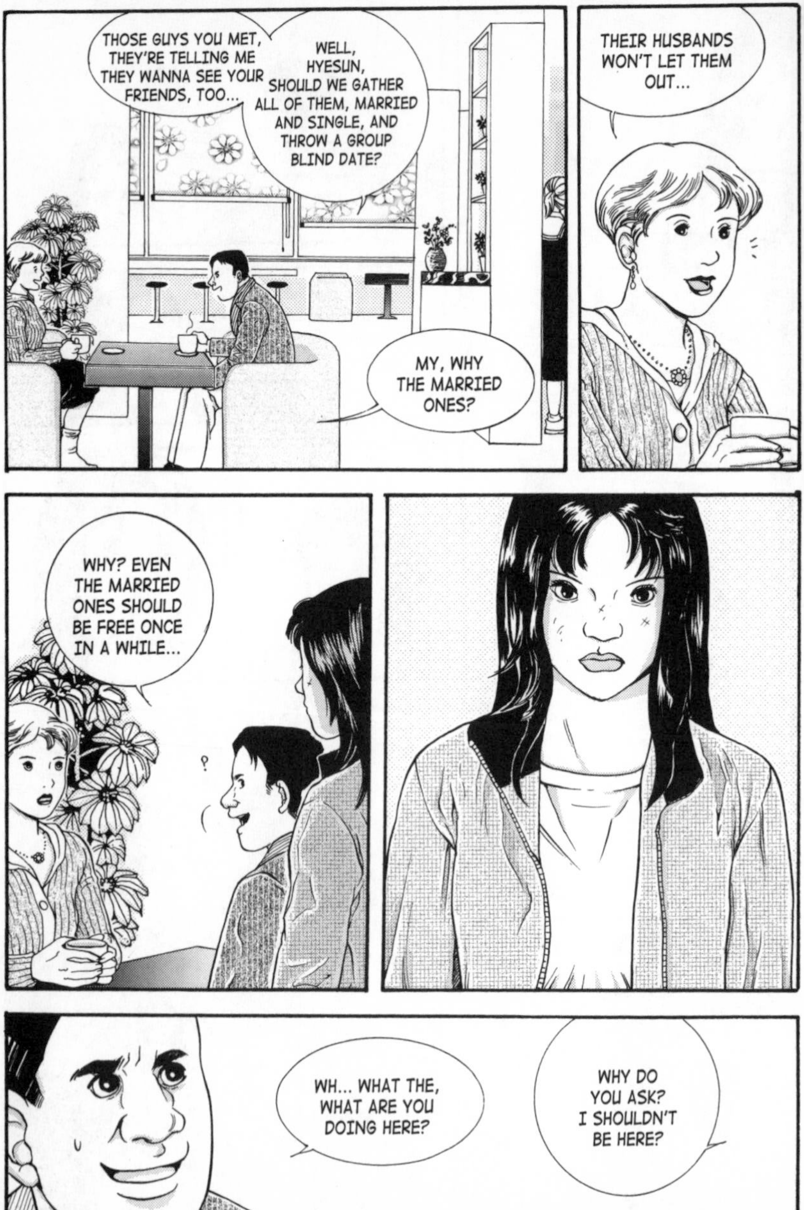
THOSE GUYS YOU MET, THEY'RE TELLING ME THEY WANNA SEE YOUR FRIENDS, TOO...
WELL, HYESUN, SHOULD WE GATHER ALL OF THEM, MARRIED AND SINGLE, AND THROW A GROUP BLIND DATE?
MY, WHY THE MARRIED ONES?
THEIR HUSBANDS WON'T LET THEM OUT...
WHY? EVEN THE MARRIED ONES SHOULD BE FREE ONCE IN A WHILE...
?
WH... WHAT THE, WHAT ARE YOU DOING HERE?
WHY DO YOU ASK? I SHOULDN'T BE HERE?

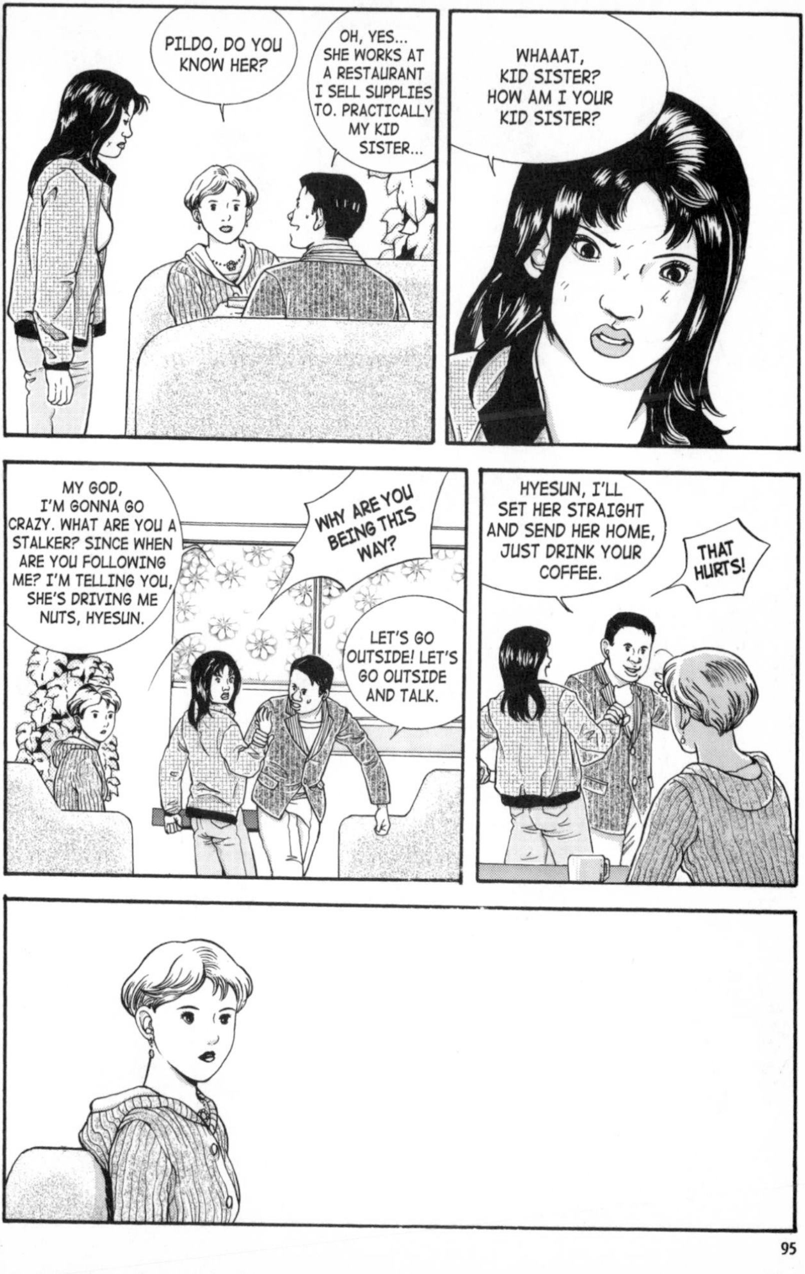
PILDO, DO YOU KNOW HER?
OH, YES... SHE WORKS AT A RESTAURANT I SELL SUPPLIES TO. PRACTICALLY MY KID SISTER...
WHAAAT, KID SISTER? HOW AM I YOUR KID SISTER?
MY GOD, I'M GONNA GO CRAZY. WHAT ARE YOU A STALKER? SINCE WHEN ARE YOU FOLLOWING ME? I'M TELLING YOU, SHE'S DRIVING ME NUTS, HYESUN.
WHY ARE YOU BEING THIS WAY?
LET'S GO OUTSIDE! LET'S GO OUTSIDE AND TALK.
HYESUN, I'LL SET HER STRAIGHT AND SEND HER HOME, JUST DRINK YOUR COFFEE.
THAT HURTS!

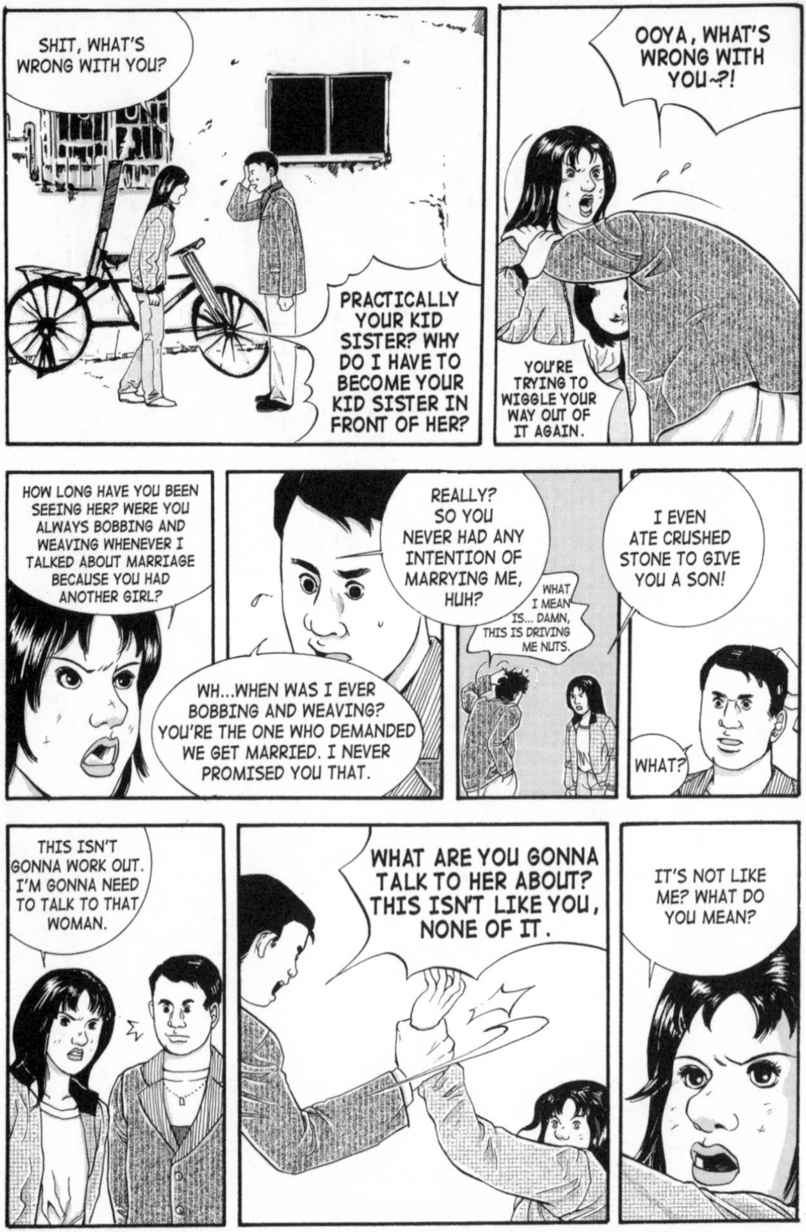
SHIT, WHAT'S WRONG WITH YOU?
PRACTICALLY YOUR KID SISTER? WHY DO I HAVE TO BECOME YOUR KID SISTER IN FRONT OF HER?
OOYA, WHAT'S WRONG WITH YOU~?!
YOU'RE TRYING TO WIGGLE YOUR WAY OUT OF IT AGAIN.
HOW LONG HAVE YOU BEEN SEEING HER? WERE YOU ALWAYS BOBBING AND WEAVING WHENEVER I TALKED ABOUT MARRIAGE BECAUSE YOU HAD ANOTHER GIRL?
WH...WHEN WAS I EVER BOBBING AND WEAVING? YOU'RE THE ONE WHO DEMANDED WE GET MARRIED. I NEVER PROMISED YOU THAT.
REALLY? SO YOU NEVER HAD ANY INTENTION OF MARRYING ME, HUH?
WHAT I MEAN IS... DAMN, THIS IS DRIVING ME NUTS.
I EVEN ATE CRUSHED STONE TO GIVE YOU A SON!
WHAT?
THIS ISN'T GONNA WORK OUT. I'M GONNA NEED TO TALK TO THAT WOMAN.
WHAT ARE YOU GONNA TALK TO HER ABOUT? THIS ISN'T LIKE YOU, NONE OF IT.
IT'S NOT LIKE ME? WHAT DO YOU MEAN?

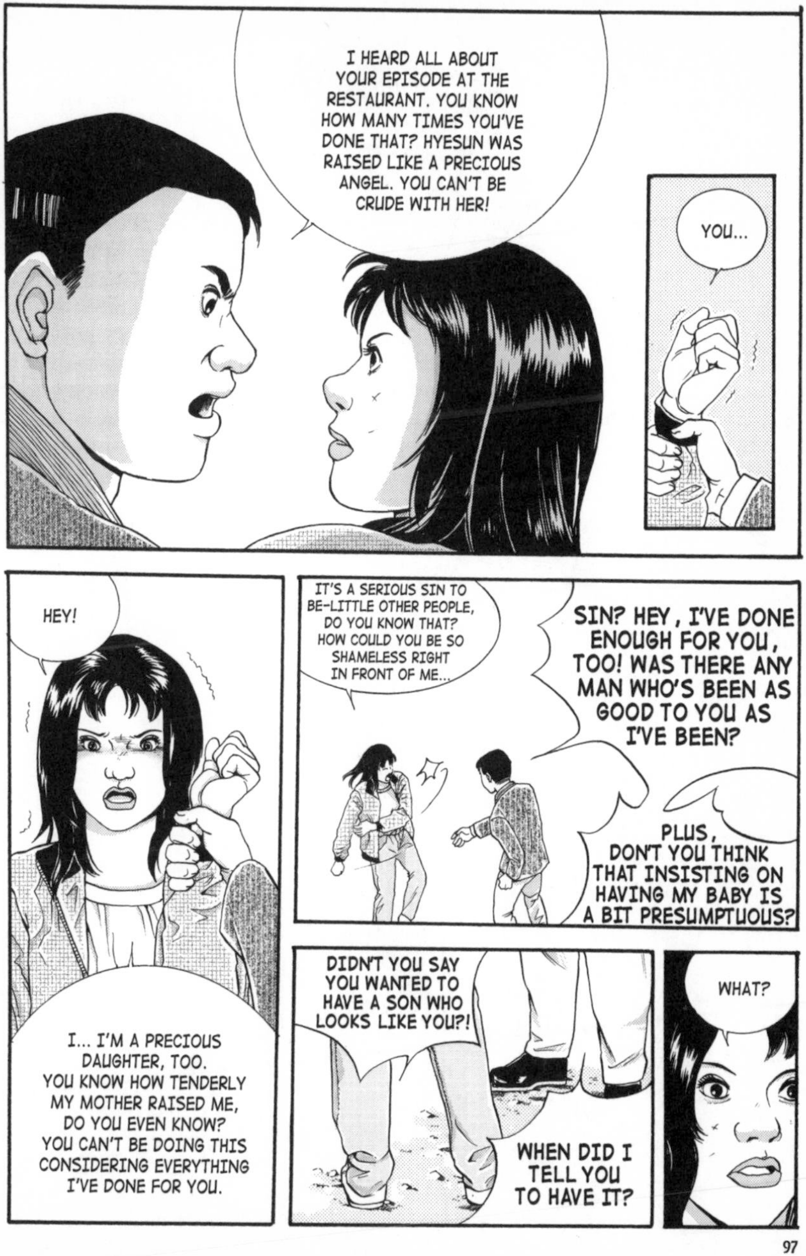
I HEARD ALL ABOUT YOUR EPISODE AT THE RESTAURANT. YOU KNOW HOW MANY TIMES YOU'VE DONE THAT? HYESUN WAS RAISED LIKE A PRECIOUS ANGEL. YOU CAN'T BE CRUDE WITH HER!
YOU...
HEY!
I... I'M A PRECIOUS DAUGHTER, TOO. YOU KNOW HOW TENDERLY MY MOTHER RAISED ME, DO YOU EVEN KNOW? YOU CAN'T BE DOING THIS CONSIDERING EVERYTHING I'VE DONE FOR YOU.
IT'S A SERIOUS SIN TO BE-LITTLE OTHER PEOPLE, DO YOU KNOW THAT? HOW COULD YOU BE SO SHAMELESS RIGHT IN FRONT OF ME...
SIN? HEY, I'VE DONE ENOUGH FOR YOU, TOO! WAS THERE ANY MAN WHO'S BEEN AS GOOD TO YOU AS I'VE BEEN?
PLUS, DON'T YOU THINK THAT INSISTING ON HAVING MY BABY IS A BIT PRESUMPTUOUS?
DIDN'T YOU SAY YOU WANTED TO HAVE A SON WHO LOOKS LIKE YOU?!
WHEN DID I TELL YOU TO HAVE IT?
WHAT?

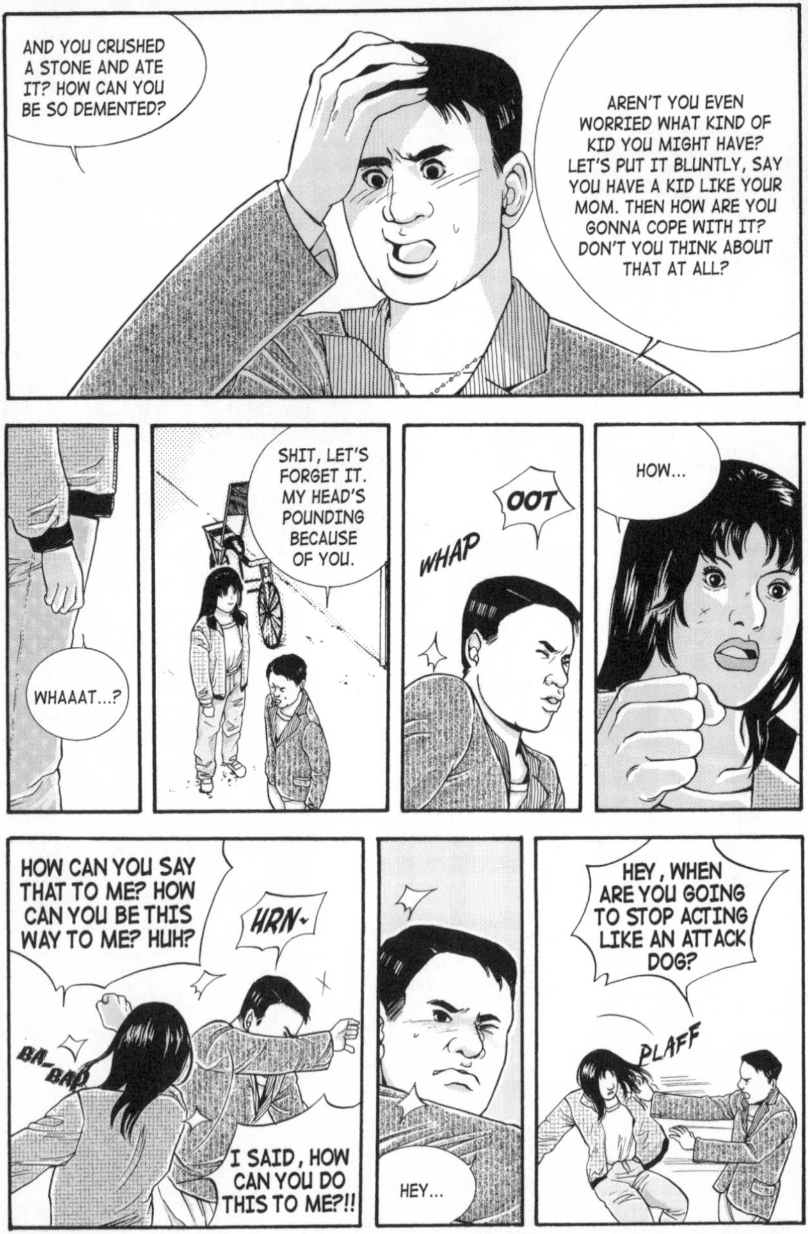

AND YOU CRUSHED A STONE AND ATE IT? HOW CAN YOU BE SO DEMENTED?
AREN'T YOU EVEN WORRIED WHAT KIND OF KID YOU MIGHT HAVE? LET'S PUT IT BLUNTLY, SAY YOU HAVE A KID LIKE YOUR MOM. THEN HOW ARE YOU GONNA COPE WITH IT? DON'T YOU THINK ABOUT THAT AT ALL?
WHAAAT...?
SHIT, LET'S FORGET IT. MY HEAD'S POUNDING BECAUSE OF YOU.
OOT
WHAP
HOW...
HOW CAN YOU SAY THAT TO ME? HOW CAN YOU BE THIS WAY TO ME? HUH?
URN
BA-BAP
I SAID, HOW CAN YOU DO THIS TO ME?!!
HEY...
HEY, WHEN ARE YOU GOING TO STOP ACTING LIKE AN ATTACK DOG?
PLAFF

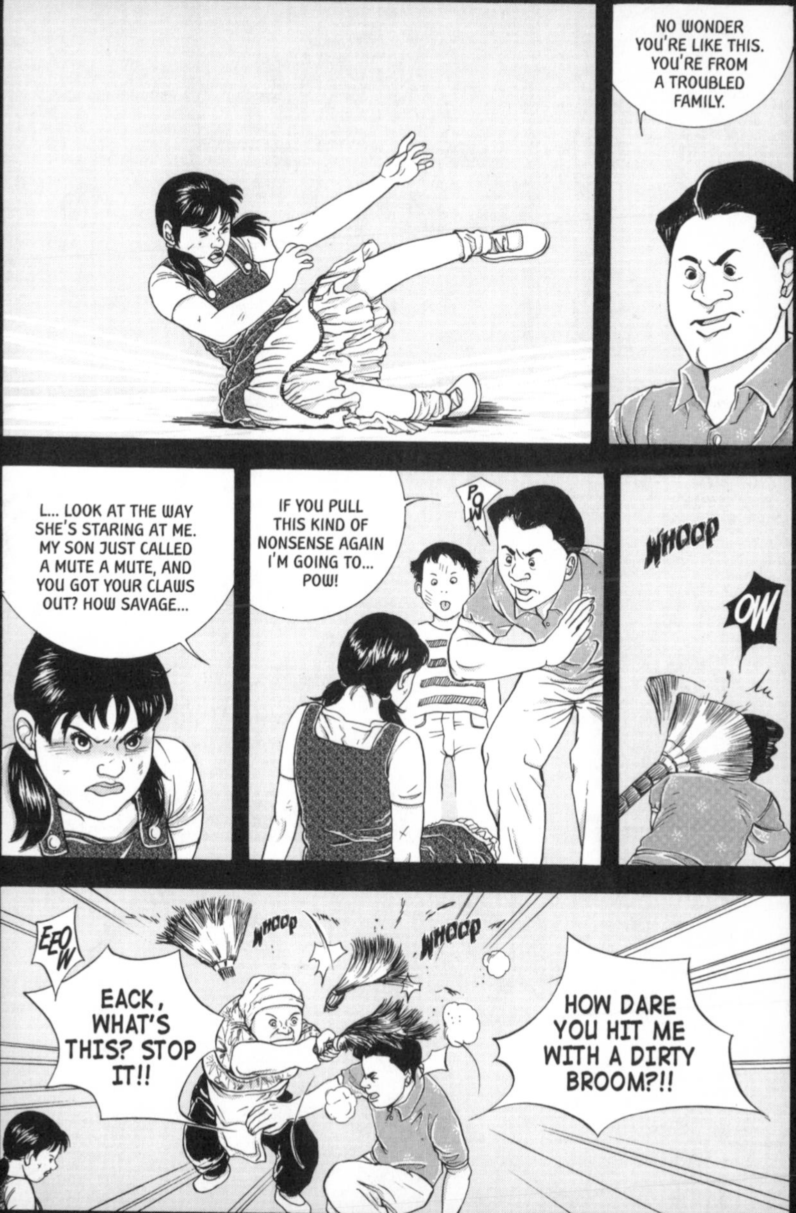
NO WONDER YOU'RE LIKE THIS. YOU'RE FROM A TROUBLED FAMILY.
L... LOOK AT THE WAY SHE'S STARING AT ME. MY SON JUST CALLED A MUTE A MUTE, AND YOU GOT YOUR CLAWS OUT? HOW SAVAGE...
IF YOU PULL THIS KIND OF NONSENSE AGAIN I'M GOING TO... POW!
POW
WHOOP
OW
EEOW
WHOOP
WHOOP
EACK, WHAT'S THIS? STOP IT!!
HOW DARE YOU HIT ME WITH A DIRTY BROOM?!!

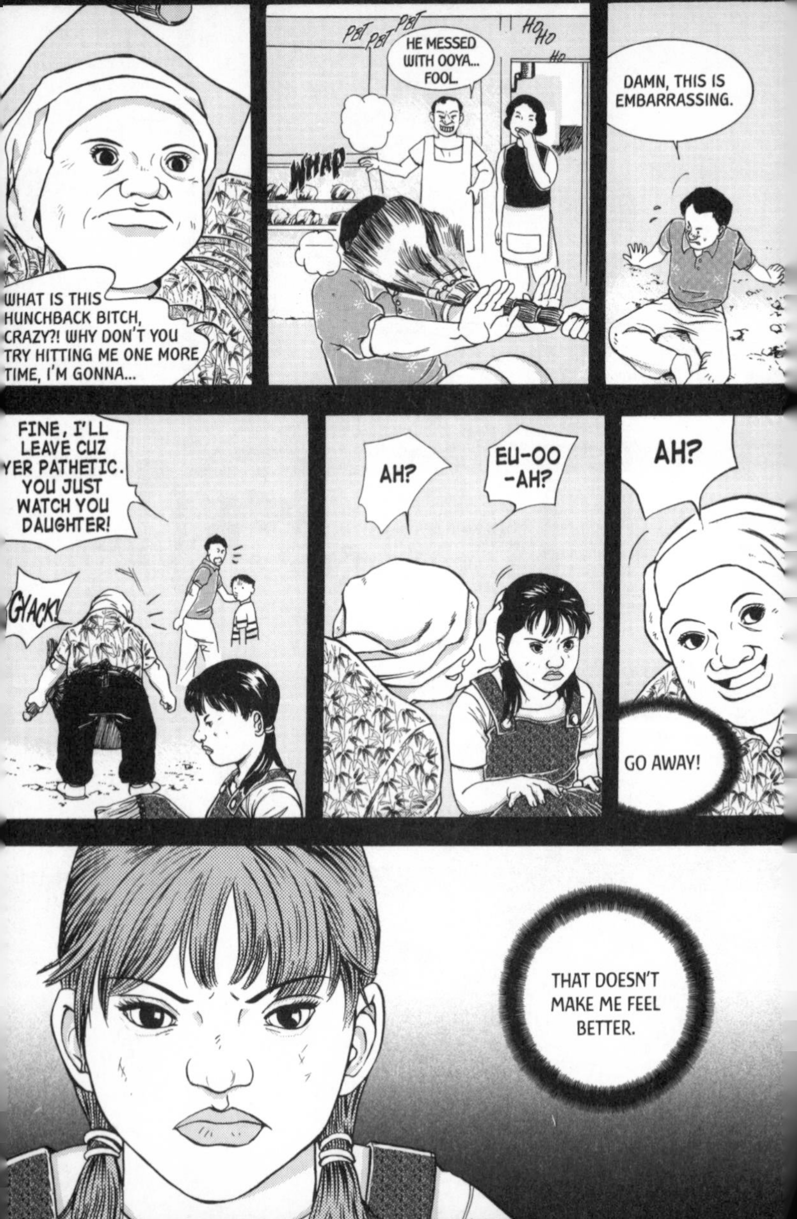
WHAT IS THIS HUNCHBACK BITCH, CRAZY?! WHY DON'T YOU TRY HITTING ME ONE MORE TIME, I'M GONNA...
PBT PBT PBT
HO HO HO
HE MESSED WITH OOYA... FOOL.
WHAP
DAMN, THIS IS EMBARRASSING.
FINE, I'LL LEAVE CUZ YER PATHETIC. YOU JUST WATCH YOU DAUGHTER!
GYACK!
AH?
EU-OO -AH?
AH?
GO AWAY!
THAT DOESN'T MAKE ME FEEL BETTER.

BECAUSE ALL OF THIS IS YOUR FAULT!

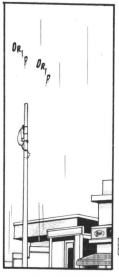

DR1P DR1p

DR1P DR1P

DR1p

OOYA, WHY DON'T YOU BE THE BIGGER PERSON AND LET IT GO?

HOW CAN I REFUSE WHEN A WOMAN LIKE THAT SAYS SHE LIKES ME?

THIS OPPORTUNITY IS HEAVEN SENT, A CHANCE TO MAKE UP FOR THE SLOPPY LIFE I LEAD AS AN IMMATURE GUY.

WAS EVERYTHING THAT I'VE DONE FOR YOU ALL THIS TIME SLOPPY, TOO?

N...NO. I DO KNOW THAT YOU'RE A GOOD PERSON, KID. BUT... DAMN, I DON'T KNOW!

DON'T BE LYING ON YOUR BUTT LIKE THAT, GO HOME. WHEN YOU LOOK LIKE THAT IT MAKES ME FEEL BAD. IT'S RAINING, OOYA. COME ON!

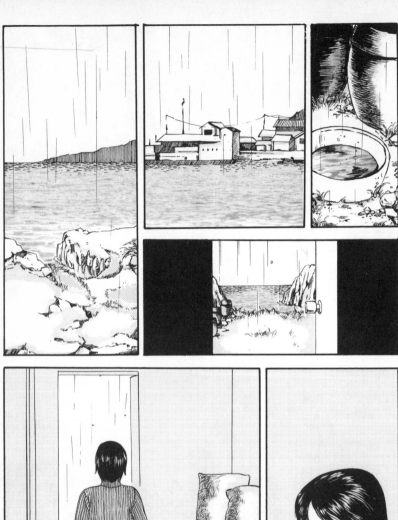

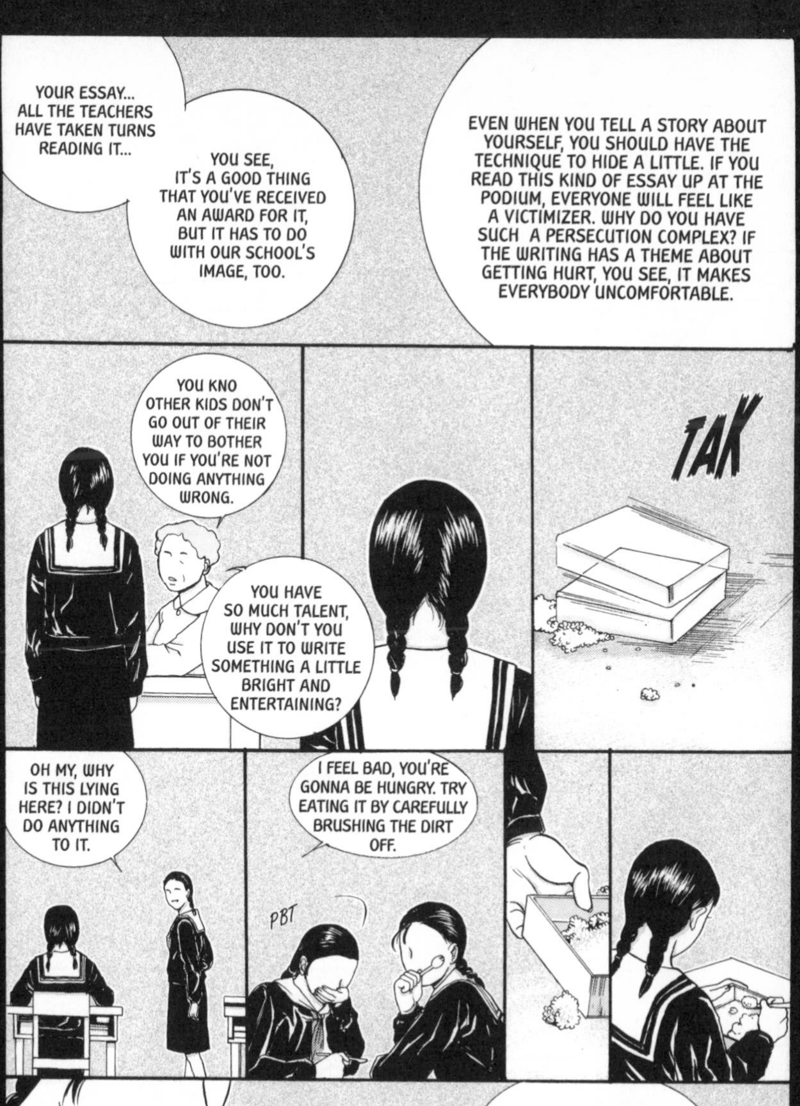
YOUR ESSAY... ALL THE TEACHERS HAVE TAKEN TURNS READING IT...
YOU SEE, IT'S A GOOD THING THAT YOU'VE RECEIVED AN AWARD FOR IT, BUT IT HAS TO DO WITH OUR SCHOOL'S IMAGE, TOO.
EVEN WHEN YOU TELL A STORY ABOUT YOURSELF, YOU SHOULD HAVE THE TECHNIQUE TO HIDE A LITTLE. IF YOU READ THIS KIND OF ESSAY UP AT THE PODIUM, EVERYONE WILL FEEL LIKE A VICTIMIZER. WHY DO YOU HAVE SUCH A PERSECUTION COMPLEX? IF THE WRITING HAS A THEME ABOUT GETTING HURT, YOU SEE, IT MAKES EVERYBODY UNCOMFORTABLE.
YOU KNO OTHER KIDS DON'T GO OUT OF THEIR WAY TO BOTHER YOU IF YOU'RE NOT DOING ANYTHING WRONG.
YOU HAVE SO MUCH TALENT, WHY DON'T YOU USE IT TO WRITE SOMETHING A LITTLE BRIGHT AND ENTERTAINING?
TAK
OH MY, WHY IS THIS LYING HERE? I DIDN'T DO ANYTHING TO IT.
I FEEL BAD, YOU'RE GONNA BE HUNGRY. TRY EATING IT BY CAREFULLY BRUSHING THE DIRT OFF.
PBT
EEK, SHE'S REALLY EATING IT. LOOKS LIKE THAT WEIRDO DOESN'T EVEN HAVE ANY PRIDE.

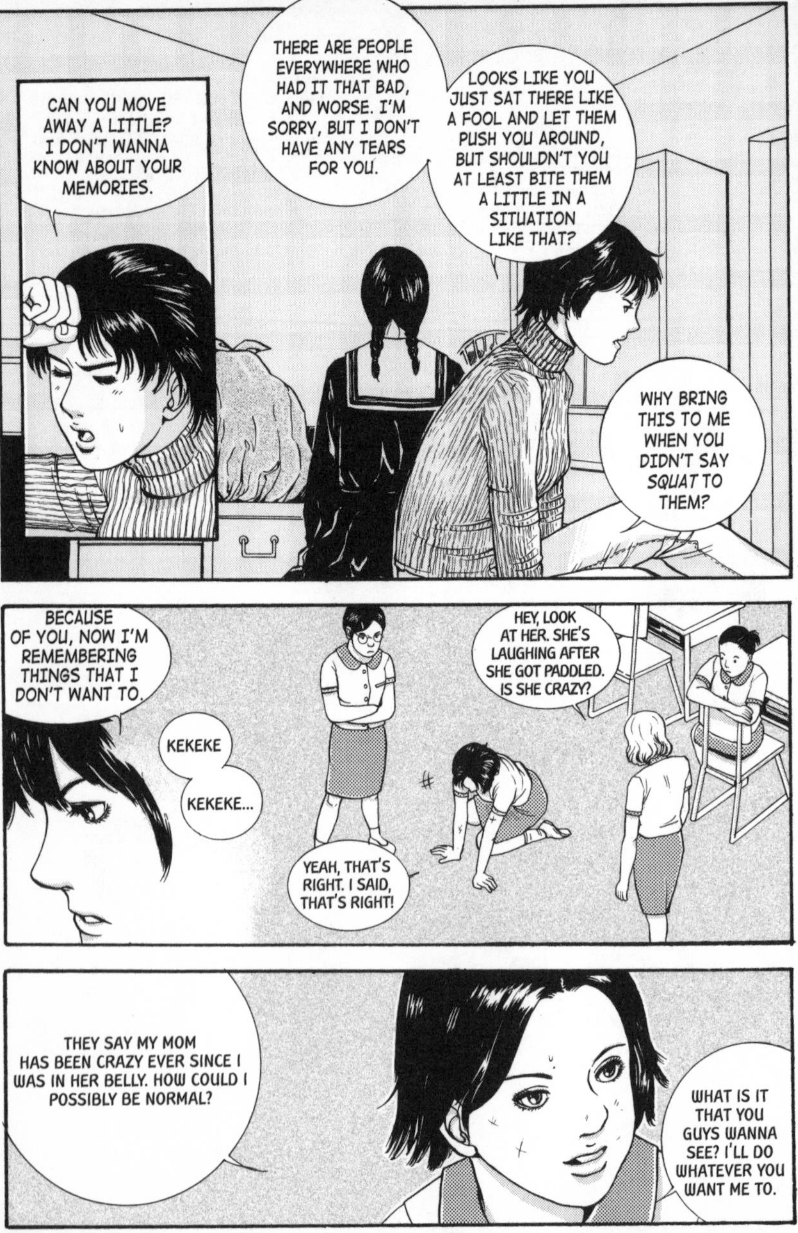
THERE ARE PEOPLE EVERYWHERE WHO HAD IT THAT BAD, AND WORSE. I'M SORRY, BUT I DON'T HAVE ANY TEARS FOR YOU.
LOOKS LIKE YOU JUST SAT THERE LIKE A FOOL AND LET THEM PUSH YOU AROUND, BUT SHOULDN'T YOU AT LEAST BITE THEM A LITTLE IN A SITUATION LIKE THAT?
CAN YOU MOVE AWAY A LITTLE? I DON'T WANNA KNOW ABOUT YOUR MEMORIES.
WHY BRING THIS TO ME WHEN YOU DIDN'T SAY *SQUAT* TO THEM?
BECAUSE OF YOU, NOW I'M REMEMBERING THINGS THAT I DON'T WANT TO.
HEY, LOOK AT HER. SHE'S LAUGHING AFTER SHE GOT PADDLED. IS SHE CRAZY?
KEKEKE
KEKEKE...
YEAH, THAT'S RIGHT. I SAID, THAT'S RIGHT!
THEY SAY MY MOM HAS BEEN CRAZY EVER SINCE I WAS IN HER BELLY. HOW COULD I POSSIBLY BE NORMAL?
WHAT IS IT THAT YOU GUYS WANNA SEE? I'LL DO WHATEVER YOU WANT ME TO.

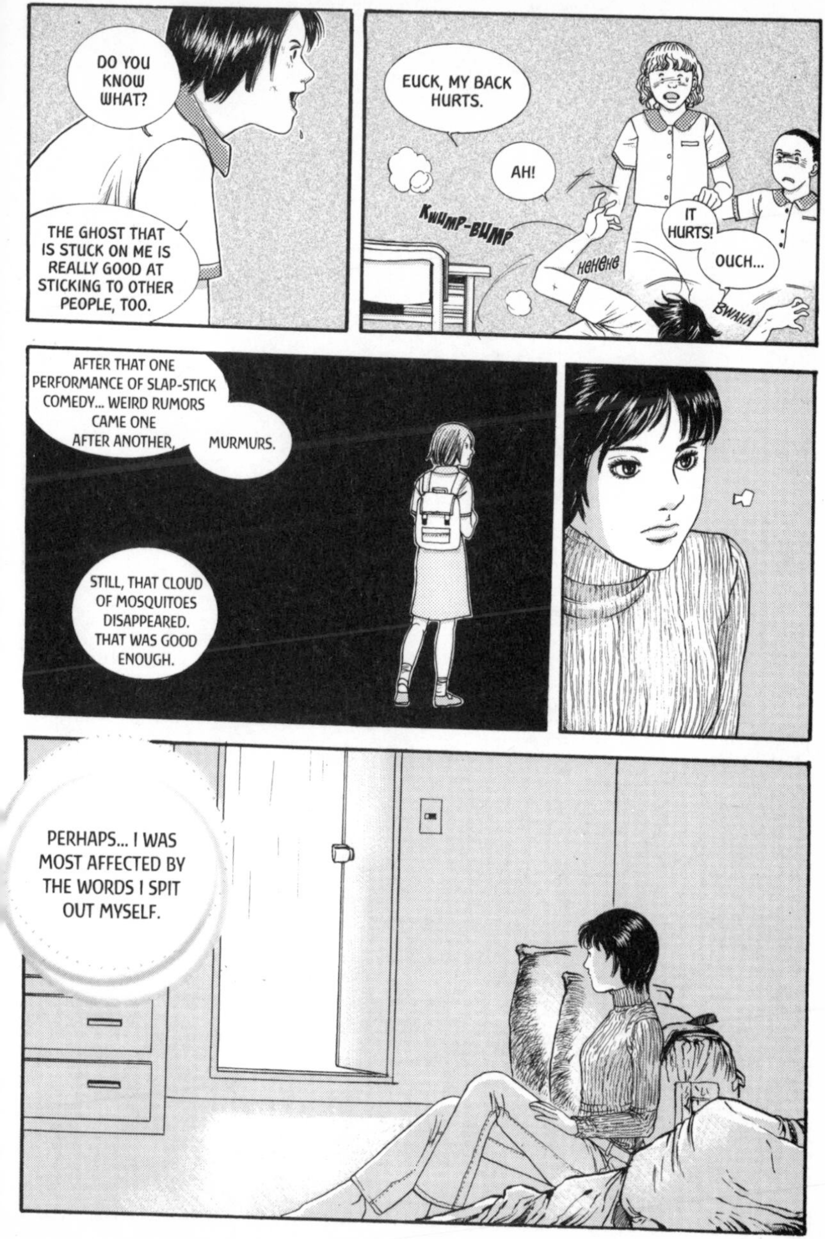
DO YOU KNOW WHAT?
THE GHOST THAT IS STUCK ON ME IS REALLY GOOD AT STICKING TO OTHER PEOPLE, TOO.
EUCK, MY BACK HURTS.
AH!
KWUMP-BUMP
IT HURTS!
OUCH...
HEHEHE
BWAHA
AFTER THAT ONE PERFORMANCE OF SLAP-STICK COMEDY... WEIRD RUMORS CAME ONE AFTER ANOTHER,
MURMURS.
STILL, THAT CLOUD OF MOSQUITOES DISAPPEARED. THAT WAS GOOD ENOUGH.
PERHAPS... I WAS MOST AFFECTED BY THE WORDS I SPIT OUT MYSELF.

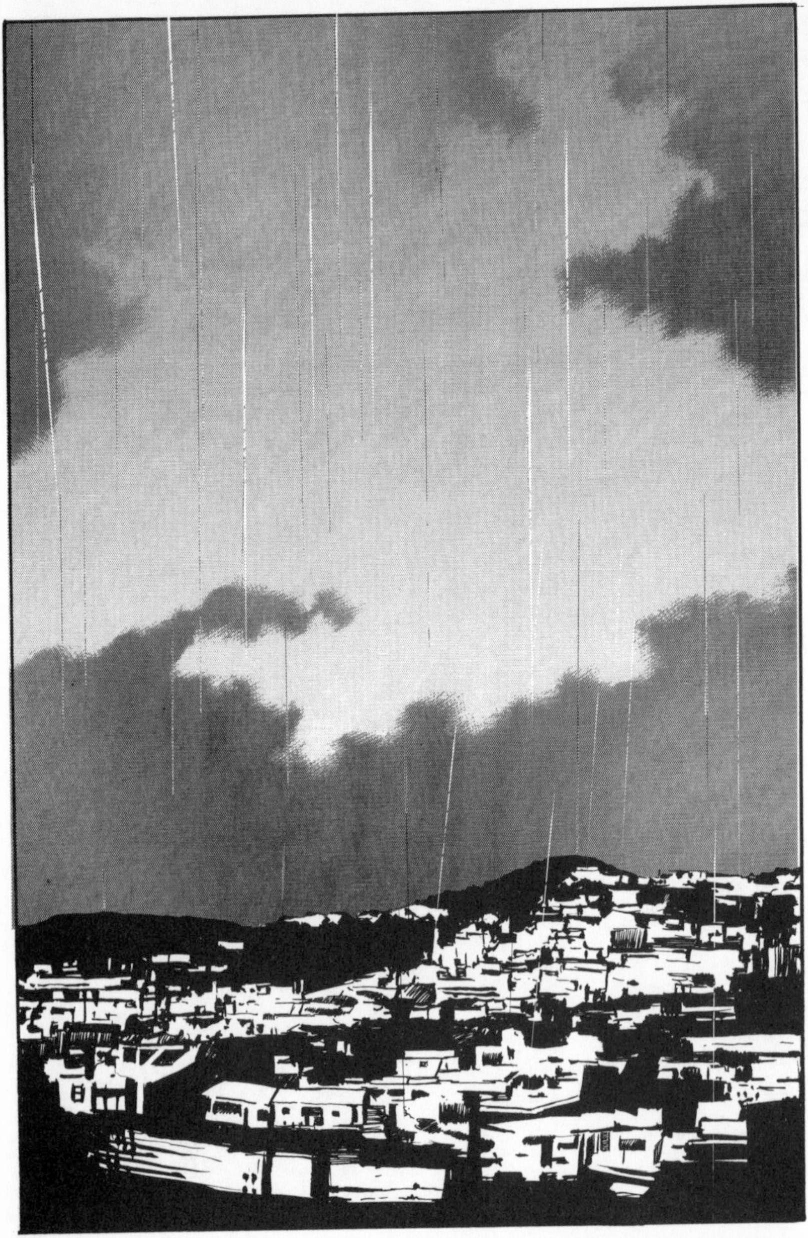

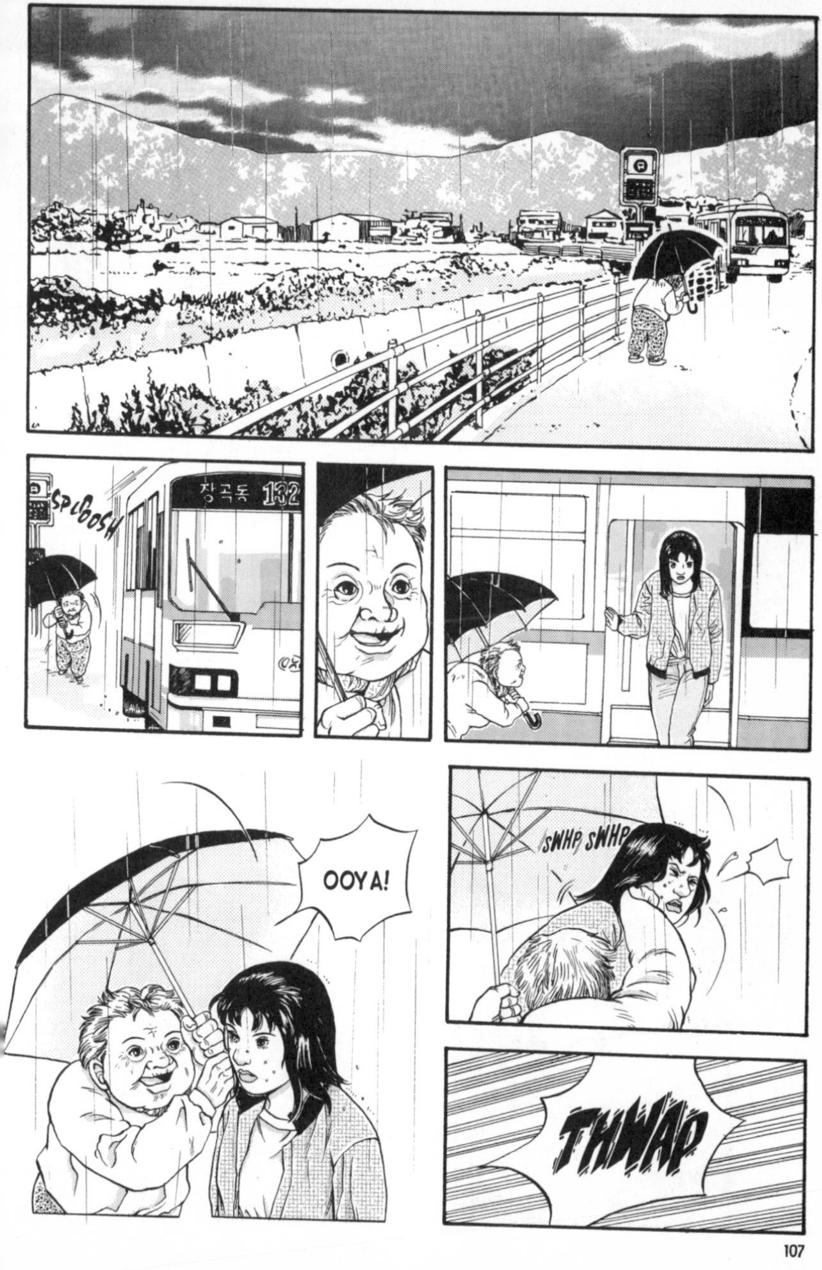

SPLOOSH
장곡동 132
OOYA!
SWHP SWHP
THWAP

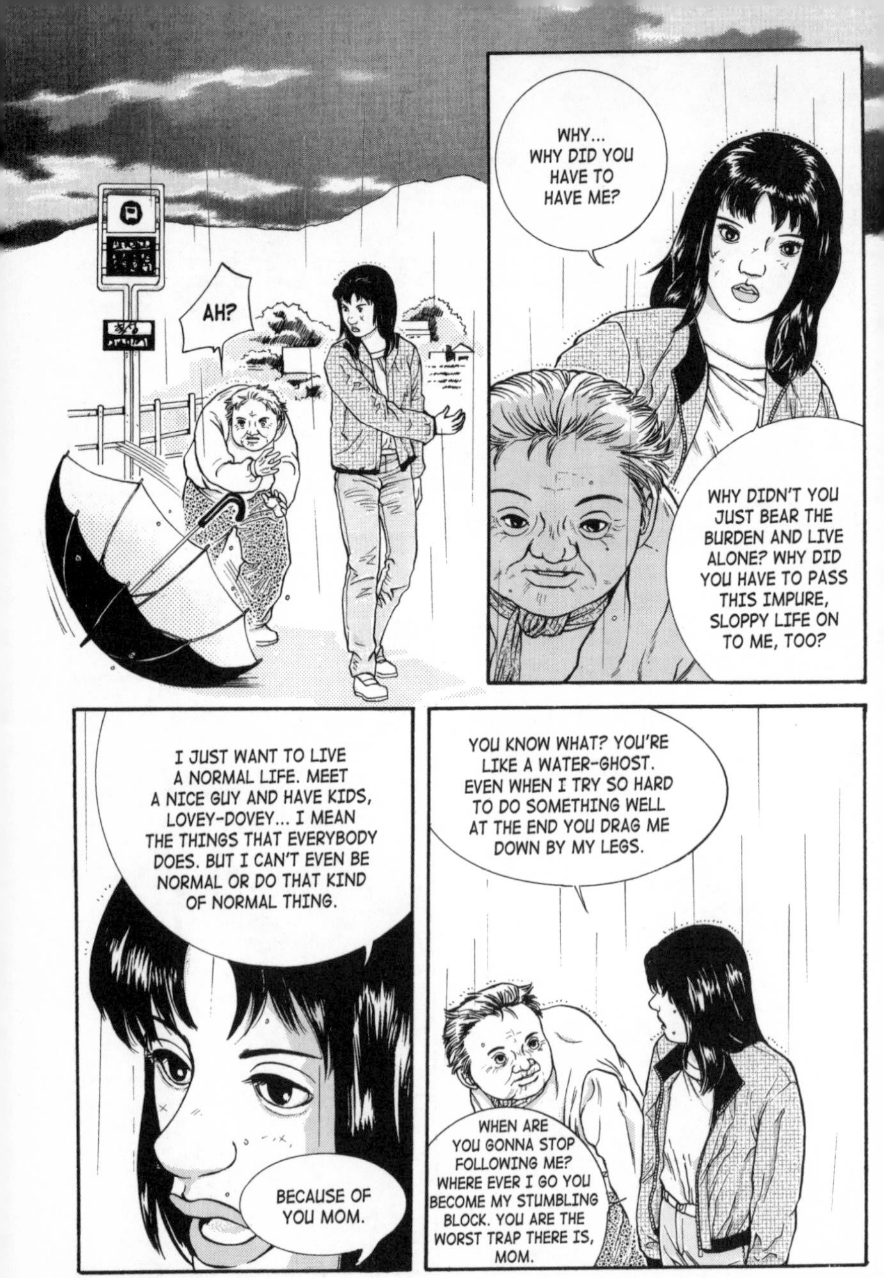
AH?
WHY...
WHY DID YOU
HAVE TO
HAVE ME?
WHY DIDN'T YOU
JUST BEAR THE
BURDEN AND LIVE
ALONE? WHY DID
YOU HAVE TO PASS
THIS IMPURE,
SLOPPY LIFE ON
TO ME, TOO?
I JUST WANT TO LIVE
A NORMAL LIFE. MEET
A NICE GUY AND HAVE KIDS,
LOVEY-DOVEY... I MEAN
THE THINGS THAT EVERYBODY
DOES. BUT I CAN'T EVEN BE
NORMAL OR DO THAT KIND
OF NORMAL THING.
BECAUSE OF
YOU MOM.
YOU KNOW WHAT? YOU'RE
LIKE A WATER-GHOST.
EVEN WHEN I TRY SO HARD
TO DO SOMETHING WELL
AT THE END YOU DRAG ME
DOWN BY MY LEGS.
WHEN ARE
YOU GONNA STOP
FOLLOWING ME?
WHERE EVER I GO YOU
BECOME MY STUMBLING
BLOCK. YOU ARE THE
WORST TRAP THERE IS,
MOM.

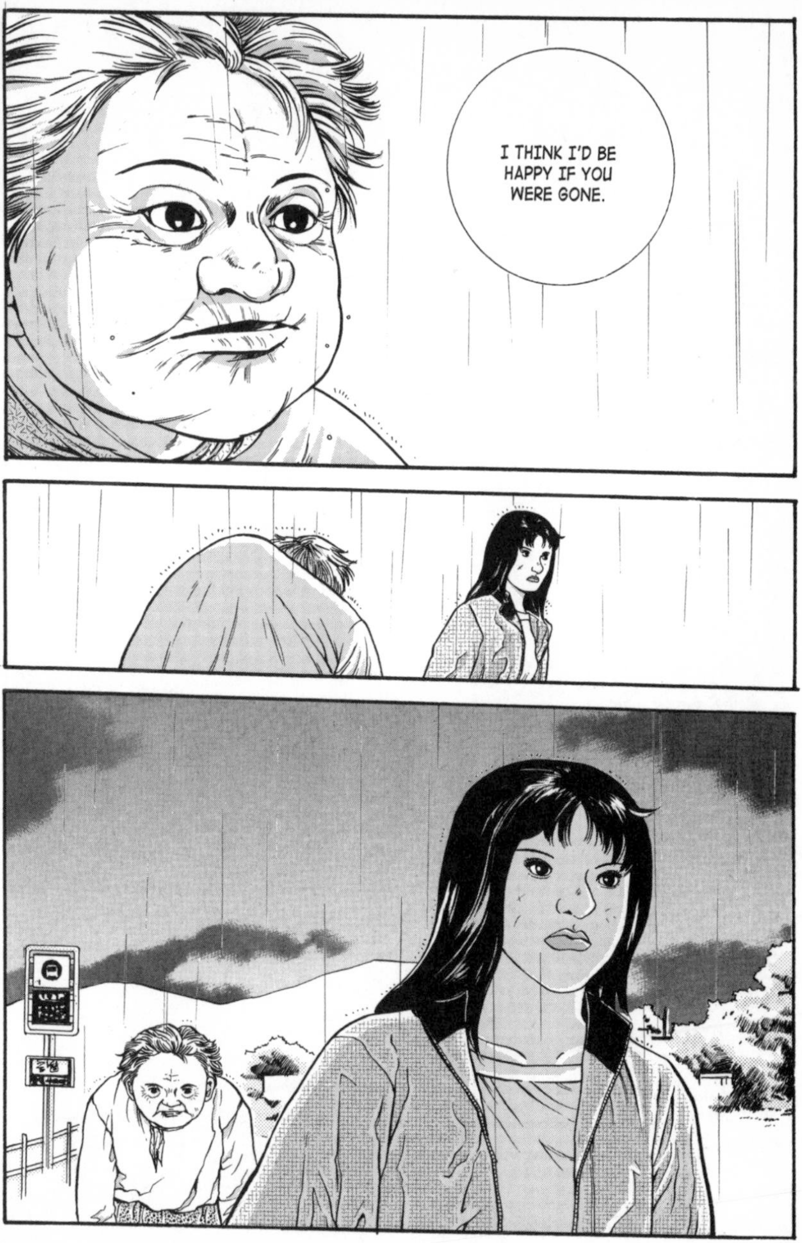
I THINK I'D BE HAPPY IF YOU WERE GONE.

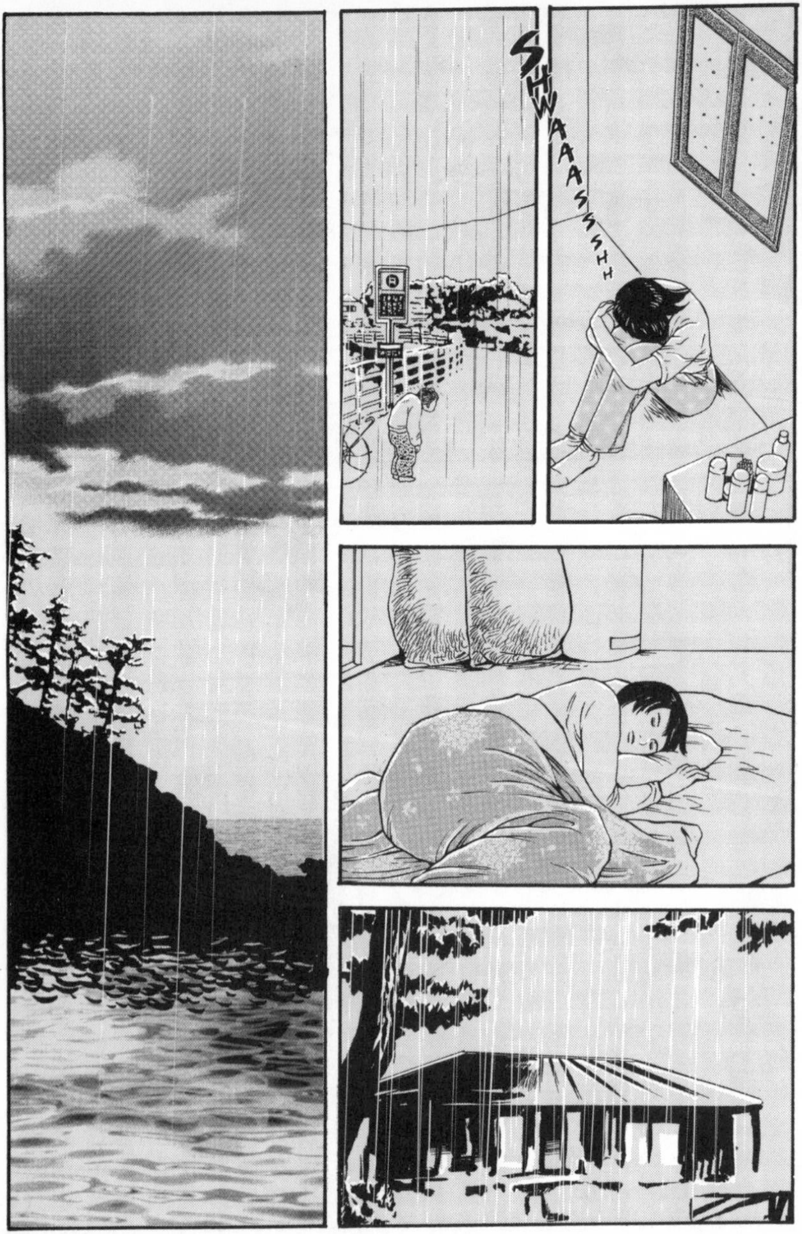
SHWAAASSSHH

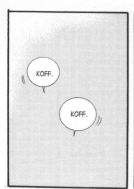

KOFF.

KOFF.

OW, MY THROAT'S SORE. MAYBE I'M GETTING A COLD...

DRRK

CLICK

PLOOOP

I'M DOG-TIRED, DOG-TIRED. I'M TORTURED BY DREAMS NIGHT AND DAY, SO I'M EXHAUSTED EVEN THOUGH I HAVEN'T DONE ANYTHING.

HOO-WOO

THAT PATHETIC UNIFORM HAS DISAPPEARED AGAIN WITHOUT A SOUND. I BET SHE'S BUSY GOING TO AND FROM SCHOOL, IN HER OWN WAY.

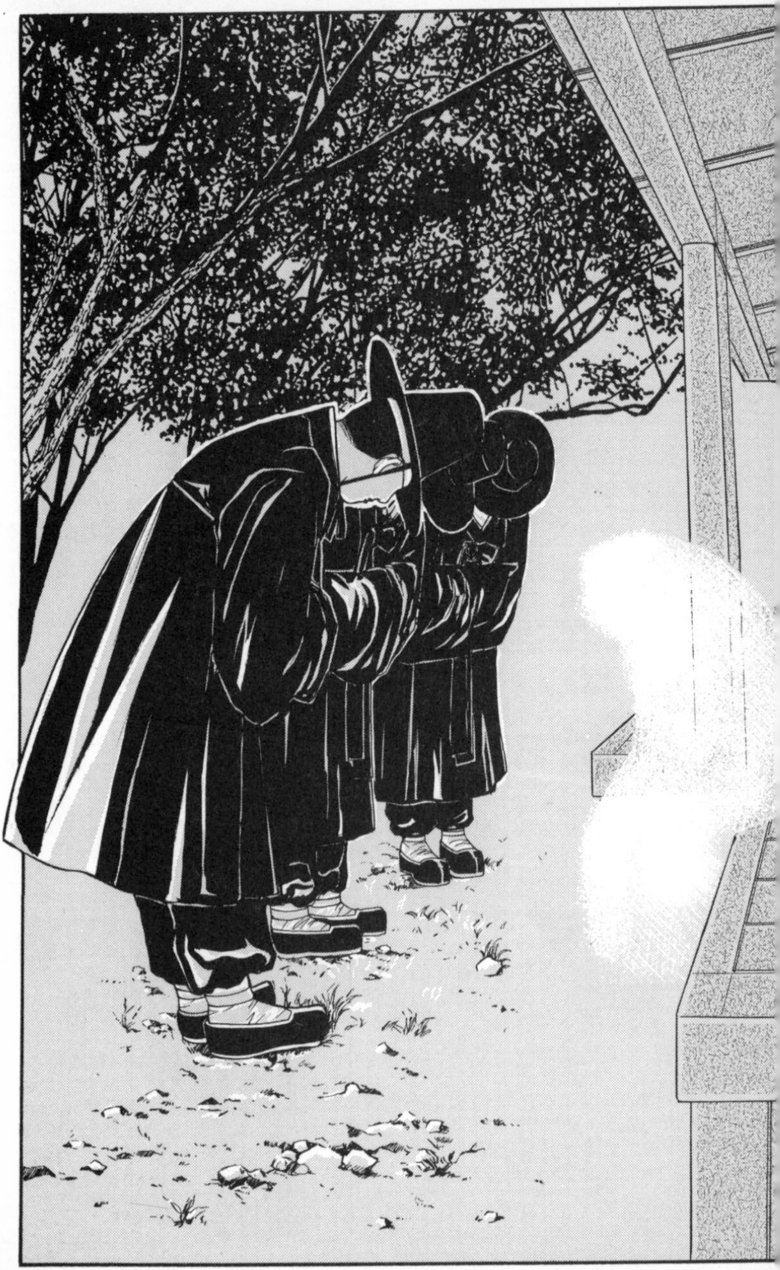

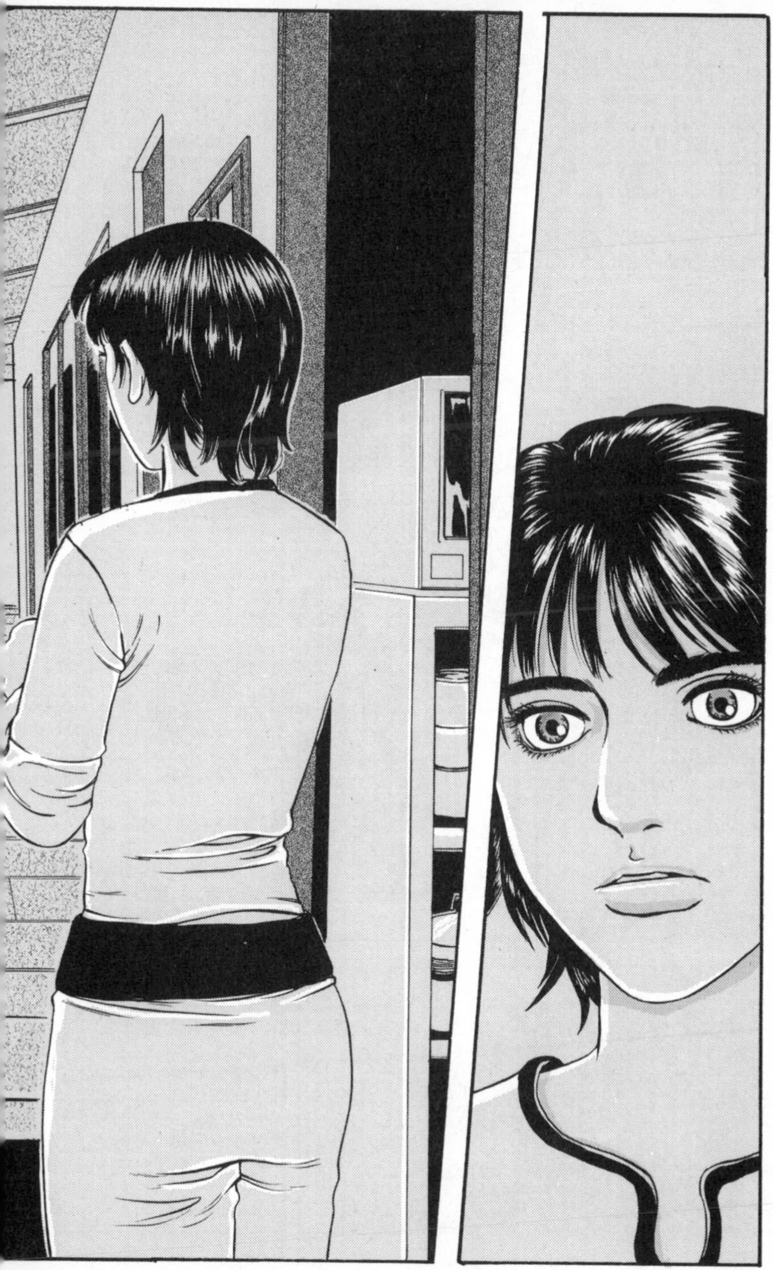

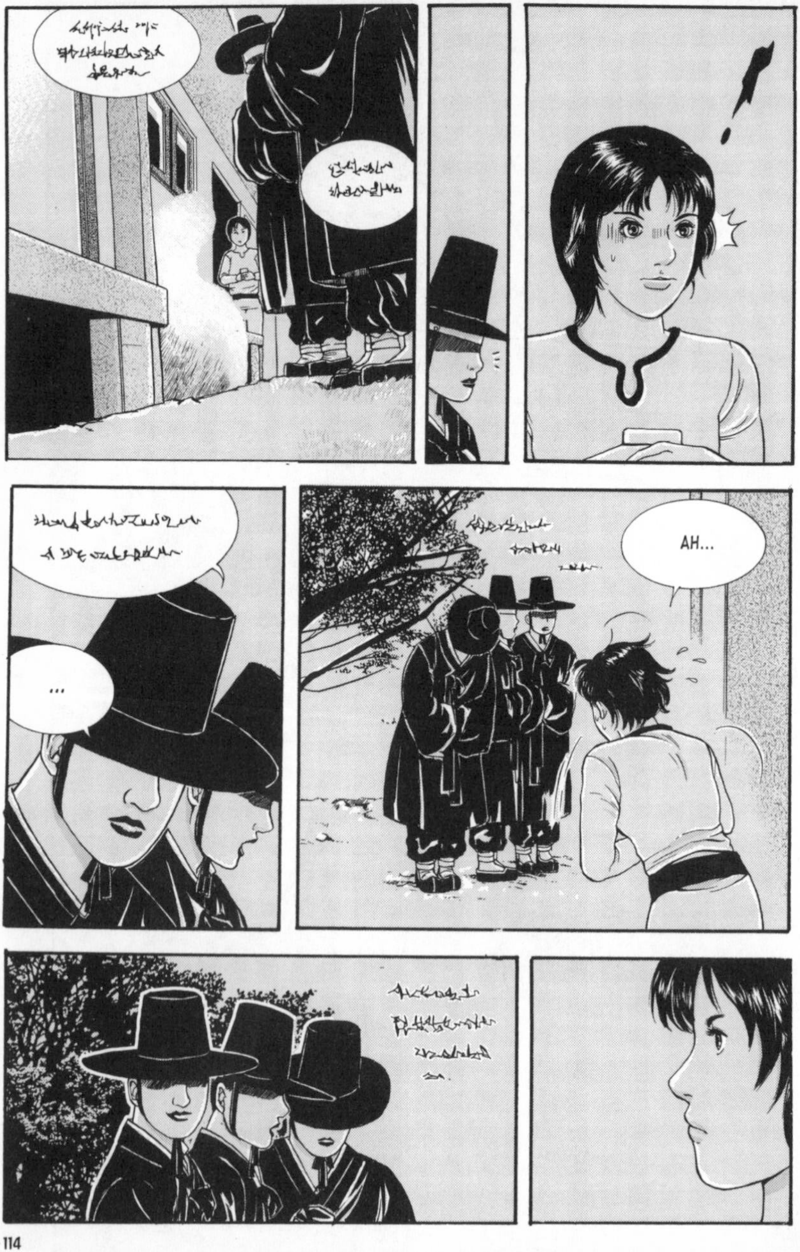
!
...
AH...

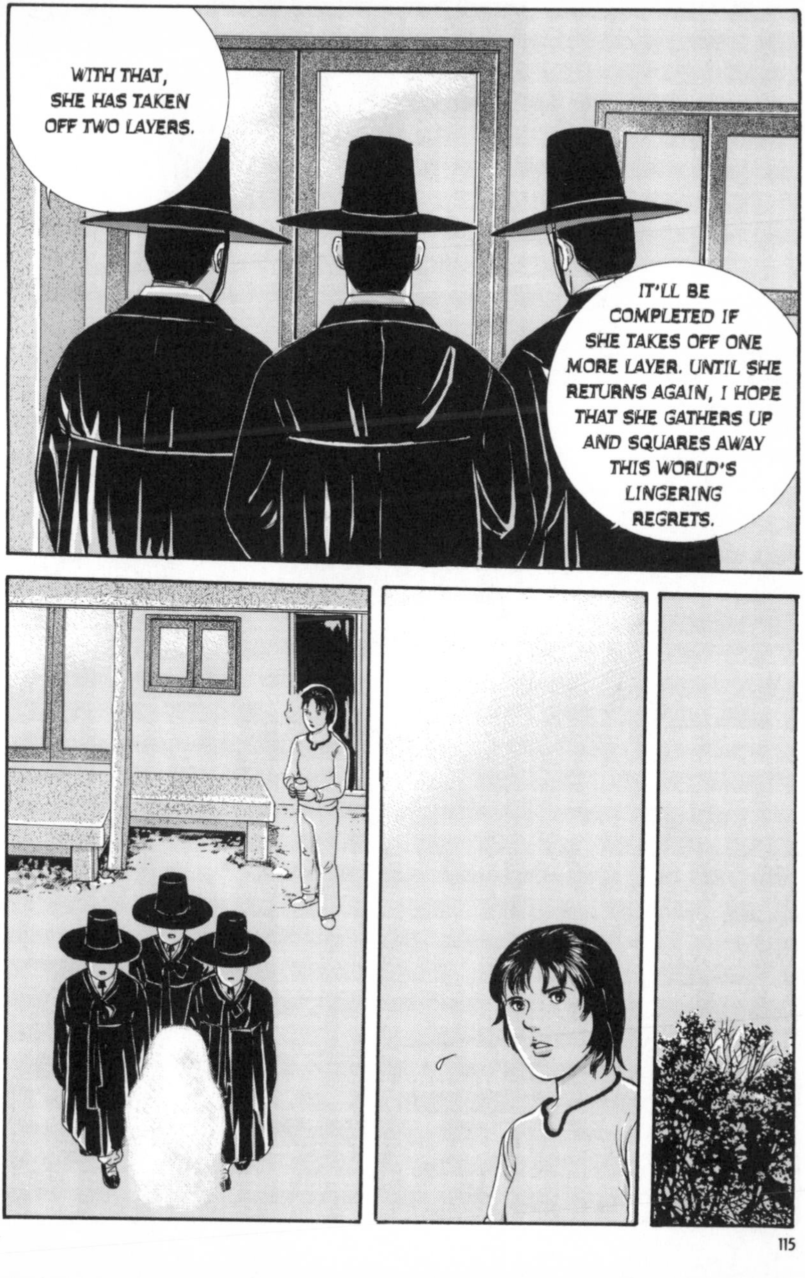
WITH THAT, SHE HAS TAKEN OFF TWO LAYERS.
IT'LL BE COMPLETED IF SHE TAKES OFF ONE MORE LAYER. UNTIL SHE RETURNS AGAIN, I HOPE THAT SHE GATHERS UP AND SQUARES AWAY THIS WORLD'S LINGERING REGRETS.

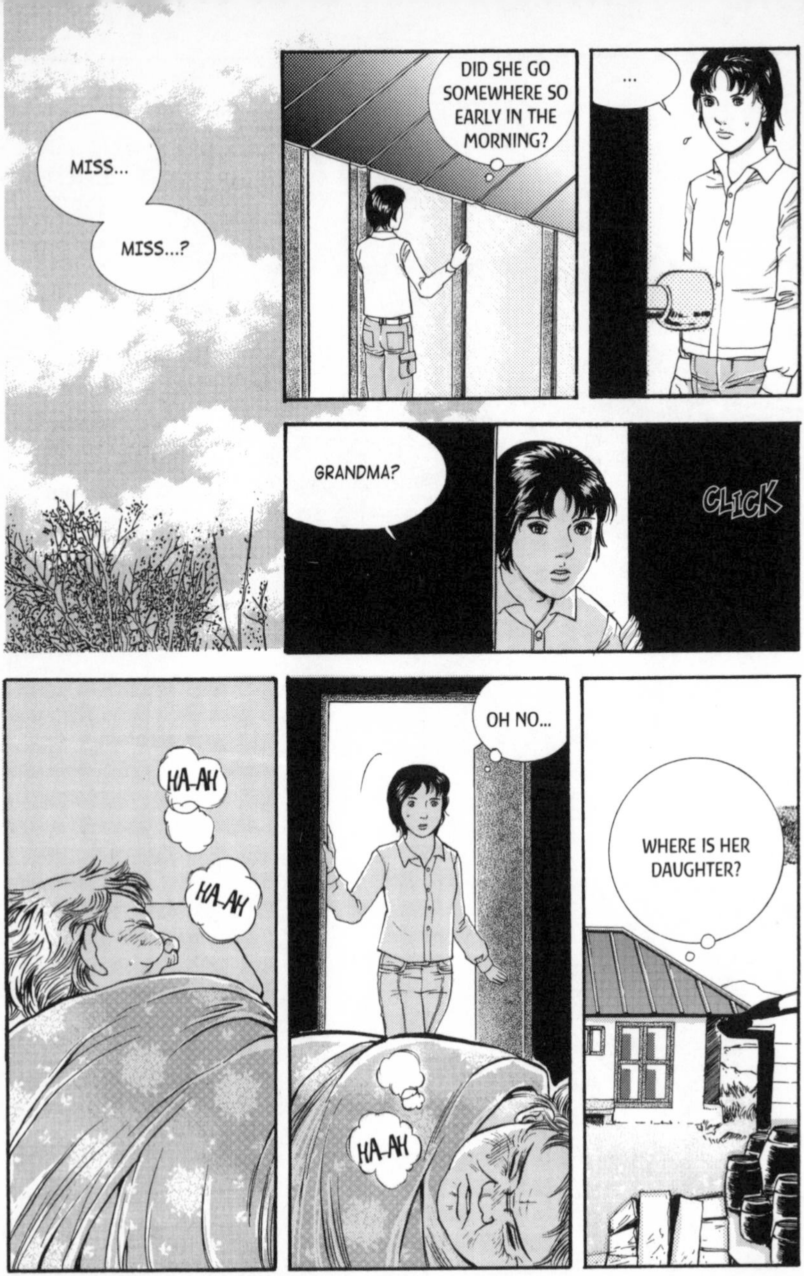
MISS...
MISS...?
DID SHE GO SOMEWHERE SO EARLY IN THE MORNING?
...
GRANDMA?
CLICK
HA-AH
HA-AH
OH NO...
HA-AH
WHERE IS HER DAUGHTER?

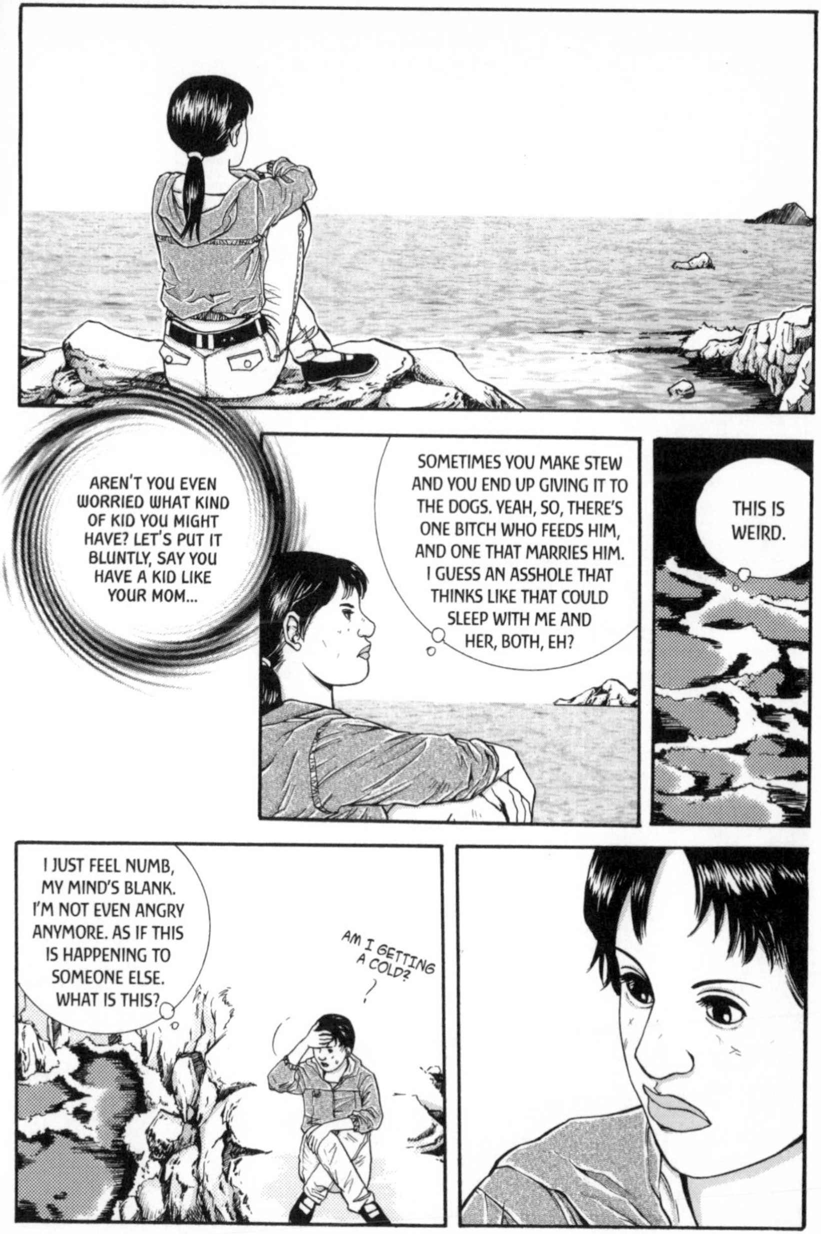
AREN'T YOU EVEN WORRIED WHAT KIND OF KID YOU MIGHT HAVE? LET'S PUT IT BLUNTLY, SAY YOU HAVE A KID LIKE YOUR MOM...
SOMETIMES YOU MAKE STEW AND YOU END UP GIVING IT TO THE DOGS. YEAH, SO, THERE'S ONE BITCH WHO FEEDS HIM, AND ONE THAT MARRIES HIM. I GUESS AN ASSHOLE THAT THINKS LIKE THAT COULD SLEEP WITH ME AND HER, BOTH, EH?
THIS IS WEIRD.
I JUST FEEL NUMB, MY MIND'S BLANK. I'M NOT EVEN ANGRY ANYMORE. AS IF THIS IS HAPPENING TO SOMEONE ELSE. WHAT IS THIS?
AM I GETTING A COLD?

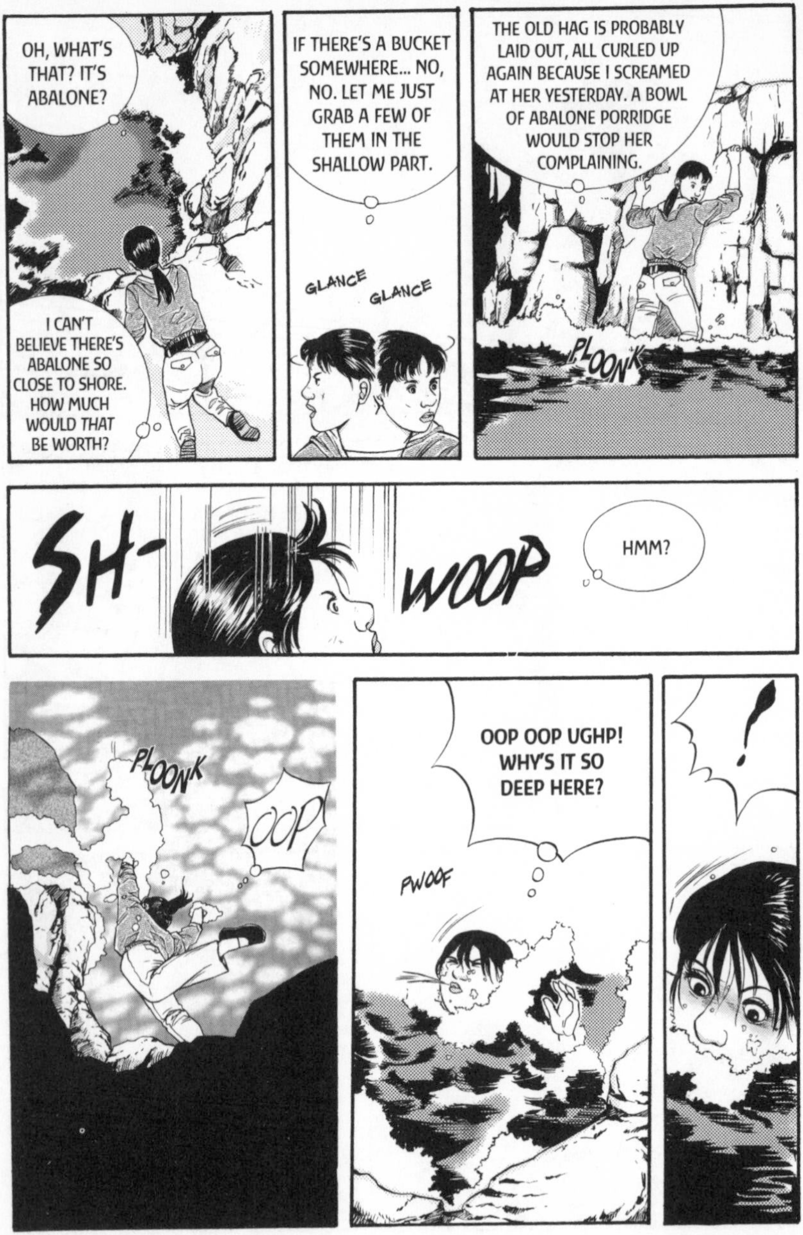

OH, WHAT'S THAT? IT'S ABALONE?
I CAN'T BELIEVE THERE'S ABALONE SO CLOSE TO SHORE. HOW MUCH WOULD THAT BE WORTH?
IF THERE'S A BUCKET SOMEWHERE... NO, NO. LET ME JUST GRAB A FEW OF THEM IN THE SHALLOW PART.
GLANCE GLANCE
THE OLD HAG IS PROBABLY LAID OUT, ALL CURLED UP AGAIN BECAUSE I SCREAMED AT HER YESTERDAY. A BOWL OF ABALONE PORRIDGE WOULD STOP HER COMPLAINING.
PLOONK
SH-WOOP
HMM?
PLOONK
OOP
OOP OOP UGHP! WHY'S IT SO DEEP HERE?
PWOOF
!

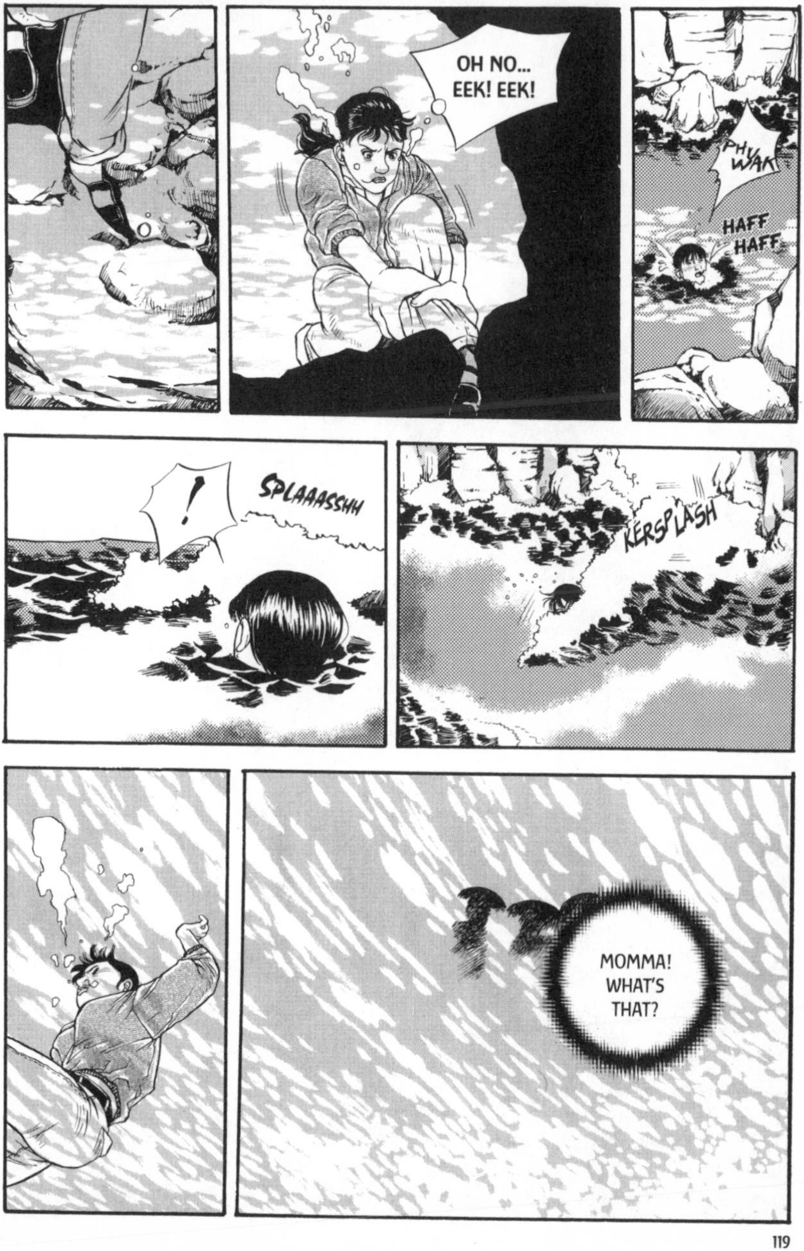

OH NO...
EEK! EEK!
PHWAK
HAFF
HAFF
!
SPLAAASSHH
KERSPLASH
MOMMA!
WHAT'S
THAT?

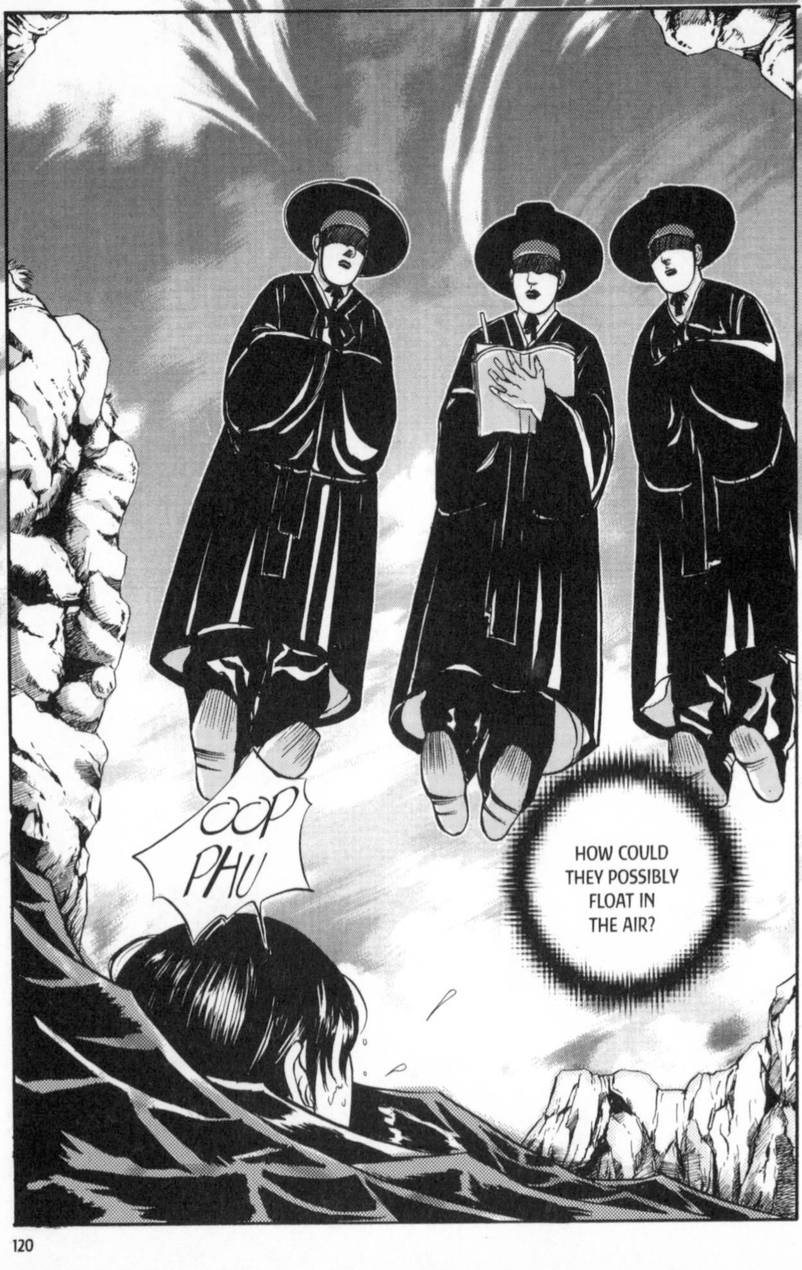
OOP
PHU
HOW COULD THEY POSSIBLY FLOAT IN THE AIR?

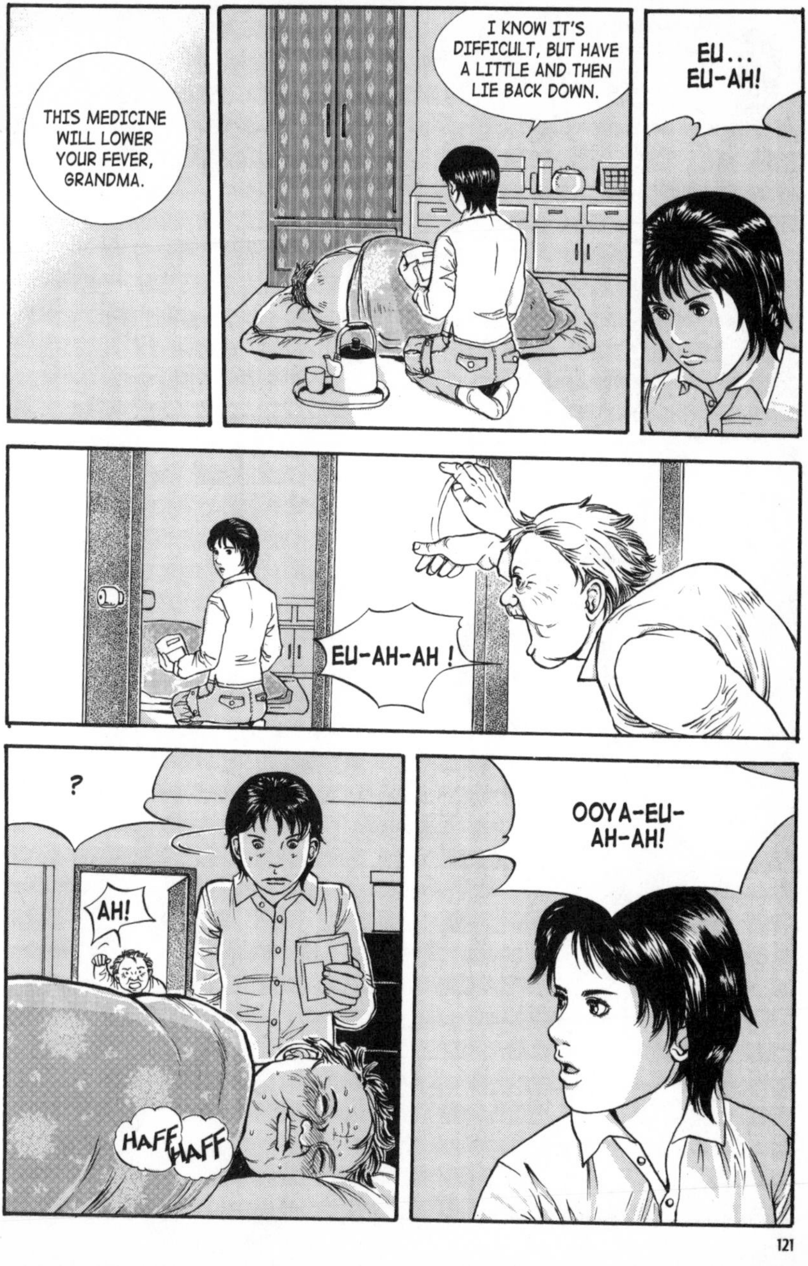
THIS MEDICINE WILL LOWER YOUR FEVER, GRANDMA.
I KNOW IT'S DIFFICULT, BUT HAVE A LITTLE AND THEN LIE BACK DOWN.
EU... EU-AH!
EU-AH-AH !
?
AH!
HAFF HAFF
OOYA-EU-AH-AH!

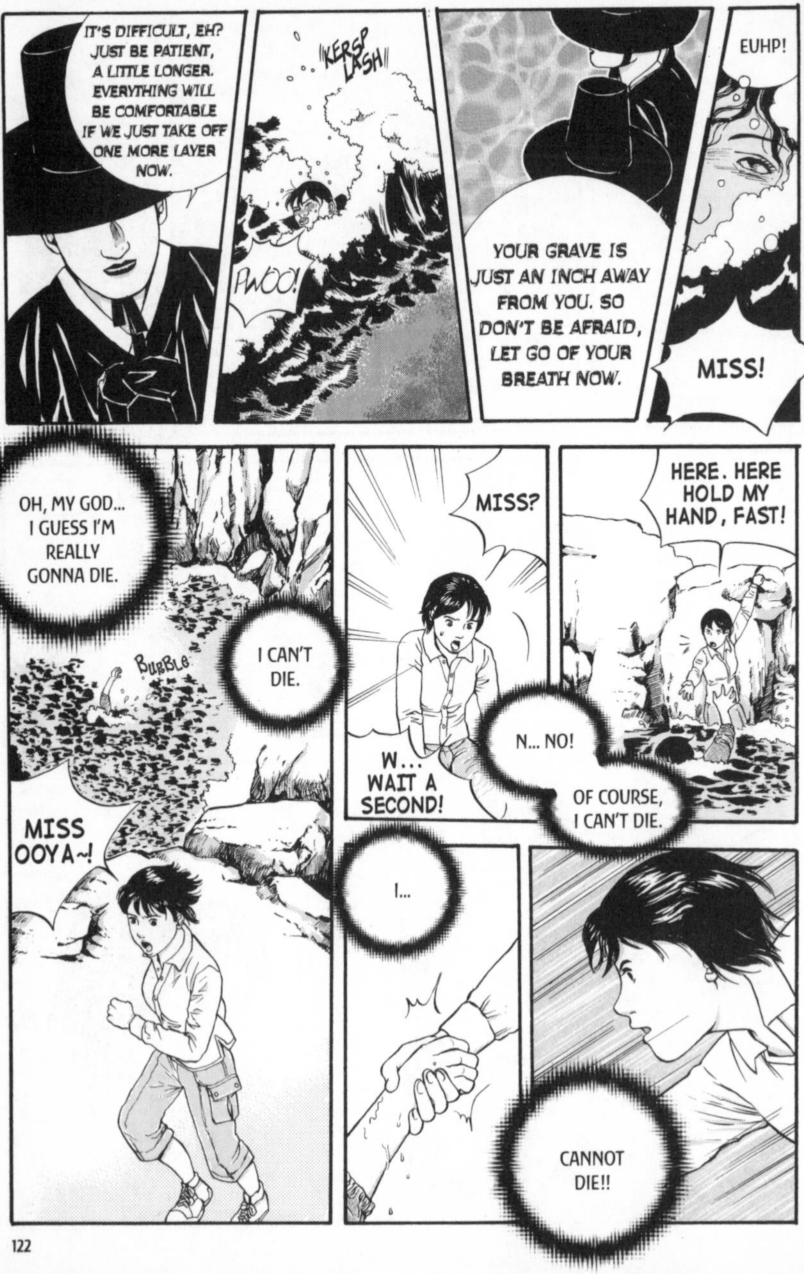
IT'S DIFFICULT, EH? JUST BE PATIENT, A LITTLE LONGER. EVERYTHING WILL BE COMFORTABLE IF WE JUST TAKE OFF ONE MORE LAYER NOW.
KERSP LASH
PWOO!
YOUR GRAVE IS JUST AN INCH AWAY FROM YOU. SO DON'T BE AFRAID, LET GO OF YOUR BREATH NOW.
EUHP!
MISS!
OH, MY GOD... I GUESS I'M REALLY GONNA DIE.
BUBBLE
I CAN'T DIE.
MISS OOYA~!
MISS?
W... WAIT A SECOND!
HERE. HERE HOLD MY HAND, FAST!
N... NO!
OF COURSE, I CAN'T DIE.
I...
CANNOT DIE!!

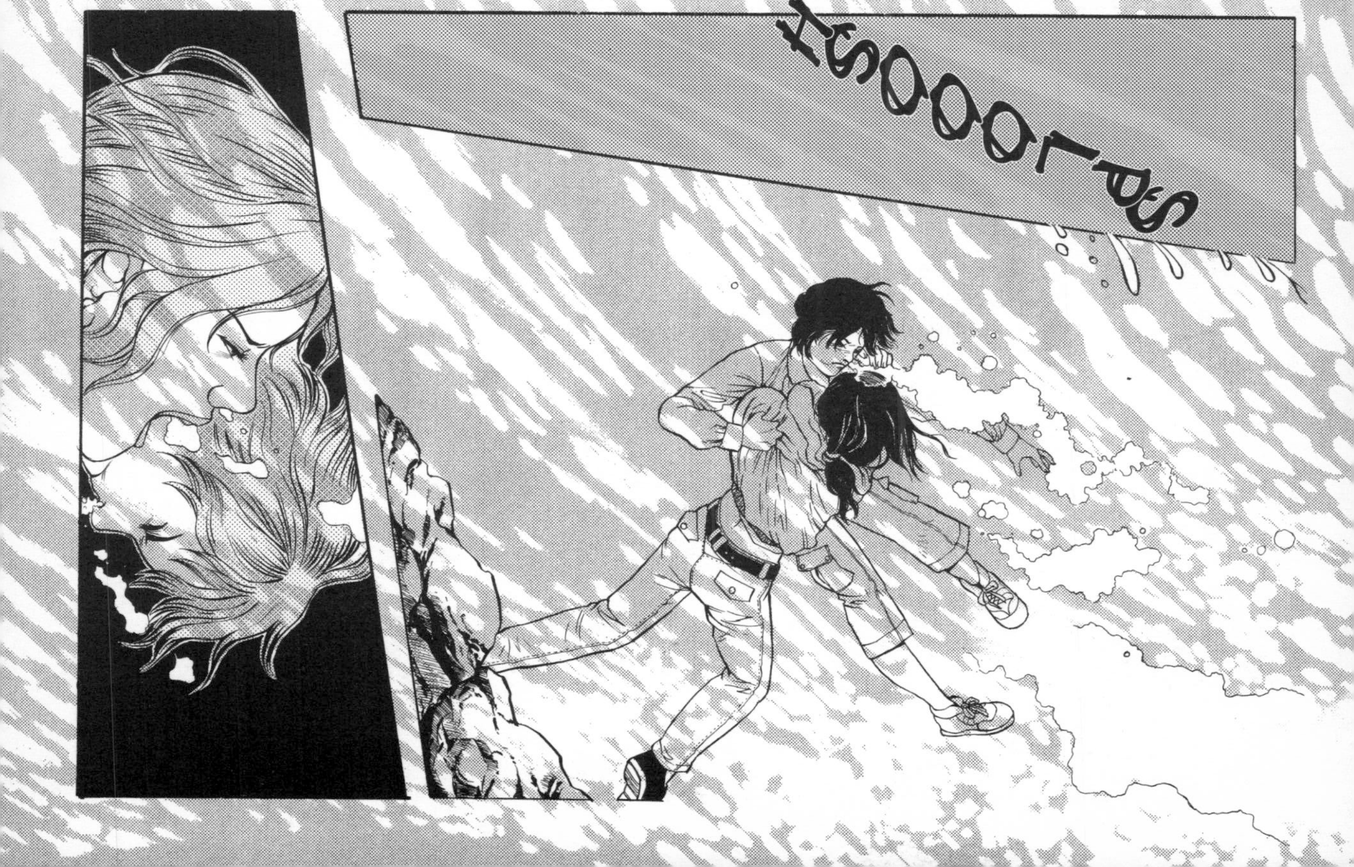
SPLOOOOSH

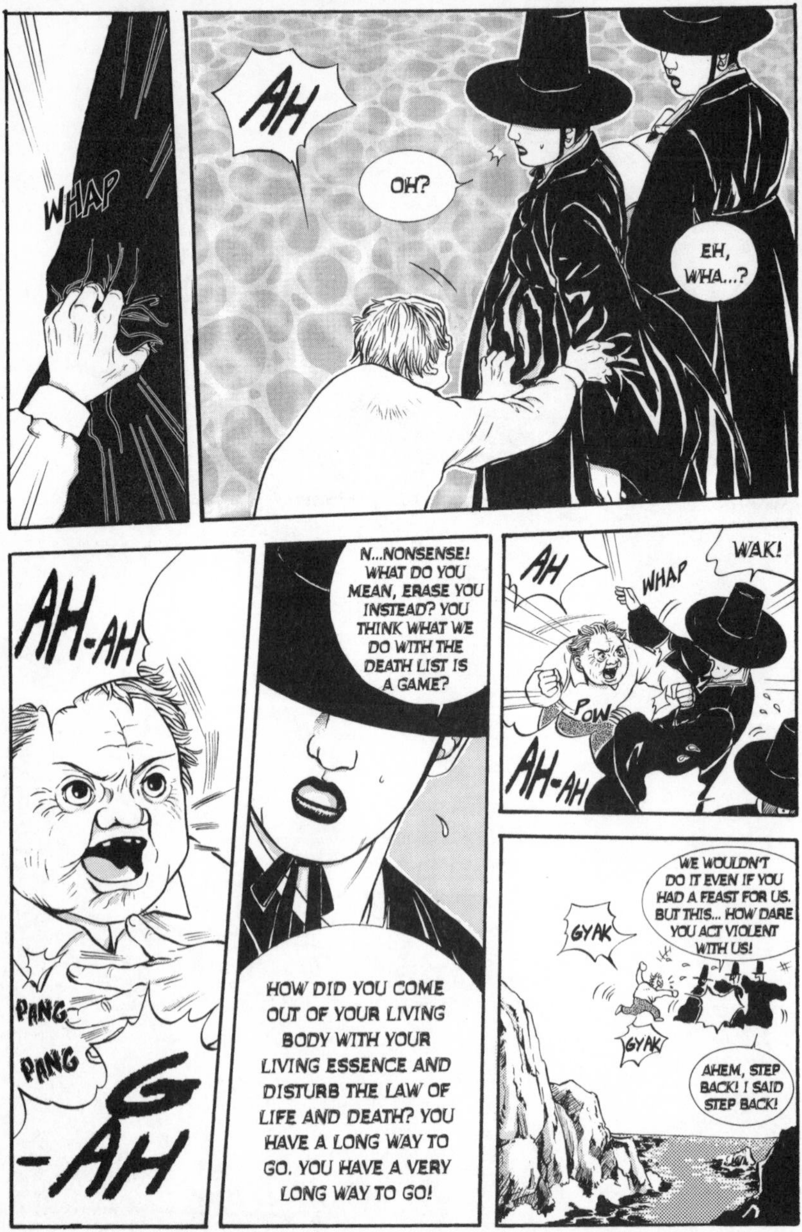
WHAP
AH
OH?
EH, WHA...?
AH-AH
N...NONSENSE! WHAT DO YOU MEAN, ERASE YOU INSTEAD? YOU THINK WHAT WE DO WITH THE DEATH LIST IS A GAME?
HOW DID YOU COME OUT OF YOUR LIVING BODY WITH YOUR LIVING ESSENCE AND DISTURB THE LAW OF LIFE AND DEATH? YOU HAVE A LONG WAY TO GO. YOU HAVE A VERY LONG WAY TO GO!
PANG
PANG
G-AH
AH
WHAP
WAK!
POW
AH-AH
WE WOULDN'T DO IT EVEN IF YOU HAD A FEAST FOR US. BUT THIS... HOW DARE YOU ACT VIOLENT WITH US!
GYAK
GYAK
AHEM, STEP BACK! I SAID STEP BACK!

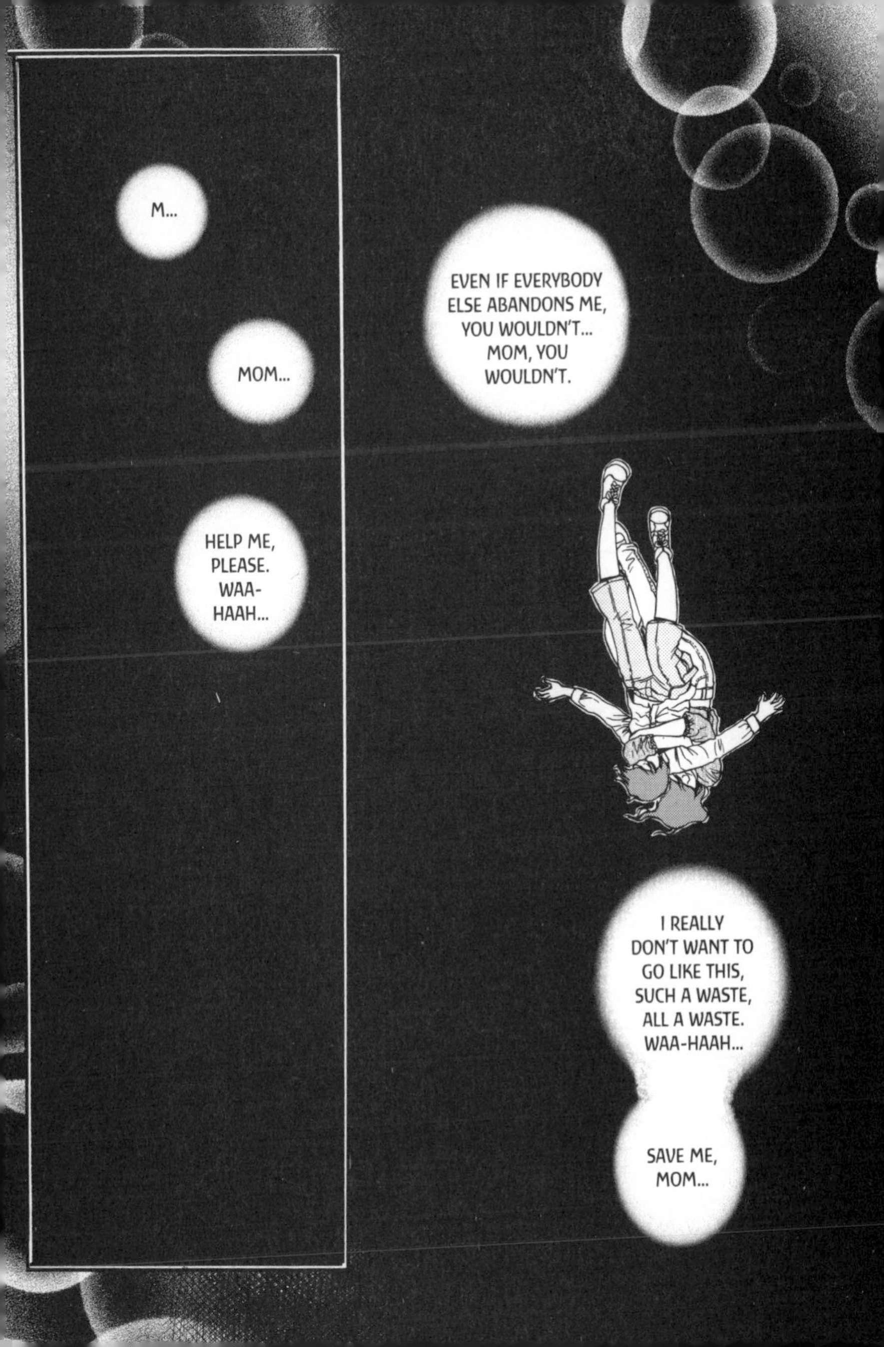
EVEN IF EVERYBODY ELSE ABANDONS ME, YOU WOULDN'T... MOM, YOU WOULDN'T.
M...
MOM...
I REALLY DON'T WANT TO GO LIKE THIS, SUCH A WASTE, ALL A WASTE. WAA-HAAH...
SAVE ME, MOM...
HELP ME, PLEASE. WAA-HAAH...

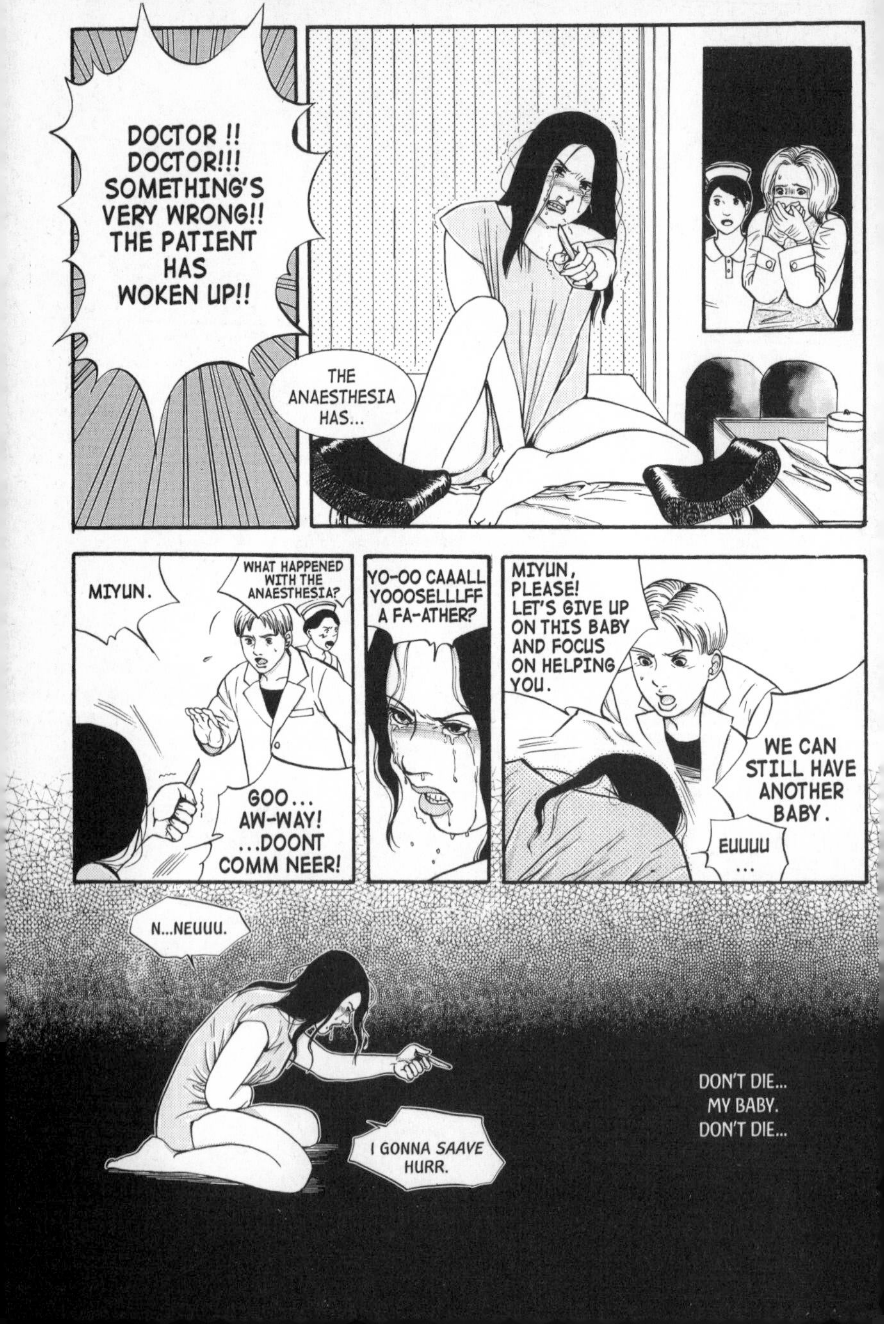
DOCTOR !! DOCTOR!!! SOMETHING'S VERY WRONG!! THE PATIENT HAS WOKEN UP!!
THE ANAESTHESIA HAS...
MIYUN.
WHAT HAPPENED WITH THE ANAESTHESIA?
GOO... AW-WAY! ...DOONT COMM NEER!
YO-OO CAAALL YOOOSELLLFF A FA-ATHER?
MIYUN, PLEASE! LET'S GIVE UP ON THIS BABY AND FOCUS ON HELPING YOU.
WE CAN STILL HAVE ANOTHER BABY.
EUUUU ...
N...NEUUU.
I GONNA *SAAVE* HURR.
DON'T DIE... MY BABY. DON'T DIE...

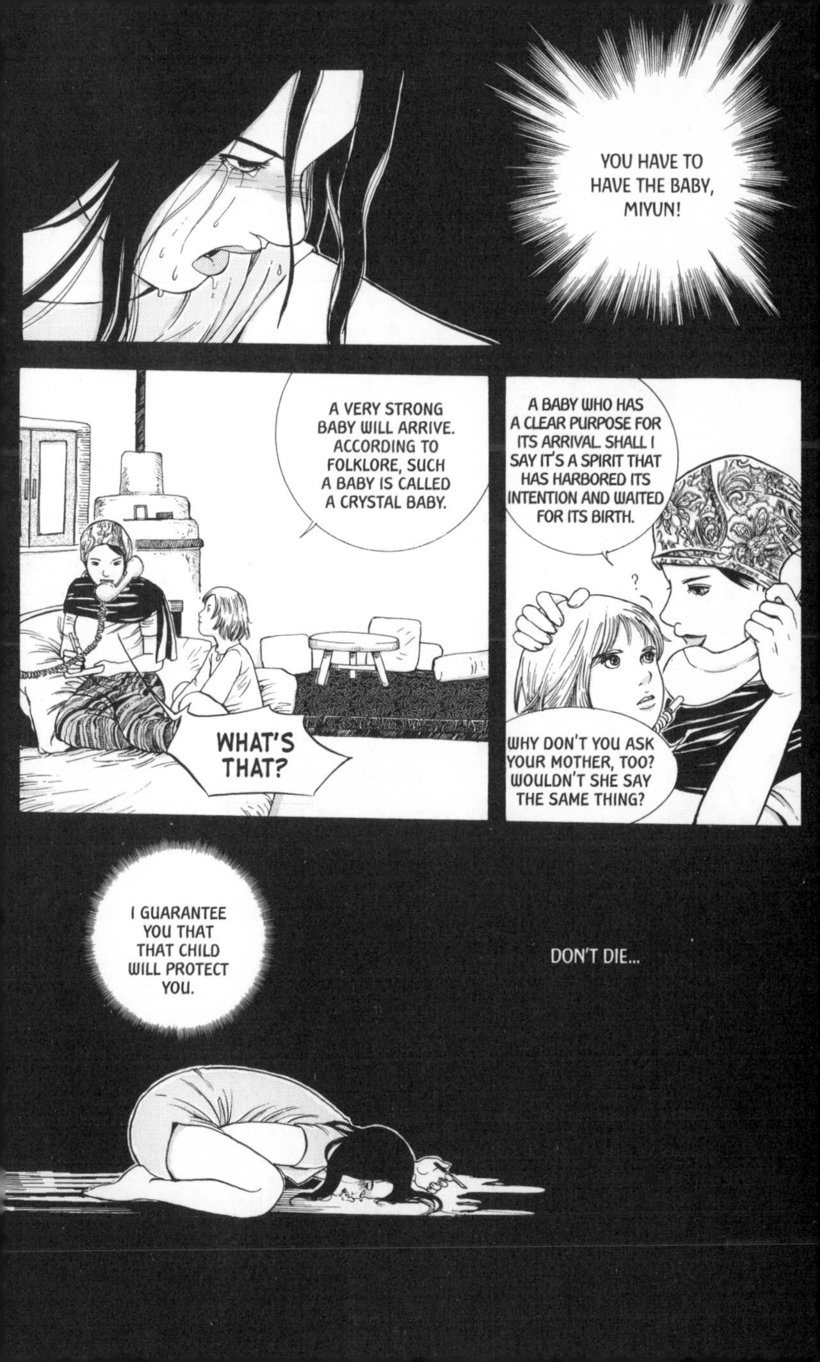
YOU HAVE TO HAVE THE BABY, MIYUN!
A VERY STRONG BABY WILL ARRIVE. ACCORDING TO FOLKLORE, SUCH A BABY IS CALLED A CRYSTAL BABY.
WHAT'S THAT?
A BABY WHO HAS A CLEAR PURPOSE FOR ITS ARRIVAL. SHALL I SAY IT'S A SPIRIT THAT HAS HARBORED ITS INTENTION AND WAITED FOR ITS BIRTH.
?
WHY DON'T YOU ASK YOUR MOTHER, TOO? WOULDN'T SHE SAY THE SAME THING?
I GUARANTEE YOU THAT THAT CHILD WILL PROTECT YOU.
DON'T DIE...

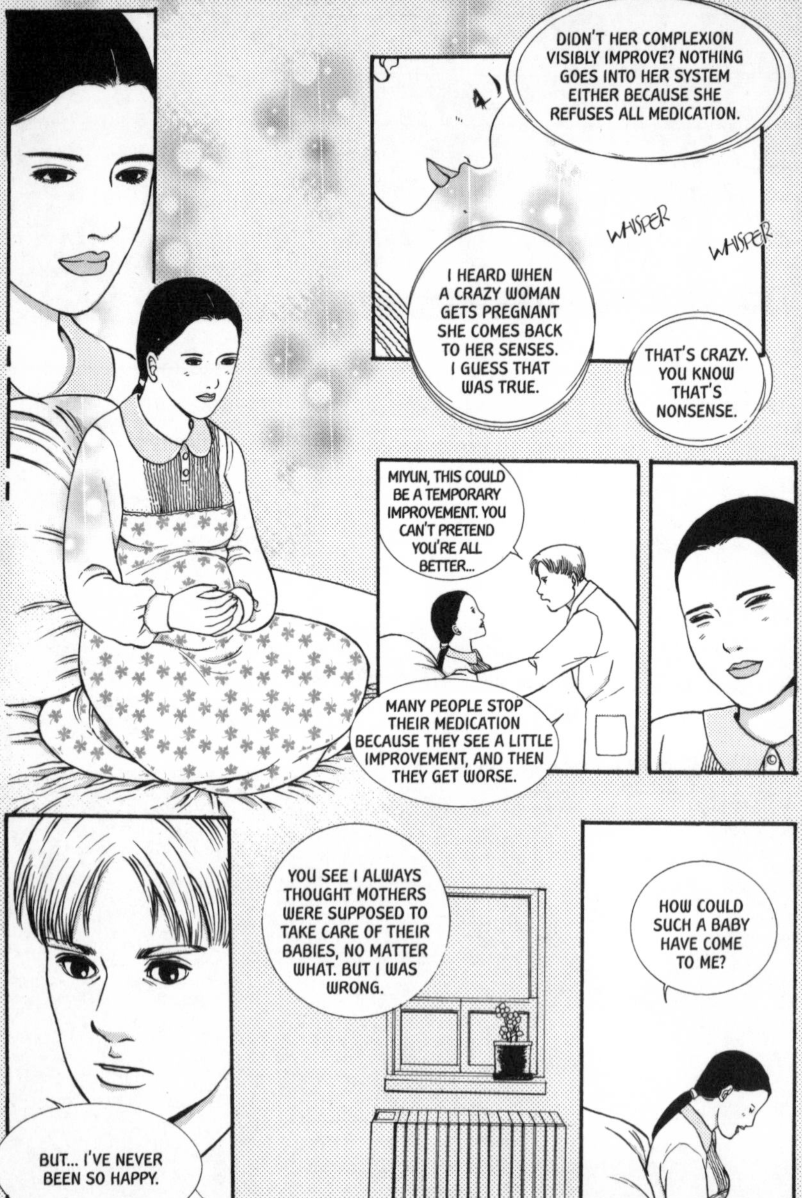
DIDN'T HER COMPLEXION VISIBLY IMPROVE? NOTHING GOES INTO HER SYSTEM EITHER BECAUSE SHE REFUSES ALL MEDICATION.
WHISPER
WHISPER
I HEARD WHEN A CRAZY WOMAN GETS PREGNANT SHE COMES BACK TO HER SENSES. I GUESS THAT WAS TRUE.
THAT'S CRAZY. YOU KNOW THAT'S NONSENSE.
MIYUN, THIS COULD BE A TEMPORARY IMPROVEMENT. YOU CAN'T PRETEND YOU'RE ALL BETTER...
MANY PEOPLE STOP THEIR MEDICATION BECAUSE THEY SEE A LITTLE IMPROVEMENT, AND THEN THEY GET WORSE.
BUT... I'VE NEVER BEEN SO HAPPY.
YOU SEE I ALWAYS THOUGHT MOTHERS WERE SUPPOSED TO TAKE CARE OF THEIR BABIES, NO MATTER WHAT. BUT I WAS WRONG.
HOW COULD SUCH A BABY HAVE COME TO ME?

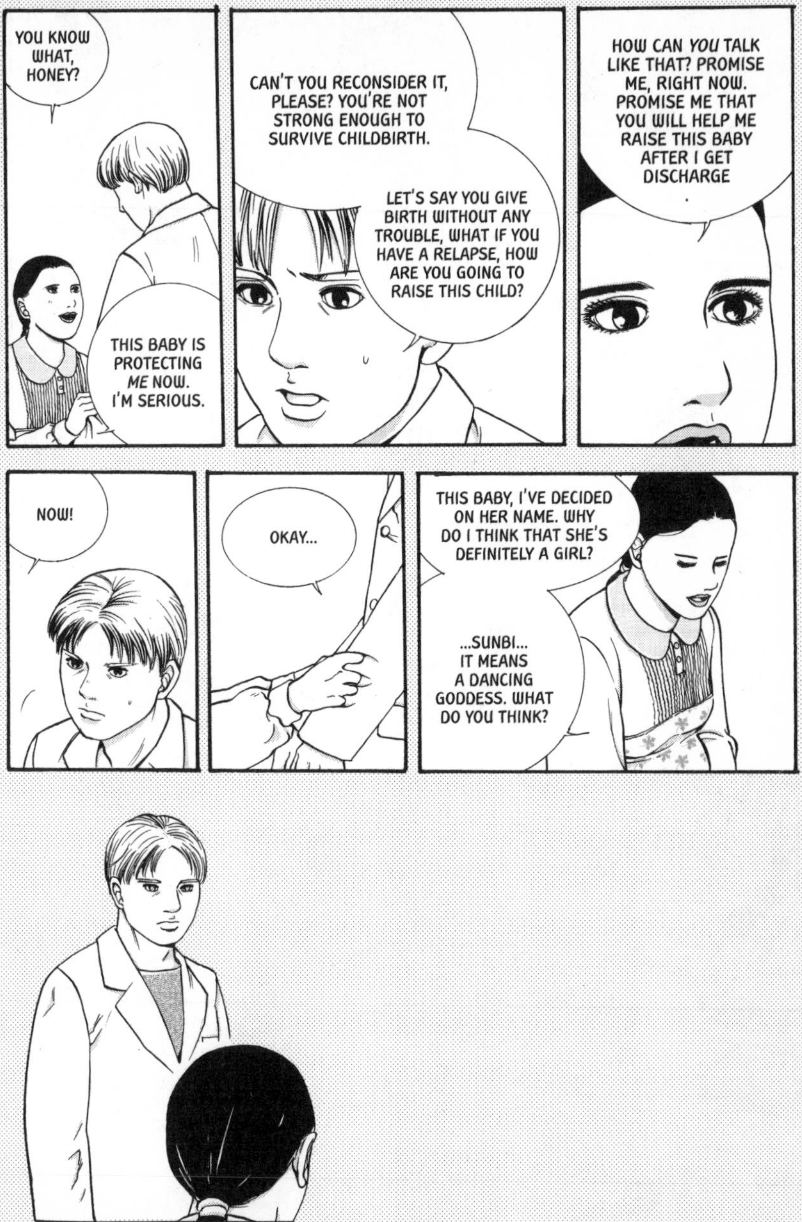
YOU KNOW WHAT, HONEY?
THIS BABY IS PROTECTING *ME* NOW. I'M SERIOUS.
CAN'T YOU RECONSIDER IT, PLEASE? YOU'RE NOT STRONG ENOUGH TO SURVIVE CHILDBIRTH.
LET'S SAY YOU GIVE BIRTH WITHOUT ANY TROUBLE, WHAT IF YOU HAVE A RELAPSE, HOW ARE YOU GOING TO RAISE THIS CHILD?
HOW CAN *YOU* TALK LIKE THAT? PROMISE ME, RIGHT NOW. PROMISE ME THAT YOU WILL HELP ME RAISE THIS BABY AFTER I GET DISCHARGE.
NOW!
OKAY...
THIS BABY, I'VE DECIDED ON HER NAME. WHY DO I THINK THAT SHE'S DEFINITELY A GIRL?
...SUNBI... IT MEANS A DANCING GODDESS. WHAT DO YOU THINK?

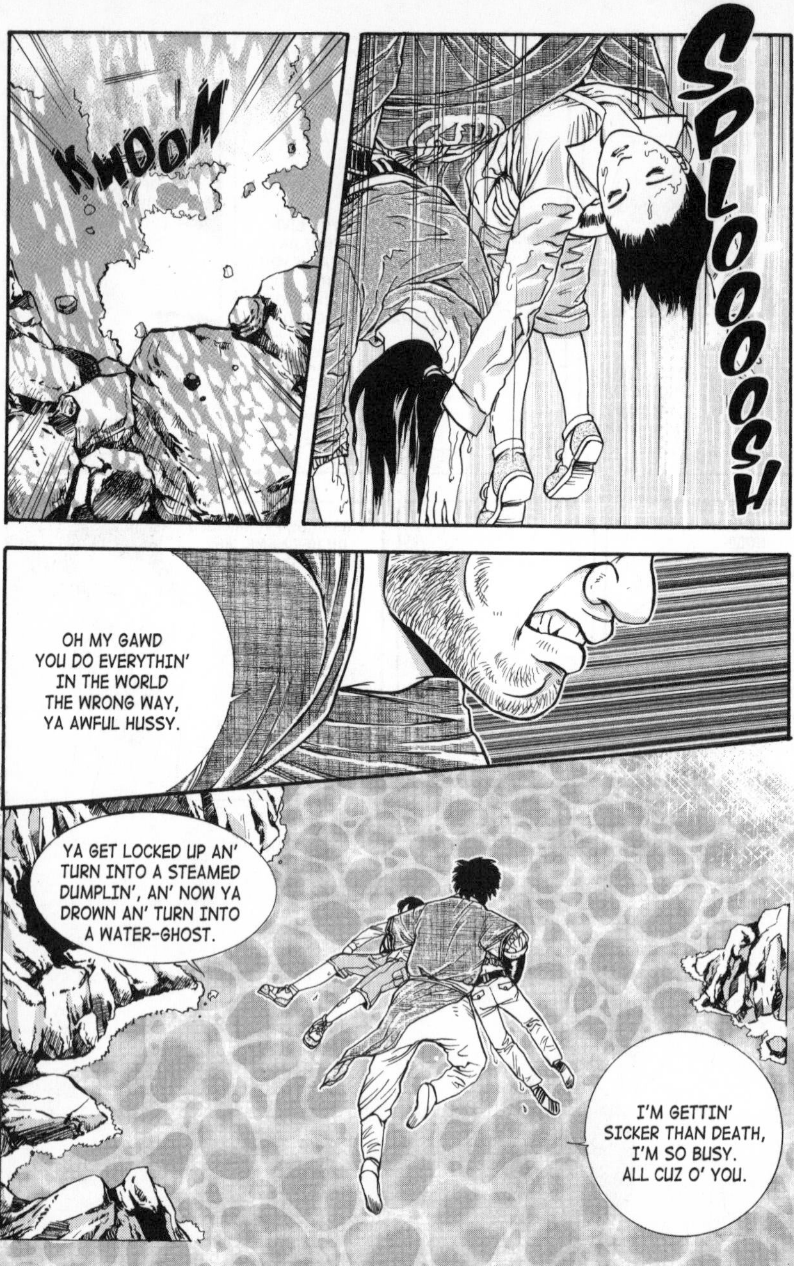
SPLOOOOOOSH
KWOOM
OH MY GAWD YOU DO EVERYTHIN' IN THE WORLD THE WRONG WAY, YA AWFUL HUSSY.
YA GET LOCKED UP AN' TURN INTO A STEAMED DUMPLIN', AN' NOW YA DROWN AN' TURN INTO A WATER-GHOST.
I'M GETTIN' SICKER THAN DEATH, I'M SO BUSY. ALL CUZ O' YOU.

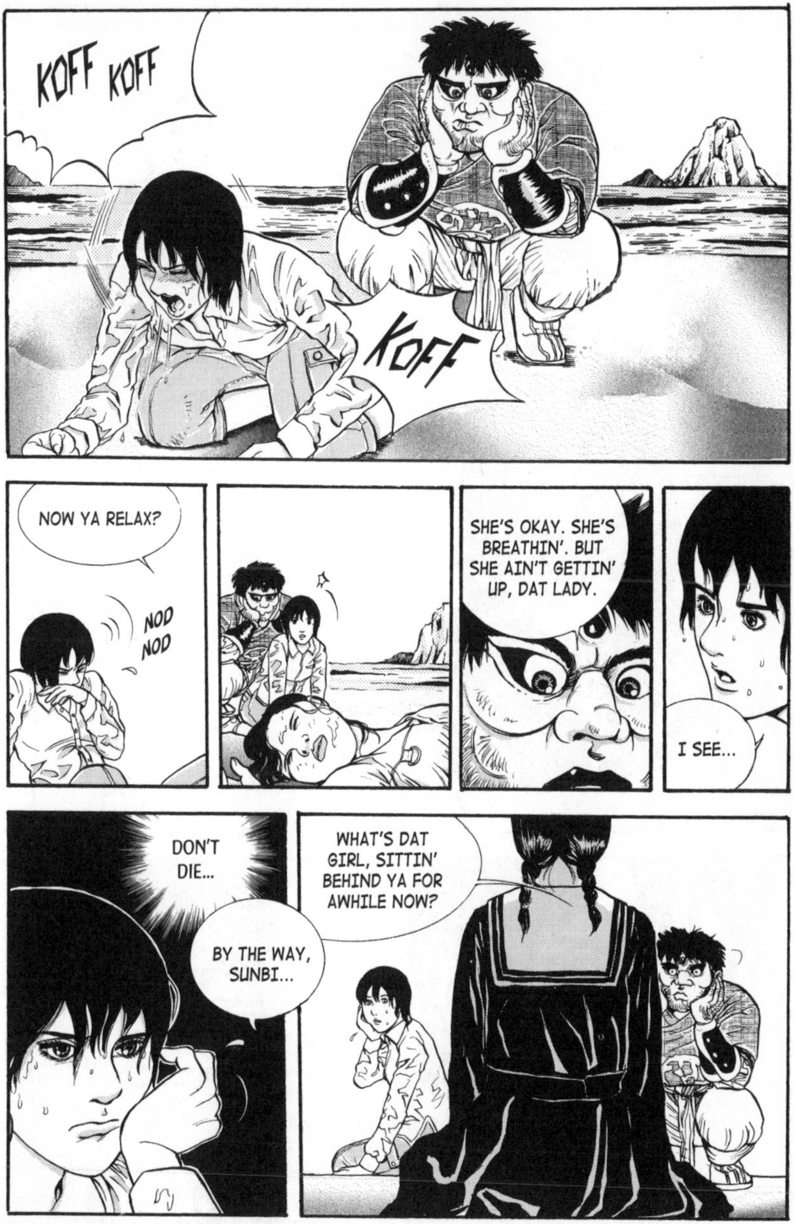
KOFF KOFF
KOFF
NOW YA RELAX?
NOD NOD
SHE'S OKAY. SHE'S BREATHIN'. BUT SHE AIN'T GETTIN' UP, DAT LADY.
I SEE...
DON'T DIE...
WHAT'S DAT GIRL, SITTIN' BEHIND YA FOR AWHILE NOW?
BY THE WAY, SUNBI...

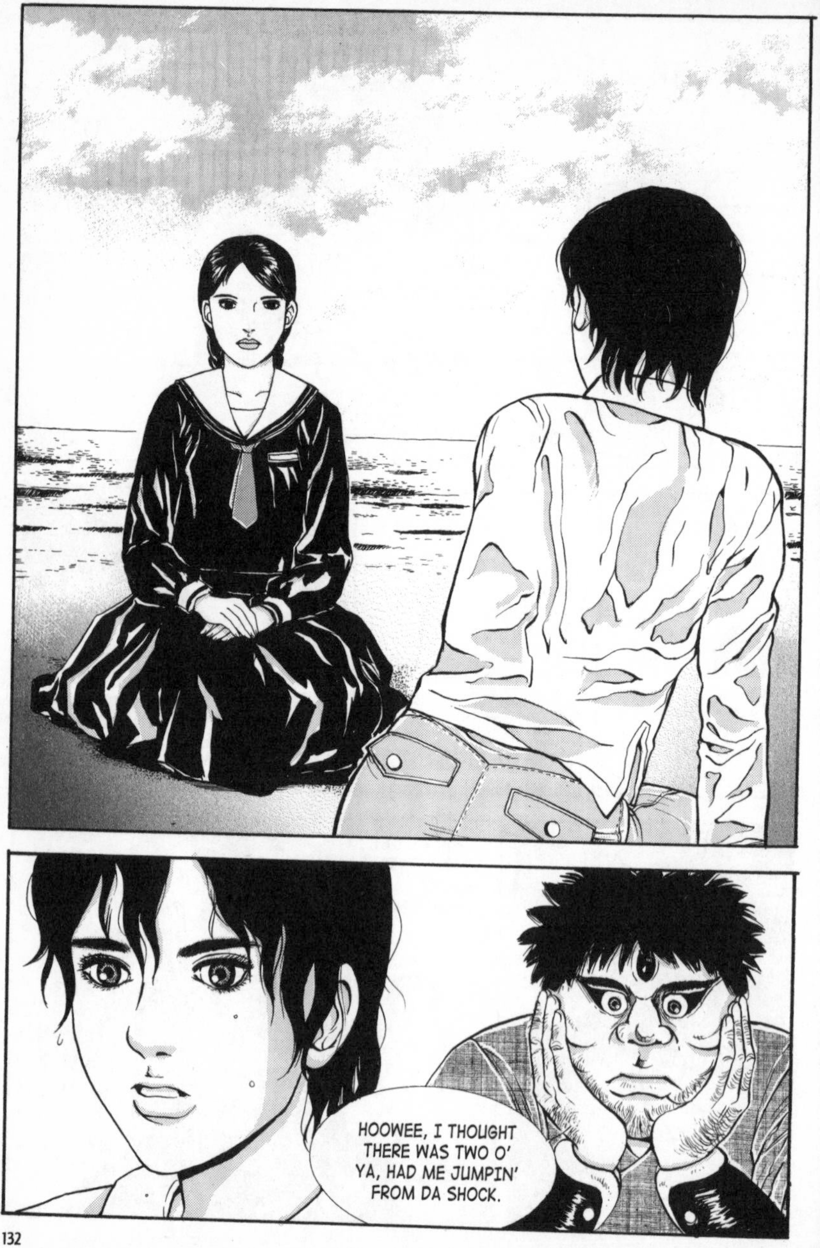
HOOWEE, I THOUGHT THERE WAS TWO O' YA, HAD ME JUMPIN' FROM DA SHOCK.

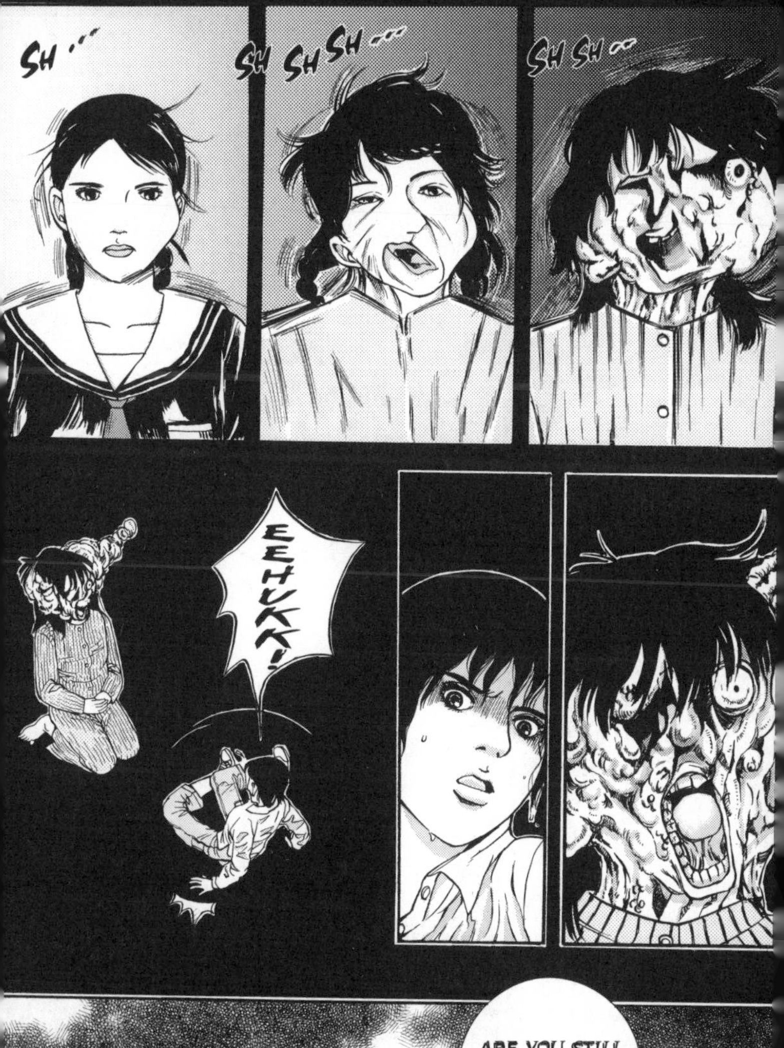
SH ...
SH SH SH ...
SH SH ...
EEHUKK!
ARE YOU STILL AFRAID OF YOUR MOM?

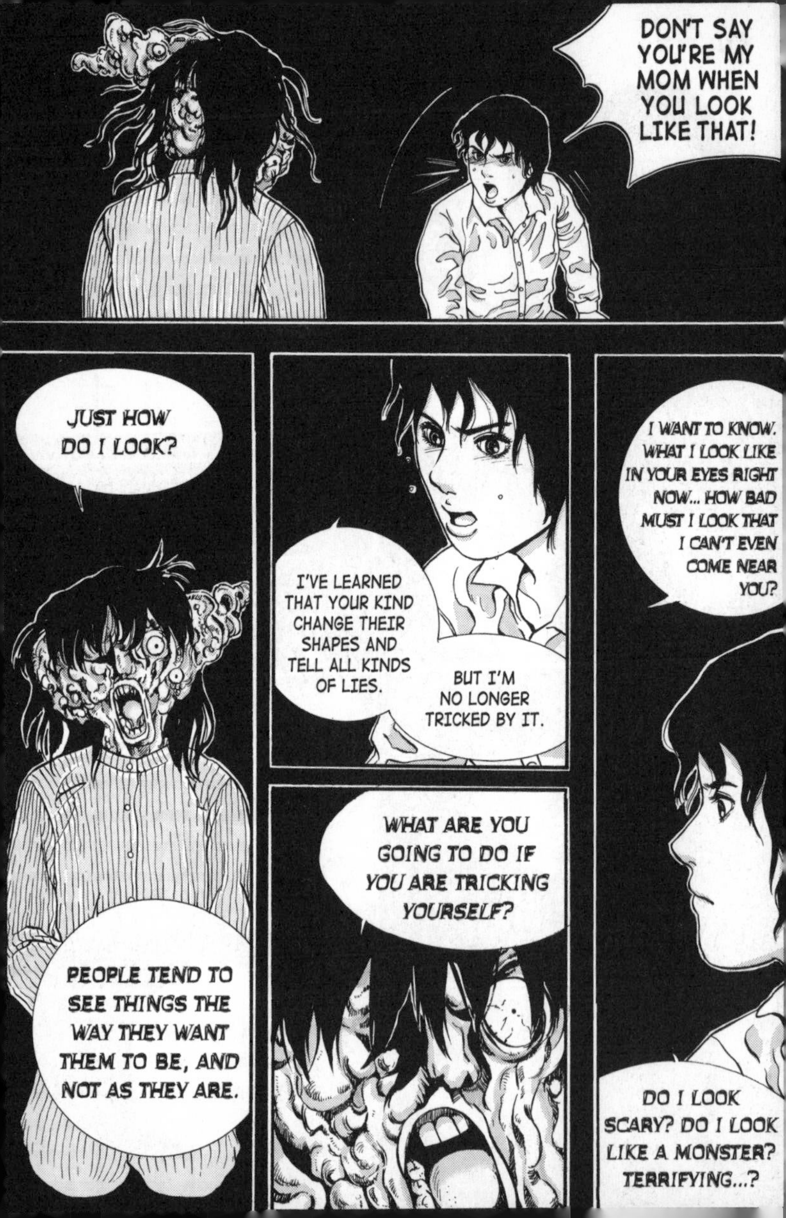
DON'T SAY YOU'RE MY MOM WHEN YOU LOOK LIKE THAT!
JUST HOW DO I LOOK?
PEOPLE TEND TO SEE THINGS THE WAY THEY WANT THEM TO BE, AND NOT AS THEY ARE.
I'VE LEARNED THAT YOUR KIND CHANGE THEIR SHAPES AND TELL ALL KINDS OF LIES.
BUT I'M NO LONGER TRICKED BY IT.
WHAT ARE YOU GOING TO DO IF YOU ARE TRICKING YOURSELF?
I WANT TO KNOW. WHAT I LOOK LIKE IN YOUR EYES RIGHT NOW... HOW BAD MUST I LOOK THAT I CAN'T EVEN COME NEAR YOU?
DO I LOOK SCARY? DO I LOOK LIKE A MONSTER? TERRIFYING...?

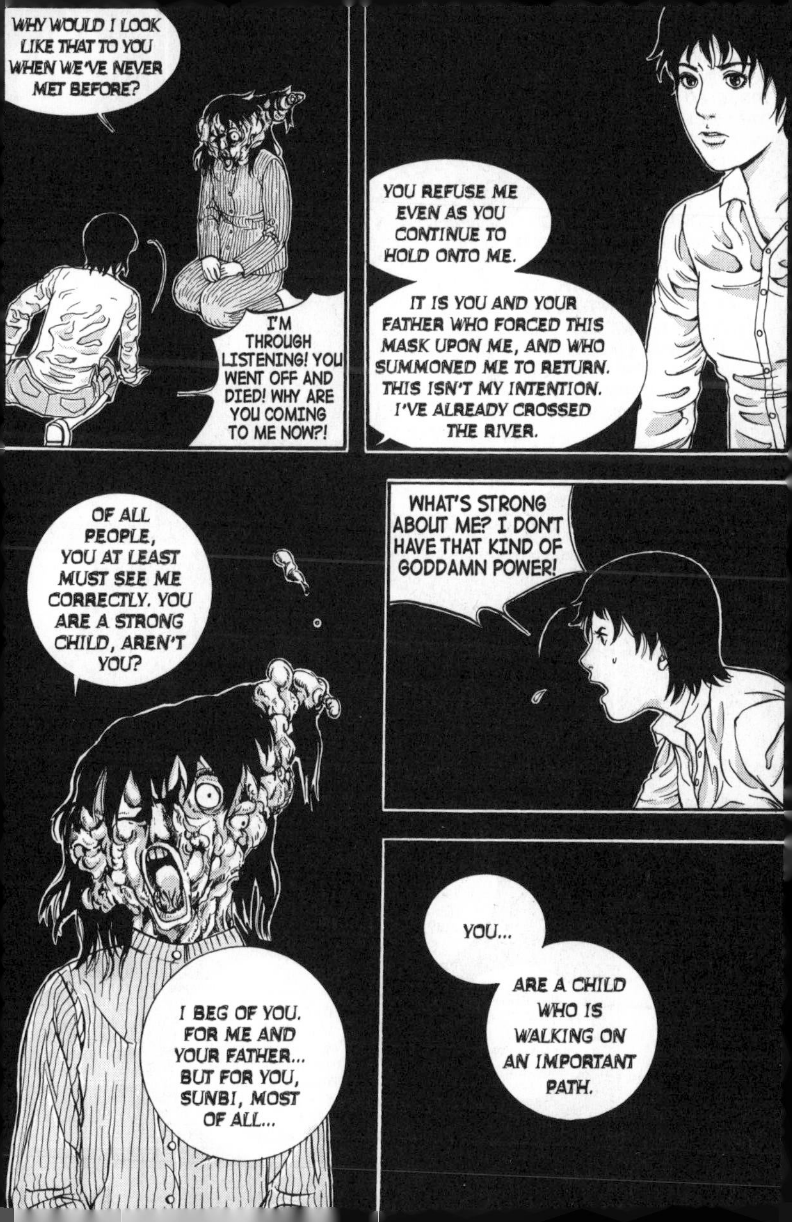
WHY WOULD I LOOK LIKE THAT TO YOU WHEN WE'VE NEVER MET BEFORE?
I'M THROUGH LISTENING! YOU WENT OFF AND DIED! WHY ARE YOU COMING TO ME NOW?!
YOU REFUSE ME EVEN AS YOU CONTINUE TO HOLD ONTO ME.
IT IS YOU AND YOUR FATHER WHO FORCED THIS MASK UPON ME, AND WHO SUMMONED ME TO RETURN. THIS ISN'T MY INTENTION. I'VE ALREADY CROSSED THE RIVER.
OF ALL PEOPLE, YOU AT LEAST MUST SEE ME CORRECTLY. YOU ARE A STRONG CHILD, AREN'T YOU?
WHAT'S STRONG ABOUT ME? I DON'T HAVE THAT KIND OF GODDAMN POWER!
I BEG OF YOU. FOR ME AND YOUR FATHER... BUT FOR YOU, SUNBI, MOST OF ALL...
YOU...
ARE A CHILD WHO IS WALKING ON AN IMPORTANT PATH.

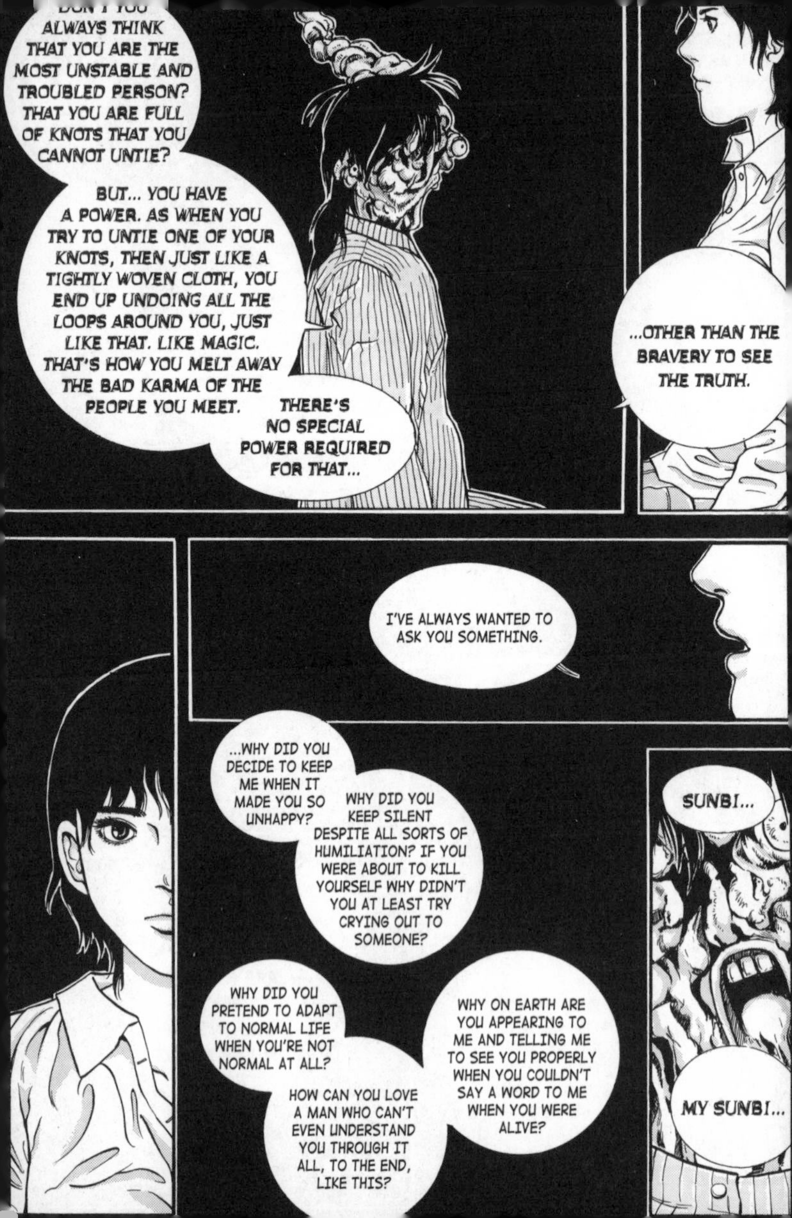
ALWAYS THINK THAT YOU ARE THE MOST UNSTABLE AND TROUBLED PERSON? THAT YOU ARE FULL OF KNOTS THAT YOU CANNOT UNTIE?
BUT... YOU HAVE A POWER. AS WHEN YOU TRY TO UNTIE ONE OF YOUR KNOTS, THEN JUST LIKE A TIGHTLY WOVEN CLOTH, YOU END UP UNDOING ALL THE LOOPS AROUND YOU, JUST LIKE THAT. LIKE MAGIC. THAT'S HOW YOU MELT AWAY THE BAD KARMA OF THE PEOPLE YOU MEET.
THERE'S NO SPECIAL POWER REQUIRED FOR THAT...
...OTHER THAN THE BRAVERY TO SEE THE TRUTH.
I'VE ALWAYS WANTED TO ASK YOU SOMETHING.
...WHY DID YOU DECIDE TO KEEP ME WHEN IT MADE YOU SO UNHAPPY?
WHY DID YOU KEEP SILENT DESPITE ALL SORTS OF HUMILIATION? IF YOU WERE ABOUT TO KILL YOURSELF WHY DIDN'T YOU AT LEAST TRY CRYING OUT TO SOMEONE?
WHY DID YOU PRETEND TO ADAPT TO NORMAL LIFE WHEN YOU'RE NOT NORMAL AT ALL?
HOW CAN YOU LOVE A MAN WHO CAN'T EVEN UNDERSTAND YOU THROUGH IT ALL, TO THE END, LIKE THIS?
WHY ON EARTH ARE YOU APPEARING TO ME AND TELLING ME TO SEE YOU PROPERLY WHEN YOU COULDN'T SAY A WORD TO ME WHEN YOU WERE ALIVE?
SUNBI...
MY SUNBI...

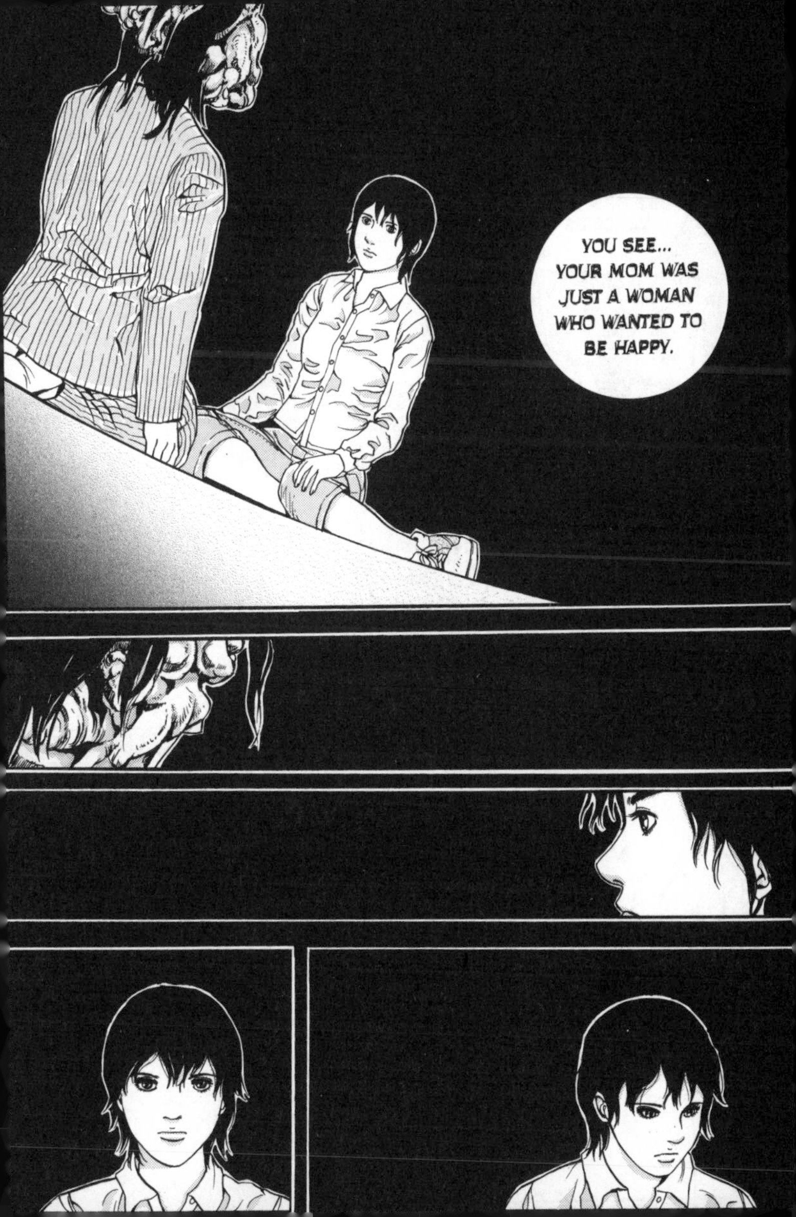
YOU SEE... YOUR MOM WAS JUST A WOMAN WHO WANTED TO BE HAPPY.

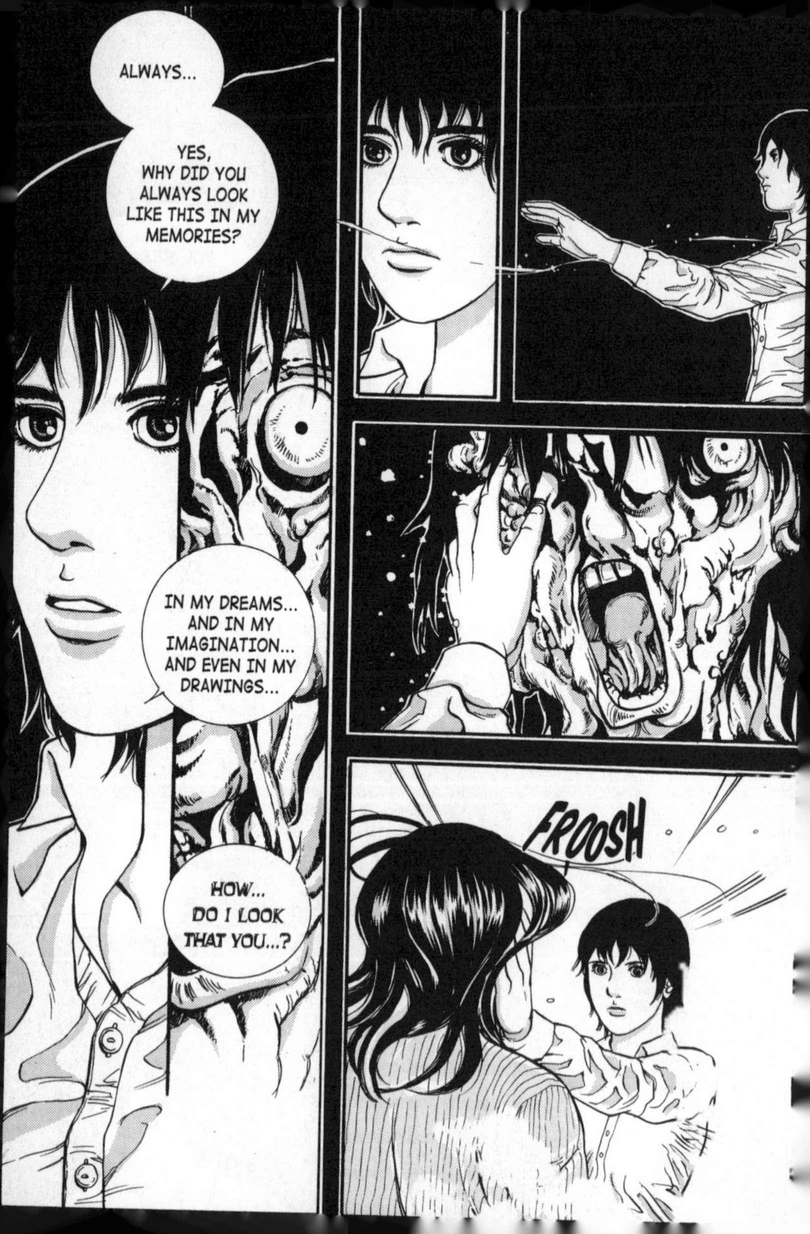
ALWAYS...
YES, WHY DID YOU ALWAYS LOOK LIKE THIS IN MY MEMORIES?
IN MY DREAMS... AND IN MY IMAGINATION... AND EVEN IN MY DRAWINGS...
HOW... DO I LOOK THAT YOU...?
FROOSH

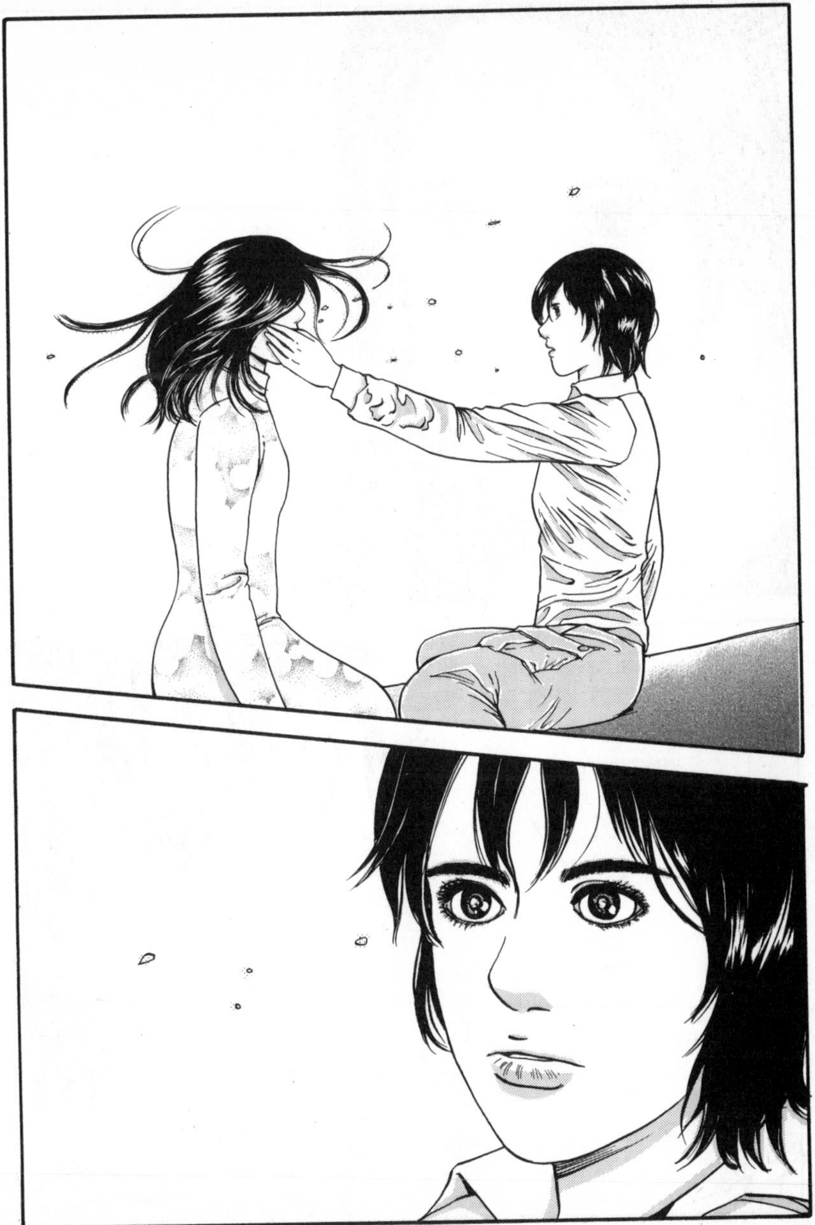

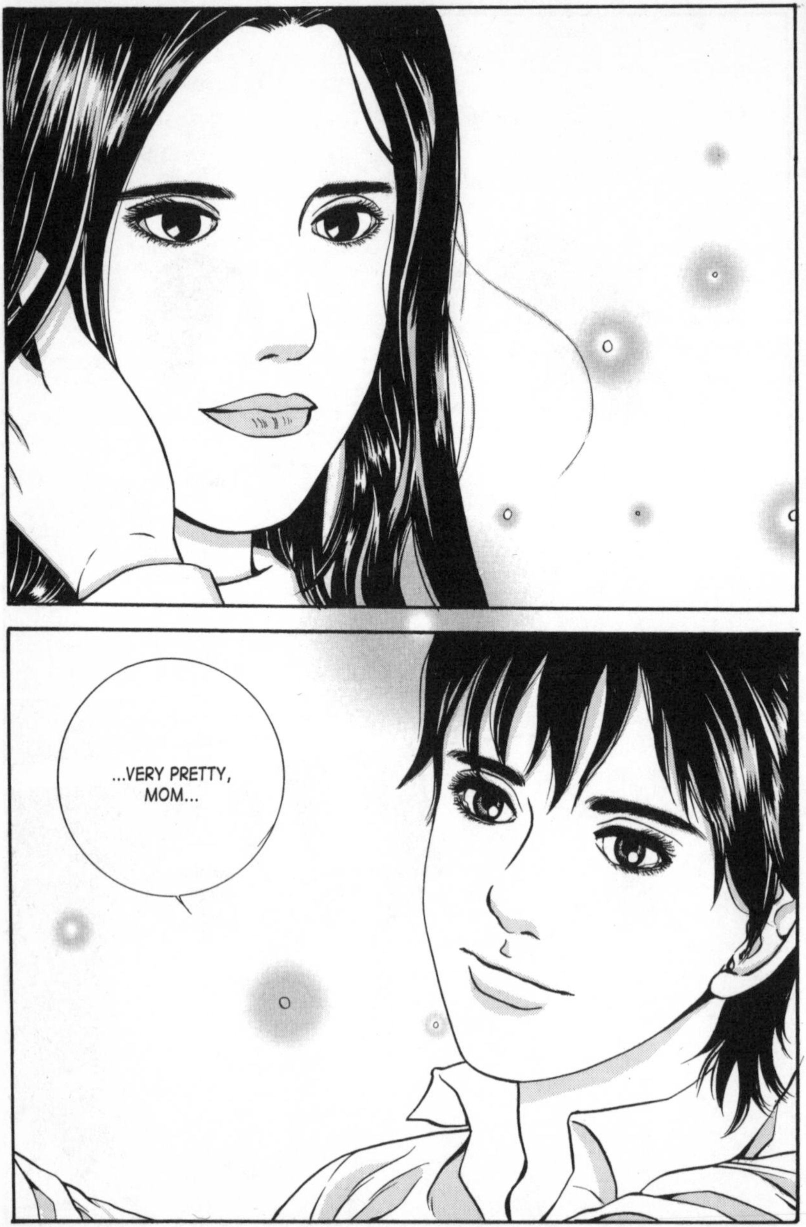
...VERY PRETTY,
MOM...

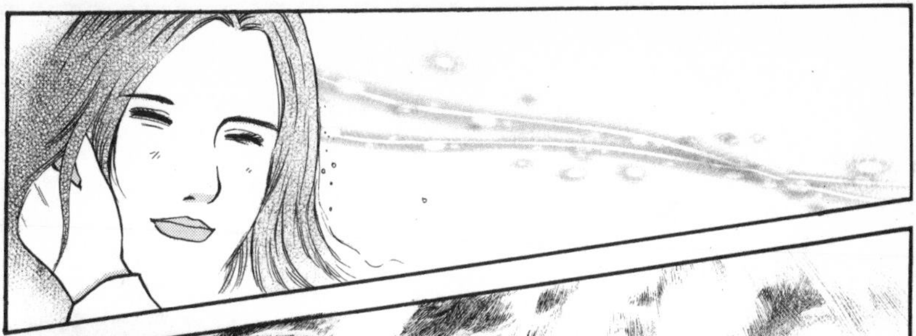

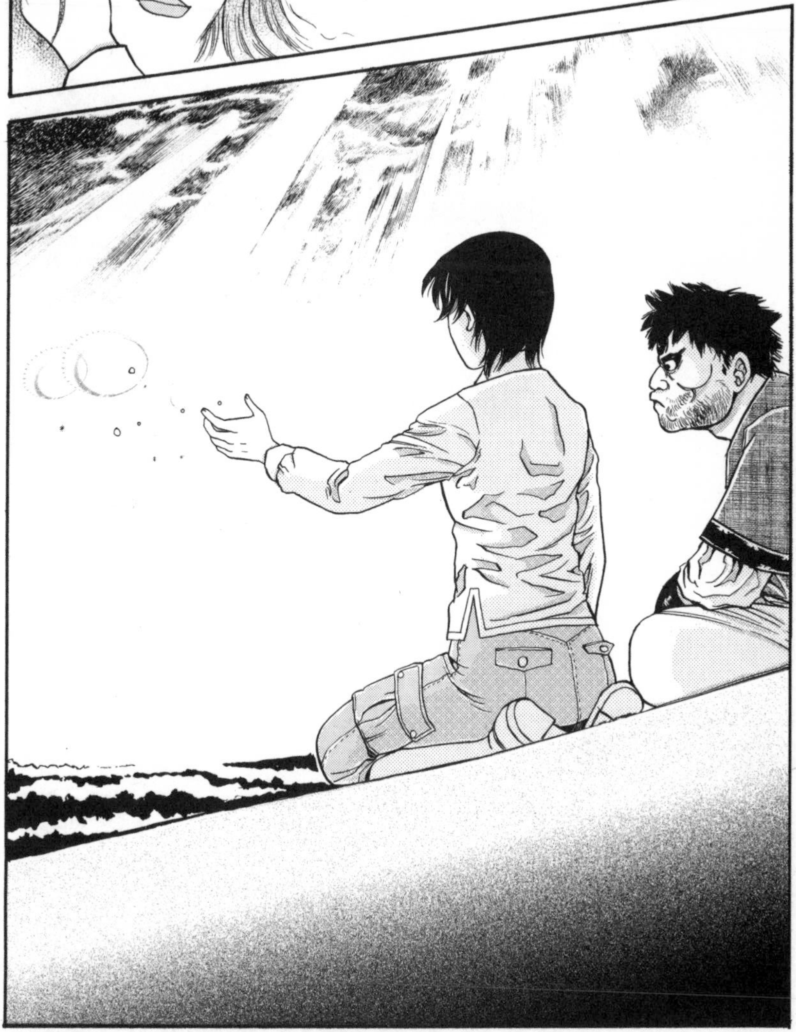

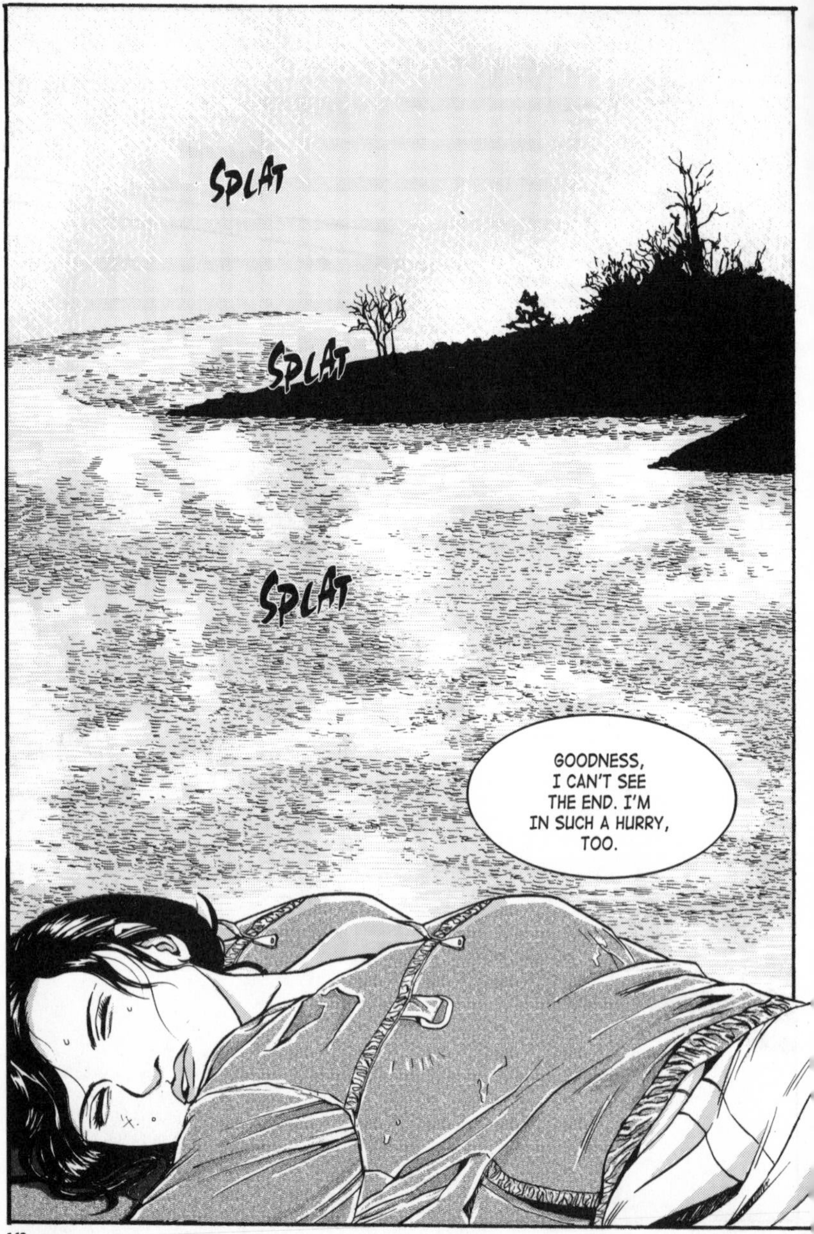
SPLAT
SPLAT
SPLAT
GOODNESS, I CAN'T SEE THE END. I'M IN SUCH A HURRY, TOO.

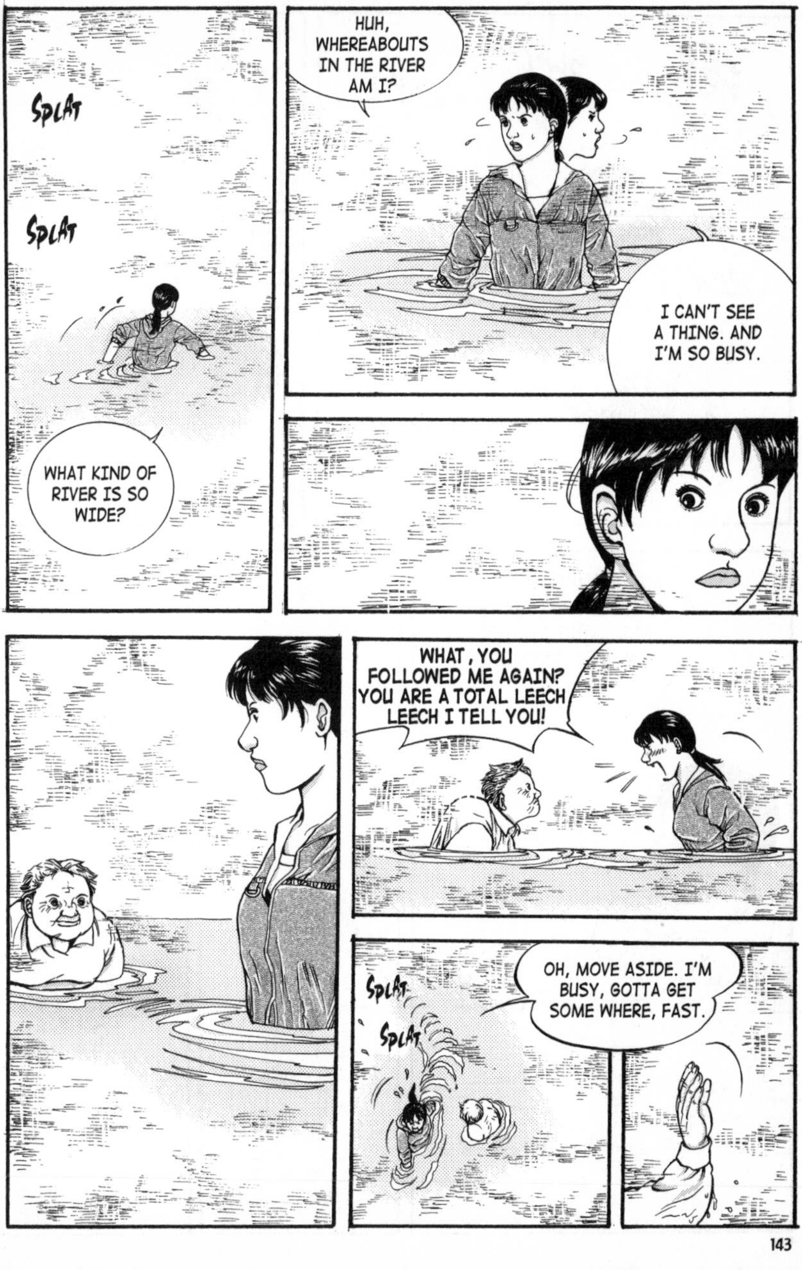
SPLAT
SPLAT
WHAT KIND OF RIVER IS SO WIDE?
HUH, WHEREABOUTS IN THE RIVER AM I?
I CAN'T SEE A THING. AND I'M SO BUSY.
WHAT, YOU FOLLOWED ME AGAIN? YOU ARE A TOTAL LEECH LEECH I TELL YOU!
OH, MOVE ASIDE. I'M BUSY, GOTTA GET SOME WHERE, FAST.
SPLAT
SPLAT

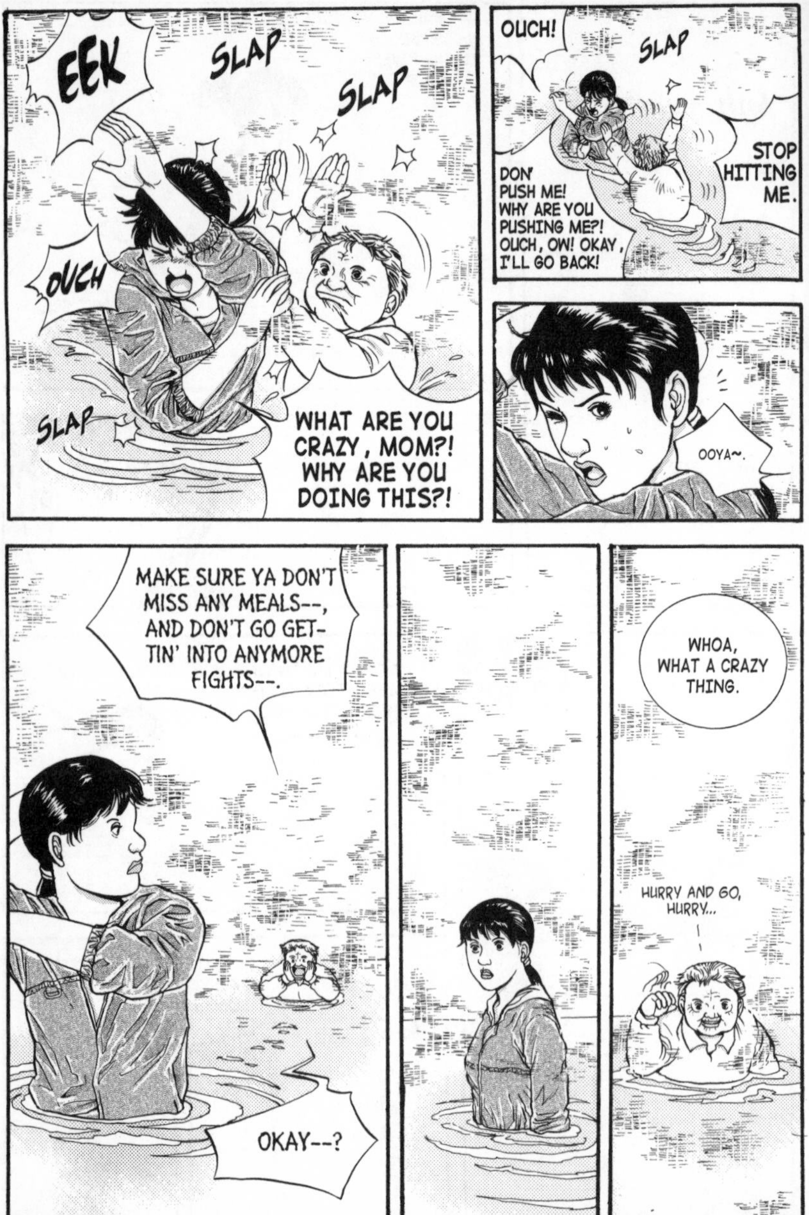
EEK
SLAP
SLAP
OUCH
SLAP
WHAT ARE YOU CRAZY, MOM?! WHY ARE YOU DOING THIS?!
OUCH!
SLAP
DON' PUSH ME! WHY ARE YOU PUSHING ME?! OUCH, OW! OKAY, I'LL GO BACK!
STOP HITTING ME.
OOYA~.
MAKE SURE YA DON'T MISS ANY MEALS--, AND DON'T GO GET-TIN' INTO ANYMORE FIGHTS--.
OKAY--?
WHOA, WHAT A CRAZY THING.
HURRY AND GO, HURRY...

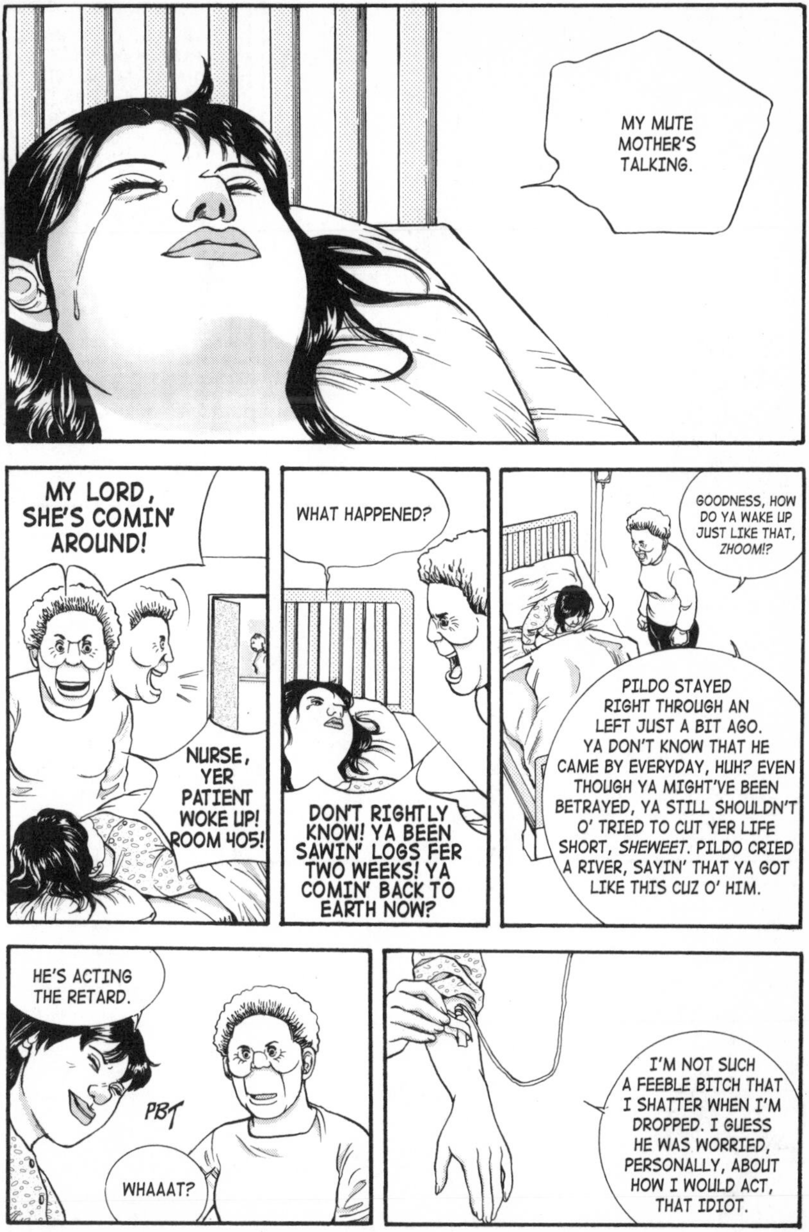

MY MUTE MOTHER'S TALKING.
MY LORD, SHE'S COMIN' AROUND!
NURSE, YER PATIENT WOKE UP! ROOM 405!
WHAT HAPPENED?
DON'T RIGHTLY KNOW! YA BEEN SAWIN' LOGS FER TWO WEEKS! YA COMIN' BACK TO EARTH NOW?
GOODNESS, HOW DO YA WAKE UP JUST LIKE THAT, *ZHOOM!?*
PILDO STAYED RIGHT THROUGH AN LEFT JUST A BIT AGO. YA DON'T KNOW THAT HE CAME BY EVERYDAY, HUH? EVEN THOUGH YA MIGHT'VE BEEN BETRAYED, YA STILL SHOULDN'T O' TRIED TO CUT YER LIFE SHORT, *SHEWEET*. PILDO CRIED A RIVER, SAYIN' THAT YA GOT LIKE THIS CUZ O' HIM.
HE'S ACTING THE RETARD.
PBT
WHAAAT?
I'M NOT SUCH A FEEBLE BITCH THAT I SHATTER WHEN I'M DROPPED. I GUESS HE WAS WORRIED, PERSONALLY, ABOUT HOW I WOULD ACT, THAT IDIOT.

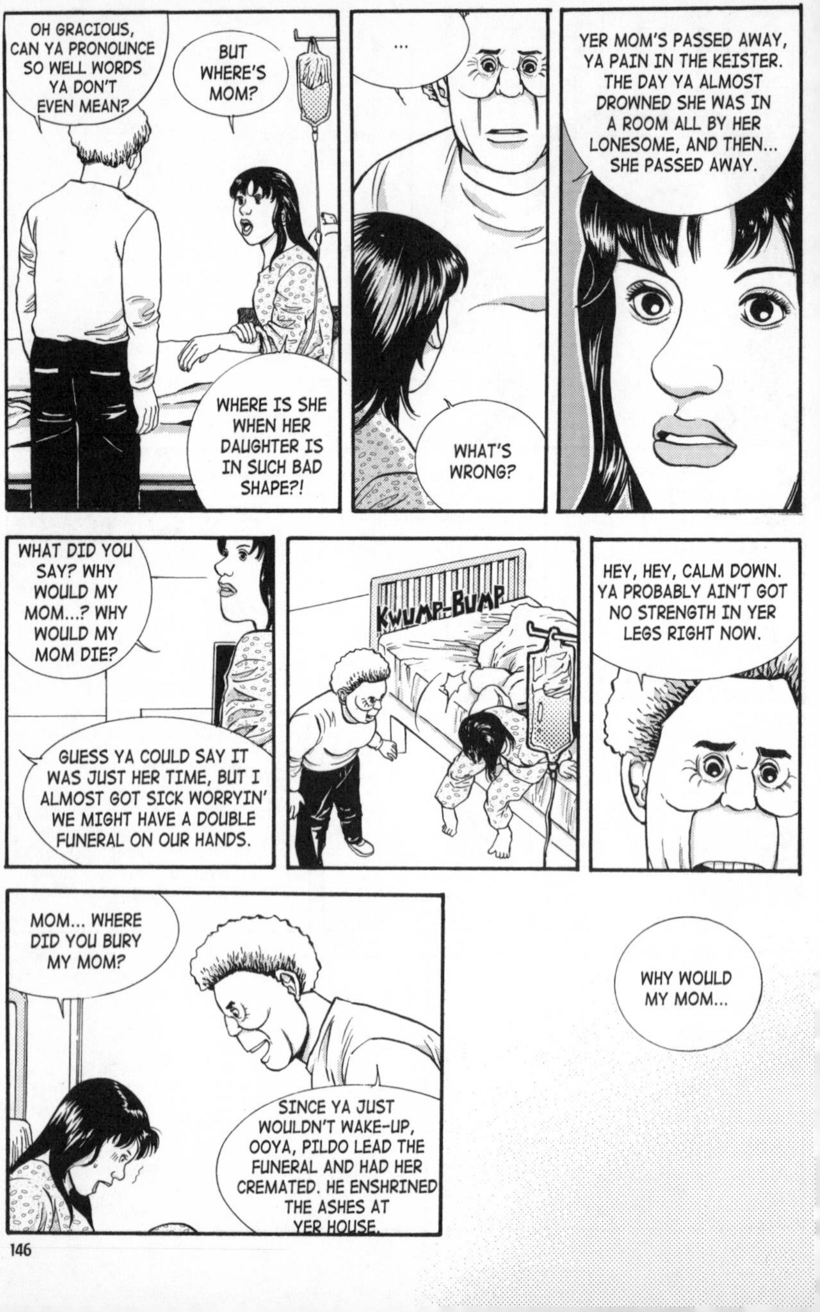
OH GRACIOUS, CAN YA PRONOUNCE SO WELL WORDS YA DON'T EVEN MEAN?
BUT WHERE'S MOM?
WHERE IS SHE WHEN HER DAUGHTER IS IN SUCH BAD SHAPE?!
...
WHAT'S WRONG?
YER MOM'S PASSED AWAY, YA PAIN IN THE KEISTER. THE DAY YA ALMOST DROWNED SHE WAS IN A ROOM ALL BY HER LONESOME, AND THEN... SHE PASSED AWAY.
WHAT DID YOU SAY? WHY WOULD MY MOM...? WHY WOULD MY MOM DIE?
GUESS YA COULD SAY IT WAS JUST HER TIME, BUT I ALMOST GOT SICK WORRYIN' WE MIGHT HAVE A DOUBLE FUNERAL ON OUR HANDS.
KWUMP-BUMP
HEY, HEY, CALM DOWN. YA PROBABLY AIN'T GOT NO STRENGTH IN YER LEGS RIGHT NOW.
MOM... WHERE DID YOU BURY MY MOM?
SINCE YA JUST WOULDN'T WAKE-UP, OOYA, PILDO LEAD THE FUNERAL AND HAD HER CREMATED. HE ENSHRINED THE ASHES AT YER HOUSE.
WHY WOULD MY MOM...

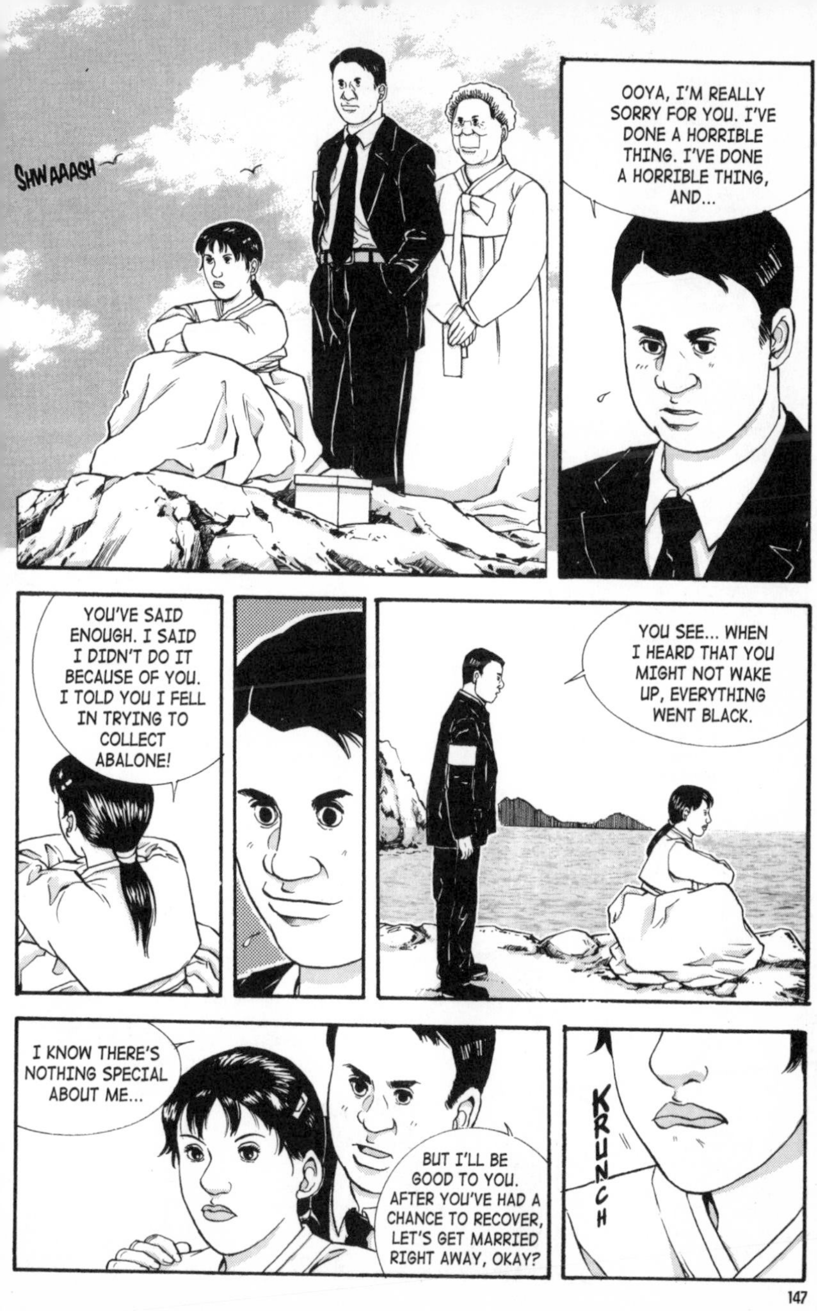
SHWAAASH
OOYA, I'M REALLY SORRY FOR YOU. I'VE DONE A HORRIBLE THING. I'VE DONE A HORRIBLE THING, AND...
YOU'VE SAID ENOUGH. I SAID I DIDN'T DO IT BECAUSE OF YOU. I TOLD YOU I FELL IN TRYING TO COLLECT ABALONE!
YOU SEE... WHEN I HEARD THAT YOU MIGHT NOT WAKE UP, EVERYTHING WENT BLACK.
I KNOW THERE'S NOTHING SPECIAL ABOUT ME...
BUT I'LL BE GOOD TO YOU. AFTER YOU'VE HAD A CHANCE TO RECOVER, LET'S GET MARRIED RIGHT AWAY, OKAY?
KRUNCH

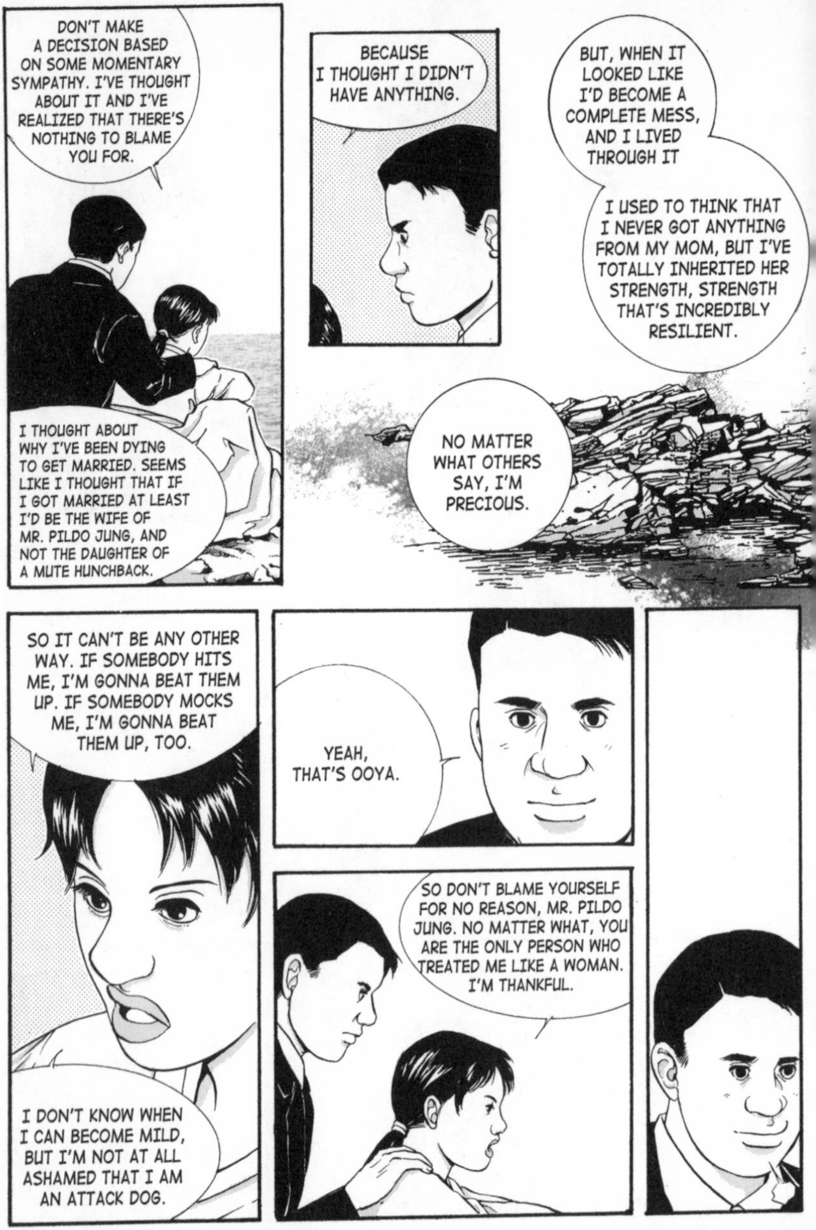

DON'T MAKE A DECISION BASED ON SOME MOMENTARY SYMPATHY. I'VE THOUGHT ABOUT IT AND I'VE REALIZED THAT THERE'S NOTHING TO BLAME YOU FOR.
I THOUGHT ABOUT WHY I'VE BEEN DYING TO GET MARRIED. SEEMS LIKE I THOUGHT THAT IF I GOT MARRIED AT LEAST I'D BE THE WIFE OF MR. PILDO JUNG, AND NOT THE DAUGHTER OF A MUTE HUNCHBACK.
BECAUSE I THOUGHT I DIDN'T HAVE ANYTHING.
BUT, WHEN IT LOOKED LIKE I'D BECOME A COMPLETE MESS, AND I LIVED THROUGH IT
I USED TO THINK THAT I NEVER GOT ANYTHING FROM MY MOM, BUT I'VE TOTALLY INHERITED HER STRENGTH, STRENGTH THAT'S INCREDIBLY RESILIENT.
NO MATTER WHAT OTHERS SAY, I'M PRECIOUS.
SO IT CAN'T BE ANY OTHER WAY. IF SOMEBODY HITS ME, I'M GONNA BEAT THEM UP. IF SOMEBODY MOCKS ME, I'M GONNA BEAT THEM UP, TOO.
I DON'T KNOW WHEN I CAN BECOME MILD, BUT I'M NOT AT ALL ASHAMED THAT I AM AN ATTACK DOG.
YEAH, THAT'S OOYA.
SO DON'T BLAME YOURSELF FOR NO REASON, MR. PILDO JUNG. NO MATTER WHAT, YOU ARE THE ONLY PERSON WHO TREATED ME LIKE A WOMAN. I'M THANKFUL.

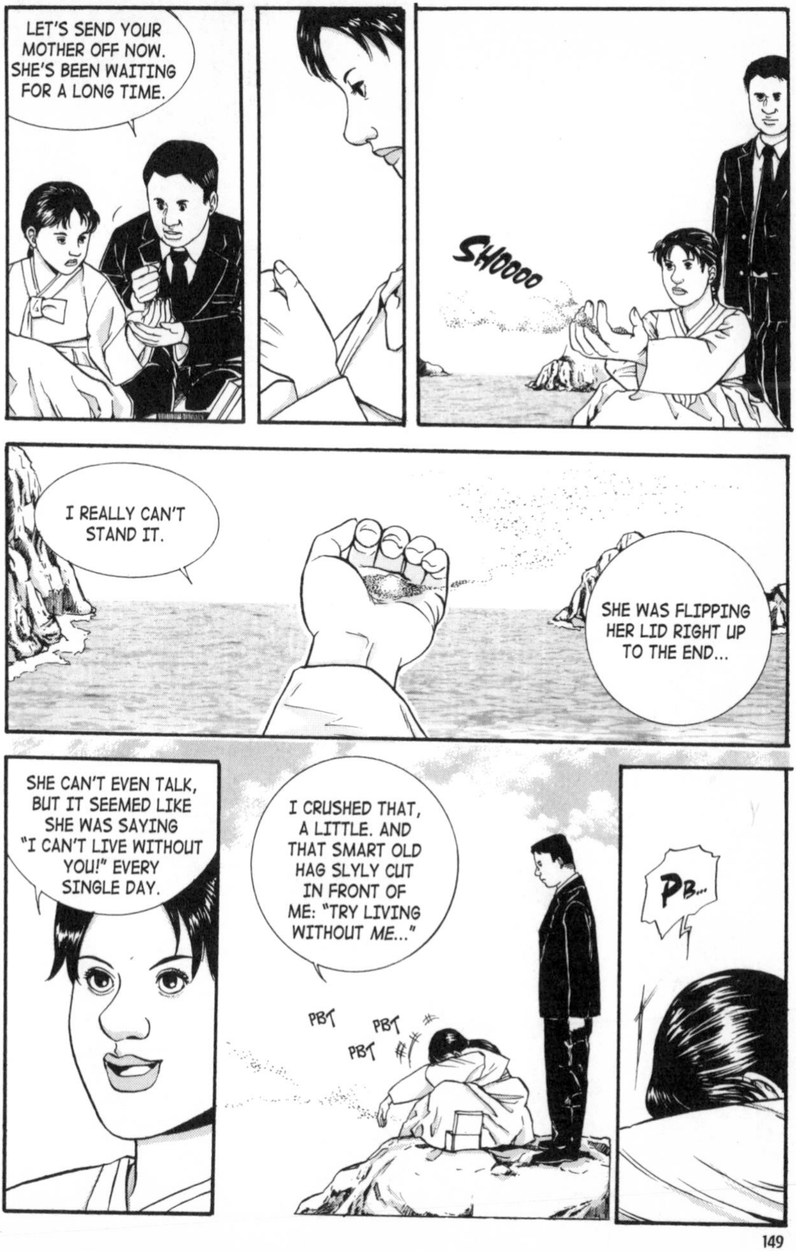
LET'S SEND YOUR MOTHER OFF NOW. SHE'S BEEN WAITING FOR A LONG TIME.
SHOOOO
I REALLY CAN'T STAND IT.
SHE WAS FLIPPING HER LID RIGHT UP TO THE END...
SHE CAN'T EVEN TALK, BUT IT SEEMED LIKE SHE WAS SAYING "I CAN'T LIVE WITHOUT YOU!" EVERY SINGLE DAY.
I CRUSHED THAT, A LITTLE. AND THAT SMART OLD HAG SLYLY CUT IN FRONT OF ME: "TRY LIVING WITHOUT ME..."
PBT
PBT
PBT
PB...

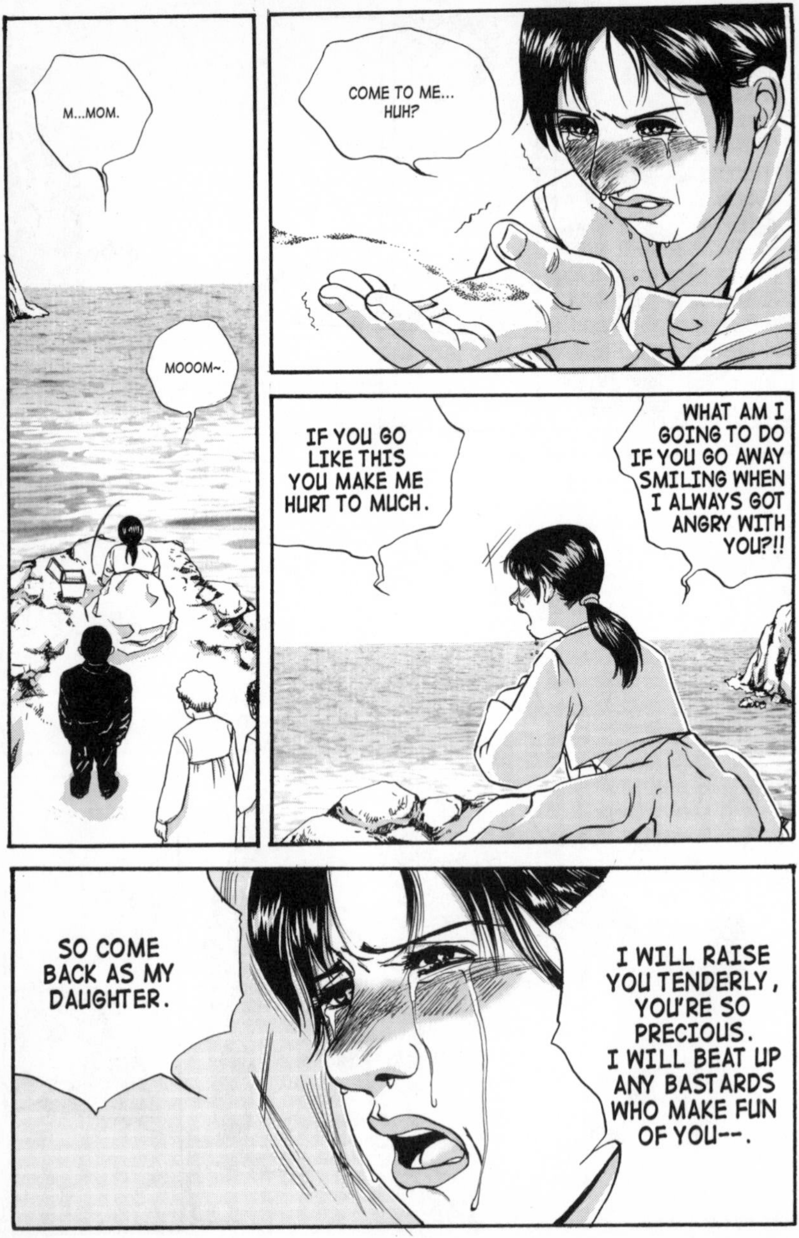
M...MOM.
MOOOM~.
COME TO ME... HUH?
WHAT AM I GOING TO DO IF YOU GO AWAY SMILING WHEN I ALWAYS GOT ANGRY WITH YOU?!!
IF YOU GO LIKE THIS YOU MAKE ME HURT TO MUCH.
SO COME BACK AS MY DAUGHTER.
I WILL RAISE YOU TENDERLY, YOU'RE SO PRECIOUS. I WILL BEAT UP ANY BASTARDS WHO MAKE FUN OF YOU--.

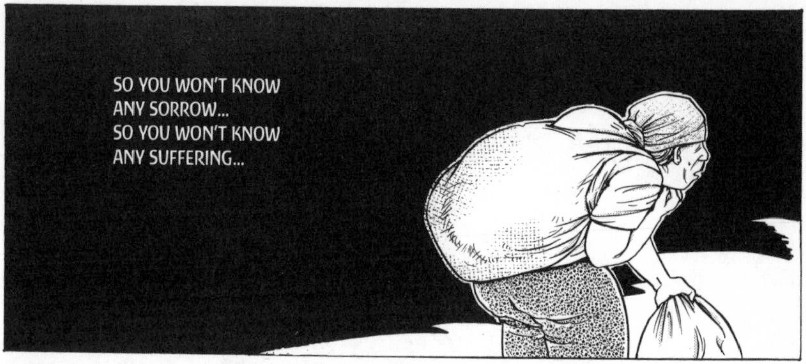
SO YOU WON'T KNOW
ANY SORROW...
SO YOU WON'T KNOW
ANY SUFFERING...

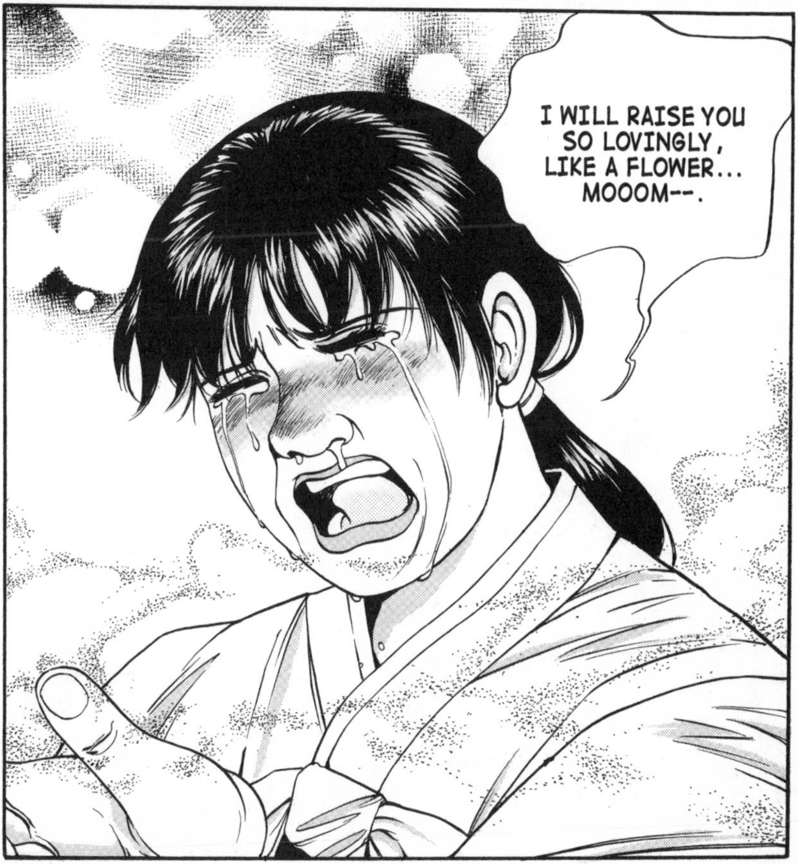
I WILL RAISE YOU
SO LOVINGLY,
LIKE A FLOWER...
MOOOM--.

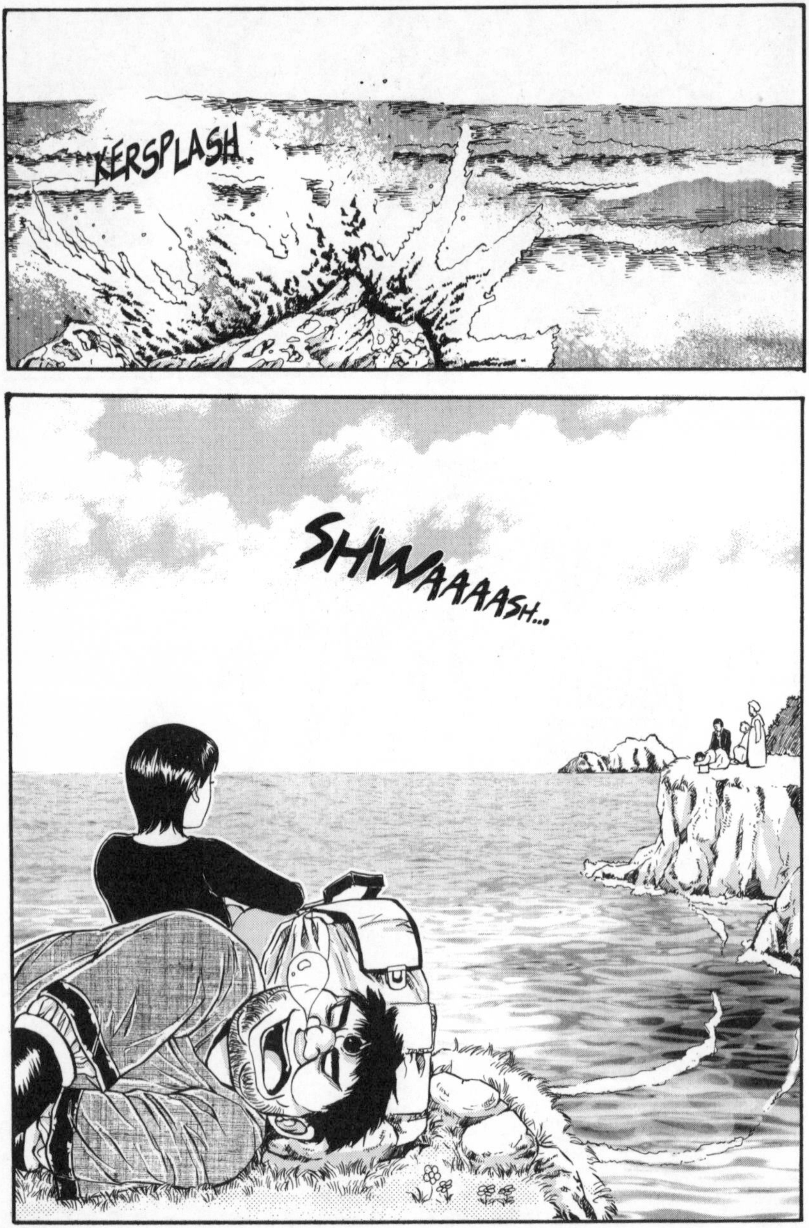
KERSPLASH
SHWAAAAASH...

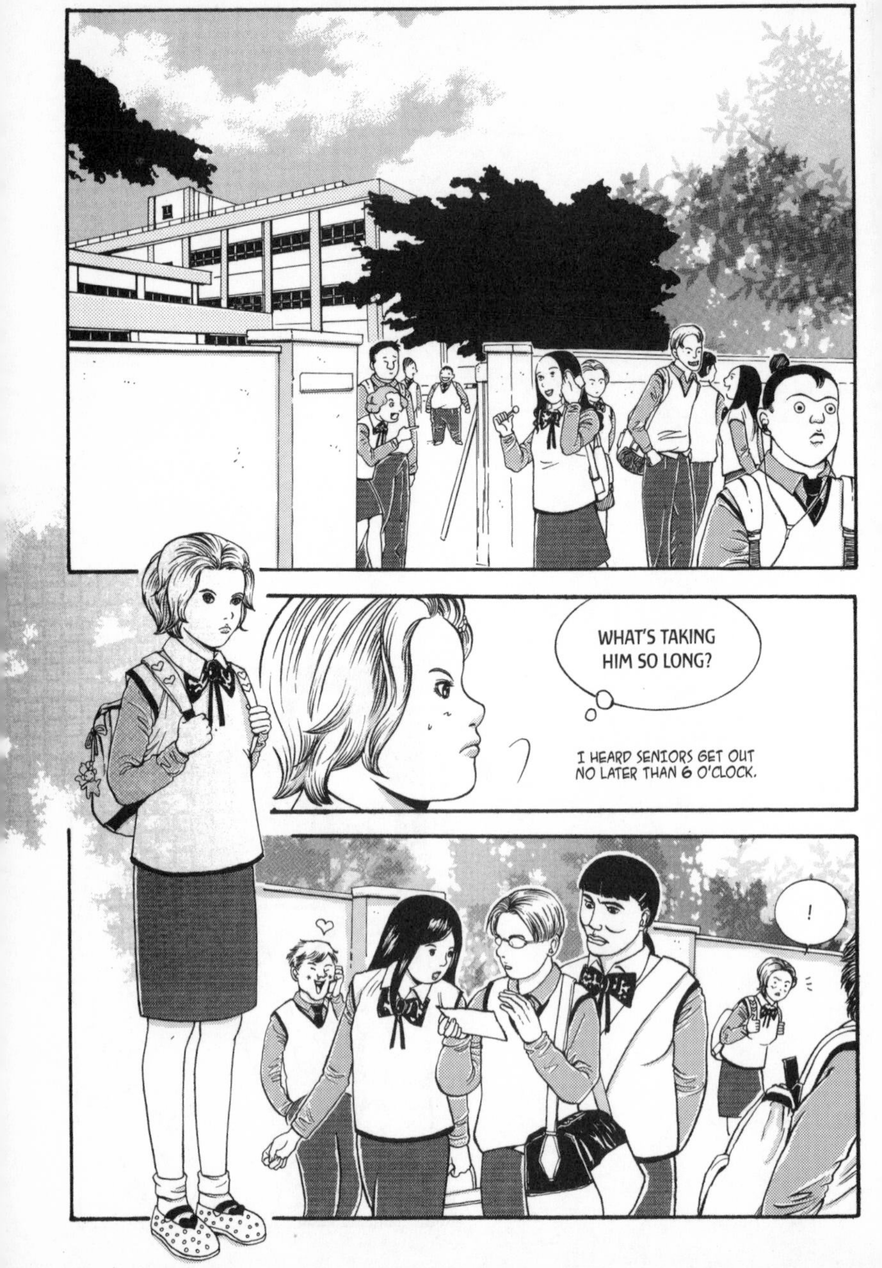
WHAT'S TAKING HIM SO LONG?
I HEARD SENIORS GET OUT NO LATER THAN 6 O'CLOCK.
!

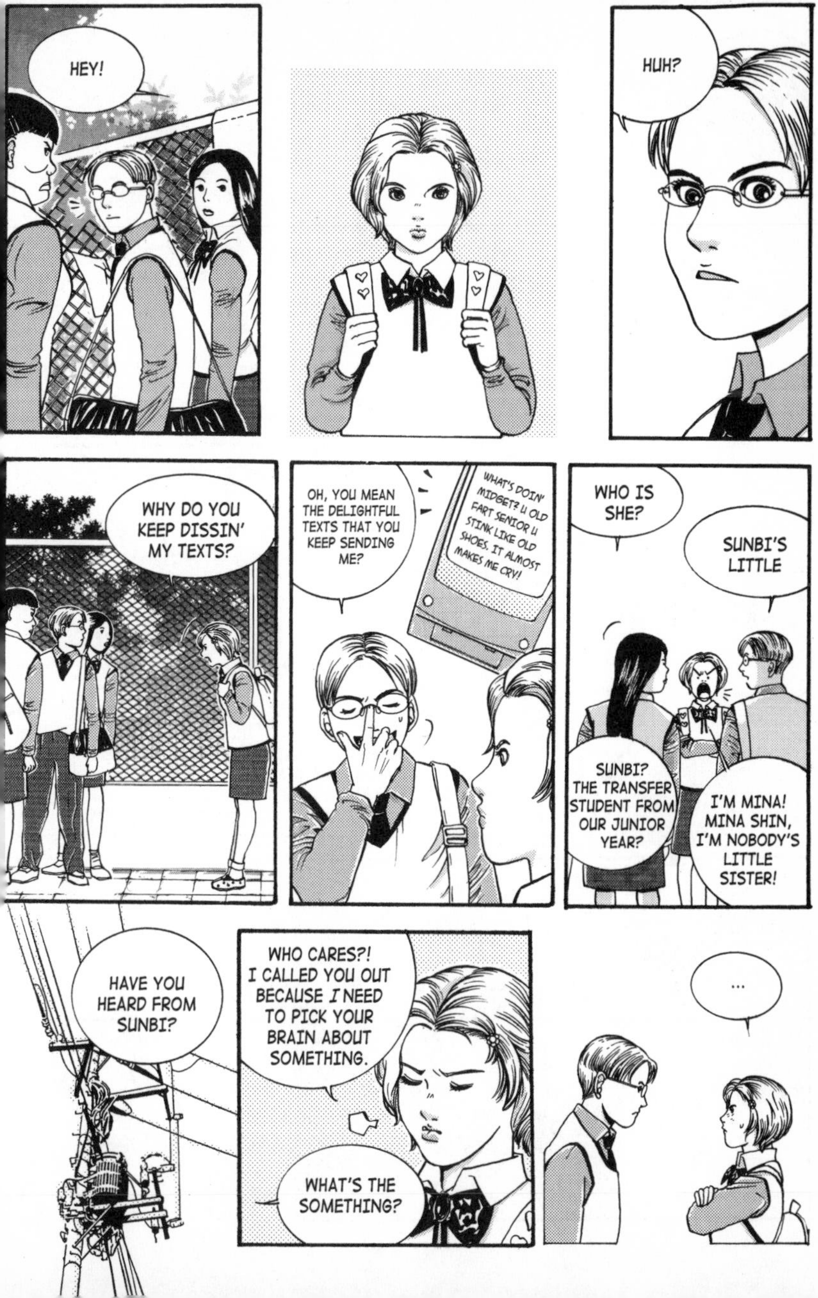
HEY!
HUH?
WHY DO YOU KEEP DISSIN' MY TEXTS?
OH, YOU MEAN THE DELIGHTFUL TEXTS THAT YOU KEEP SENDING ME?
WHAT'S DOIN' MIDGET? U OLD FART SENIOR U STINK LIKE OLD SHOES. IT ALMOST MAKES ME CRY!
WHO IS SHE?
SUNBI'S LITTLE
SUNBI? THE TRANSFER STUDENT FROM OUR JUNIOR YEAR?
I'M MINA! MINA SHIN, I'M NOBODY'S LITTLE SISTER!
HAVE YOU HEARD FROM SUNBI?
WHO CARES?! I CALLED YOU OUT BECAUSE I NEED TO PICK YOUR BRAIN ABOUT SOMETHING.
WHAT'S THE SOMETHING?
...

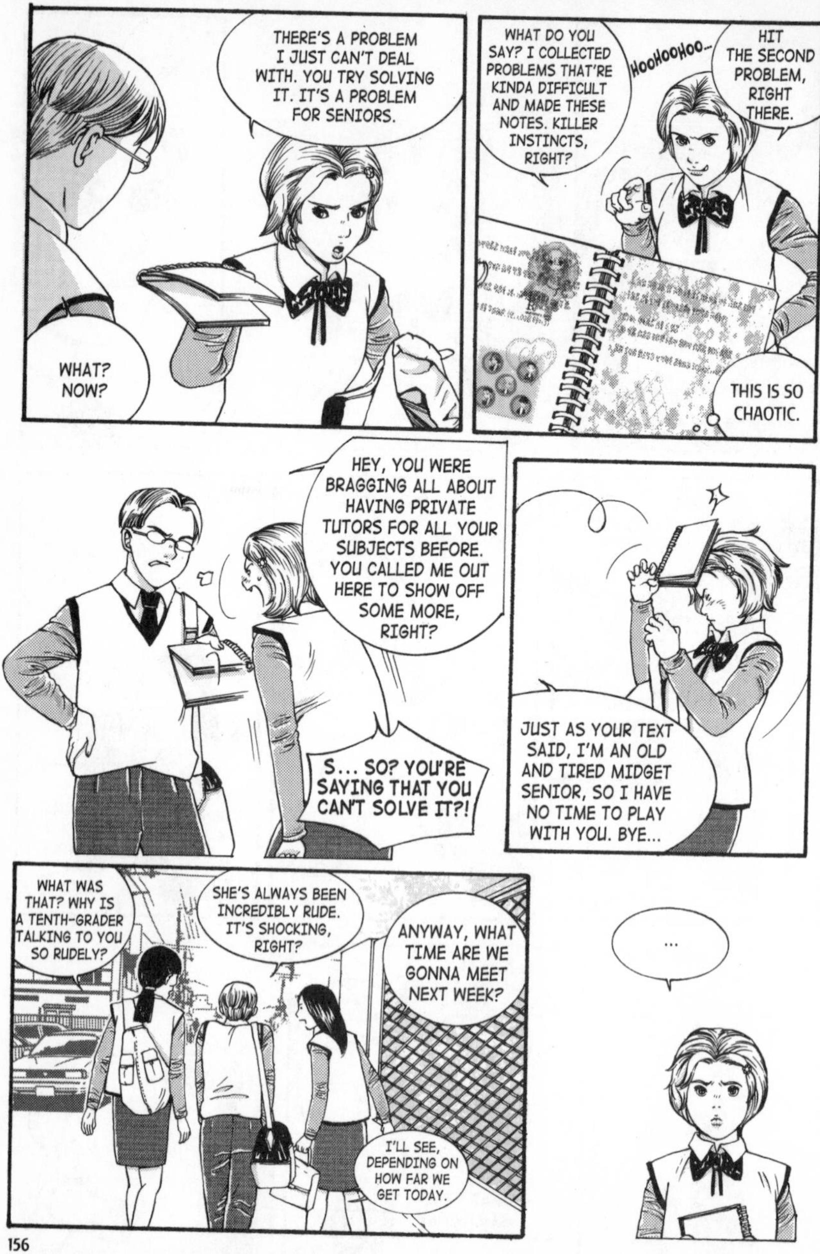
THERE'S A PROBLEM I JUST CAN'T DEAL WITH. YOU TRY SOLVING IT. IT'S A PROBLEM FOR SENIORS.
WHAT? NOW?
WHAT DO YOU SAY? I COLLECTED PROBLEMS THAT'RE KINDA DIFFICULT AND MADE THESE NOTES. KILLER INSTINCTS, RIGHT?
HOOHOOHOO...
HIT THE SECOND PROBLEM, RIGHT THERE.
THIS IS SO CHAOTIC.
HEY, YOU WERE BRAGGING ALL ABOUT HAVING PRIVATE TUTORS FOR ALL YOUR SUBJECTS BEFORE. YOU CALLED ME OUT HERE TO SHOW OFF SOME MORE, RIGHT?
S... SO? YOU'RE SAYING THAT YOU CAN'T SOLVE IT?!
JUST AS YOUR TEXT SAID, I'M AN OLD AND TIRED MIDGET SENIOR, SO I HAVE NO TIME TO PLAY WITH YOU. BYE...
WHAT WAS THAT? WHY IS A TENTH-GRADER TALKING TO YOU SO RUDELY?
SHE'S ALWAYS BEEN INCREDIBLY RUDE. IT'S SHOCKING, RIGHT?
ANYWAY, WHAT TIME ARE WE GONNA MEET NEXT WEEK?
I'LL SEE, DEPENDING ON HOW FAR WE GET TODAY.
...

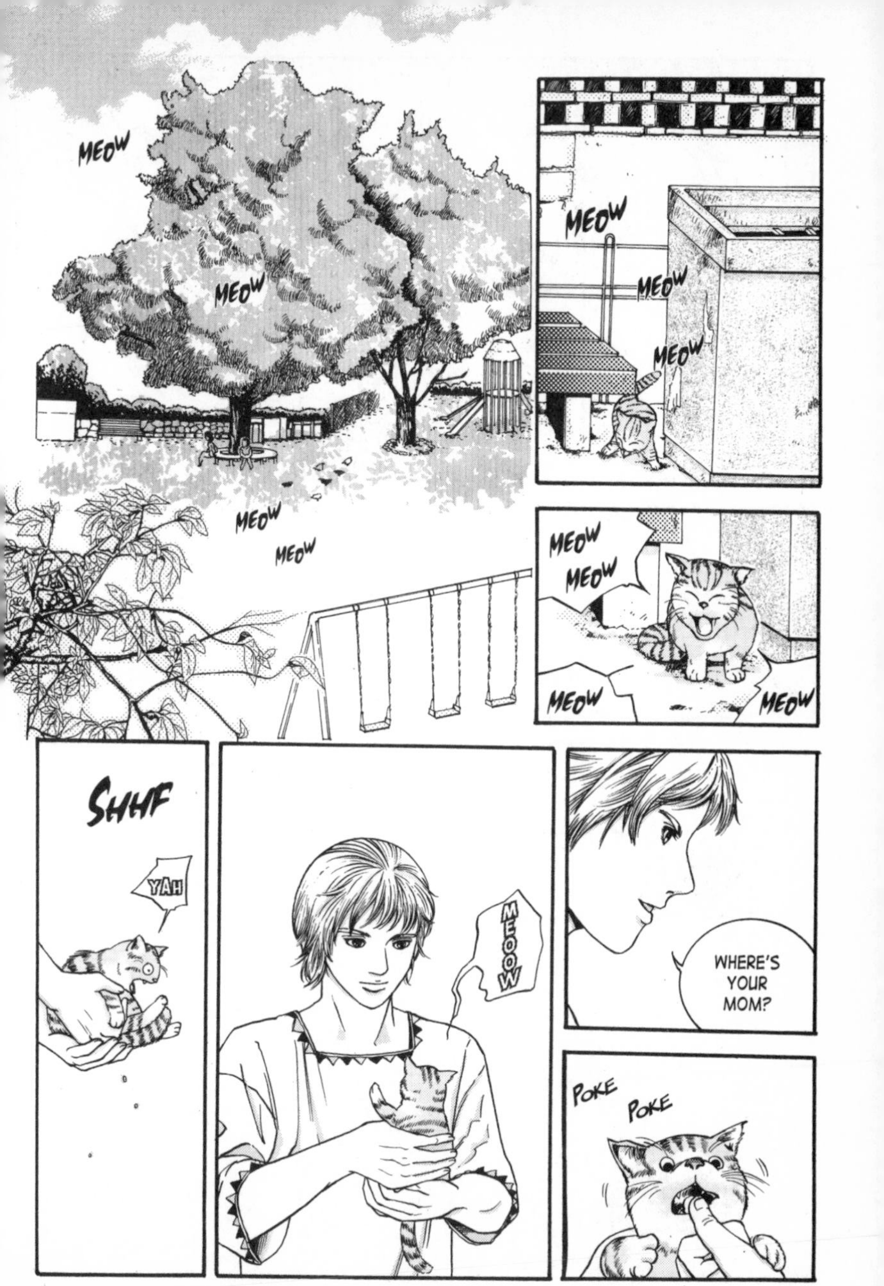
MEOW
MEOW
MEOW
MEOW
MEOW
MEOW
MEOW
MEOW
MEOW
MEOW
MEOW
SHHF
YAH
MEOOW
WHERE'S YOUR MOM?
POKE
POKE

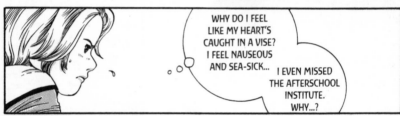

WHY DO I FEEL LIKE MY HEART'S CAUGHT IN A VISE? I FEEL NAUSEOUS AND SEA-SICK... I EVEN MISSED THE AFTERSCHOOL INSTITUTE. WHY...?

DAMN.

MEOW

MEOW

MEOW! MEOW!

MEOW!

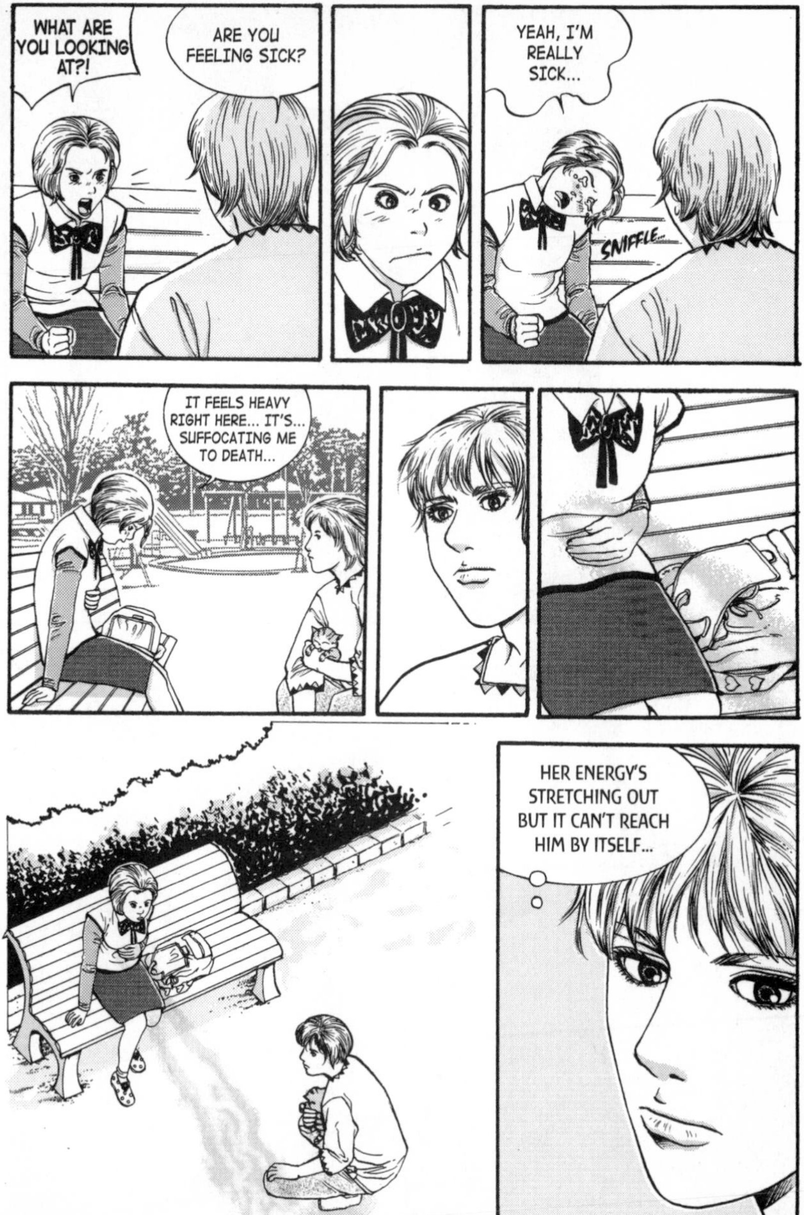
WHAT ARE YOU LOOKING AT?!
ARE YOU FEELING SICK?
YEAH, I'M REALLY SICK...
SNIFFLE...
IT FEELS HEAVY RIGHT HERE... IT'S... SUFFOCATING ME TO DEATH...
HER ENERGY'S STRETCHING OUT BUT IT CAN'T REACH HIM BY ITSELF...

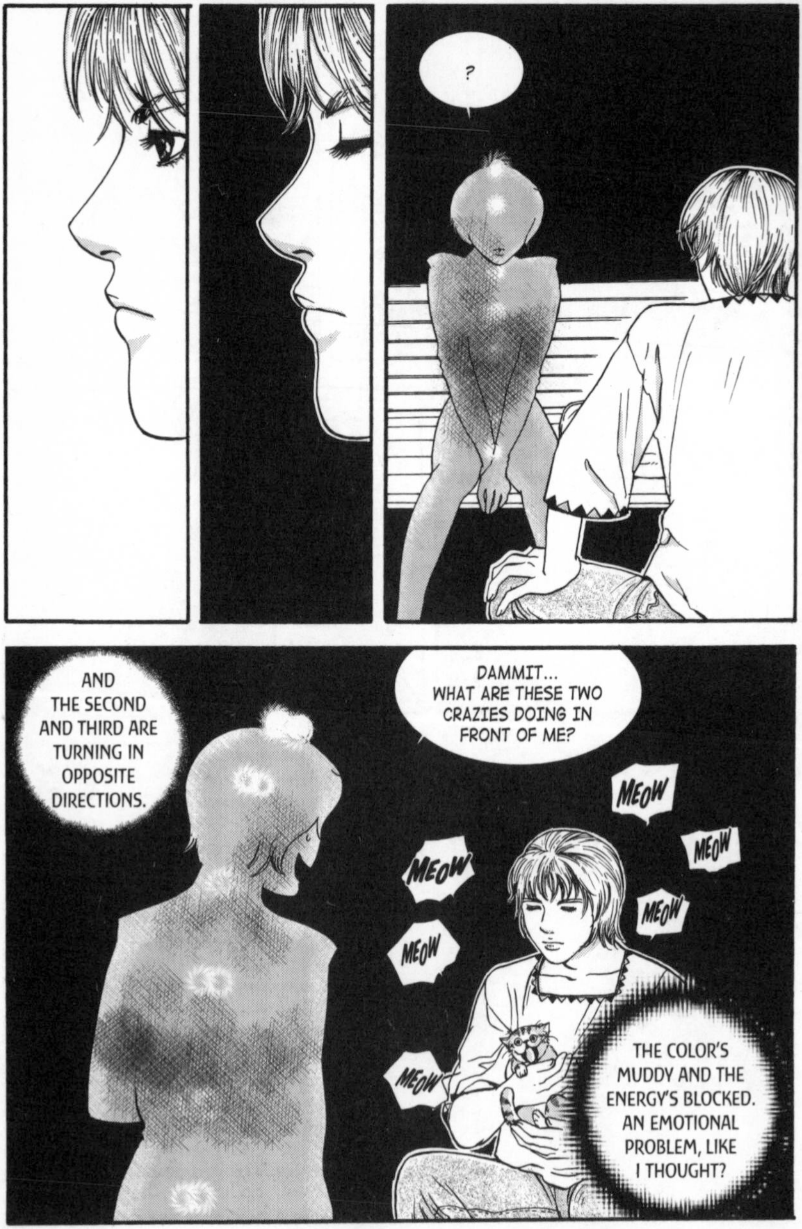
?
AND THE SECOND AND THIRD ARE TURNING IN OPPOSITE DIRECTIONS.
DAMMIT... WHAT ARE THESE TWO CRAZIES DOING IN FRONT OF ME?
MEOW
MEOW
MEOW
MEOW
MEOW
MEOW
THE COLOR'S MUDDY AND THE ENERGY'S BLOCKED. AN EMOTIONAL PROBLEM, LIKE I THOUGHT?

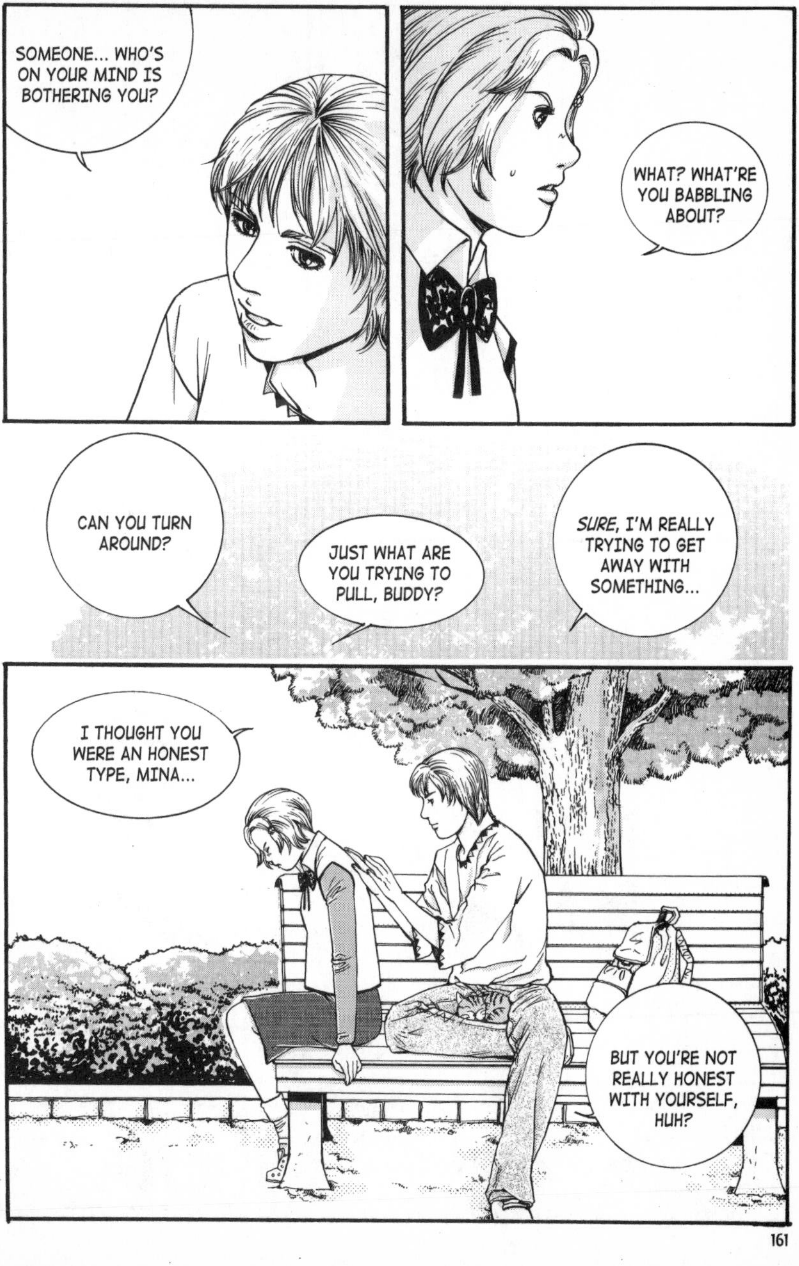
SOMEONE... WHO'S ON YOUR MIND IS BOTHERING YOU?
WHAT? WHAT'RE YOU BABBLING ABOUT?
CAN YOU TURN AROUND?
JUST WHAT ARE YOU TRYING TO PULL, BUDDY?
SURE, I'M REALLY TRYING TO GET AWAY WITH SOMETHING...
I THOUGHT YOU WERE AN HONEST TYPE, MINA...
BUT YOU'RE NOT REALLY HONEST WITH YOURSELF, HUH?

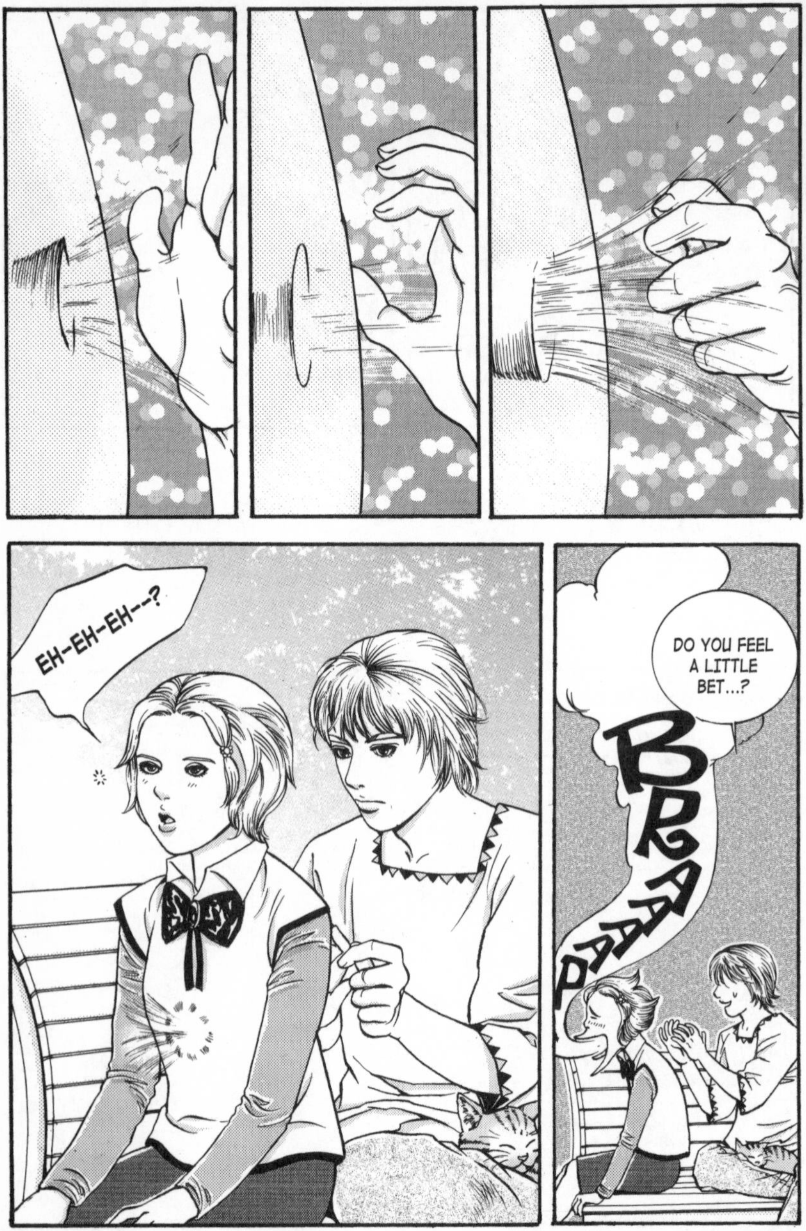
EH-EH-EH--?
DO YOU FEEL A LITTLE BET...?
BRAAAAP

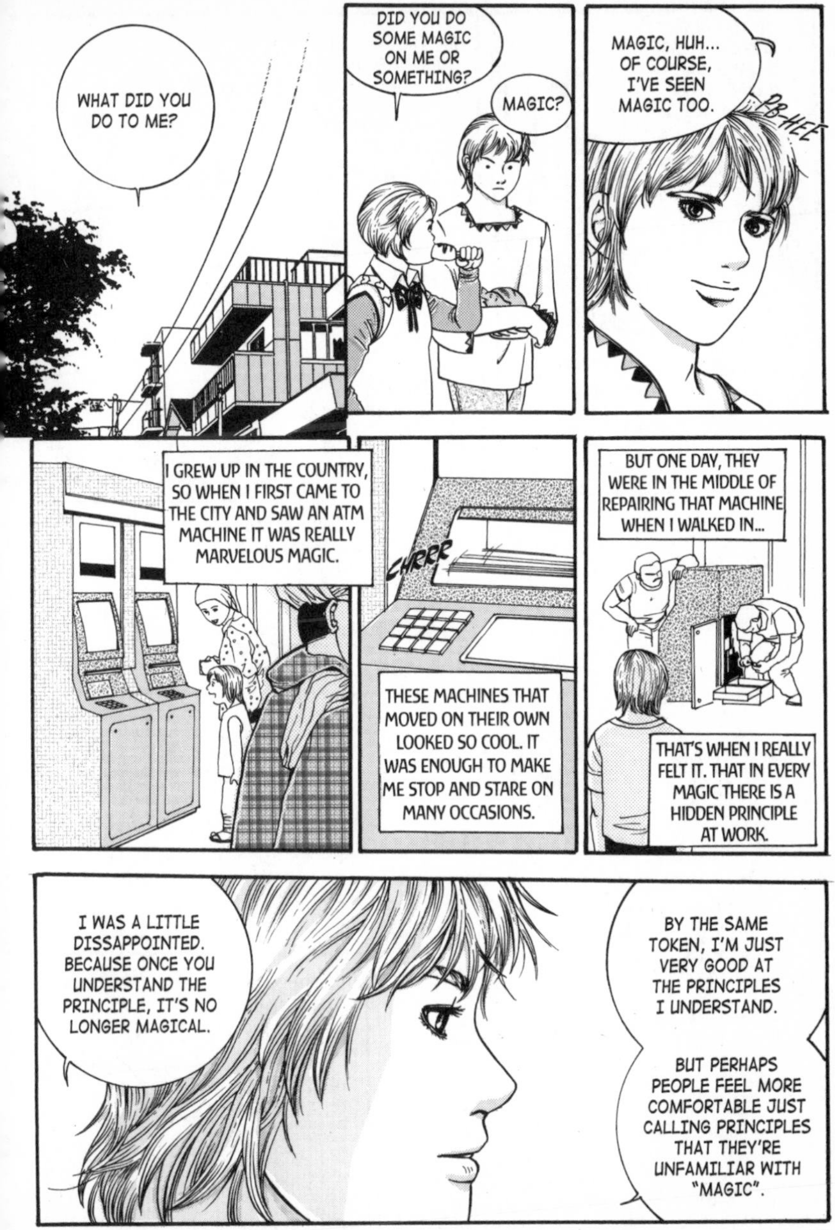
WHAT DID YOU DO TO ME?
DID YOU DO SOME MAGIC ON ME OR SOMETHING?
MAGIC?
MAGIC, HUH... OF COURSE, I'VE SEEN MAGIC TOO.
PB-HEE
I GREW UP IN THE COUNTRY, SO WHEN I FIRST CAME TO THE CITY AND SAW AN ATM MACHINE IT WAS REALLY MARVELOUS MAGIC.
CHRRR
THESE MACHINES THAT MOVED ON THEIR OWN LOOKED SO COOL. IT WAS ENOUGH TO MAKE ME STOP AND STARE ON MANY OCCASIONS.
BUT ONE DAY, THEY WERE IN THE MIDDLE OF REPAIRING THAT MACHINE WHEN I WALKED IN...
THAT'S WHEN I REALLY FELT IT. THAT IN EVERY MAGIC THERE IS A HIDDEN PRINCIPLE AT WORK.
I WAS A LITTLE DISSAPPOINTED. BECAUSE ONCE YOU UNDERSTAND THE PRINCIPLE, IT'S NO LONGER MAGICAL.
BY THE SAME TOKEN, I'M JUST VERY GOOD AT THE PRINCIPLES I UNDERSTAND.
BUT PERHAPS PEOPLE FEEL MORE COMFORTABLE JUST CALLING PRINCIPLES THAT THEY'RE UNFAMILIAR WITH "MAGIC".

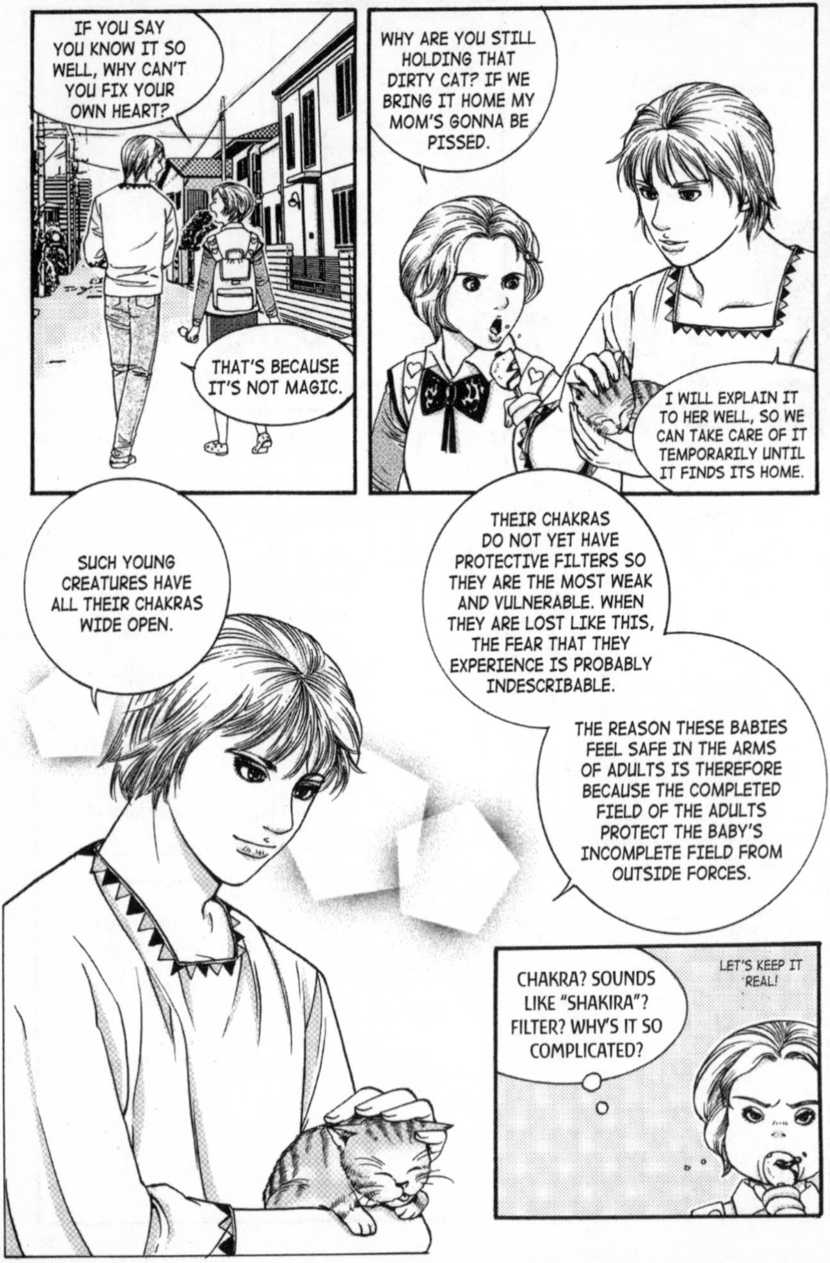
IF YOU SAY YOU KNOW IT SO WELL, WHY CAN'T YOU FIX YOUR OWN HEART?
THAT'S BECAUSE IT'S NOT MAGIC.
WHY ARE YOU STILL HOLDING THAT DIRTY CAT? IF WE BRING IT HOME MY MOM'S GONNA BE PISSED.
I WILL EXPLAIN IT TO HER WELL, SO WE CAN TAKE CARE OF IT TEMPORARILY UNTIL IT FINDS ITS HOME.
SUCH YOUNG CREATURES HAVE ALL THEIR CHAKRAS WIDE OPEN.
THEIR CHAKRAS DO NOT YET HAVE PROTECTIVE FILTERS SO THEY ARE THE MOST WEAK AND VULNERABLE. WHEN THEY ARE LOST LIKE THIS, THE FEAR THAT THEY EXPERIENCE IS PROBABLY INDESCRIBABLE.
THE REASON THESE BABIES FEEL SAFE IN THE ARMS OF ADULTS IS THEREFORE BECAUSE THE COMPLETED FIELD OF THE ADULTS PROTECT THE BABY'S INCOMPLETE FIELD FROM OUTSIDE FORCES.
CHAKRA? SOUNDS LIKE "SHAKIRA"? FILTER? WHY'S IT SO COMPLICATED?
LET'S KEEP IT REAL!

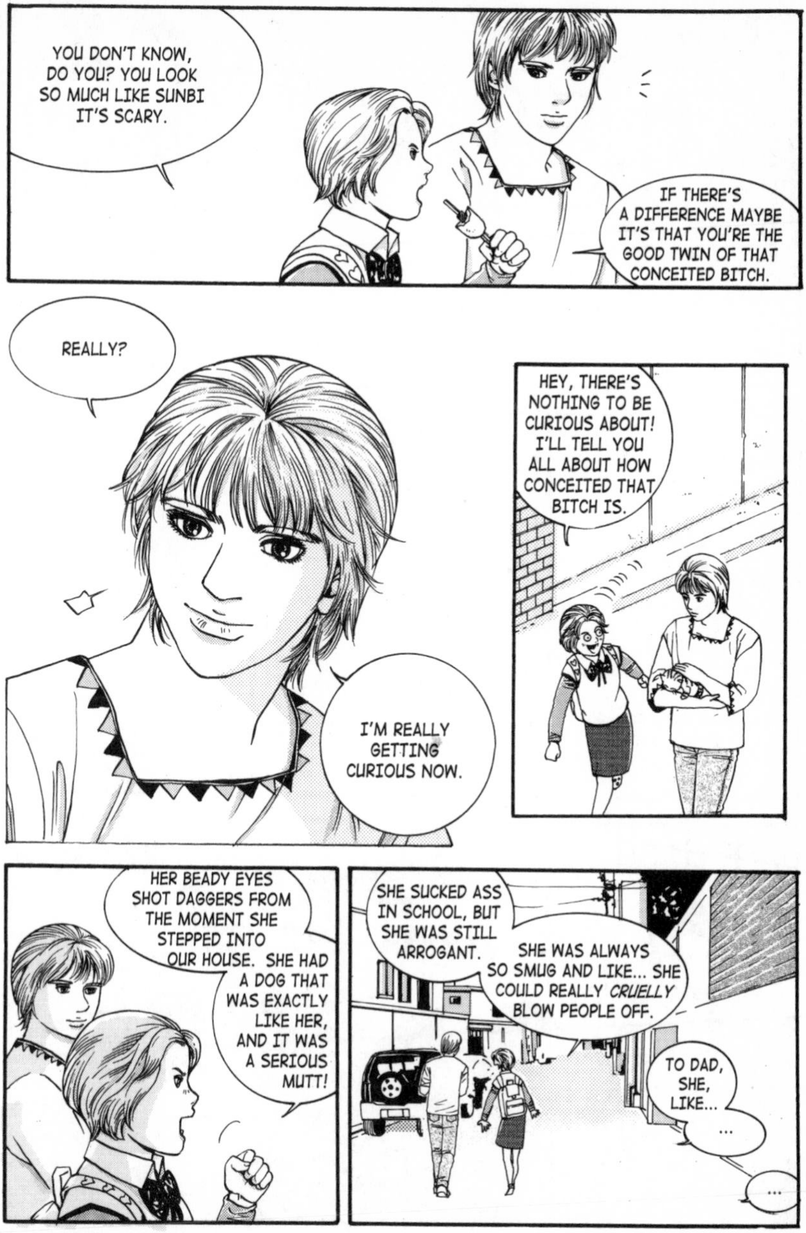
YOU DON'T KNOW, DO YOU? YOU LOOK SO MUCH LIKE SUNBI IT'S SCARY.
IF THERE'S A DIFFERENCE MAYBE IT'S THAT YOU'RE THE GOOD TWIN OF THAT CONCEITED BITCH.
REALLY?
I'M REALLY GETTING CURIOUS NOW.
HEY, THERE'S NOTHING TO BE CURIOUS ABOUT! I'LL TELL YOU ALL ABOUT HOW CONCEITED THAT BITCH IS.
HER BEADY EYES SHOT DAGGERS FROM THE MOMENT SHE STEPPED INTO OUR HOUSE. SHE HAD A DOG THAT WAS EXACTLY LIKE HER, AND IT WAS A SERIOUS MUTT!
SHE SUCKED ASS IN SCHOOL, BUT SHE WAS STILL ARROGANT.
SHE WAS ALWAYS SO SMUG AND LIKE... SHE COULD REALLY *CRUELLY* BLOW PEOPLE OFF.
TO DAD, SHE, LIKE...
...
...

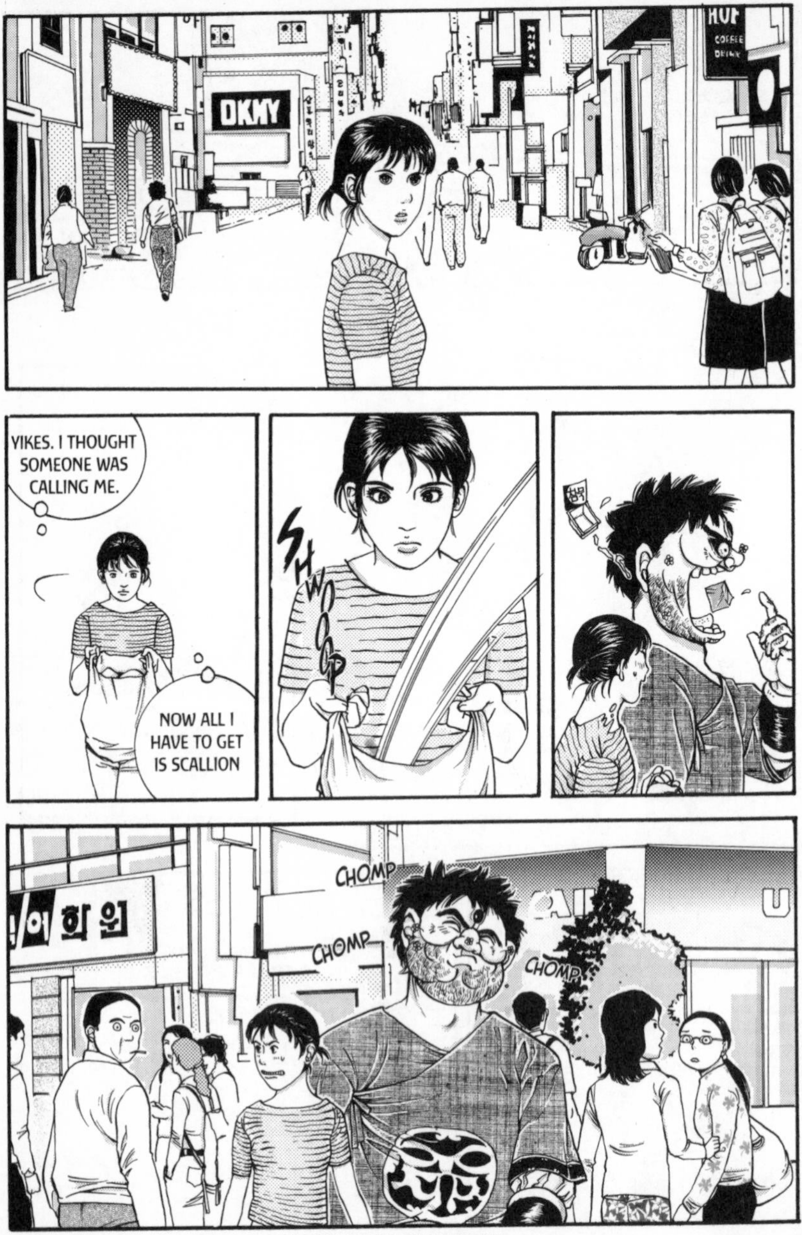
DKNY
COFFEE
YIKES. I THOUGHT SOMEONE WAS CALLING ME.
NOW ALL I HAVE TO GET IS SCALLION
SHWOOOP
CHOMP
CHOMP
CHOMP

* THE PACKAGE LABEL IN THE FOURTH PANEL READS "PURE JELLY"

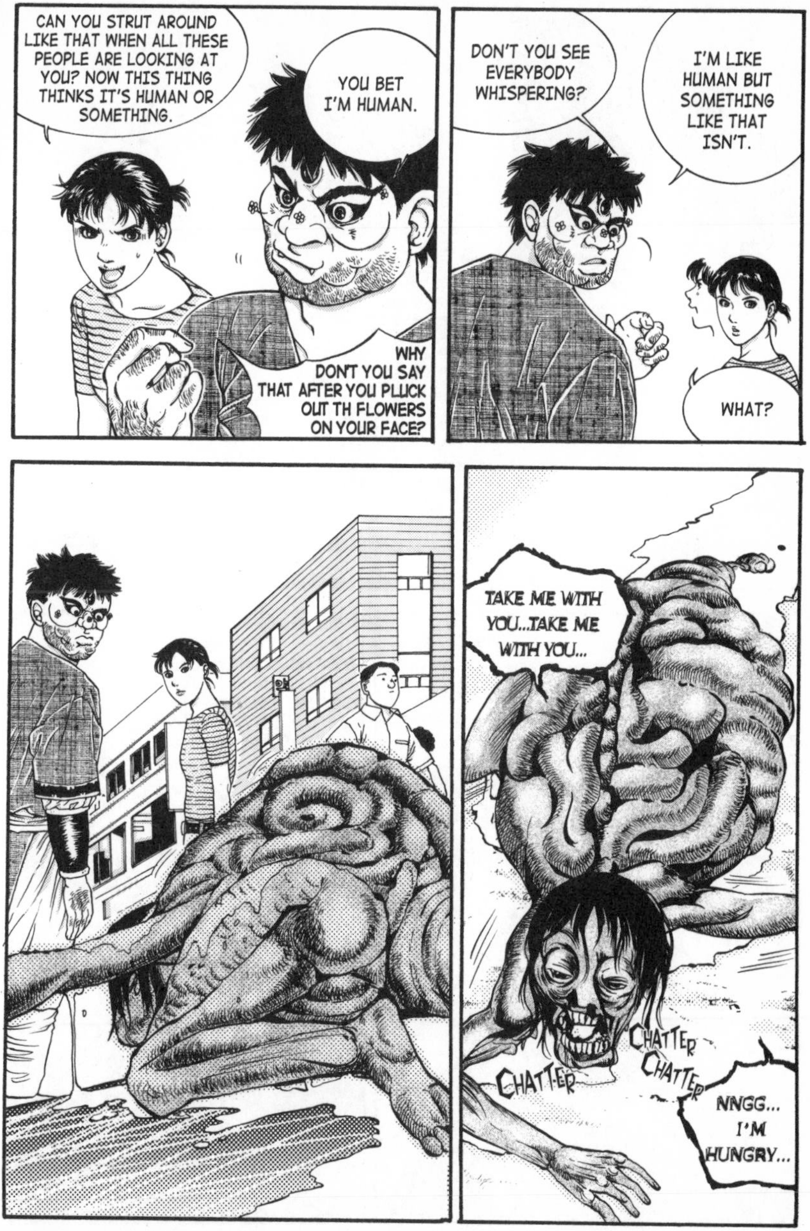
CAN YOU STRUT AROUND LIKE THAT WHEN ALL THESE PEOPLE ARE LOOKING AT YOU? NOW THIS THING THINKS IT'S HUMAN OR SOMETHING.
YOU BET I'M HUMAN.
WHY DON'T YOU SAY THAT AFTER YOU PLUCK OUT TH FLOWERS ON YOUR FACE?
DON'T YOU SEE EVERYBODY WHISPERING?
I'M LIKE HUMAN BUT SOMETHING LIKE THAT ISN'T.
WHAT?
TAKE ME WITH YOU...TAKE ME WITH YOU...
CHATTER
CHATTER
CHATTER
NNGG... I'M HUNGRY...

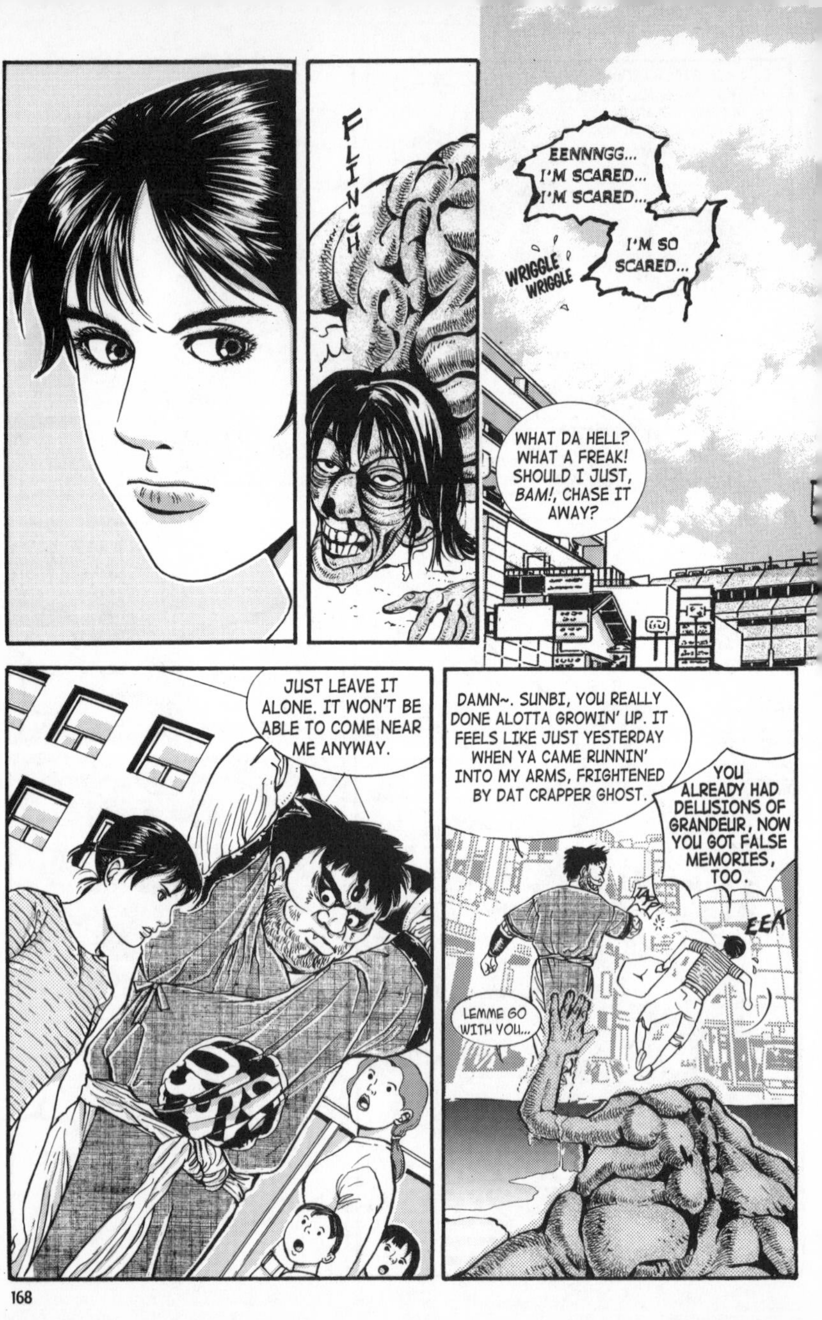
FLINCH
EENNNGG... I'M SCARED... I'M SCARED...
I'M SO SCARED...
WRIGGLE WRIGGLE
WHAT DA HELL? WHAT A FREAK! SHOULD I JUST, BAM!, CHASE IT AWAY?
JUST LEAVE IT ALONE. IT WON'T BE ABLE TO COME NEAR ME ANYWAY.
DAMN~. SUNBI, YOU REALLY DONE ALOTTA GROWIN' UP. IT FEELS LIKE JUST YESTERDAY WHEN YA CAME RUNNIN' INTO MY ARMS, FRIGHTENED BY DAT CRAPPER GHOST.
YOU ALREADY HAD DELUSIONS OF GRANDEUR, NOW YOU GOT FALSE MEMORIES, TOO.
EEK
LEMME GO WITH YOU...

HA HA HA HA...

THAT MAKES NO SENSE.

NO CENTS? DOES IT MAKE ANY DIMES?

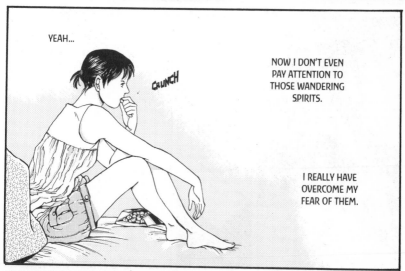

YEAH...

CRUNCH

NOW I DON'T EVEN PAY ATTENTION TO THOSE WANDERING SPIRITS.

I REALLY HAVE OVERCOME MY FEAR OF THEM.

* THE SIGN READS "HYOSUNG STATE EXAM PREPARATION INSTITUTE, 3RD AND 4TH FLOORS"

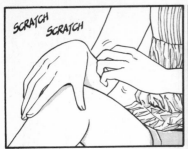

SCRATCH
SCRATCH

SCRATCH

SKRT
SKRT
SKRT
SKRT

I DON'T KNOW HOW YOU SURVIVE AS A COMEDIAN WITH THAT KIND OF JOKE...

OUCH!

OH NO, I'M BLEEDING... IT'S COMPLETELY SWOLLEN UP. HOW STUPID...

THAT ARM, YOUR BODY REMEMBERS IT, SEE?

STOP, LET'S STOP THINKING ABOUT THAT.

I'D HAVE TO BE STUPID TO PLAY ALONG WITH THAT KIND OF TRICK AGAIN.

CHIKA
CHIKA

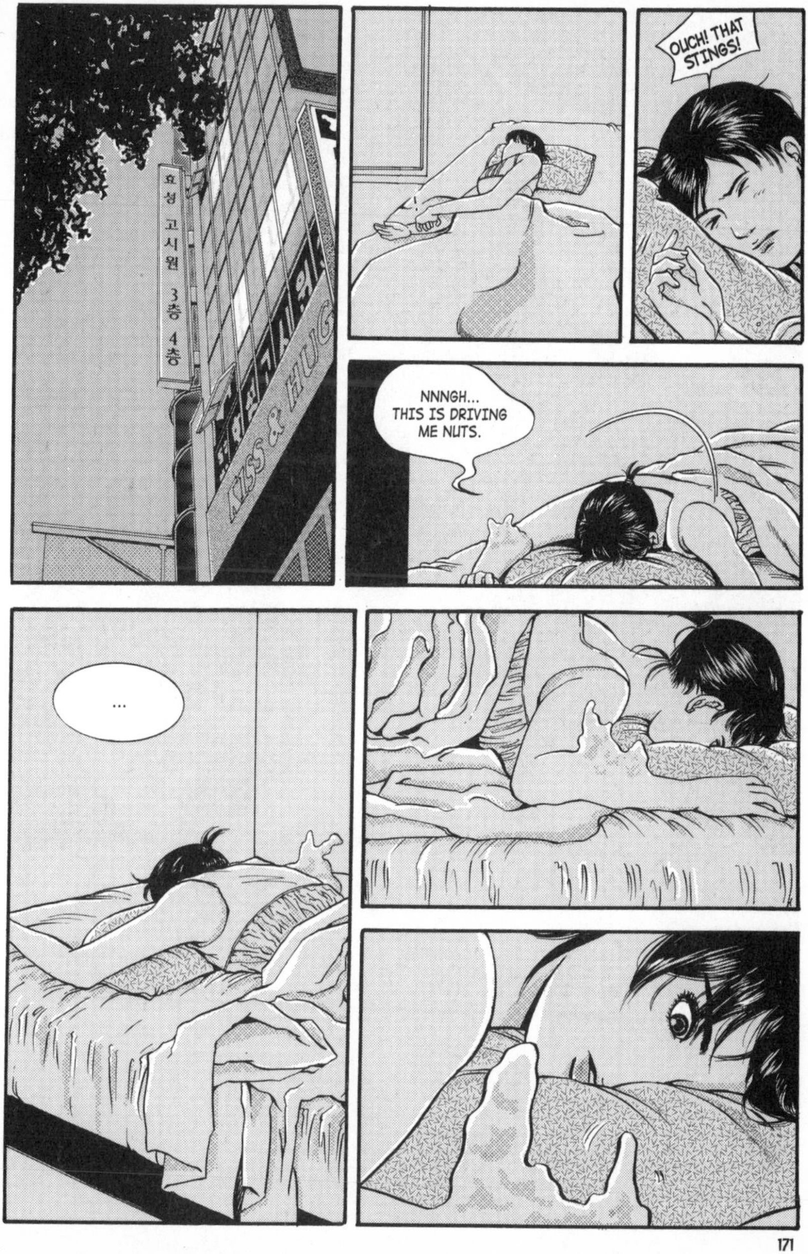
효성 고시원 3층 4층
KISS & HUG
OUCH! THAT STINGS!
NNNGH... THIS IS DRIVING ME NUTS.
...

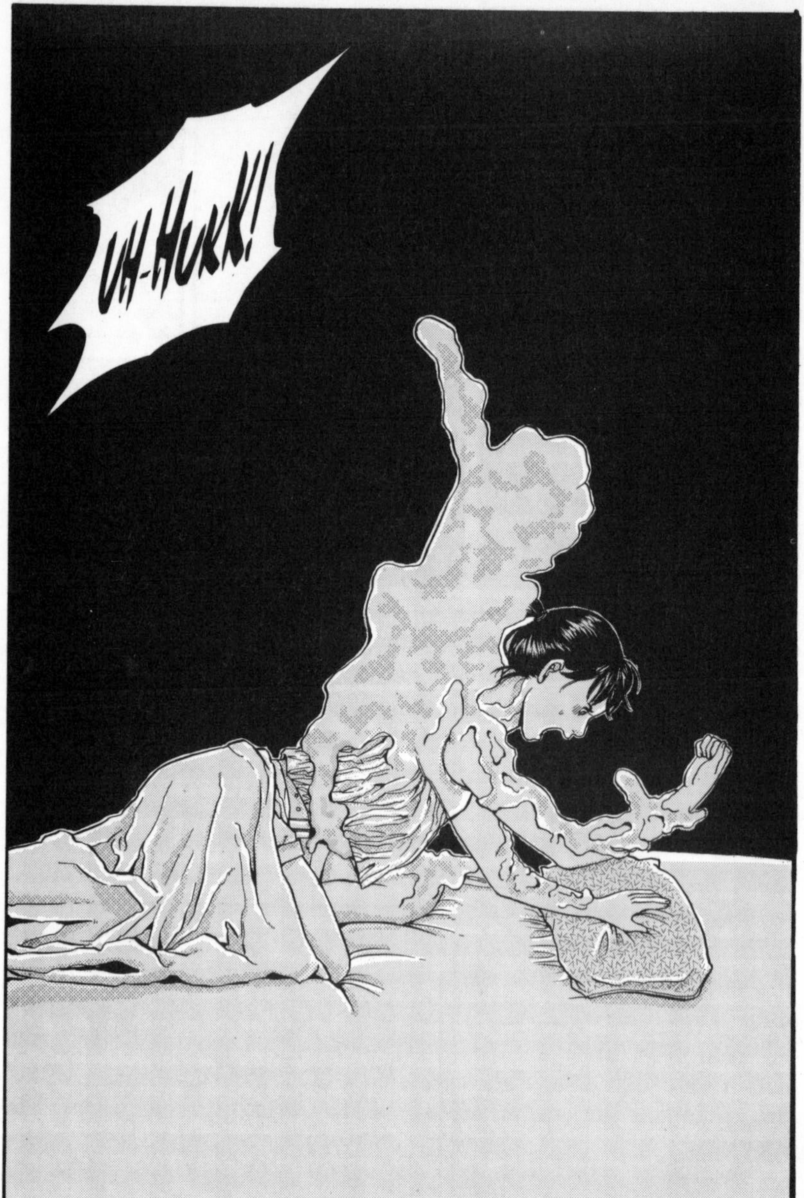
UH-HUKK!!

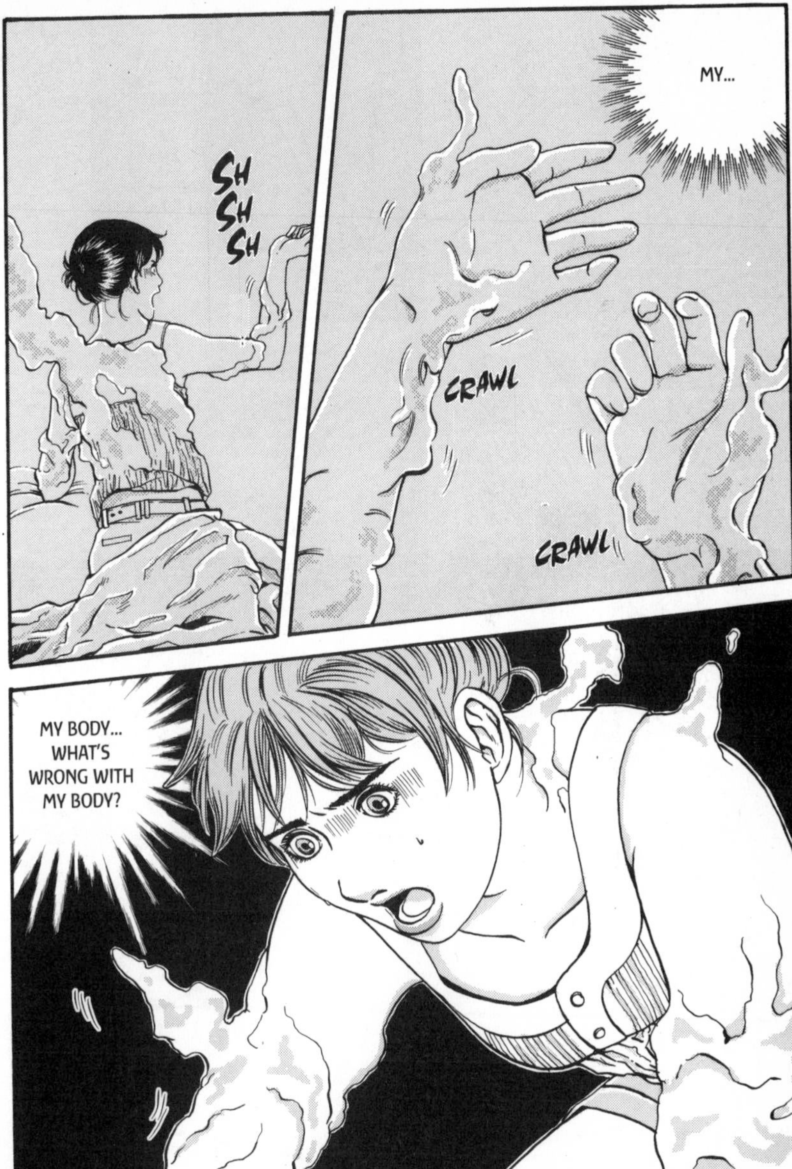
SH
SH
SH
MY...
CRAWL
CRAWL
MY BODY... WHAT'S WRONG WITH MY BODY?

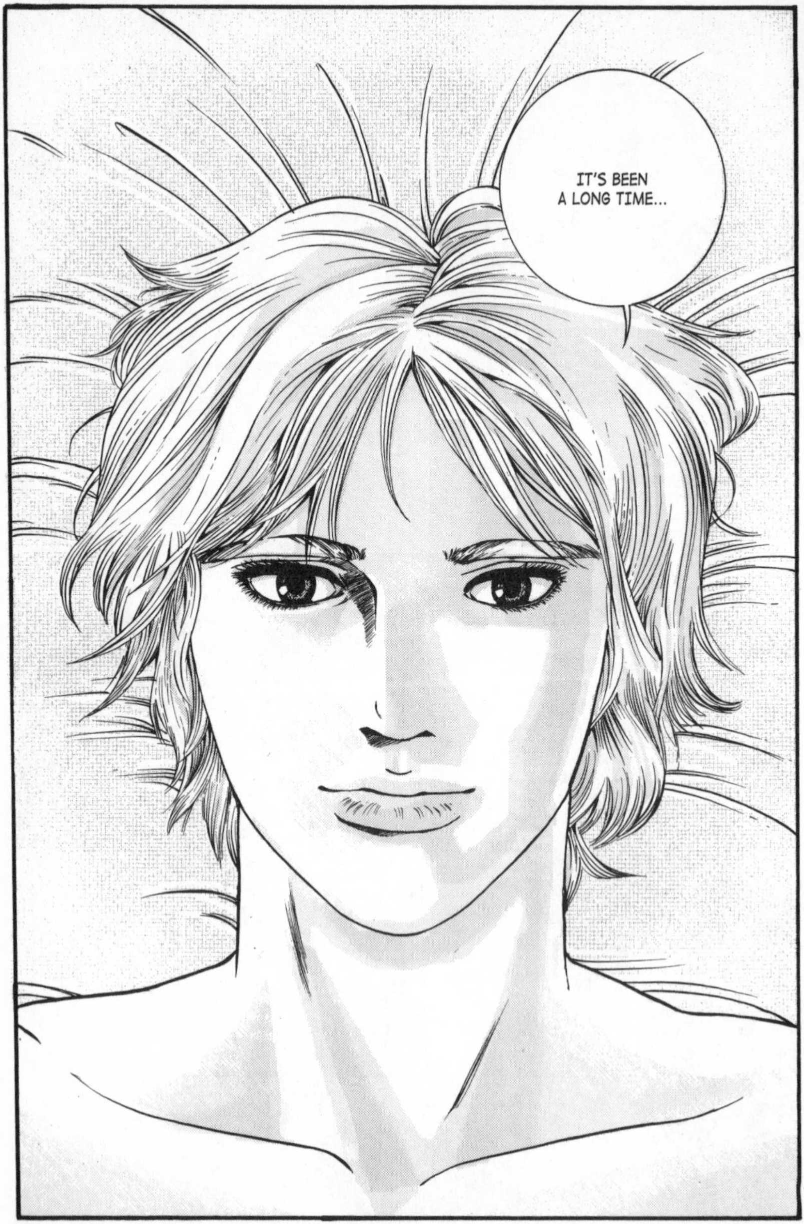
IT'S BEEN
A LONG TIME...

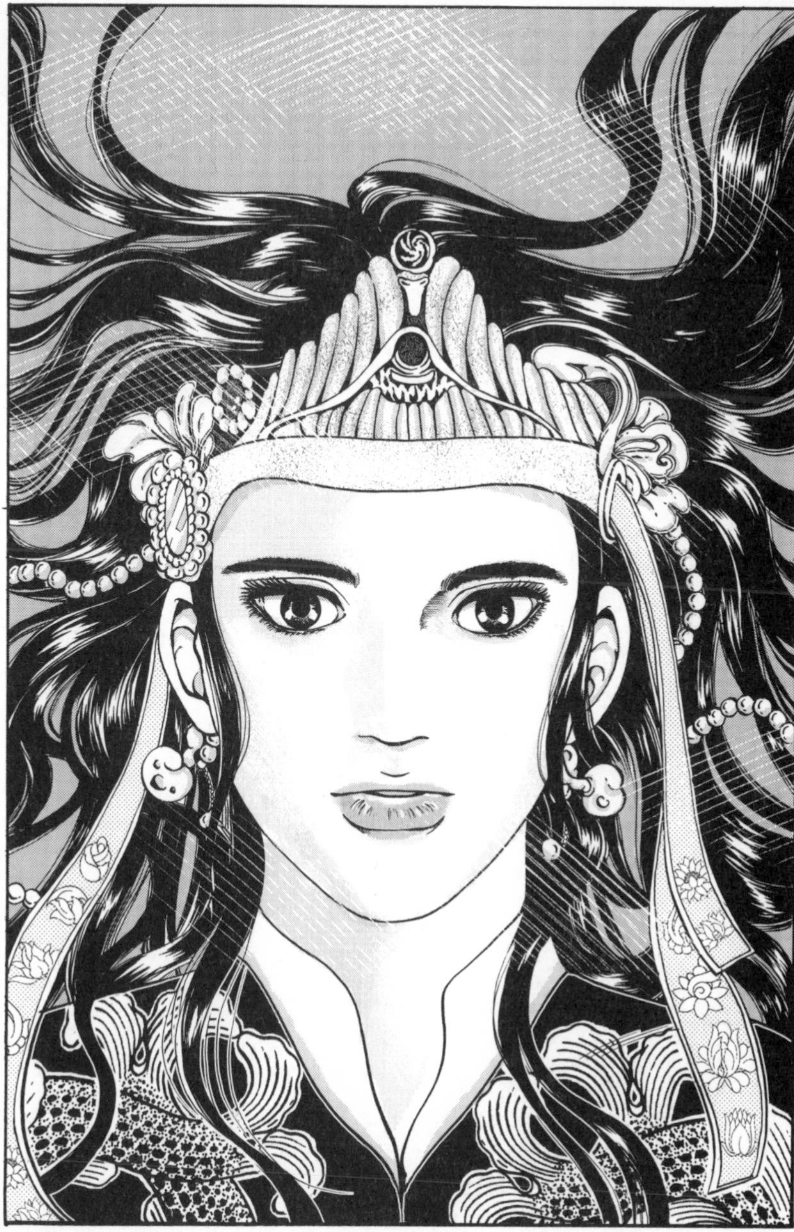

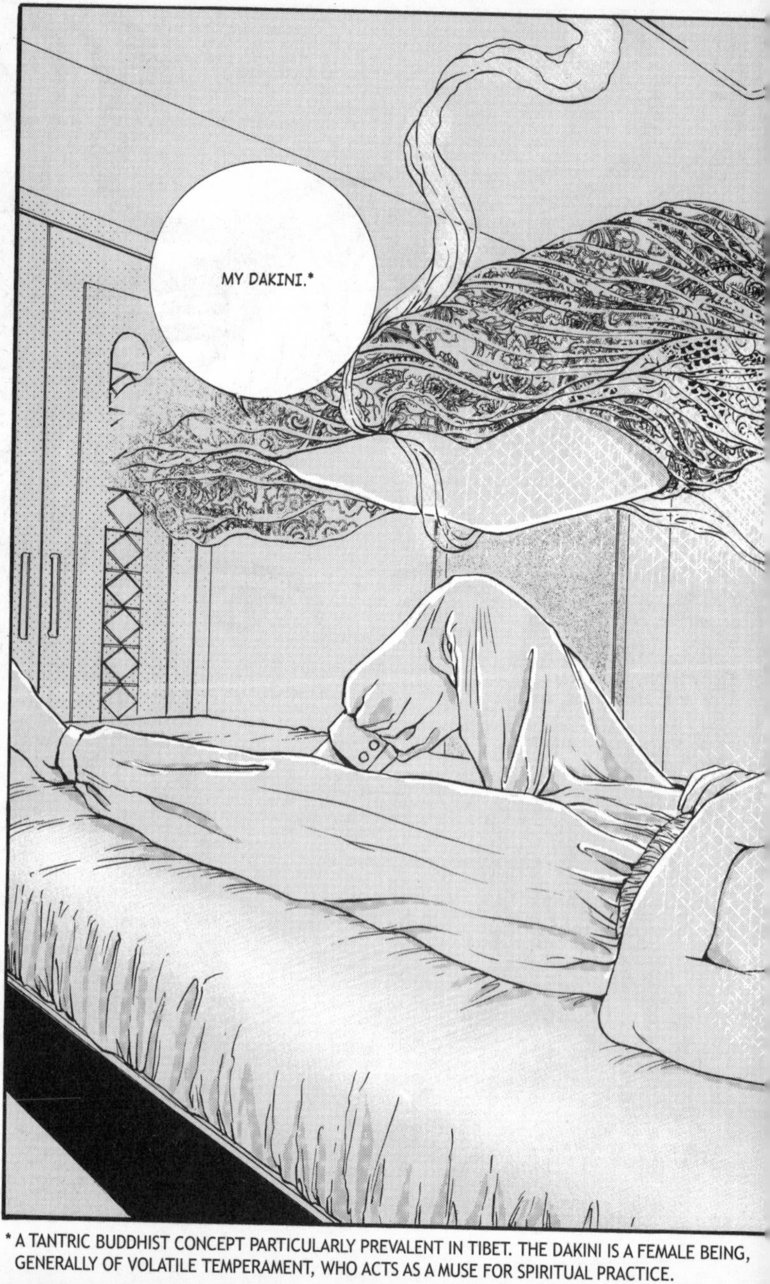
MY DAKINI.*

* A TANTRIC BUDDHIST CONCEPT PARTICULARLY PREVALENT IN TIBET. THE DAKINI IS A FEMALE BEING, GENERALLY OF VOLATILE TEMPERAMENT, WHO ACTS AS A MUSE FOR SPIRITUAL PRACTICE.

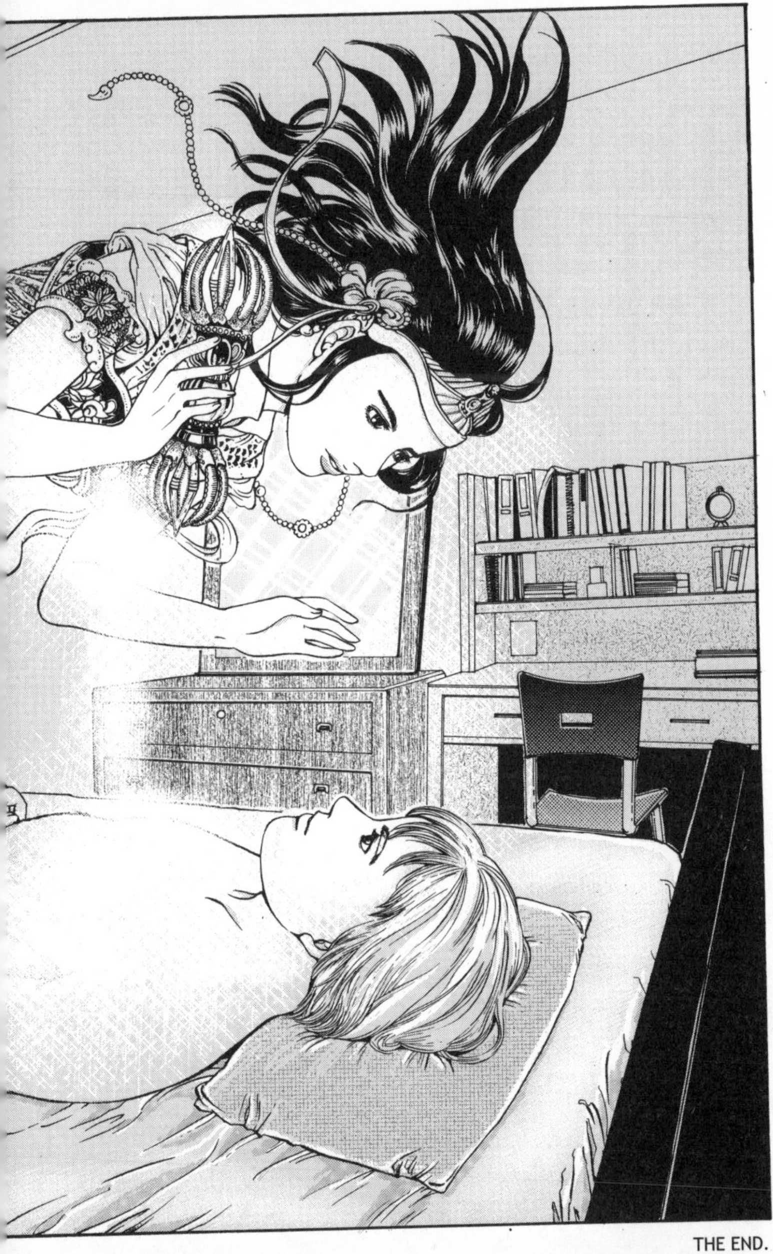

THE END.
To be continued in Volume 7.

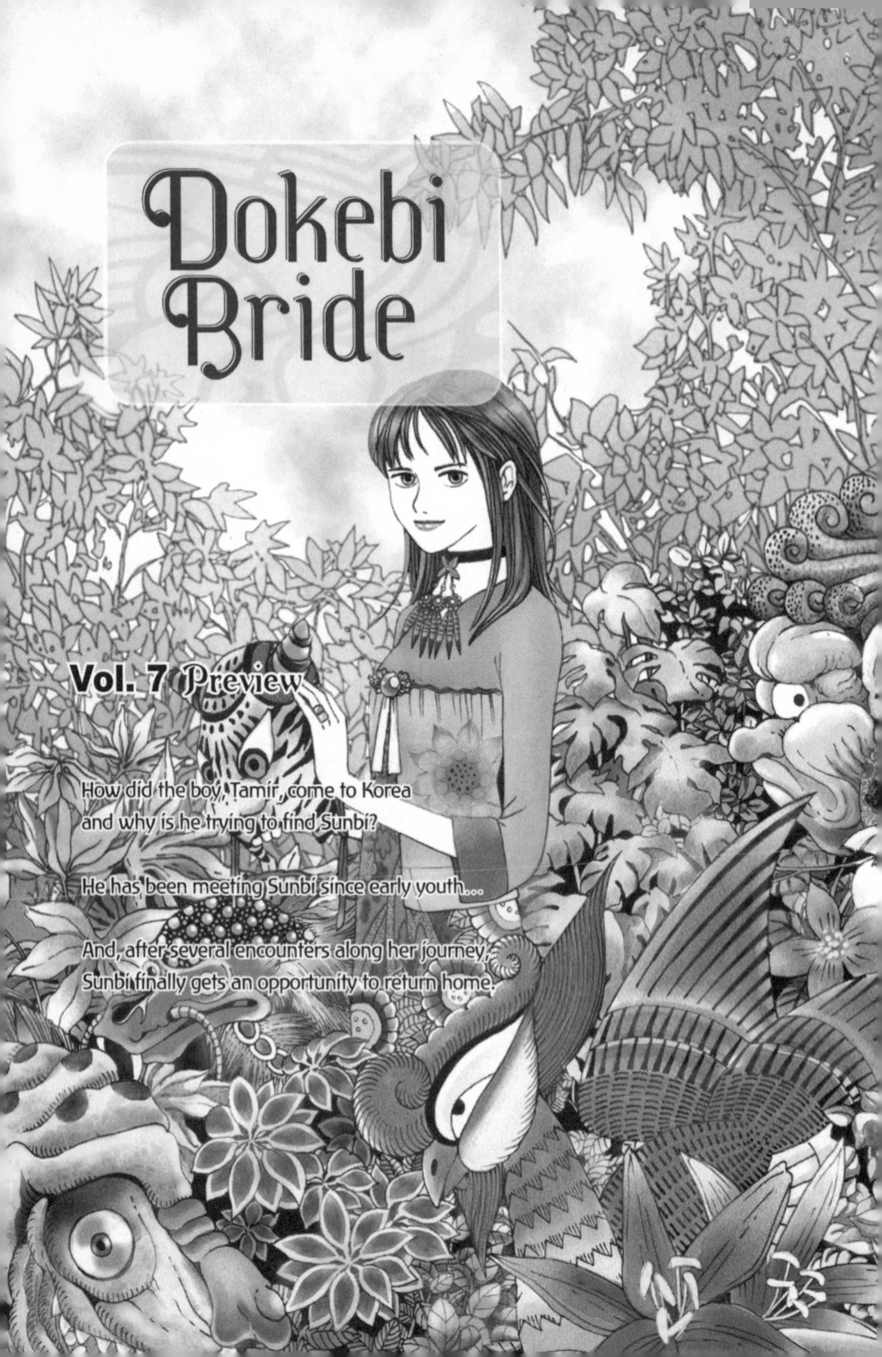
Dokebi Bride
Vol. 7 Preview
How did the boy, Tamir, come to Korea and why is he trying to find Sunbi?
He has been meeting Sunbi since early youth...
And, after several encounters along her journey, Sunbi finally gets an opportunity to return home.

AEGIS Vol.5

by Jinha Yoo

Chaos threatens everywhere—from the farthest corner of the galaxy to around the next street corner—in the fifth chapter of this mind-bending science fiction saga. Total war has broken out between AEGIS and the Lexy… and after a vengeful hacker turns U.S. military defenses against the people of Earth, Izare's efforts to keep his brother Jino safe may have all been for nothing. Jino himself, meanwhile, is off trying to lead a normal life—normal, that is, except when he's being stalked by a "former classmate," harassed by a local gang, or pursued by the mysterious entity known only as "Master!"

Let's Be Perverts Vol.4

by Youjung Lee

After hours of watching porn, Perverto and his pervert pals have it all figured out: Get a call-girl! Will they know what to do with her when they find her? Hongdan and Mr. Pi keep falling into each other's arms, so Mr. Pi exposes his lusty deeds. Hongdan is impressed! But she can't stop thinking of Perverto, and Perverto can't stop thinking of girls. Nerdy Eunwul struggles to hide her shameful past, but school rumors can't be stopped. Is it too late for Perverto to score? How does Mr. Pi decide to assist Hongdan?! Will anyone find true love and happiness? Hearts, minds, and entire identities flip-flop and hop-frog each other in the surprising conclusion to this naughty-but-nice series, *Let's Be Perverts*!

Roureville Vol.2

by E.Hae

Evan Pryce made his name investigating dangerous mysteries, but nothing can prepare him for the small, sleepy town of Roureville. Evan settles in to the quiet life, living with good-natured Jayce and writing his novel. However, when a violent attempt is made on his life, Evan realizes he's very close to uncovering the town's dirty little secret. He renews his investigation and discovers there are as many secrets in Roureville as there are people. Indeed, the biggest secret may have been living with him right under his nose: Jayce. Meanwhile, Evan's fiancée Cleo arrives in Roureville along with his brother Eric. And Evan learns that even living in Roureville cannot prevent one's past from catching up.

Try this!

10, 20, and 30

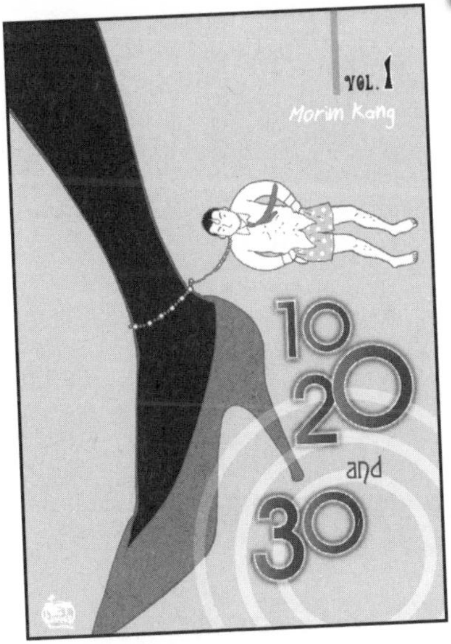
VOL. 1
Morim Kang
10
20
and
30

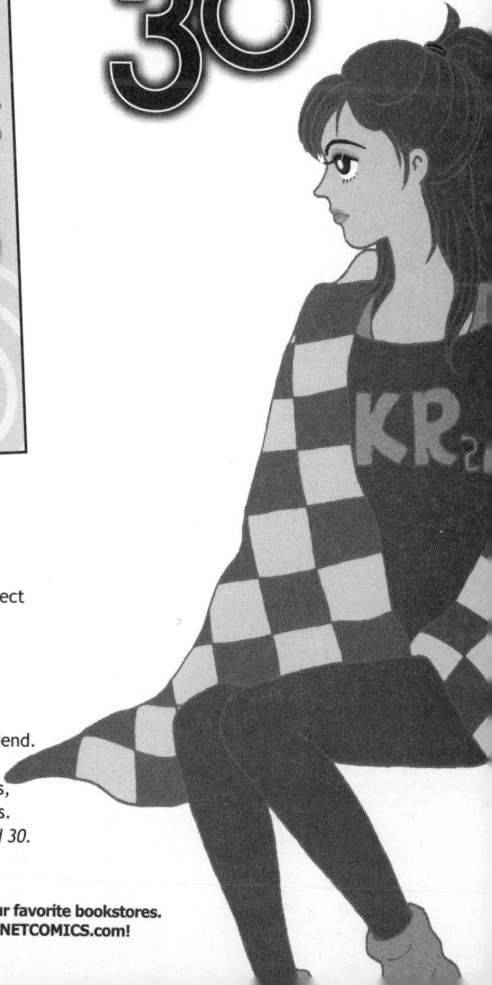

by Morim Kang

Three extraordinary women in three age groups with three unforgettable lives intersect in Morim Kang's fascinating *10, 20, and 30*. Yuhrin is a clumsy, scatterbrained widow in her 30's whose teenage daughter, Kangae, is forced to take care of her. Meanwhile, Kangae's jaded, twenty-something cousin Ami suffers a messy breakup with her boyfriend. Finally, Kangae, who dreads the thought of growing up and its attendant responsibilities, hates men and is sure to complicate matters. Get ready for one wild ride with *10, 20, and 30*.

Available now at your favorite bookstores.
Read it at www.NETCOMICS.com!

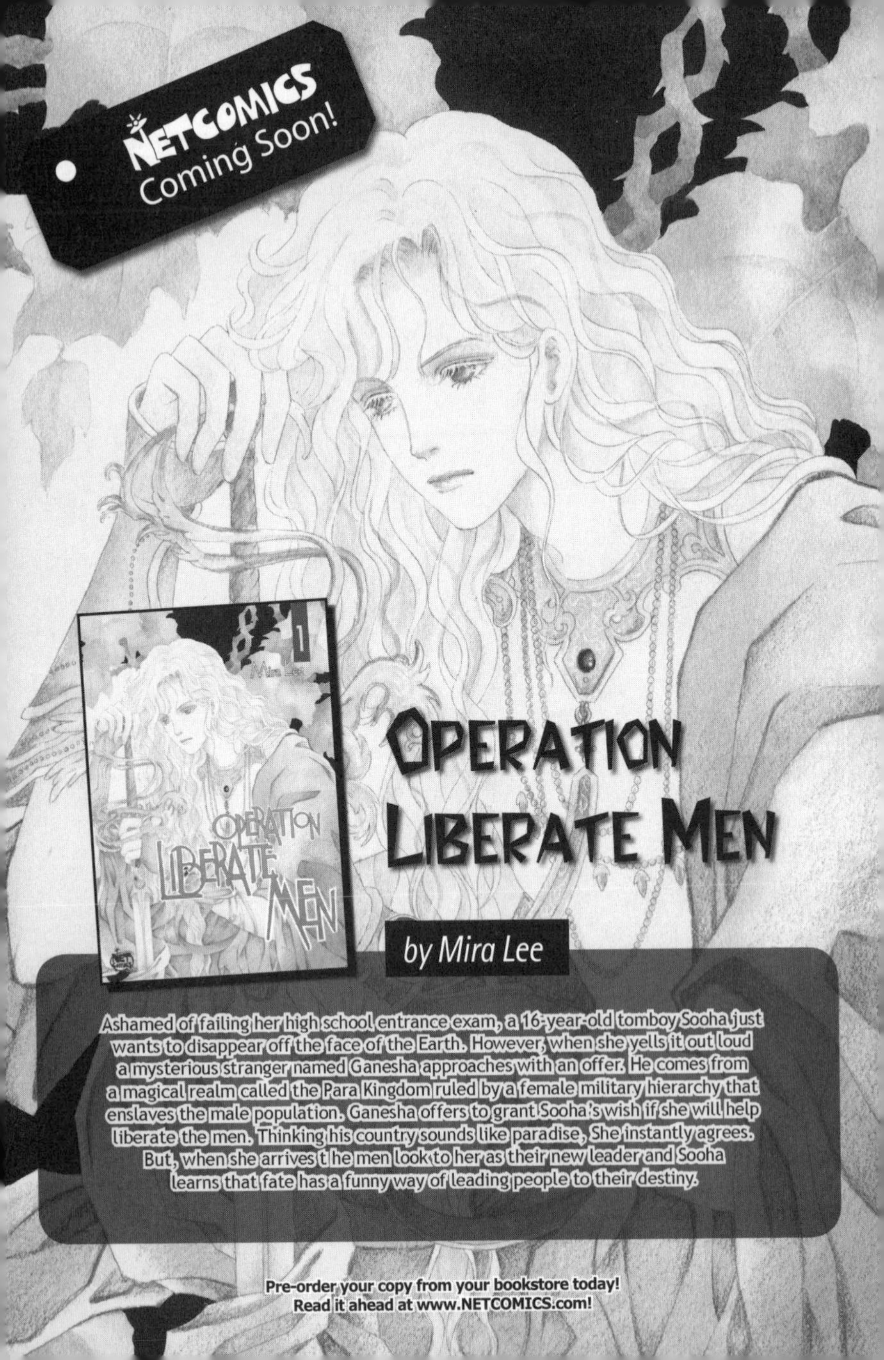
NETCOMICS
Coming Soon!
1
Mira Lee
OPERATION LIBERATE MEN
OPERATION LIBERATE MEN
by Mira Lee
Ashamed of failing her high school entrance exam, a 16-year-old tomboy Sooha just wants to disappear off the face of the Earth. However, when she yells it out loud a mysterious stranger named Ganesha approaches with an offer. He comes from a magical realm called the Para Kingdom ruled by a female military hierarchy that enslaves the male population. Ganesha offers to grant Sooha's wish if she will help liberate the men. Thinking his country sounds like paradise, She instantly agrees. But, when she arrives t he men look to her as their new leader and Sooha learns that fate has a funny way of leading people to their destiny.
Pre-order your copy from your bookstore today!
Read it ahead at www.NETCOMICS.com!

A brand-new title from Kyungok Kang, author of *In the Starlight* & *Narration of Love at 17*

Two Will Come

Ordinary high school girl Jina discovers that she is heir to a terrible legacy handed down from her family's sinister history. Long ago, her ancestors killed a magical serpent known as an Imugi, believing that it would bring them good luck. Unfortunately, the creature cursed them as it died, decreeing that one family member of each generation for that day forth will be killed by two people closely acquainted with that person. In this day and age, no one wants to believe in such outmoded superstitions, but one of Jina's relatives has been murdered without fail in every generation. Now, Jina has been informed that she will be next to die...

Two Will Come

1

Kyungok Kang

New 2007!

PASSIONATE TWO-FACE

by Youjung Lee

In despair over the loss of Hyeji, his one true love, Sangbaek runs into a very special make-up artist... and suddenly becomes the best-looking guy on the scene. The catch is, he has to give the artist every right to his life—including his real face. Sangbaek's handsome new mug attracts everyone's attention, but his mind is set on nothing but winning back his beloved Hyeji. But can he really recapture Hyeji when she's already given her heart to a rich and powerful man? Youjung Lee's dramatic wizardry in *Passionate Two-Face* will leave *you* mulling over the true face of love.